Mishima on Stage

Michigan Monograph Series in Japanese Studies
Number 59

Center for Japanese Studies
The University of Michigan

Mishima on Stage

The Black Lizard and Other Plays

Edited and with an Introduction by
Laurence Kominz

Foreword by Donald Keene

Center for Japanese Studies
The University of Michigan
Ann Arbor 2007

Published by the Center for Japanese Studies,
The University of Michigan
1007 E. Huron St.
Ann Arbor, MI 48104-1690

Library of Congress Cataloging-in-Publication Data

Mishima, Yukio, 1925–1970.
Mishima on stage : the Black Lizard and other plays / edited and with an introduction by Laurence Kominz.
p. cm. — (Michigan monograph series in Japanese studies ; no. 59)
ISBN 978-1-929280-42-1 (cloth : alk. paper) — ISBN 978-1-929280-43-8 (pbk. : alk. paper)
1. Mishima, Yukio, 1925–1970—Translations into English. I. Kominz, Laurence, 1952– II. Title. III. Title: Black Lizard and other plays. IV. Series.

PL833.I7A6 2007
895.6′25—dc22

2007033084

This book was set in Palatino Macron.

This publication meets the ANSI/NISO Standards for Permanence of Paper for Publications and Documents in Libraries and Archives (Z39.48—1992).

Printed in the United States of America

Contents

Illustrations

Foreword

Mishima's Kabuki Plays

Mishima Yukio was probably the most prodigiously endowed Japanese writer of the twentieth century. Although he was only forty-five when he died, under spectacular circumstances that brought him worldwide fame, he had already completed a more voluminous oeuvre than most writers who live twice that long. His writings extended to every genre. Although he was best known as a novelist, he excelled also as a short-story writer. His works of fiction ranged from the philosophic to the farcical; he could write in whatever style was appropriate to each. He published numerous essays on literary, political, cultural and purely journalistic topics. He was also the most successful playwright of his generation.

Mishima once said of his plays that they were his "mistress," as opposed to his novels, his "wife." This formula may suggest that he thought of the theatre as a welcome escape from the serious business of the novel, but his work in the theatre meant far more to him than it did to novelists who only occasionally wrote plays. At the exhibition displaying facets of his career held in Tokyo shortly before his death, he divided his activities in four "rivers," one of which was the theatre.

Mishima drew inspiration for his plays from many sources. His modern plays—that is, the plays that did not borrow the plots or acting styles from the traditional Japanese theatre—often were indebted to European drama, even if they were set in Japan and had only Japanese characters. One of the most successful, *The Fall of the House of Suzaku (Suzaku Ke no metsubo)*, 1967, was based on the *Heracles* of Euripides, though the action takes place in Japan during and after the Pacific War. *The Tropical Tree (Nettaiju)*, 1960, also set in Japan, originated in a newspaper account Mishima heard about that described certain events in the south of France. *Madame de Sade (Sado Koshaku Fujin)*, 1965, was based on translations of de Sade's writings by Shibusawa Tatsuhiko. In addition, several plays (including Racine's *Brittanicus*), translated by other men, were rewritten by Mishima to make them more effective on the Japanese stage.

Distinct from these plays are those Mishima wrote in the manner of the different varieties of traditional Japanese theatre—noh, *kyōgen*, and kabuki. Mishima's *Five Modern Noh Plays (Kindai nōgaku shū)*, 1956, though based on noh plays and given their titles, all dealt with contemporary Japan, in keeping with Mishima's view of noh as an absolute theatre whose validity did not depend on time or place.

The plays Mishima wrote for kabuki have varied sources. The most striking as a text is perhaps *The Blush on the White Hibiscus Blossom: Lady Fuyo and the True History of the Ōuchi Clan (Fuyo no tsuyo Ōuchi jikki),* 1955, an extraordinary adaptation and condensation of Racine's *Phèdre*. The work, intended for performance by kabuki actors, is cast for the most part into the traditional alternating lines of seven and five syllables. Some passages are sung by a narrator, not a member of the cast, who sets the scene or comments on what the actors have said. This play might be dismissed as a mere tour-de-force if it were not so assured in its observance of the language and prosody of a kabuki play in the tradition of *jōruri* (the puppet theatre), even while faithfully following the plot of Racine's tragedy. Probably no other playwright of Mishima's generation could have handled the classical language with such confidence. No doubt his frequent attendance at kabuki performances from the time he was child helped him to acquire mastery of the conventions of kabuki, including those derived from the repertory of the *jōruri* theatre.

Mishima's most popular kabuki play was *The Sardine Seller's Net of Love (Iwashiuri koi no hikiami),* 1954, based on a Japanese story dating back to the medieval period. In this play Mishima did not uniformly observe the traditional metrics, but he employed the style so convincingly that the play might be mistaken for the text of a newly discovered kabuki play, not exactly contemporary in its language but close enough for members of the audience to understand the dialogue without difficulty. This play was written specifically with the great *onnagata* Nakamura Utaemon in mind. Utaemon rarely appeared in humorous plays, and this may be one reason why the play found exceptional favor with audiences.

Another of Mishima's kabuki plays that continues to enjoy popularity is *Hell Screen (Jigokuhen),* 1953, his dramatization of the novella by Akutagawa Ryūnosuke. In this play, too, Mishima makes use of a narrator who comments in metrical language on the terrible events that are taking place before the eyes of the audience.

I had a small part in the creation of *Busu,* a comedy based on a celebrated work of the medieval *kyōgen* repertory. In 1957, not long after my translation of Mishima's *Five Modern Noh Plays* was published, Mishima arrived in New York. The book aroused a surprising amount of interest, and various people immediately asked Mishima's permission to stage the works in New York. He chose two young men who, though of undoubted ability, unfortunately lacked experience in raising money. Frustrated in their search for money without strings attached, they at one point decided that they would have more success finding a backer if, following the Japanese practice of staging a comedy in between two serious plays, the program could feature a Mishima comedy in between two of his modern noh plays.

Mishima, knowing of my special fondness for *kyōgen*, wrote to me in Japan asking if I would make a modern version of the *kyōgen* play *Hanago*. I did my best, but the humor simply did not go over as a modern play. For example, I thought it would not seem very humorous to an American audience when the lady of the house threatens to kill her servant if he fails to do what she commands. I tried making *Hanago* into a seventeenth-century play, rendering the name Hanago as Miss Flora, and calling the servant Dorcas, but it still did not work. Mishima, giving up on me, instead wrote his delightful *Busu*, naming two characters after the young producers. This still did not attract a backer. The producers next decided that Americans did not like one-act plays and asked Mishima rewrite three of his noh plays as a single three-act play. Although surely his patience must have been exhausted by this time, Mishima did as requested. He gave the play that resulted the English title *Long After Love*, a play on words that suggested Mishima's feeling for English. It was performed in Washington some years ago.

Each of Mishima's kabuki plays reveals some aspect of his many-faceted abilities, especially his extraordinary skill in writing an artificial but beautiful language that today no one speaks and extremely few people can write. His success in these plays was not, however, that of pastiche; the plays carry genuine dramatic conviction, and demonstrate that the methods of kabuki still make for valid and effective theatre.

DONALD KEENE

Acknowledgments

Books can never be written alone, and if not for the support and friendship of many wonderful people, this project would have ended in disappointment and frustration. I cannot adequately express my gratitude to co-translator and good friend, Mark Oshima, who read and closely critiqued every play and essay in the book. His insights about translation for the stage have been invaluable, and he translated the longest work in this anthology. Mark devoted hundreds of hours to the project, and it has become as much his as it is mine. Co-translator Jonah Salz discovered *Yuya* and *Busu* in the early nineties, and we worked together to prepare a translation of *Yuya* for his student production at Franklin & Marshall College in 1994. It was thanks to a joint research project with Jonah in 1998 that I was in Japan to see *The Sardine Seller's Net of Love* at the Shochiku-za in Osaka. I was entranced by the play and recognized it as a tour de force, unlike any other kabuki play written in the postwar era, and unlike any Mishima play I had read. Donald Keene's stories of times spent with Mishima, and of remarkable plays that had gone unnoticed in world literature piqued my interest and set me on the right track in my search for plays to translate. He supported the project from the first time I mentioned it to him, in 1998. I went back to Mishima's complete works and found many long-ignored masterpieces among them. So it was that *Mishima on Stage* became my latest obsession.

It is one thing to be obsessed with a literary study and quite another to persuade a publisher and agents that one's personal enthusiasm can be converted into a book that will actually engage readers and make a significant contribution to scholarship. Bruce Willoughby and Leslie Pincus of the Center for Japanese Studies at the University of Michigan were supportive from the outset, as was Jin Auh of the Wylie Agency in New York, who represents the Mishima estate.

Even when playwrights are no longer with us, theatre is made by living human beings, and I wanted to meet and talk with actors and directors who had experience directing, producing, and acting in the plays in this anthology. Dōmoto Masaki, Nagayama Takeomi, Bandō Tamasaburō, Nakamura Kanzaburō XVIII, and Ōzasa Yoshio are very busy men, but they all graciously made time to talk with me regarding their work in and opinions about Mishima's plays.

Arranging photographs for the book was a daunting task. Permission has to be obtained from every owner of a photograph, every photographer, and every person pictured. Arranging this was the author's responsibility, and with no funding for a secretary to handle correspondence, there were times when I wanted to give up on photographs altogether. I am grateful for the help given to me by the two museums that provided the pictures: The Tsubouchi Memorial Theatre Museum at Waseda University, and Heshiki Naoko at the Mishima Yukio Bungakukan. I especially want to thank Bandō Tamasaburō for generously allowing us to use a photo of him on the book jacket. He is playing Tsuyukusa in the climactic scene of Mishima's *Hell Screen* at Shinbashi Enbujō in 1978. Funding for photograph reproduction and rights was partially provided by a research allowance from the Center for International Education at Waseda University during my stay there in 2001–2002.

I badgered various friends and family members into reading play translations and essays during the two years I worked on the project. My thanks to colleagues Karin Magaldy-Unger, Adrian Pinnington, and Mark Driscoll, and to my father, David, mother, Eleanor, and step-father, Peter Condliffe for reading bits and pieces of the manuscript when our paths crossed. Finally, I have to say again how grateful I am to have a wife and children who tolerate my running off to the university to work late, or off on out-of-town trips to collect materials or give presentations, leaving them fatherless and husbandless. Toshimi, Leo, and Maya, thank-you. And to Toshimi special thanks for editing everything I have had to write in Japanese to keep this project running.

Introduction

Laurence Kominz

The world remembers Mishima Yukio because of his dramatic ritual suicide in 1970 after a failed attempt to convince Japanese army troops to rise and restore the emperor to his former glory. Only forty-five years old, Mishima died at the peak of his career as one of the world's greatest twentieth-century novelists. During his lifetime almost all of his major works of fiction, some twenty-eight novels and short stories, were translated into English and other foreign languages, earning him millions of devoted readers and critical acclaim around the globe. Outside Japan, what is much less well known is that Mishima was the premiere playwright of Japan's postwar era. Many of his plays are masterpieces, every bit as gripping, disturbing, and sumptuous as his novels. The world's ignorance of Mishima's achievements in drama is due to so few plays having been available in translation, and because Mishima's non-Japanese biographers have shown little concern for his work in theatre.[1]

The scope of Mishima's activity as a playwright and his popularity with audiences were unrivalled in Japan during the 1950s and 1960s, the two decades he worked in the theatre. He wrote plays in a wide range of genres: straight drama, kabuki, dance drama, screenplays, musical drama, radio drama, opera libretti. The vast majority of them were for Japan's modern, realist stage (*shingeki*) and for kabuki. Almost every one of Mishima's plays was mounted professionally, and there were years when he utterly dominated the Tokyo theatre. In the calendar year 1955, for example, nine different Mishima plays were produced for the theatre-going public. This level of activity attracted the sort of media attention usually reserved for star performers, not playwrights, and Mishima became a theatre celebrity.

Literary critics and scholars were just as impressed with Mishima's plays as were his audiences. During Mishima's lifetime many of his plays won prestigious literary awards. Scholars admired the structural elegance of his plays, his attention to the nuances of language, and his ability to create classical forms populated with contemporary characters and infused with his own personal values. A 1995 survey of fifty-four Japanese theatre scholars and critics concluded that Mishima was Japan's greatest postwar playwright, and that his play, *Madame de Sade,* is Japan's finest twentieth-century play.[2] Mishima's popularity with audiences has never waned. In

Figure 1. Mishima Yukio in front of a poster for his play *The Harp of Joy*, 1964. The poster reproduces his handwritten essay about the play. Photograph courtesy of the Mishima Yuko Literary Museum and Shinchōsha.

the thirty-six years since his death, half of his plays have been produced on professional stages in Japan, and his best work is presented repeatedly.

Mishima wrote plays in a wide range of genres, plays that have surprised, delighted, and challenged Japanese audiences over the years. Among them in this anthology are *The Sardine Seller,* the best new kabuki play of the postwar era, and a charming, romantic parody unlike any other work Mishima wrote; *Yuya,* an elegant, modern noh play with a disturbing message about the beauty of deceit; and *The Black Lizard,* featuring Mishima's most dangerous heroine, a cunning lady jewel thief, in a battle of wits with Japan's most brilliant detective. This romantic tragicomedy illuminates in clear and dramatic fashion Mishima's ideas about the relationship between beauty and death.

Mishima's convictions about drama and his approach to playwriting were the product of his broad reading in classical and modern Japanese literature and world drama but, even more importantly, the result of extensive theatre viewing when he was a youth, beginning when he entered middle school. Mishima made detailed notes about the more than one hundred plays he attended during his middle school, high school, and college years. The productions that Mishima viewed were in three radically different genres: noh, kabuki, and *shingeki.* To understand Mishima's work as a playwright—how and why he wrote plays that were so different from each other—it is essential to have some knowledge of these theatrical genres.

Noh is a classical form dating back to the 1300s. It is a fusion of music, dance, and a chanted text. The language of noh texts is intensely poetic and allusive, and so archaic that educated Japanese cannot understand it when recited unless they have studied it in advance. The music and dance of noh are austere in the extreme. Noh actors are members of hereditary acting families, and they perform in no other genre of theatre. Male actors use masks to perform all kinds of roles—women, gods, warriors, and ghosts. Each noh drama seeks to use all of its elements to illuminate the passions and explore the soul of a single character, often a long dead warrior or poet.

Kabuki too is classical theatre, but considerably more lively than noh. Noh's stage is small and bare of properties, but kabuki's is a huge tapestry of color that resembles a scene from a woodblock print landscape or cityscape come to life. Kabuki characters speak in the language of eighteenth- and nineteenth-century Japan, different from modern Japanese, but intelligible and expressive for modern audiences. Kabuki's dance and music are much livelier than their counterparts in noh. Kabuki plays are romantic melodramas, acted in a histrionic style. All actors are male, but they use make-up, not masks. Noh actors play both male and female roles, but in kabuki, actors called *onnagata* specialize in women's roles. *Onnagata* use falsetto voices and feminine posture and gait to create women characters. Every scene, every line, every movement in kabuki is aesthetically beautiful—even scenes of terrible cruelty and torture.

Shingeki ("new theatre"), Japan's version of modern, psychological realist drama, began in the 1920s by presenting translations of Western plays. Shakespeare came to Japan at the same time as Ibsen, and because *shingeki* sought to create a style that could present both, directing and acting were, and continue to be, considerably more presentational than their counterparts in the West. From the outset *shingeki* companies were committed to using actresses for women's roles.

Playwriting in *shingeki* evolved along with modernization movements in poetry and fiction. Playwrights rejected the classical language of kabuki and strove to use the language of everyday speech in their texts. *Shingeki* playwrights espoused rules of Western dramaturgy, such as maintaining unity of time, place, and action. Emerging Japanese playwrights wrote parlor room dramas that were peopled by characters whose actions and feelings were true to their psychologies, and who spoke in an idiom true to their gender and class.

In the 1920s *shingeki* had been a theatre by and for intellectuals, but a large and energetic proletarian wing took theatre to the masses in the 1930s, leading professional and amateur productions in factories and the countryside, as well as staging more traditional productions in theatres. The proletarian *shingeki* movement was brutally suppressed in 1940, and only one *shingeki* company was allowed to remain in operation during the war. *Shingeki* did enjoy a resurgence after World War II, however. Even though Mishima is well known for reanimating the classical traditions of noh and kabuki, most of his important theatrical writing was for *shingeki* productions.

Mishima's childhood experience in the theatre was almost entirely in kabuki. He attended over one-hundred kabuki productions and, by his own admission, became obsessed by kabuki, reading plays at home and taking his notebook to the theatre to jot down his thoughts about what he saw taking place on stage. Kabuki had a profound impact on his approach to all of his theatrical writing.

First and foremost, kabuki taught Mishima to value classical conventions of language and to admire the purity of a theatrical genre's stage presentation. Mishima would become the great formalist playwright of postwar Japan. In traditional kabuki plays, poetic lyrics and dialogue in classical Japanese, visual splendor, music, and dance create a powerful, beautiful, unified aesthetic and emotional experience. Mishima attended *shin kabuki* ("new kabuki"), plays written in the twentieth century and couched in modern Japanese with just enough archaic language to give a "feel" of old Japan. These plays are acted in a static way, without movements based on dance, without lyrical narration. Mishima found these mixed *shingeki*/kabuki plays to be pallid and weak. For Mishima the playwright, whether he was writing for *shingeki* or kabuki, remaining true to the language and stage requirements of the genre was a must. He believed that purity of form was the basis of strong plays, mixing and matching language and presentational elements from different genres was bad.

Mishima learned from kabuki that the classics could be moving and accessible. For most Japanese of the modern era, classical and foreign languages are an impediment to comprehension, and therefore an impediment to emotional engagement in a text or in a performance. Kabuki can provide a wonderful antidote to this difficulty. In kabuki, music, physical bravado, and histrionic declamation all contribute to infuse archaic language with unmistakable meanings and intense emotions. Mishima was by all accounts an intellectual genius, and he quickly mastered classical Japanese and several foreign languages. Archaic language soon became a conduit, not a barrier, for the young Mishima, and he readily grasped the meaning of the texts and could feel the emotions of characters in works that would remain foreign and remote to most Japanese: Greek tragedy, Racine, the Bible, not to mention Japanese classical literature.

Thanks to this unique childhood in the theatre, Mishima became a classicist and a formalist, and he was unlike any other playwright in postwar Japan. The direction of Japanese theatre since World War II has been strongly away from traditional values, away from formalism, and toward freedom of expression. Starting in the 1950s and increasing in the 1960s with the emergence of avant-garde drama, playwrights and directors engaged in a wide range of theatrical experimentation, using noh, kabuki, and *shingeki* actors in hybrid productions. Avant-garde dramatists sought to eliminate the tyranny of verbal semantics, and sometimes dispensed with written texts altogether, creating movement-based theatre that became a major stream of the avant-garde. During all of this experimental ferment, Mishima remained true to his commitment to writing pure *shingeki* and pure kabuki. He took the characters from classical noh plays and gave them contemporary psyches in his modern noh plays, but these plays were written in the modern Japanese idiom and were meant to be performed by *shingeki* actors following the stage conventions and values of *shingeki*. In *Lady Fuyo*, Mishima put Racine's *Phaedra* on the kabuki stage. His text was entirely in classical Japanese, and the play was performed using kabuki dance and traditional lyrical recitation, following all of the presentational forms of traditional kabuki. It was a pure, classical kabuki play.

When Mishima did, upon occasion, use heterodox conventions in a play, it was almost always done in a way entirely opposite to what every other experimental dramatist espoused. Instead of freeing theatrical genres from traditional constraints, Mishima imposed new rigidity on freer forms, using classical and formal elements from outside the tradition. For example, in his kabuki play *Hell Screen*, Mishima reined in the usual free-wheeling flow of time and space in kabuki by subjecting his play to the three unities of Western classical drama. In his *shingeki* play, *Madame de Sade*, Mishima recreated a static, Racinian drama consisting of a series of speeches by the principal characters who are all women.[3] Unlike most of his playwright peers, Mishima clearly felt that adherence to formal requirements in drama assisted and strengthened his writing for the stage.

Mishima's love of classical formalism set him apart from his contemporaries, and so did his political convictions. Postwar Japanese theatre has enthusiastically supported progressive social agendas. First *shingeki* and then the avant-garde led the Japanese arts into new territory, criticizing the traditional values that had given rise to militarism, exposing racial and ethnic prejudice, sexism, and other forms of social injustice, and attacking the dehumanization of corporate industrial and postindustrial Japan. Through the 1950s, all theatre troupes espoused liberal values, labor socialism, or even communism. In the 1960s, the avant-garde embraced the radical left. Guerilla theatre, street theatre, tent theatre, "happenings," all began in that decade.

For the first ten years of Mishima's theatrical career, politics had no place in his playwriting. Mishima explored the individual psyche, and its struggles for power with other psyches in the pursuit of control, security, or sexual gratification. He was fascinated by the tyranny of forbidden carnal desire, by the allure, the passion, and the danger inherent in beauty, transgression, and death. Mishima was obsessed by visual and physical beauty of every sort. Some of his plays were in themselves gorgeous spectacles. In other plays characters are forced confront the fragility of human beauty, or to ponder the value of beauty in comparison with other things that they value. In the 1960s, when the avant-garde turned far to the left, Mishima became deeply interested in political issues, but he turned right, championing military values and loyalty to the emperor in drama, novels, and essays.

Politically and stylistically Mishima differed from his playwright peers, yet during his lifetime he inspired many fine actors and directors to work with him on his projects. Mishima's plays were insightful, witty, but also disturbing, and leading actors and directors were eager to stage them. By the mid-fifties Mishima had matured into an experienced theatre professional who enjoyed working collaboratively on theatrical projects, sometimes even directing his own plays. In the 1960s Mishima emerged as a theatre company leader, and he occasionally directed major stage productions. By the time of his death, Japan recognized Mishima as one of the most innovative and versatile dramatists of the century.

Mishima had one serious advantage over his fellow playwrights. He was a first-rate novelist who also wrote plays. His breadth of knowledge, his probing curiosity about the human condition, and his mastery of the written word surpassed that of any other playwright of his time. Mishima believed that his work in serious fiction and his playwriting strengthened each other. In 1955 he wrote, "These days I'm writing fiction and plays at the same time, and I don't feel any conflict in working this way. The theatre and my study are at opposite ends of the see-saw that is my life."[4]

It was common enough for novelists to dabble in theatre, but rare indeed for a novelist to maintain a career as a major playwright for the duration of his life, much less to dominate the world of theatre as Mishima did. What made Mishima so special in this regard? In 1954 Mishima wrote about the challenges he faced in an extended essay entitled, "Why Novelists Don't Write Plays." Financial reasons of course head Mishima's list of reasons why novelists do not write plays. In Japan writing plays is much less lucrative than writing novels, but there were plenty of artistic reasons keeping fiction writers away from theater. Few novelists enjoy submitting their creative work to the formal constraints imposed by requirements of the stage, or to the intense and usually critical scrutiny of directors and actors who may change his text. Established novelists rarely attend plays and do not feel at home with actors or working in the theatre. When on rare occasions they attempt a theatre project, even with a supportive company, they cannot help but feel like incompetent amateurs. Mishima concluded that in order to put up with all of the artistic restrictions, financial privations, and personal humiliations involved in sustaining a serious career as a playwright, one has to know theatre intimately and must be deeply in love with it.[5] This was very rare in Japanese novelists. Mishima himself loved the theatre intensely, and it was this love that sustained him in his difficult struggle to become a great playwright, and in his dedication to pursue his career in the theatre for his entire life.

In November of 1970, less than two weeks before Mishima committed suicide, the Tōbu Department Store art gallery ran a five-day Mishima exhibition that Mishima carefully designed himself. Mishima divided his life into "Four Rivers: The River of Books, the River of the Stage, the River of the Body, and the River of Action." In retrospect it is clear that this was Mishima's formal summing up of his life, his work, his philosophy, and his ideals. This anthology is an exploration of Mishima's "River of the Stage," and the next section of the introduction is a narrative account of Mishima's life in the theatre, an account that until now has been neglected by English-language biographers and translators. It is beyond the scope of a play anthology to travel down Mishima's other three rivers—to analyze in detail his work as a fiction writer, or to trace the development of his political philosophy, or to delve into the mysteries of his sexuality. We shall see, however, that Mishima's Four Rivers were not separately flowing watercourses, but constantly intermingling and intersecting streams. Following Mishima's River of the Stage through its still pools and raging cataracts reveals the struggles and triumphs of a playwright of exceptional complexity and ambition, a playwright whose works have become classics in Japan and are destined to become such in the world at large.

A LIFE IN THE THEATRE

Childhood and Youth: An Obsession with Kabuki, 1937–45

Mishima Yukio (his real name was Hiraoka Kimitake—he began using the pen name Mishima Yukio at age sixteen) was born in 1925 into a family of the upper middle class, but one with aristocratic pretensions and aspirations. Mishima's mother and grandmother were great fans of kabuki, and when Mishima entered his first year of junior high at the Peers School, they felt he was ready to see kabuki and noh, and they began taking him regularly to see these two very different forms of traditional theatre. It was during these years that Mishima learned to love the formal language and stage conventions of Japan's great classical theatre forms, and to appreciate the work of fine actors.

Mishima remembered his first kabuki, when he saw the *onnagata* Nizaemon XII (1882–1946) playing Kaoyo in *Chūshingura*: "It was impossible to believe that the actor, old and wrinkled, was the beautiful woman who had caused the tragedy. I was stunned that a man could produce such a voice. Kabuki was indescribably strange to me. It had a rancid flavor to it, but even as a boy I could tell that it would be a strangely delicious flavor were I to taste it."[6] Mishima tasted of kabuki, and soon was in its thrall, attending shows at least once a month whenever he was in Tokyo until shortly before his suicide in 1970. Soon after his first trip to the Kabuki-za, kabuki had become serious fun: "In middle school and high school I would take the texts with me to the theatre, and stare intensely at the stage all the while writing with my pencil, never looking at the page I was writing on. I was terribly obsessed with kabuki at that age."[7]

Mishima was exposed to noh at an even earlier age than kabuki, thanks to hearing his mother practicing *utai*—noh chanting—at home. When he was in seventh grade she took him to see the god play *Miwa*,[8] and even as a child Mishima was impressed by noh's formal beauty and structure. Mishima recognized that language and stage convention in noh and kabuki were inextricably linked, creating a beautiful aesthetic whole. He later wrote, "From noh I learned that words are actions."[9]

Experiences at the theatre had a strong impact on Mishima's selection of personal reading material. He read *bunraku* plays by Chikamatsu, kabuki plays by Tsuruya Namboku, and noh plays as well. In school he was introduced to classical European drama and the Bible, and both impressed him. While a second-year middle-school student he wrote a four-act, twenty-eight character, four hundred page-long play centered on the immaculate conception of Christ, entitled "Distance."[10] The play begins with a chorus of angels announcing to Satan the conception of Christ, at which Satan trembles in fear. At the end of the play the angel Gabriel orders Mary to go forth, and with her divine child, to bring great changes to the world. The structure and depth of characterization in "Distance" are remarkable for a fourteen-year old.[11] This was Mishima's first long work of literature, but he also wrote shorter plays. As a student, Mishima was an avid writer of poetry and fiction, making frequent, award-winning submissions to Peers School literary magazines. "Distance" demonstrates that drama was just as important to him as were poetry and fiction in his early years, and demonstrates that as early as middle school, Mishima was capable of being deeply moved by non-Japanese literary material and yearned to express in his native language strong feelings inspired by foreign culture.

At age seventeen Mishima began writing extended critical essays about almost every play he went to see.[12] It was then 1942 and Japan's military government had closed down all but one *shingeki* theatre, the Bungaku-za. Although kabuki theatres were staging regular programs, the government encouraged the presentation of plays about martial heroism and discouraged plays that glorified romantic love.

Mishima wrote most of his essays using classical Japanese grammar. If he began an essay in classical grammar, he maintained it throughout. He probably could not have suspected it at that time, but this precocious and archaic exercise would serve as training for later work as a kabuki playwright. When it came to evaluating kabuki plays, Mishima stood on the side of classicism and tradition. He criticized actors whose delivery or movements seemed at all modern. Since early in the twentieth century playwrights had written new kabuki plays (*shin kabuki*) using the modern Japanese language, presented without sung narration or dance-based movement. Mishima was contemptuous of these new plays and felt they had none of the power or beauty of classical kabuki plays.

Toita Yasuji, a noted critic and scholar of kabuki was impressed with the perceptiveness and honesty of Mishima's critical essays.[13] Mishima frequently singled out individual lines of speech and minutely analyzed the strengths and weaknesses of the actor's delivery. He sometimes copied out long monologues that especially impressed him, many of them established *mei-serifu* or "great lines from classic plays." This love of dramatic monologue would influence Mishima's playwriting throughout his career and in every genre.[14] These critical essays show that Mishima had a clear understanding of what makes kabuki successful or unsuccessful in performance. Success was determined more by actors and acting than by any other factor, but he recognized the necessity of a fusion of various arts and first-rate talent, which of course included playwriting.

Mishima admired the work of many kabuki actors and wrote extensively about their appearances and performance styles. It was as a young man, sitting in the audience, that he first saw the actors and actresses with whom he would work a decade later. He first wrote about Nakamura Utaemon VI (1917–2001) (then called Shikan) in January of 1944. "With his style and physique he was the epitome of a princess. His timing, and the way he moved his body so ostentatiously in contrast to the stillness of the actor he was partnering . . . it was a flawless performance."[15] Mishima would later become more devoted to this actor than any other, and he would write some of his most evocative and haunting character descriptions in any genre about this man.

In December of 1944, Mishima went alone to see *shimpa*, a theatre form that contains elements of kabuki and *shingeki* (it uses both actresses and *on-*

nagata), and that presents melodramas set mainly in the Meiji Era. Mishima noted that the audience was meager due to the air raids, and that the properties were shabby, but he also observed that Mizutani Yaeko (1905–79), the leading *shimpa* actress of her day, did a fine job with her two roles.[16] In early April of 1945 Mishima went to a *shingeki* play for the first time in his life.[17] He saw Sugimura Haruko (1907–97) at the Bungaku-za in "A Woman's Life," the play that made her Japan's biggest star of the stage. She would be the central figure in Mishima's rise to fame as a playwright exactly ten years later. He wrote nothing about the play at the time. All of his early 1945 entries are sparse, perhaps because he was preoccupied with the worsening war situation and the prospect of being drafted. Fortunately, he failed his physical examination, and he was sent to the nearby naval arsenal at Zama. He worked as a civilian under orders of the Imperial Navy, along with his fellow Tokyo University law students.

Writing, Publishing, and Directing Plays, 1945–52

Even though Mishima knew less about the *shingeki* stage than he did about either noh or kabuki, as a writer it was to *shingeki* that he turned his attention after the war. Mishima was eager to establish himself as both a novelist and serious playwright, and in the late forties he wrote and began to publish short stories and novels. Mishima began writing plays before he had any notion of whether or not he would be able to get them published or performed. He had worthy role models to emulate in his playwriting. In the prewar era, several authors of serious fiction had written *shingeki* plays that had been well received by both critics and the public, and Mishima admired the work of the leading Japanese *shingeki* playwright, Kishida Kunio (1890–1954).

Mishima's first two one-act plays, *The Burning House* and *Lighthouse,* were produced by a first-rate *shingeki* company in 1949 and 1950. *The Burning House* was a rocky maiden voyage for Mishima as a playwright, and *Lighthouse,* an excellent play, was undermined by his inexperience as a director. Finally, with his first three modern noh plays (1950–52), a subgenre of *shingeki* that Mishima would turn into his trademark, Mishima achieved success at the most prestigious *shingeki* theatres in Tokyo.

When the war ended, the theatre world turned upside down. Many of kabuki's big theatres had been destroyed in the fire bombings of Japan's major cities, and kabuki struggled to find venues to mount its plays. In 1946 it seemed that the occupation regime might threaten kabuki even more than the bombing raids had done. Kabuki, which had been prevented from presenting romantic or erotic material by the Japanese military regime, now found the martial and historical half of its repertory suppressed by the American Occupation authorities. Many of kabuki's greatest masterpieces were on the black list, and actors specializing in martial roles were out of work. It was not until 1947 that kabuki producers were allowed to present the full repertory of kabuki plays.[18]

While kabuki struggled, *shingeki* thrived. *Shingeki* dramatists who had spent the war years in jail for leftist tendencies emerged from prison as heroes of the new, democratizing Japan. Professional and amateur *shingeki* troupes sprang up in Tokyo and all over Japan. The two major *shingeki* companies were the Bungaku-za and Haiyū-za in Tokyo. The Bungaku-za had almost collapsed during the war, but the hugely successful play, *A Woman's Life*, rescued the company and catapulted actress Sugimura Haruko into stardom and a leadership role in the company. Bungaku-za means "The Literary Theatre," and it was committed to "avoiding pedantry, or subservience to politics while offering the intelligent general public, through the medium of the stage, a glimpse of a 'genuine entertainment for the soul.'"[19] The Bungaku-za presented a mixture of Western classics and work by established Japanese playwrights.

The leader of the Haiyū-za was actor-director Senda Koreya (1904–94), a former member of the Tsukiji Shogekijō, the first *shingeki* company, founded in 1924. Senda had led the finest of the proletarian theatre troupes in the late twenties and early thirties but spent most of the war in jail as a leftist activist. "Haiyū-za" means "Actors' Theatre." Its repertory was similar to that of the Bungaku-za, but it occasionally produced left-leaning plays, and its leadership, its actors, and its staff were more committed to labor and socialist causes than were their counterparts at the Bungaku-za. Labor unions, which had been suppressed in prewar Japan, thrived in the postwar era, and labor organizations around the country produced extensive all-Japan tours of the best *shingeki* plays. Both Bungaku-za and Haiyū-za ran two different performance series: on the main stage, one-month-long runs of multiact classic plays and plays by established playwrights, and, on a smaller stage, five-to-ten-day-long productions of new works. Bungaku-za called their short, new works series "Atelier Performances," and Haiyū-za called theirs "Study Performances" (Benkyō-kai).

During the five years after World War II, Mishima struggled to find a place in Japan's literary world. His main aspiration was as a novelist, and he was given encouragement in difficult times by the finest of mentors, Kawabata Yasunari (1899–1972), later Japan's first Nobel laureate in literature. Mishima graduated from the Law Department of Tokyo University in 1947 and took a prestigious, entry-level position at the Ministry of Finance. For just under a year he led a dual life as writer and elite junior bureaucrat. Despite university and then professional duties, these were prolific years for Mishima. In addition to writing several short stories and two long novels, he wrote six one-act plays and one four-act play. Mishima also began to put his talents as a theatre critic to use, publishing critical essays in newspapers and in theatre magazines. He also began to join literary societies that included novelists, academics, playwrights, and dramatists.

Kawabata, Mishima's mentor, had considerable clout with *Ningen*

(*Humanity*), a leading literary journal, and in 1946 Kawabata helped Mishima publish his first important short story, "Cigarette," in it. In November 1948 *Ningen* published Mishima's play, *The Burning House (Kataku)*, which he had finished earlier that year. Mishima had at last published his first play. It was noticed by Yashiro Seiichi (1929–98), a professor of French literature at Waseda University who was also on the production committee of the Haiyū-za.[20] Yashiro convinced his colleagues to stage the play in their small-stage "Benkyō-kai series" for new works.

It was an amazing stroke of luck for Mishima. His very first play production would be by one of the two most prestigious theatres in Japan, would be directed by Aoyama Sugisaku (1889–1956), a distinguished pioneer of *shingeki*, and would star Senda Koreya himself. *The Burning House* is a drawing-room play about a dysfunctional aristocratic family, set in contemporary postwar Japan. The main character is the father (played by Senda) who is incapable of recognizing his family's decline in status and income after the war, and who remains blind to the illicit sexual relationships his children are having. The play concludes with the report of a love suicide by the daughter and a lodger that may in fact be a lie, and a fire in the house that may in fact be an illusion. In *The Burning House* Mishima shows how strong perceptions can become reality and convincing lies can become the truth.

But Mishima did not experience any satisfaction watching his first play come to life on stage during rehearsals. The weakness and faults of the play stood out more clearly than he had anticipated.[21] He was mortified as he watched rehearsals progress. He wrote that "it was like one of my worst nightmares, when all of a sudden I find myself walking around Ginza barefoot, dressed only in pajamas."[22] The play had many flaws. Because the Buddhist parable of the title was unknown to audiences, it baffled rather aided comprehension of the text; the play was filled with monologues a half-page long, almost impossible for even the best *shingeki* actor to deliver with conviction. Audiences never understood what was illusory and what was real. Mishima wrote that he had crafted "a play in which no dramatic events take place,"[23] but critics wrote that "it was a play that moved no one."[24] Yashiro wrote that the "disastrous production was bitter but effective medicine that taught Mishima the difference between plays and novels."[25] Mishima saw the failure as primarily his own responsibility, but he knew that this was his maiden voyage and he could write much better plays. He also must have wanted better, more sensitive direction, and perhaps this is why he chose to direct his next play at the Haiyū-za himself.[26]

Mishima's second play to be produced (and the first play in this anthology) was *The Lighthouse (Tōdai)*. He wrote it in March of 1949 while he was working on *Confessions of a Mask*, the semi-autobiographical best-selling novel that won him celebrity status in Japan. *The Lighthouse* was published in May, and two productions were mounted in November and December in Osaka and Kyoto. The real test for *The Lighthouse* was its Tokyo premiere in

February 1950, once again in the Haiyū-za's small-stage series, but this time with Mishima directing his own play.

The Lighthouse tells the story of an upperclass family that is threatened with destruction because the son, age twenty-five, is in love with his stepmother, who is just five years older. The nineteen-year-old daughter of the family is an innocent schoolgirl at the beginning of the play, but during the course of the play she is confronted with coercive sexual play at a party of friends and with her brother's obsessive love for their stepmother. *The Lighthouse* was clearly inspired by Mishima's favorite classical European play, Racine's *Phaedra,* as well as works from the Japanese classics in which ill-fated love between stepmothers and stepsons drives characters to deceive and destroy people they love and trust. In *The Lighthouse* Mishima was hoping to show his audience that the forbidden passions that inspired classical works like *Phaedra* are still with us today, and although they take less dramatic form in our everyday lives, they are no less destructive. Mishima was also presenting masks in this play, which he wrote while working on his landmark novel, *Confessions of a Mask.* The son, Noboru, is the one character who wants to cast away the mask of deception and declare his love openly, but his stepmother, and more importantly, his sister, prevent him. Mishima seems to be saying that only by submitting to the falsity of masked existence is family life possible.

The Lighthouse is a much better play than *The Burning House.* It is full of lively, quirky, convincing dialogue, and energetic physical movement. Long monologues only occur when they make sense psychologically.

Once again, fate was to deny Mishima his first theatrical triumph. Despite his role as director of the play, Mishima was an outsider and had no say at all in the casting of the play. According to Dōmoto Masaki, Mishima's friend, theatrical colleague, and biographer, the play was terribly miscast. Not only were the actors too old for their parts, but they were accustomed to playing workers and peasants rather than aristocrats.[27] The actress who played the alluring stepmother was a mannish, left-wing veteran of proletarian theatre. Mishima, unable to establish a rapport with his actors, sat in his director's chair with his face in the script as the actors struggled with their roles on stage. The actors resented his apparent indifference, commenting that if all Mishima wanted to do was to read his play by himself, he should never have attempted to direct the play.[28]

Late 1949 was the high-water mark for the dream of socialist revolution in Japan, and there was a feeling among leftists that at this crucial juncture, "People who aren't with us are against us."[29] The administration and production staff of the Haiyū-za were even more dedicated to socialism than the cast, and they despised Mishima.[30] Mishima was a celebrity novelist, an aristocrat fresh out of the Finance Ministry. He was ignorant of theatre vocabulary and knew nothing of the technical requirements of production. According to Dōmoto, the production staff saw Mishima as an amateur, haute-bourgeois, overpaid outsider, and they made his work very difficult. They dismissed the play as an anachronistic bourgeois bedroom drama with no redeeming value since it was oblivious to the class struggle.[31] With no direction from Mishima and with the cast unenthusiastic about the play, it seemed headed for disaster when Aoyama Sugisaku stepped in and became co-director, in effect taking over directorial responsibility.

Even with Aoyama's assistance the play was uninspired, lacking the depth and mythic overtones that Mishima intended. This is not surprising when we examine Aoyama's director's notes analyzing the main characters. They are amazingly superficial for a director of his experience.[32] Mishima criticized Aoyama in his program notes in the play program in one of the more remarkable examples of veiled criticism ever released to the public. Mishima couched the entire experience of creating the production in terms of a ship on a voyage. This followed both the maritime imagery of the title of the play, and a famous essay by Osanai Kaoru (1881–1928), the founder of Tsukiji Shogekijō, in which Osanai described the work of the theatre in terms of the building and sailing of a great ship. Osanai likened the playwright to a ship designer and builder and the director to the captain who decides the destination and steers the ship and all its crew (staff and actors) and passengers (audience) safely to port. Mishima admitted that this ship had had a baby (himself) for its captain, and that the ship was rocking dangerously and some of the crew were even getting mutinous.[33] "But then Aoyama stepped in, aiding the baby in this crisis with words of advice. He strode the deck calmly under clear skies. Without even looking at the compass he could tell how the ship had gone off course."[34] Mishima's subtext is that Aoyama never really took the trouble to discover what course Mishima had intended for the ship, and set it on the same sort of course Aoyama had sailed many times before.

After *The Lighthouse,* Mishima felt it was time to part ways with the Haiyū-za, and he approached Bungaku-za, the other major *shingeki* company in Tokyo. Ever since Mishima had begun to read *shingeki* plays, he had admired Kishida Kunio, a co-founder and the leading playwright of the Bungaku-za; and the company was considerably less socialist than the Haiyū-za. Mishima grew close to Kishida through Kumo no Kai (The Cloud Society), a literary society that Kishida founded in 1950. Kumo no Kai was a loosely knit group of authors, actors, directors, and design artists, and Kishida founded it in the hopes of discovering creative young artists and writers who could contribute to the growth of postwar theatre. Mishima joined Kumo no Kai after *The Lighthouse,* made the acquaintance of Kishida, and visited him regularly at his house.[35] Kishida developed a real liking for the young playwright, and the feeling was mutual.

Mishima also established a close friendship with Akutagawa Hiroshi (1920–81), son of the great novelist Akutagawa Ryūnosuke (1892–1927), and one of the leading directors and actors in Bungaku-za. Mishima asked

Akutagawa Hiroshi to lend him noh texts to help him with his next exciting theatrical endeavor—writing modern plays based on classical noh plays. We know from an essay published in November 1949 that Mishima was already intrigued by the never performed prewar adaptations of noh to *shingeki* by the author Kōri Torahiko (1890–1924) and felt that such plays had potential for the stage.[36] Dōmoto Masaki states that in 1950 Mishima already had all the noh texts he needed and had been working on his modern noh plays for some time, but he borrowed texts from Akutagawa to give this important Bungaku-za figure a sense of participation in the project.[37] If Mishima was being disingenuous with Akutagawa, Akutagawa never learned about it, or did not care. He was enthusiastic, and he convinced Bungaku-za to produce *Kantan,* Mishima's first modern noh play, in their "atelier" production in December 1950, with Akutagawa directing.

Mishima had learned from *The Burning House* and *The Lighthouse* that if he was going to rework classical drama he would have to make his antecedents clearer, and make the connections between the modern world and the classical world far less subtle than he had done in those two plays. Mishima also had learned that he needed a director who shared his values and his sense of what theatre should and could be, and in Akutagawa he had found a man he could work with for a long time.

The original noh play about the magical dream pillow of Kantan is based on a Chinese fable. A young man setting out to seek his fortune in public life stops at an inn where he sleeps on the pillow. In a dream he sees himself embark on an illustrious career that takes him to the pinnacle of power and fame, only to be cruelly overthrown and killed. He awakes to find that the vision was a dream. The dream inspires him to repent of his secular desires and set out to follow the Buddha's way.

In Mishima's *shingeki* play, set in modern Japan, a disillusioned young man comes home to find that only his housekeeper remains. She has the pillow of Kantan and it has already magically transported four men away, never to return. The young man sleeps on the pillow, "wakes up," and encounters numerous temptations, promising power, fame, and the love of beautiful women. Even though he cynically rejects all temptations, he rises to power and wealth despite himself, finally becoming a great dictator. But his cynical detachment foils the inevitable assassination plot, and he "returns" to the house and his former maid with a new sense of the meaning and importance of common, day-to-day existence.[38]

The play is elegantly and wittily written, full of parody and social satire, and it includes a singing chorus and dancers, inspired by the noh drama. It is a purely *shingeki* play, written in contemporary Japanese, and meant to be produced using the conventions of the modern stage. Supernatural events take place in Mishima's play, but the supernatural experiences are lived by contemporary characters who attempt to make sense of these experiences in ways that make sense psychologically, to themselves and to the audience.

Kantan was a critical success that impressed the Bungaku-za. It inspired Mishima to work on more modern noh plays, and he wrote a total of nine of them between 1950 and 1962. They became his signature works and they are the most frequently performed of his one-act plays, both in Japan and around the world. *Kantan* also marked the beginning of a thirteen-year-long relationship between Mishima and the Bungaku-za that was, until their bitter parting, harmonious and productive for both parties.

Mishima's success with *Kantan* at the Bungaku-za in December 1950, caught the attention of the *shingeki* world, and he found himself once again planning projects with the Haiyū-za leadership. Both Bungaku-za and Haiyū-za were eager to present his modern noh plays in their small-stage series for new works, and both did in 1952. Bungaku-za premiered *Sotoba Komachi* and Haiyū-za premiered *The Damask Drum* within a few days of each other in February.

Sotoba Komachi is recognized as one of the very best plays among Mishima's nine modern noh plays. Mishima's source is a classical noh play, which tells the ninth-century story of the courtier Fukakusa's fatal obsession with the heartless beauty and poetess, Ono no Komachi, and his hundred-night vigil in her garden, waiting in vain for her to acknowledge his love. Mishima's play is set in postwar Tokyo. In a park one night a romantic young poet encounters a hideous old beggar lady who tells him that in the 1880s she was a beautiful young aristocratic girl named Komachi. The beggar lady is transformed in the poet's eyes into the gorgeous creature she was in the past, and he becomes her suitor, an officer named Fukakusa. They go to a ball in the famous Rokumeikan pavilion, and he declares his eternal love for her. The beggar entreats the poet to perceive the reality of her ugliness and old age—if he cannot, he will die, but the poet replies, "If I think something is beautiful, I must say it is beautiful, even if I die for it."[39] The poet's obsession with romance and beauty, and his inability to recognize reality, lead him to death in a single night just as surely as the same failings led Fukakusa to his death after his one-hundred-night vigil a millennium earlier. In *Sotoba Komachi* Mishima pits romanticism against cynicism, beauty against death, and dream against reality in a gripping, modern existential debate.

In the late forties and in the first years of the fifties, Mishima wrote and published many essays on theatre. Mishima wrote one of his most important, "Notes by a Novelist who Enjoys Writing Plays," in 1949, between his first two Haiyū-za plays. The essay ranges over a wide number of topics. In it Mishima compares the essential nature of *shingeki* and kabuki; of fiction and drama; of Germanic literature, Latinate literature, and Japanese literature; and he enters the debate about who is the better playwright, Shakespeare or Racine. Mishima also states his personal tastes (it is here that we learn that his favorite play of all time is Racine's *Phaedra*) and reasons for writing drama. "There are times when I really want to write plays," he begins, "usually in the middle of writing fiction or essays. It's hard to analyze just why.

It is like going from a routine family meal to a pleasant but not ostentatious evening party. Writing plays puts me in a good mood."[40]

In the debate between form and content Mishima comes out solidly on the side of form. "Passion and form come together to make theatre, but naturalism, proletarian literature, and postwar plays stress content, and their authors show contempt for form with the result that they have lost artistic quality. *Shingeki* reeks of pedantry, didacticism, elitism, condescension, and spineless intellectual pettiness. Exciting theatre won't be possible until it banishes these qualities altogether. The solution is to learn from kabuki. Theatre should be about scandal. We need a *shingeki* play that opens immediately with a scene of a pastor strangling a policeman to death."[41] In this diatribe, Mishima criticizes the content of *shingeki,* not its form. Mishima was committed to making *shingeki* more intense and immediate, and he put his convictions into practice in his modern noh plays. Mishima went on to denounce literature used as a political tool, even for "enlightenment," declaring that "it is time for artists to return to art."[42]

Kabuki Playwright Extraordinaire, 1953–58

The years 1953 to 1958 were Mishima's glory years. During these years Mishima amazed the world of the stage by writing five classical kabuki plays, four of which appear in this anthology. His opus was called "Mishima Kabuki," and his kabuki plays were entirely unique fusions of classical staging and language with characters possessing contemporary personalities and moral values. During these six years Mishima also wrote many successful *shingeki* plays and became a member of the Bungaku-za company. From 1953 to 1958 Mishima produced an amazing series of novels and short stories, each so different from the other that it was almost impossible to imagine that the same man had written them all. In 1953 he published "Death in Midsummer," a probing and sympathetic exploration of the feelings of a mother who loses her two small children in an accident. At the same time he was writing *Forbidden Colors,* a portrait of the lives of homosexual men in Tokyo, revealing Mishima's convictions about beauty and the impossibility of love. Soon after completing his Daphnis and Chloe love story, *The Sound of Waves,* he embarked on the creation of the tortured psyche of the young monk who set fire to Japan's greatest architectural treasure in what some consider the finest novel of his career, *The Temple of the Golden Pavilion.*

It was during these years that Mishima embarked on a path that no major novelist had ever pursued—he became a kabuki playwright, contributing a new work almost every year to the most important shows at kabuki's premiere venue, the Kabuki-za. Mishima had been unconsciously, or perhaps subconsciously, preparing himself for this career for sixteen years. From his first year in middle school, he had attended kabuki every month whenever he was in Tokyo. He continued to write his personal journal of theatre criticism until the end of 1947. The one hundred entries over a five-year period prepared Mishima to be perhaps the most eloquent kabuki critic of the postwar era. From 1948 he published regularly in newspapers and kabuki journals. In some of his articles he analyzed kabuki as an art form, and explained why it appealed to him. In 1948 he wrote that "the force behind all of kabuki is evil. Kabuki's power is based on twin curses of cruelty and stupidity. Its beauty is suffused with danger, its ugliness must have the fascination of the demonic."[43] He quoted Shakespeare, saying that in kabuki "foul is fair and fair is foul."[44]

No topic or person elicited more creative prose from Mishima than did Nakamura Utaemon VI (1917–2001), the leading *onnagata* of the second half of the twentieth century. It is safe to say that without Utaemon, Mishima would not have become a kabuki playwright. Between 1948 and 1953 Mishima wrote five long essays about Utaemon. The actor and his art are best described in Mishima's words. Mishima began by writing that "the appeal of the actor is entirely physical. His acting is in no way intellectual, nor can a brilliant actor be analyzed intellectually. If you can, then he is not a great actor."[45] Having denied the validity of intellectual analysis, Mishima went on, over the years, to exhaust his descriptive powers in his attempt to do the impossible. "Utaemon may not look like a classical *onnagata,* with his eyes that tilt upward and his protruding lower lip, but he makes you feel that this is how *onnagata* in the past must have played their roles."[46] "Utaemon is a blend of classical form and modern melancholy that lead us to the heart of kabuki."[47] "He has a cold, desolate strength, like fire freezing over, and when you touch it you will burn your hands."[48] "You sense danger, and vulnerability, when, as Yukihime, he bends backward, and you feel he'll snap in two, but then, with a frightful deliberateness he bends even more, and cherry petals fall into his breast."[49]

Mishima did not try to meet Utaemon personally until 1952, and when he did, he requested that Utaemon meet him while in full makeup and costume. This made Utaemon feel somewhat uncomfortable because, committed *onnagata* that he was, he felt he had to be in character as a woman when dressed that way.[50] Nevertheless, the meeting between ardent fan and kabuki star went well enough, and a year later Mishima would write his first kabuki play for the actor he admired above all others.

Mishima loved kabuki for its aesthetic beauty more than anything else, and he was strongly attracted to kabuki dance plays, *buyō* dance, and dance in general. Later in the 1950s, after watching Bandō Mitsugorō VII (1882–1961), one of the greatest *buyō* dancers of the century, perform in a New Year's kabuki show, Mishima wrote about the essence of dance:

> When an audience sees good dance the viewers feel that *this* is what the human body was meant to do. It is a vision of the freedom and beauty that the body can become. Dance is joy. Even if a dance portrays grief, the means it uses to portray grief is joyful. Dance

> burdens the body with the incredibly severe restriction of music, killing one's ability to exercise free will over one's own body, and pulls humans back to the essential rhythms of our existence. What is strange is that humans can only be free when they have submitted to the powerful restraint of a human invention—music—a force totally outside our bodies. But though music seems to be the invention of man, it in fact conforms to the basic natural laws of the universe, so though we look and feel free when we dance, that feeling in fact is the result of returning to a primordial state that precedes human life.[51]

It is significant that Mishima senses freedom in one of Japan's most formal and disciplined genres of dance.

Mishima's first creative writing in classical Japanese was not for kabuki, but instead took the form of dance drama texts. *Buyō* dance drama texts include lyrical and allusive poetry to be sung by one or more musical ensembles, and frequently employ dialogue for the dancers. Mishima wrote his first dance drama in 1944, a never performed but remarkably precocious *jiuta* spin-off of the *Chūshingura* story (the forty-seven loyal retainers).[52] In 1951 he wrote a three-act dance drama text entitled *The Girl Who Longed To Be a Chikamatsu Heroine (Tsuya Kurabe Chikamatsu Musume)* for a major *buyō* recital by the Yanagibashi Midorikai, a geisha ensemble, with lyrics for both *kiyomoto* and *tokiwazu* musicians. It is an original play about a girl who is obsessed with Chikamatsu's love suicide plays and stages a sham love suicide with her lover in order to be with him. The ghosts of dead lovers from a Chikamatsu play appear before the girl and her lover and dance for them. When the girl prays for the repose of the ghosts' souls, they reward her by helping her to remain forever with the man she loves.[53] In 1952 and 1953 Mishima wrote two more *buyō* dance dramas and a Western-style danced operetta set at the Carnival in Rio de Janeiro.

Mishima's love of kabuki and admiration for Utaemon and his work as a kabuki critic and dance drama playwright did not escape the notice of the Shochiku Corporation, the huge entertainment company that owns major theatres like the Kabuki-za, Tōgeki, and Shimbashi Enbujō, and which produced most kabuki performances in the early 1950s. In 1949, when he went to see a show at Tōgeki Theatre, Mishima ran into an old school acquaintance, Nagayama Takeomi (1925–2006), who was then working in the theatre manager's office.[54] Nagayama would later become president of the Shochiku Corporation. Nagayama and Mishima were both born in 1925, but because Mishima was born in January and Nagayama in August, Mishima was one year his senior at the Peers School. Their paths rarely crossed at school, but each admired the other from afar: Mishima cheered star catcher Nagayama at baseball games, and Nagayama was amazed by Mishima's contributions to the school's literary magazines.[55] What they did not know was that both had mothers who loved kabuki and took their sons regularly.

In 1953 the director of production at the Kabuki-za recommended to Ōtani Takejirō, then president of Shochiku, that they ask Mishima to write a kabuki play.[56] In a conference they agreed that they would suggest an adaptation of Akutagawa Ryunosuke's famous short story "Hell Screen," the story of a cruel and capricious minister of state who orders a master artist to paint a hell screen, the completion of which requires the painter to witness his own daughter's death inside a carriage that has been set on fire. The Shochiku leadership decided on this story because of Akutagawa's stellar reputation, and because the short story had three major characters that could be easily converted into a play with a unique love triangle.[57]

Nagayama was sent to make the request because by this time he and Mishima were good friends. He went along with the general manager of the Kabuki-za to Mishima's home in Meguro. As Nagayama remembers it, Mishima answered at once: "Akutagawa's 'Hell Screen.' It sounds interesting. But the play I write for you will be nothing at all like what you are expecting."[58] Mishima was familiar with a prewar *shin kabuki* adaptation of the story, done for Ichikawa Sadanji II (1880–1940) which transposed the original story almost verbatim onto the kabuki stage.[59] After a very brief discussion of the project, the Shochiku men enjoyed a long afternoon talking about kabuki with Mishima and his mother.

Mishima promised to deliver the play by autumn, and he spent a long, hard summer working on it. What made it so difficult was that he was writing original lyrics in classical poetic Japanese to be sung by a *gidayū* narrator, interwoven into the dialogue of the play in the manner of a traditional historical drama. Unlike the more ornamental lyrics of his earlier dance dramas, this narration had to sustain the plot and characterizations of the play more directly. It had to be *gidayū* because Mishima believed that "*gidayū bushi* may be the most expressive theatrical medium in the world, because it has the artistic means to express violent emotions."[60] "Powerful and violent emotions cannot be expressed in the language of *shingeki*."[61] Mishima felt contempt for standard new kabuki plays "composed in modern Japanese or in some mixed modern/classical idiom."[62] He would write kabuki in the language of Chikamatsu or Mokuami, not Mayama Seika. Further, Mishima loved the rhythm of Edo period Japanese as it was delivered on the kabuki stage. Mishima had a point to prove with this play.

The task Mishima set for himself was a difficult one. He described the challenge later in an essay:

> To bring to life lines of *gidayū bushi*, full of simple humor and vulgarity, was truly difficult. You need to do an incredible amount of study in a wide variety of areas. You have to take the stance of a antiquarian. The heads of Edo period *jōruri* authors were filled with the arcana of Japan and China, but when they wrote *jōruri* they never let learning impede entertainment. And today when we listen to *jōruri*, we listen with the same ears that listen to Heifetz,

> and when we stop at a bar on the way home from the theatre we argue about Sartre. In these circumstances to write *jōruri* is almost absurd. It was a strange and unhealthy effort, so much so that I thought at times it would make me ill.[63]

Mishima sent progress reports to Nagayama, who met with his staff in September to devise a conflagration for the play. Kabuki had a rich repertoire of tried and true special effects, but burning carriages was not on the list.[64] Mishima was finished by mid-October, and when he gave the script to Nagayama he shouted exultantly, "It's in *gidayū bushi!*" This was what he meant by a text that Nagayama was not expecting.[65]

At the first reading of the script Mishima revived a custom that had gone into abeyance in the Meiji period. Just like the company head playwrights of old, he read the entire text himself, with kabuki delivery for each character. The director, Kubota Mantarō (1889–1963), was so excited that he joined Mishima, and they read together.[66] Mishima would do this *hon yomi* for his actors at the first cast meeting before every one of his kabuki plays.

Utaemon, who would play the leading woman's role, was amazed by the text.[67] He had never seen a new kabuki piece like it. It was a tour-de-force, almost unimaginable in a first-time kabuki playwright. The *gidayū* text was written in flawless *shichi-gochō* (seven-five syllable poetic meter), ready to be set to music without any changes necessary. Provisions were made for *geza* music and lyrics (incidental music from the concealed musicians' room, stage right). The entire play reads as if it were written in the late Edo period. Thus, Mishima held true to his convictions about the language of the play. The actors had no difficulty delivering Mishima's lines just as they were written, all the while using traditional kabuki acting techniques. It was a piece made to order for Utaemon, with the actor's physically frail but spiritually indominatable beauty subjected to unspeakable cruelty in the climactic carriage-burning scene. Utaemon later wrote that he had never had such a positive experience with a new kabuki play.[68] The only major cut in the script made during rehearsal was the elimination of most of the narration and dialogue during the carriage-burning scene. The visual impact was so strong that the director felt that words were superfluous, and Mishima willingly accepted this change. He wrote that his greatest satisfaction as playwright came when he saw audiences rapt in horror during the climax of the play.[69]

Hell Screen was a financial and critical success in 1953, although it has been criticized in hindsight, when compared to his later, more original kabuki plays. Mishima had turned the original narrative fiction into a dialogue-centered text. He had also rewritten the play in a classical idiom, changed the structure of the tale to fit the European three unities, and added three significant new characters. All the same, many felt his play was too similar to Akutagawa's original tale. Mishima himself wanted to do a more original play for his next kabuki.[70] In any case, Mishima's *Hell Screen* text, and his support of the company during rehearsals, convinced Shochiku and its leading actors, especially Utaemon and lead male role actor Nakamura Kanzaburō XVII (1909–88), to work with him on future kabuki projects.

Mishima's next kabuki play was *The Sardine Seller's Net of Love,* a romantic comedy entirely different from *Hell Screen.* This play would turn out to be the all-time favorite Mishima kabuki, enjoying repeated performances over the fifty years since Kanzaburō first trod the boards of the Kabuki-za in 1954 as the lovelorn peddler of sardines, with Utaemon as his beloved courtesan.

In 1953, thanks in part to a successful revival of the 1698 hit play *Keisei Asamagatake,* Mishima was discovering the joys of Genroku kabuki and its "cheerful, refreshing, generous, bright, dialogue-based plays."[71] The Genroku era, at the turn of the eighteenth century, was the period when the first great actors and playwrights created the first sophisticated kabuki plays. The plays of that period were full of light-hearted word play and physical comedy. For *The Sardine Seller* Mishima borrowed from a medieval folk tale *(otogizōshi)* and a parody of *The Tale of the Heike,* in which all of the protagonists are animals, but the overall story was an original creation done in homage to Genroku kabuki, with its disguises, parodies, and playful love affairs.

The story of *The Sardine Seller* is silly and charming at the same time. Sarugenji, the son of a wealthy fish wholesaler, catches a glimpse of a high-ranking courtesan riding in a palanquin and falls so hopelessly in love that he collapses and is unable to sell sardines. His father agrees to assist him in the seemingly hopeless task of meeting a lady normally reserved only for the wealthiest patrons. They will rent costumes and a horse, and Sarugenji will pose as a feudal lord to gain access to the lofty courtesan, Hotarubi.

Happy revelry ensues in the pleasure district, during which Sarugenji, pressed to recount his exploits in battle, recites the "Fish Battle of Ichinotani," a punning "fish *jōruri*" tour-de-force in the spirit of Chikamatsu that only a genius like Mishima would even think of attempting in this day and age. Presently the inebriated sardine seller dozes off, head resting on his beloved's lap. In his sleep he begins to intone his sardine seller's spiel. When awakened and questioned by Hotarubi, Sarugenji gamely supports his false identity by deftly citing classical poems. Convinced that the young man is indeed a feudal lord, Hotarubi collapses in tears. She is really a princess who fell in love with a sardine seller when, from her castle tower, she heard him call out his spiel in a beautiful voice. She was later kidnapped and sold to a Kyoto brothel, but she has never forsaken her first, true love. The princess resolves to become a fishmonger's wife, and join him, singing out the vendor's calls, selling sardines all over the Kyoto region.

The response to *Sardine Seller* in 1954 was unanimous popular and critical acclaim. Mishima knew his audience intimately, and all were charmed by this play. Hotarubi is beautiful and elegant and Sarugenji is a short, earnest, little fool. Despite his fishy smell, the sardine vendor is the only man for Hotarubi. A love so incongruous just had to be true. Unlike traditional kabuki tragedies, in this joyful play love conquered all, and postwar Japanese audiences seemed to enjoy a play that disavowed rigid Edo period class rules.

The critics were just as entranced as audiences. Toita Yasuji called the play "a very fresh sardine, capturing the essence of one of the glories of Japan."[72] Akiyama Yasusaburō wrote, "It is remarkably enjoyable. I am amazed at the degree to which a young author has assimilated the essence of kabuki humor and wordplay."[73] After *Sardine Seller* kabuki critics and producers jokingly suggested to Mishima that he should give up fiction writing and become a full-time kabuki playwright.

At the cast read-through of the play Kanzaburō remarked to Mishima that he must have been in a happy mood when he wrote the play.[74] On this second effort archaic Japanese flowed from Mishima's pen with ease.[75] Utaemon loved the play and the Hotarubi role. He was now in a remarkable position for a postwar kabuki actor—he had a talented playwright doing new material especially for him. Utaemon later said that it was after *Sardine Seller* that he resolved to "go with Mishima in kabuki wherever he led."[76] What a thrill it must have been for Mishima to be working so closely with his idol.

Early in 1955 Mishima adapted the noh play *Yuya* to kabuki as a *shosagoto* dance drama. The noh play was a favorite of Utaemon's, and he specifically requested the work of Mishima to present in February at his privately produced kabuki recital, called Tsubomi no Kai.

Mishima wrote *Yuya* in two months. It was set to *nagauta* music, a new challenge for Mishima. Mishima also redesigned the play's dramaturgical concept. In the noh play Yuya is a dancing girl who is the mistress of Grand Minister Taira no Munemori. Although she has word that her mother is gravely ill, she must stifle her grief and dance and entertain gaily at a cherry-blossom viewing party held by her patron. The appeal of the play lies in the contrast of the grieving beauty who is denied permission to visit her mother with the splendor and joy of the Capital bedecked in blossoms. Munemori's character is thinly sketched in the original play, but Mishima made him something of a medieval epicurean sadist. Yuya (Utaemon) retained much of her character from the noh play, but Munemori was done in pure kabuki style, and Mishima added a temple priest, done in quasi-*shingeki* style.

Mishima directed the play and had a much better rapport with his cast and production colleagues than he had during his directorial debut at the Haiyū-za five years before. Of course the director of a kabuki dance drama is responsible only for the overall aesthetics of the production and for the relationship between speaking parts and danced parts. The choreographer is responsible for dance and the acting within dance that is at the core of the play. *Yuya* was presented at the Kabuki-za in the regular program in April of

Figure 2. Mishima (left) at the Kabuki-za in 1957 at a rehersal of the kabuki dance drama *Yuya*, with actor Nakamura Utaemon VI (right) and choreographer Fujima Kanjūrō VI (center). Photograph courtesy of the Mishima Yukio Literary Museum. Photograph by Yoshida Chiaki.

1957. Utaemon danced it twice more for kabuki, and it entered his personal repertory of favorite dance dramas. Reviews were increasingly positive each time the play was performed.

Mishima had provided Shochiku with two hit plays for its gala November Kaomise productions in 1953 and 1954, and the kabuki world was expecting another in 1955. It was to be the kabuki play Mishima most wanted to write, his adaptation of Racine's *Phaedra* to the kabuki stage. He had been thinking about the task for four or five years already. Mishima understood the challenge that he was facing. He realized that "the structures of Racinian drama and kabuki are as different as oil and water."[77] The original could not simply be translated and put on a kabuki stage; it would have to be more like an adaptation of Racine's *Phaedra* to ballet or opera.[78] Mishima reset the play in Japan's feudal era, and made it entirely native in spirit because he wanted to create the intimacy and power that could only come when audiences view a work from their own cultural heritage. With this play Mishima hoped to provide "the experiential equivalent of a French mother taking her middle school-age son to see *Phaedra* at the Comedie Francaise. To do this requires a scale and grandeur impossible to achieve in a *shingeki* production. It had to be kabuki, and Phaedra had to be played by Utaemon."[79] Mishima directed the play himself.

The play was entitled *The Blush on the White Hisbiscus Blossom: Lady Fuyo and the True Account of the Ōuchi Clan (Fuyo no tsuyu Ōuchi jikki).* It has proven to be Mishima's least successful kabuki play, and has never been restaged. During rehearsals Mishima had to scramble to rewrite a scene for Ichikawa En'ō (1888–1963) (playing the counterpart to Theseus) who complained that his part was too small. Mishima made the requested substantial changes in a matter of hours so that rehearsals could proceed without delay. With only four or five days to completely rehearse a brand new play, time was of the essence. Mishima swallowed his pride as director and playwright and gave in to the demands by the famous kabuki actor that he revise the play. Utaemon had been Mishima's dream Phaedra, but Utaemon found Lady Fuyo a difficult role to play. To an extent, Utaemon blamed himself for the lack of success of the play, but he also wrote that Mishima was a much better playwright than director.[80]

Reviews were mixed, but much more negative than for *Hell Screen* or *Sardine Seller.* Some reviewers said it was weak because it was an adaptation of a foreign play, not an original work.[81] Toita wrote that it was based on visual beauty and a stringing together of the weakest aspects of kabuki dramaturgy.[82] The most favorable reviewer wrote, "The absurdity of kabuki perfectly suits the impossibility of adapting foreign works to our culture. It is a small-scale curiosity. Not impressive, but a cleverly done one-act play."[83] Mishima said of the reviews, "These people understand nothing."[84]

No kabuki plays by Mishima were performed in 1956, but in 1957 *The Sardine Seller* and *Yuya* were produced at the Meiji-za and the Kabuki-za to popular and critical acclaim. In August 1957 Utaemon joined with Shochiku to co-produce a combined Tsubomi Kai and Shimpa show. For this show Utaemon requested a *shimpa* play from Mishima. The result was *Morning Azaleas (Asa no Tsutsuji),* in which Utaemon played a Viscountess in a declining aristocratic family who is forced to submit to the advances of a nouveau riche boor in order to secure money to save her family. All in all it was an undistinguished performance in an undistinguished play.[85] It was probably a good thing that Mishima was in New York that August.

Mishima wrote his last one-act kabuki play, *Musume Gonomi Obitori no Ike (The Sash Stealing Pond),* a comedy, for presentation at the 1958 November Kaomise at the Kabuki-za. This time Mishima set out to parody historical drama, specifically the most exalted secular act that takes place on the Edo stage—the pursuit of blood revenge. The mid-fifties had seen something of a Chikamatsu revival. In a 1958 essay Mishima wrote that he admired Chikamatsu's art, but unlike his contemporaries who held Chikamatsu's domestic tragedies in highest esteem, Mishima now preferred the history plays. He loved fighting heroes like Coxinga, and he admired Chikamatsu's parody scenes in the history plays.[86]

Mishima borrowed a setting and the lead male character for *Sash Stealing Pond* from a piece of an obscure nineteenth-century adventure story by Santo Kyōden (1761–1816). The character was the Toad Bandit (Gama-maru), who used a magic potion to help him rob and drown victims in a pond north of Kyoto. The play's plot and all other characters were original.

The heroine of the play is Princess Kiku (Utaemon) who is on a quest to take revenge on the man who robbed and murdered her mother. Toad Bandit has been using Kiku's mother's sash to lure travelers to the pond, so Kiku is convinced that he is the man who murdered her mother. But it turns out that although Toad Bandit waylaid and raped her mother, her mother chose to become the bandit's wife. Princess Kiku expresses humiliation and revulsion at her mother's depravity, but later she has to admit that her assumption of the high moral ground is hypocritical. She is in love with the handsome, young family retainer Samanosuke, but their difference in station prevents her from marrying him. The play concludes when all the principal characters agree to keep the liaison between the Toad Bandit and the mother secret from the world so that Princess Kiku and Samanosuke can travel around the country on a sham revenge quest and share the same bed as husband and wife when they spend the night at inns.

Kiku and her mother engage in immoral behavior, both by Edo period standards and the standards of Japanese society in 1958. One marries her rapist and the other fakes the sacred act of blood revenge to cover up an illicit love affair. Kabuki audiences seem to love them nevertheless. As in the *Sardine Seller,* the feudal hierarchy is repudiated when two aristocratic ladies consummate their love with a servant and a bandit. In traditional kabuki plays, mothers in the samurai class are always sticklers for moral propriety who sternly counsel their daughters to beware of irresponsible affairs of the heart. Mishima turned kabuki convention on its head by having a daughter reprimand her mother for her immoral behavior.[87] In *Sash Stealing Pond* Mishima questions conventional moral values much as he did in serious novels like *Forbidden Colors* and *The Temple of the Golden Pavilion*, but instead of denying the possibility of love, as he had in these two novels, in *Sash Stealing Pond* Mishima made apparently immoral relationships acceptable for middle-class kabuki audiences by having true love conquer all, as it had in *The Sardine Seller*.

Sash Stealing Pond was the first play to use the Kabuki-za's recently redesigned stage machinery. This is one reason why Mishima put more special effects scenes in this play than in any previous work. Spectacular effects included swimming and swooping sashes, an actor-swallowing pond, a huge flying kite, and a dramatic *gandōgaeshi* scene change in which the entire set for scene one rotates upward, revealing scene two. Kabuki fans and critics loved the play for its quirky characters, unexpected plot twists, its playful eroticism, and spectacular staging. There was "a special esprit in this ridiculous story . . . it was a play that captured the spirit of late Edo, but which attracts modern audiences to kabuki."[88] Utaemon enjoyed the play, and it restored his confidence in Mishima after *Morning Azaleas*.

After *Sash Stealing Pond*, Mishima wrote no more kabuki plays for Shochiku. His love of kabuki remained, but his participation took other directions. In 1959 he edited a sumptuous book of photographs and essays dedicated to Utaemon. He had already paid tribute to Utaemon in the short story *Onnagata* (1957), a sensitive character sketch of a *shingeki* director's complex feelings about a kabuki actor, with the portrait of the actor based closely on Mishima's idol. Mishima also assisted Shochiku with the reconstruction of a lost classic by Tsuruya Namboku, *The Scarlet Princess of Edo (Sakura Hime Azuma Bunsho)*.

For most of the 1960s Mishima did not work in kabuki. Nagayama suggests that the time and energy Mishima had previously reserved for kabuki he devoted to films during those eight years.[89] In the late sixties Mishima once again turned to kabuki, writing and directing the longest and most ambitious kabuki play of his career, *The Moon Drawn Like a Bow (Chinzetsu Yumihari Zuki)*, produced just before his death. In this endeavor Mishima followed the prescription he set forth for *Sash Stealing Pond* in 1958: "Newly composed kabuki plays should be couched in the idiom of traditional kabuki, and should partake of the beauty, stage mechanics, and all of the acting conventions, just as they are used in traditional kabuki. I believe that within this framework, contemporary themes and modern humor and wit must be interwoven into a new and original work."[90] Mishima did much more than this in his kabuki plays. He infused his own personality and convictions into plays that were written in classical Japanese and presented following Edo period stage conventions. No playwright had done this for a half a cen-

Figure 3. Mishima (left) onstage at the Kabuki-za in 1958 for a rehersal of *Sash Stealing Pond*, with, from right to left, Ichikawa Ennosuke II, director Kubota Mantarō, and Nakamura Utaemon VI. Photograph courtesy of the Mishima Yukio Literary Museum. Photograph by Yoshida Chiaki.

tury prior to Mishima, and none has done it in the thirty-seven years since Mishima's death.

Shingeki Forays, 1952–55

While the years 1953–55 saw Mishima establish himself as the finest kabuki playwright of the postwar era, he was enjoying somewhat less success in the *shingeki* theatre. His one-act modern noh plays were favorites among critics, but Mishima only began to write multiact *shingeki* plays after 1950, and it was not until 1956, and his blockbuster play *Rokumeikan*, that Mishima could regularly write multiact plays that would attract large audiences for extended runs.

From 1952 to 1954 only two multiact *shingeki* plays by Mishima were produced. His first, in the summer of 1952, was *Twilight Sunflower (Yoru no Himawari)*—a play that Mishima wrote while stranded in Paris for a month without funds earlier that year. It is the story of two women, one a vindictive schemer, the other forgiving and openhearted, who compete for the affections of an ailing man whom they have each been married to and divorced from. One reviewer wrote that with long speeches and relatively little action on stage, *Twilight Sunflower* was better suited to be a novel than a play, but the characters and the story intrigued audiences and critics.[91]

In *Twilight Sunflower,* a talented young actress, Kishida Kyōko (1930–2006), performed for her first time in a Mishima play. She was Kishida Kunio's daughter, and Mishima first met her during his visits to Kishida's house. Mishima admired her for her intelligence, versatility, and calm demeanor on stage. Kishida Kyōko, who was well known outside Japan for her starring role in the film *Woman of the Dunes*, would become one of the great actresses of the late twentieth century, and she performed in more Mishima plays than any other actor or actress.

In 1953 and 1954 Mishima was preoccupied with writing for kabuki and dance drama, and he had only one *shingeki* play produced, but 1955 was a watershed year for Mishima in theatre. During that year nine of his plays were professionally produced in Tokyo: one *buyō* dance drama, one kabuki play, one musical review, three one-act *shingeki* plays, and three three-act *shingeki* plays. Nine plays produced in a single year is a record unchallenged in postwar drama and reflects an amazing productivity only possible for a playwright who could write for many different theatrical genres. This pattern would continue for Mishima throughout the 1950s. In 1955 Bungaku-za produced three of Mishima's six *shingeki* plays—one in its "atelier" series, the others in two separate five-week-long touring productions. Bungaku-za finally chose to showcase a modern noh play to a broader public as a main stage production in large theatres in Tokyo, Osaka, and Kyoto. The play was *Lady Aoi,* one of the finest of the genre.

In December one of the most important theatre innovators of the postwar period, Takechi Tetsuji (1912–88), directed an experimental production of Mishima's modern noh play *The Damask Drum*, with actors from *shingeki* (including Kishida Kyōko) as well as the traditional noh and *kyōgen* theatres. Takechi's production used noh masks, noh dance, Western music, and theatre in the round. Takechi had breathed new life into kabuki by introducing elements from noh and *kyōgen*, and had directed radically experimental noh and *kyōgen* plays that angered the hidebound authorities of those arts. He brought together performers who before the war could never have imagined working on the same stage in the same production. These experiments brought new and younger audiences to traditional performance.

Takechi's approach to directing *The Damask Drum* went against Mishima's strongest instincts about the theatre. Takechi used an eclectic mixture of theatrical conventions and made major alterations to the performance text. Mishima was initially apprehensive about turning his play over to a director like Takechi, who planned to stage the play in such a radically different way from what Mishima had in mind when he wrote it. Mishima wrote that it was like "submitting one's child to plastic surgery," but he was tactful in his evaluation of the production in his program notes, applauding "Takechi's attempt to create theatre from the same disparate elements that comprise Japanese contemporary society."[92] Mishima and Takechi never worked together again. Takechi later attributed their estrangement to disagreements over politics,[93] but their artistic differences were just as great.

Mishima's best new play of 1955 was *The Termites' Nest*, a three-act play set in the Japanese immigrant community in Brazil, staged by a new, young company called Seinen-za. It is about the forbidden passions that tear several families apart, and contains two failed attempts at double suicide by the same couple. In the play Mishima explores the contrast between romantic notions of death and its sordid reality, a theme he never tired of. *The Termites' Nest* was awarded the prestigious Kishida Prize in 1955.

Rokumeikan, *and Joining the Bungaku-za*

In 1956 the Bungaku-za celebrated the twentieth anniversary of its founding by staging four new works by Japanese playwrights. The most successful of them was Mishima's *Rokumeikan*. This play did for Mishima in drama what *Confessions of a Mask* had done for him as in the world of fiction seven years earlier—it made him a superstar of the theatre.

The last two acts of *Rokumeikan* are set in one of Japan's most famous Meiji-period cultural landmarks, the Rokumeikan, or "Baying Stag Pavilion." Built in 1883, it was a large, ornate Western-style brick building, with sitting rooms and a spacious, open ballroom on the second floor. The Japanese government used it as an official entertainment venue. Japanese politicians and government officials and their wives learned ballroom dancing so that, dressed in the latest European fashions, they could participate in European soirees at the Rokumeikan, thereby hoping to convince foreign dignitaries that Japan was a civilized nation.

Mishima was fascinated by the Rokumeikan and the cultural contradictions inherent in what took place there. He had already used it as the setting for the ghostly portion of his modern noh play, *Sotoba Komachi*. Mishima wanted to make the Rokumeikan itself a central character in the play and to interweave within the play the political conflicts of the day: the struggle against unequal treaties and the emerging nativist reaction against European "enlightenment."[94]

The play takes the form of a classic melodrama in four acts, with political intrigue at the highest level of the government inextricably connected to generational conflict between father and son, and complex romantic relationships. At the center of the story is the former geisha Asako, now married to the Prime Minister. Asako still has tender feelings for Kiyohara, her former lover and the head of the liberal opposition party whom the Prime Minister is plotting to have assassinated. Asako's son by Kiyohara is plotting to kill his father for his anti-imperial beliefs. Asako is at the very center of the action, part Machiavellian manipulator, part tenderhearted lover and mother, struggling to save the lives of her lover and son and yet remain faithful to her present husband.

Although Bungaku-za had staged six of Mishima's plays already, Sugimura Haruko, the company's star actress, had not appeared in any of them. She was too big a draw to appear in small-stage productions, and she chose her roles with care. Mishima wrote Asako's part for Sugimura, and it was a novel role for her in several respects. Bungaku-za, in order to distinguish itself from low-brow *shimpa* and other forms of popular theatre, had carefully avoided plays with major characters who were entertainers. Although Sugimura was in fact the daughter of a geisha, she had never played a geisha on stage. Second, *Rokumeikan* was a grand historical melodrama, and Mishima believed it had to be presented in a grandiose, histrionic style. It was *shingeki*, but in the spirit of kabuki or *shimpa*. "Do the part however you want, but make it big," Mishima told Sugimura.[95] "People have said that your acting is too much like *shimpa*, but that's exactly right for *Rokumeikan*. It's not a play, it's DRAMA. Do it with big, dramatic poses."[96] Mishima had secured the actress he thought best for the Asako role, as well as the director he wanted for the play, Matsuura Takeo (1926–98), who would be directing his first Mishima play.

Mishima envisioned a different form of *shingeki* for this play, a *shingeki* with style and flair: "What calls the audience out of the existing daily emotions in which it sleeps should indeed be the *style* of the play."[97] Most Japanese thought of *shingeki* as realistic theatre, but Mishima saw *shingeki* acting as no less pattern-bound than kabuki or noh acting. The key to success, he believed, was to fill the patterned acting with intense, psychologically believable emotion."[98] This formula, as practiced by Matsuura, Sugimura, and

Figure 4. *Rokumeikan*, 1956, with Sugimura Haruko as Asako Kageyama and Nakamura Nobuo as her husband, Baron Kageyama. Photograph courtesy of the Bungaku-za and Waseda University Tsubouchi Hakase Memorial Theatre Museum.

the rest of the cast, was a great success, and *Rokumeikan* was a popular sensation. After its initial one-month runs in Tokyo and the Kansai, Bungaku-za organized a thirty-five-city tour that spanned twenty-five months, ranging from Kagoshima in the south to Asahikawa in the north. In the forty-five years since its premiere, *Rokumeikan* has been performed more often than any other multiact play by Mishima.

Critics were not as friendly to *Rokumeikan* as audiences were. The most common criticism was that it was too much like "cheap melodrama, full of gorgeous sets and costumes, raging passions, but the psychological necessity for all of the passion was too thin."[99] To be fair to Mishima and his audiences, there is more to *Rokumeikan* than exotic costumes, histrionics, and assassination plots. "Asako, whose life has been dominated by love, finds herself having to deal with high political intrigue, whereas her husband, the Prime Minister, for whom life has meant politics alone, finds that he has to come to grips with tender feelings, and this is what propels the play to its catastrophe."[100]

After *Rokumeikan*, Sugimura Haruko became a devoted supporter of Mishima and appeared in many of his plays. Mishima showed his admiration by writing the one-act play *Steeplechase* expressly for her, and labeling it "for Sugimura Haruko" immediately below the play's title. Sugimura was deeply moved by this public display of admiration by the famous author.[101] *Steeplechase*, a fusion of psychological realism and shamanic ritual structure deriving from the noh drama, is about a mother whose grief for the son she lost in a steeplechase accident drives her to the brink of insanity. Bungaku-za staged the play in 1957, and it was the only Mishima "atelier" play in which Sugimura ever acted. *Steeplechase* is a tiny gem of a play that shows what Mishima could accomplish when he set his hand to writing an entirely original modern noh play, though he did not label it as such. *Steeplechase* is the representative play in this anthology of the very successful Mishima/Sugimura collaboration of the late 1950s.

In 1957 Mishima joined the Bungaku-za as an official company member. Other companies were still producing his plays, but Mishima felt most at home in the Bungaku-za, and he knew that they had the actors and directors who could do the best job with most of his plays. As a company member, Mishima was required to provide Bungaku-za with one or two new plays every year. Over the next six years Matsuura directed Bungaku-za casts headed by Sugimura in four main stage productions of multiact plays by Mishima. Bungaku-za also staged six Mishima plays in atelier and main-stage productions with casts that did not include Sugimura.

In the late 1950s and into the 1960s Mishima wrote at least one multiact *shingeki* play per year for the Bungaku-za. They fall into three broad thematic categories: (1) translations of European classics staged as *shingeki: Britannicus*, 1957; *Salome*, 1960; *Tosca*, 1963; (2) adaptations of European classics into plays set in Japan: *The Pirate and the Rose (Bara to Kaizoku)*, 1958, based on *Sleeping Beauty*; *Tropical Tree (Nettaiju)*, 1959, based on the *Oresteia* and an account of a family tragedy in France; (3) original plays set in contemporary Japan that explore the personal tragedies of characters who were committed to nationalist or right-wing causes: *Tenth-day Chrysanthemum (Tōka no Kiku)*, 1961; *The Harp of Joy (Yorokobi no Koto)*, 1963.

Of these plays *The Tropical Tree* is particularly important because it represents a 180-degree change in Mishima's thinking about the potential of *shingeki* as a medium for classical tragedy. In the late 1940s and early 1950s Mishima had written that he believed *shingeki* was only capable of expressing lukewarm emotions and was best suited to plays about the repression or suppression of intense passions. He felt that kabuki and *gidayū bushi* were better for the direct expression of violent passions. *The Tropical Tree* demonstrates Mishima's growing confidence in the expressive capacity of *shingeki* to achieve a grand and powerful presentational style commensurate with the scale and passion required by classical plays.

The Tropical Tree, an adaptation of *The Oresteia* set in contemporary Japan, comes as close to a formal Greek tragedy as any play Mishima ever wrote. In this play Mishima strove for "a stage peopled by passions only, by passions clothed in words. All must be bathed in nightmarish hues."[102] The play presents a contemporary Japanese family (mother, father, grown son, and daughter) that is riddled by incestuous relationships and murderous scheming. As in classical Greek drama, only two or three characters appear in any one scene. The role of the chorus is played by a fifth character, the family housekeeper. The action of the play takes place in a single afternoon and night.

Two poetic images dominate the play: the sea, a place of boundless freedom where human taboos have no place, and the tropical tree with its brilliant red flowers that symbolize passion and blood. In the course of the play three murders are attempted, every heterosexual liaison possible among family members is attempted, and brother and sister set out to commit love suicide. An ode by the housekeeper proclaims that only that which dies is beautiful. Mishima perceived the truth of this in many places, but nowhere more poignantly than when standing amid the ruins of the Parthenon—he felt that perhaps the Greek sculptors and architects intentionally created works that would become more beautiful as they fell into ruin.[103]

In 1957, Knopf published Donald Keene's translations of five of Mishima's modern noh plays, and that summer Mishima left Japan on a long trip to New York to promote the book and to try to get his plays produced on Broadway. Mishima discovered that while he could command the finest directors, actors, and stages in Tokyo as a matter of course, producing plays on Broadway was an altogether different and more difficult proposition. His fame and notoriety had not penetrated Manhattan, and it did not help that he was trying to sell one-act plays to a forum dedicated to multiact plays and musicals. It also did not help matters that Mishima found himself saddled with incompetent producers. Various expedients were tried to solve the former problem, including writing an interlude that would connect *Sotoba Komachi* and *Lady Aoi* to make a single play, and writing a humorous, modern *kyōgen* play that could be inserted between the two modern noh plays so as to make something like a traditional noh/*kyōgen* program.[104] The *kyōgen* play that Mishima wrote in New York is called *Busu,* and it is the only play Mishima wrote with the intention of having it performed in English, not in Japanese. It is an adaptation of the most popular play in the *kyōgen* repertory, full of physical humor and antics. Mishima poked fun at contemporary ethnic stereotypes by setting the play in a Third Avenue antique store run by an émigré Russian with American employees.

This first attempt at producing plays abroad ended in frustration and disappointment for Mishima, but thanks to the English translations, his modern noh plays were exciting interest all over the world. German and Spanish translations came out in 1958 and 1959, and several plays were presented in a very successful German tour in 1958. Mishima returned to New York in 1960 with his new wife to see *Lady Aoi* and *Hanjo* performed by an excellent Off Broadway cast. Over the next three decades this selection of five plays enjoyed more popularity around the world, both on-stage and in bookstores, than any other plays from Japan. But Mishima had dreamed of a Broadway production of his plays. Only a Broadway hit could fully satisfy his hunger for international glory and support his bid for a Nobel Prize in literature. Even now, thirty years after his death, no Mishima play has been performed on Broadway.

The Black Lizard: *Mishima Breaks His Own Rules on Dramaturgy*

In *The Black Lizard (Kuro Tokage),* Mishima's most successful play of the early 1960s, Mishima abandoned his usual commitment to the formal rules of genre and wrote a wild and exuberant play that fused disparate theatrical traditions. It is a *shingeki* play that uses the dramaturgy of kabuki and the histrionics of both kabuki and *shimpa.* Like *The Tropical Tree, The Black Lizard* took up the theme of beauty and death, but it did so in a more lighthearted fashion. It was a fun play for Mishima, a decadent tragicomedy, full of disguises, trickery, high adventure, thievery, murder, romantic love, and romantic death. *The Black Lizard* premiered in 1962 and its popularity over the years on stage and screen has been second only to *Rokumeikan.* From the outset Mishima planned the project as a "producer system" play with a director and actors from various companies combined in a one-time project team.

The original *Black Lizard* was a highly atmospheric, erotic detective novel by Edogawa Rampo (1894–1965). Rampo, who took his pen name from Edgar Allan Poe, was Japan's king of prewar pulp fiction; he wrote in a style called *eroguro* ("erotic and grotesque"). His adventure and detective stories for adults are erotic, romantic, and macabre—a sort of combination of Sherlock Holmes, H.P. Lovecraft, and *Phantom of the Opera*. Rampo's *Black Lizard* is set in Osaka and Tokyo during the Roaring Twenties. It depicts the struggle of wits between "the Black Lizard," a beautiful, brilliant, cruel lady jewel thief who is a master of disguises, and Akechi Kogorō, Rampo's very popular superdetective. *Black Lizard* was one of Mishima's favorite novels when he was a child, and he had wanted for years to adapt it to the stage.

Mishima visited Rampo to obtain the author's permission and discuss his plans for the adaptation to the stage. Rampo was impressed with Mishima from the outset, and very pleased with Mishima's plans for his stage version.[105] Mishima's most important change was to fully develop a love affair between the Black Lizard and Akechi that was only hinted at in the original novel. The producer convinced Mishima to make other changes: to move most of the action from Osaka to Tokyo, and to set the play in the 1960s. Mishima strove nevertheless to maintain the spirit of the twenties jazz age[106] and to achieve the sumptuous decadence he felt in the original story: "The play should be like a gorgeous decorator cake. But when you look carefully at the cake, it is crawling with maggots."[107]

Mishima conceived this as a playful work, and he discarded the three unities with no compunction. In kabuki fashion, the action of the play spans several weeks, and there are three acts and thirteen scenes, many requiring spectacular staging. The play's scenic requirements were as sophisticated as the most complex kabuki plays, and Mishima used several formal elements of kabuki dramaturgy, including shared delivery of lines by several actors, and long, histrionic monologues meant to express the deepest feelings of the character. Mishima had written that the fusion of aesthetic beauty and cruelty is the essence of kabuki, and he achieved that fusion in this play.

Mishima's close friend and stalwart supporter, Matsuura Takeo, directed the 1962 production, and Mizutani Yaeko (1905–79), the diva of *shimpa,* took the title role. Handsome Bungaku-za stalwart, Akutagawa Hiroshi, played Inspector Akechi. Mizutani was attracted to the role both by the opportunity to work with fresh artistic partners and the chance to try to create a new, more up-to-date drama that appealed to large audiences.[108] Mishima wrote that the title role had to be played "in the style of the great French actresses of the nineteenth century. The actress has to be a *"tres grande dame."*[109] Mizutani fulfilled his dreams on this score, and over the years a succession of great actors and actresses have made theatre history as the lady thief—among them transvestite diva Miwa Akihiro, kabuki *onnagata* superstar Bandō Tamasaburō, movie actress Matsuzaka Keiko, and former Takarazuka male-impersonation star, Asami Rei.

For Mishima *The Black Lizard* was all about the magic and the joy of theatre. He knew that literary critics would not take it seriously: it was not a play meant to enhance his bid for the Nobel Prize. Over the years, however, actors, directors, producers, and film companies have taken the play very seriously indeed, and Mishima had high ideals for *The Black Lizard* as theatre: "We strove to create not just a play that makes you laugh and cry,

Figure 5. *The Black Lizard*, 1968, with Miwa Akihiro as the Black Lizard and Mishima Yukio as one of her henchmen in the Museum of Terror, Act III. Toyoko Gekijō. Photograph courtesy of the Mishima Yukio Literary Museum.

and then forget about the next morning. We tried to create something with substance, a feeling of darkness, a sense that behind eight hundred lies, a shining truth can be seen."[110] Mishima might have written more plays like *The Black Lizard* had he not felt driven to make himself Japan's greatest twentieth century writer.[111]

1963: Fights at the Bungaku-za and an Acrimonious Departure

Bungaku-za, "The Literary Theatre," seemed just the right company for Japan's most literary playwright. From its founding the Bungaku-za had rejected the use of theatre as a political tool. Mishima, in his early essays on drama, had argued eloquently on behalf of "art for art's sake." The author and the company seemed a perfect match. But as time passed, the Bungaku-za and its leading playwright gradually changed their views about the importance of political issues, and they were coming to drastically different conclusions about the course that Japan and Japanese theatre should take. Thus, the stage was set for a bitter fight between Mishima and the Bungaku-za, culminating in a rancorous exchange of letters released to the public in newspapers that brought the Bungaku-za chapter of Mishima's career to a sudden end.

In the early 1960s Mishima was warmly ensconced at the Bungaku-za. He had placed boxing training equipment in the company's rehearsal space and was urging everyone in the company to get into shape by boxing. He continued to write fine plays for Sugimura Haruko, Kishida Kyōko, Akutagawa Hiroshi, and the other leading actors in the company. Sugimura Haruko was the soul of the company; recognized as such by the arts community at large, she was given wide-ranging leadership responsibilities. Sugimura, always fond of brilliant writers who provided star material, doted on Mishima.

The years from 1959 to 1961 saw another upswing of socialist and anti-American fervor because of the government's commitment to ratify the U.S.-Japan Security Treaty in 1960. Intellectuals and artists stood solidly in support of the labor unions and student groups that were engaging in violent and nonviolent demonstrations that they hoped would induce the government to scrap the treaty.

Sugimura Haruko had enjoyed close friendships with Chinese theatrical artists ever since World War II when the Japanese government had mandated collaborative efforts between the Bungaku-za and theatre troupes in occupied China. Chinese theatre artists had successfully navigated the treacherous waters of revolution-torn, postwar China, and by 1960, when Sugimura Haruko and the Bungaku-za visited China again, they had become devout Marxists. Their commitment to a political agenda in theatre stood in direct opposition to the official credo of the Bungaku-za, but the Chinese performers' revolutionary zeal resonated with the socialist political convictions of many in Bungaku-za, including Sugimura. In 1961 Bungaku-za broke with its apolitical tradition and staged a new-left political piece as part of its atelier series.[112]

Just at this time Mishima was beginning to express his right-wing views more openly and regularly. In 1961 he sent shock waves through the Japanese literary world with his short story "Patriotism," glorifying the bloody ritual suicides of an idealistic, emperor-worshiping young army officer and his wife at the time of the failed coup of February 1936. With *Tenth Day Chrysanthemum,* also in 1961, Mishima wrote the first of several plays that explore the psychology of characters devoted to, or who wish they could be devoted to, selfless service of the emperor. Sugimura played the leading female role in *Tenth Day Chrysanthemum,* interpreting the play, with justification, as a psychological work, not a political statement.[113]

In 1961 Sugimura became a member of a pacifist leadership organization for artists, and she remembers beginning to have arguments with Mishima over politics at this time. She recalls that in her office "he told me that when actors become political activists, that is when I quit. It hurt me, but I had been through so much in my life, I couldn't just hold it inside. He said that it was bad for actors to walk in demonstrations, but what if that was the best way to express how I really felt?"[114]

The first crisis to hit the Bungaku-za, though, was the result of internal company politics and artistic policy, not of national and international issues. It was a struggle between the old guard leadership and younger actors and directors over casting decisions and the sort of foreign material that the company should produce. In January of 1963 twenty-nine company members, including Kishida Kyōko and Akutagawa Hiroshi, left Bungaku-za to found their own new company, called Kumo (Cloud). This crisis found Sugimura and Mishima working together as staunch allies, with Mishima writing the official Bungaku-za reaction to the schism and acting as company spokesman to the press. Mishima helped the company recover its fortunes by providing Sugimura with a wonderful romantic role in his adaptation to *shingeki* of the opera *Tosca,* which enjoyed a successful one-month run in June and July. The company had an agreement with Mishima that he would provide their mainstage play for January 1964.

In the fall Sugimura joined a delegation of theatre leaders on a two-month trip to Eastern Europe and the U.S.S.R. She stopped in China for a few weeks on the way home. In China she received a letter from friends at the Bungaku-za telling her that there were difficulties with the rehearsal of Mishima's new play, *The Harp of Joy (Yorokobi no Koto).* One friend on the trip recalls that Sugimura could sense a crisis brewing, and on the plane home she said that "the time may soon come when we have to part ways with Mishima."[115]

The Harp of Joy is about a dedicated young police officer who is betrayed by superiors who turn out to be leftists in disguise. The play was a barely disguised attack on a recent court decision exonerating communist activists in the derailment of a train in 1949 (the famous "Matsukawa Incident"). The play had been read and approved by the Bungaku-za directorial board in Sugimura's absence, but during rehearsals important actors had decided that they could not in good conscience participate in a play that was clearly not only political in nature but also in opposition to their own political convictions.

Sugimura returned to Japan on November 18 and read the play immediately. On the twentieth a leadership meeting was convened and the company cancelled rehearsals and the play. Mishima was present for some of the discussions, though he probably did not take part in making the final decision. To cancel a play that was already in rehearsal for a scheduled mainstage production was an almost unheard-of action, and it immediately precipitated a crisis. On November 25 Inui Ichirō, managing director of the Bungaku-za, received a message that he should call Mishima at home. Inui called from a public phone and remembers Mishima shocking him with two pieces of information: one was that President Kennedy had just been shot, and the other was that he, Mishima, had decided to leave Bungaku-za.[116] On the twenty-seventh Mishima published an open letter in the *Asahi Shimbun* to the company and to the public. In the early part of the letter he stated the facts of the cancellation, as he understood them, and then went on to write:

> Certainly *The Harp of Joy* is quite different from my other works and includes an element of danger. But what have you been thinking about me all this while that you should be astonished by a work such as this? Have you been making a fool of me, saying that Mishima is a playwright who writes harmless dramas that gather large audiences? You set up safe criteria for "Art" all the while concealing vague political inclinations to the left, dropping the phrase "art for art's sake" from time to time. . . . Isn't this just hypocrisy and commercialism? I would like you to understand this: there is always a needle in art; there is also poison; you can't suck honey without the poison too.[117]

Inui responded for the Bungaku-za Board of Directors in a public letter on December 7, saying that Mishima had his facts wrong. At the meeting on the twentieth the consensus was to suspend the production and reconsider it for a later time, but Mishima himself had told them not to be so backhanded—to either let the play run as scheduled or cancel it. Thus pressed, the consensus had been for cancellation.[118] Borrowing Mishima's metaphor, Inui wrote that the company did not intend to "capriciously play the game of 'art for art's sake' and 'swallow the needle of art in one gulp' by presenting *The Harp of Joy* before submitting it to a thorough critical appraisal."[119]

After this exchange of public letters neither party was in a position to back down or suggest reconciliation. The break with Bungaku-za was final.

Bungaku-za would not present another Mishima play during his lifetime. Mishima and Sugimura were officially "enemies," and they never spoke again, nor did she attend his funeral.[120] Sugimura outlived Mishima by twenty-eight years, and she never acted in another Mishima play for the rest of her life.

Mishima did not leave Bungaku-za by himself. Thirteen other actors and directors followed him, including his close friend and favorite director, Matsuura Takeo. Together they founded a new company, the New Literary Theatre (NLT). NLT would produce many of Mishima's best plays in the mid-1960s.

Modern Japanese theatre companies split and recombine all the time, but rarely has a break been as acrimonious or as complete as Mishima's from the Bungaku-za. Scholars debate whether or not Mishima wrote *The Harp of Joy* as a deliberate provocation, expecting a crisis to arise and expecting to be expelled from Bungaku-za. Those who support this notion point out that Mishima knew well the political convictions of most of the company. Probably Ōzasa Yoshio's interpretation of the incident is the most accurate. He believes that Mishima expected a conflict but not a crisis, and that he was mistakenly confident that he would be able to influence the company to take a truly centrist stance by allowing plays with both leftist and rightist political coloring.[121] Ōzasa believes that Mishima's surprise at the extreme outrage felt by Sugimura and others was genuine. And the fact that thirteen of his colleagues felt strongly enough to leave the company with him shows that Mishima had been creating allies in the company who he expected would be able to sway the leadership in his favor. Mishima's Bungaku-za years were over, but his favorite director was still with him, and there were many fine artists eager to present his plays.

The NLT and Masterpieces of the Mid-Sixties

In the 1960s Mishima wrote several of the finest plays of his career as a dramatist, plays like *The Fall of the House of Suzaku*, the formalist masterpiece, *Madame de Sade*, and a three-act kabuki epic, *The Moon Drawn like a Bow*. The latter two plays are widely recognized as the finest *shingeki* play and the finest historical kabuki play written in the second half of the twentieth century. In the mid-sixties Mishima was also hard at work on the most ambitious opus of his career as a novelist, the *Sea of Fertility* tetralogy. The first volume, *Spring Snow*, came out in 1965, and it excited readers and critics alike. The concept of reincarnation ties the four novels together, and death and rebirth would become important in some of his plays as well. Mishima was also experimenting in film during these years. After a mediocre first appearance in a leading role in film in 1960, he put all of his energy into adapting "Patriotism" to the screen, which he accomplished in 1965, playing the young officer who commits *seppuku*.

Mishima and his thirteen renegade compatriots from the Bungaku-za founded NLT in January 1964. Mishima conceived of the company as a Japanese equivalent of a first-rate off-Broadway troupe, and he felt they had a group of remarkable individuals who could also work together well as a team.[122]

Mishima wanted to have the controversial *The Harp of Joy* up and running at a major theatre before his new company would be ready to mount it, so he turned to another company, Gekidan Shiki. Gekidan Shiki would later become a huge commercial company that produces musicals, but in 1964 it was a small troupe that specialized in French plays. Gekidan Shiki presented *The Harp of Joy* for three weeks in May at Nissei Theatre. The brouhaha of the previous November and December brought audiences and critics in droves. But the play's chief claim to success was its topicality and the Bungaku-za fight. Critics noted that it raised important issues about the ideological struggle in contemporary Japan, and about the decline of mutual trust in an era when economic progress was the country's only goal, but artistically it was not one of Mishima's better plays and was never performed again.[123]

NLT performed its first new Mishima play in 1965 in a one-month run of two modern noh plays, including the premiere of *Yoroboshi*. Later in the year NLT put itself on the theatrical map in Tokyo, and Mishima reaffirmed his genius as a playwright when the company presented *Madame de Sade (Sado Kōshaku Fujin)*. Mishima's inspiration for the play and his dramaturgical plan are best expressed in his own words:

> Reading *The Life of the Marquis de Sade* by Shibusawa Tatsuhiko, I was most intrigued as a writer by the riddle of why the Marquise de Sade, after having demonstrated such absolute fidelity to her husband during his long years in prison, should have left him the moment that he was at last free. This riddle served as the point of departure for my play, which is an attempt to provide a logical solution. I was sure that something highly incomprehensible, yet highly truthful, about human nature lay behind this riddle, and I wanted to examine Sade, keeping everything within this frame of reference.
>
> This play might be described as "Sade seen through women's eyes." I was obliged therefore to place Madame de Sade at the center, and to consolidate the theme by assigning all the other parts to women. Madame de Sade stands for wifely devotion; her mother, Madame de Montreuil, for law, society, and morality; Madame de Simiane, for religion; Madame de Saint-Fond, for carnal desires; Anne, Madame de Sade's younger sister, for feminine guilelessness and a lack of principles; and the servant Charlotte, for the common people. I had to involve these people with Madame de Sade and make them revolve around her, with something like the motions of the planets. I felt obliged to dispense entirely with the usual trivial stage effects, and to control the action exclusively by

> the dialogue; collisions of ideas had to create the shape of the drama, and sentiments had to be paraded throughout in the garb of reason. I thought that the necessary visual appeal would probably be provided by the beautiful Rococo costumes. Everything had to form a precise mathematical system around Madame de Sade.[124]

This is the most highly formalized play in Mishima's opus. It consists of monologues and dialogues couched in some of the most florid language Mishima ever used in *shingeki* plays. One brilliant touch, which Mishima had practiced before in the play *Steeplechase,* was to have the play dominated by a character who never appears on stage (the Marquis de Sade [Alphonse]). Every major monologue and conversation is devoted to the attempt to understand who de Sade really is, and what he means to France, to society, to politics, and to the lives of each of the women.

The solution to the riddle that induced Mishima to write the play—why Madame de Sade refused to meet her husband ever again after he left prison— is constructed from Madame de Sade's own convictions and her personal understanding of what the other women tell her about carnal desire, Christian purity and salvation, and self-preservation. Madame de Sade creates a beautiful, idealized image of her husband, in which "he piles evil on evil, and mounts on top, building a back stairway to heaven."[125] Her memories of him as a blond, handsome youth are "as if preserved in amber."[126] When told of his current physical decrepitude, Madame de Sade is unwilling to relinquish her fantasies and memories and face the sordid reality of what her husband has become.

Critics have raved about this play from its very first performance, and in the hands of fine actresses (and the occasional fine actor) it is a riveting experience for audiences. Among Mishima's multi-act plays, *Madame de Sade* has enjoyed more stage performances than any except for *Rokumeikan,* and it has a strong record of performance abroad thanks to Donald Keene's 1967 translation.

In 1967 one of Mishima's close friends, Dōmoto Masaki, an experimental director of short plays and scholar of the noh drama and homosexual theatre history, took his turn at directing two of the modern noh plays. One was the premiere of *Yuya.* Mishima had been fascinated with the classical noh play *Yuya* ever since Utaemon had asked him to write a kabuki dance drama version in 1955. Because Mishima had to make the dancing girl Yuya the center of Utaemon's kabuki play, he did not make major changes in the original story, but he was much freer in his adaptation to *shingeki.* Yuya's patron Munemori is the main character in the *shingeki* play, where he becomes a manipulative, epicurean business tycoon. In Mishima's *shingeki* version, Yuya and her patron engage in a tense battle of wits and wills, highlighting their different philosophies of life. The message in the end is dramatically different from the original play: lying and deception are the only acts that truly make life worth living.

Figure 6. *Madame de Sade*, 1965, with Tannami Yatsuko as Renee, the Marquise de Sade, and Minami Yoshie as Madame Montreuil, her mother. Photograph courtesy of Waseda University Tsubouchi Hakase Memorial Theatre Museum.

Up until the mid-1960s Mishima had not attempted to work his right-wing political convictions into adaptations of the European classics, but in *The Fall of the House of Suzaku (Suzaku Ke no Metsubo)*, staged by NLT in 1967, he infused an adaptation of Euripedes' *The Madness of Heracles* with the spirit and psychology of service to the Japanese emperor. In the original Greek play Heracles is the son of Zeus by a mortal woman, and Zeus's wife, the goddess Hera, punishes Heracles by inciting him to murder his wife and children. In *Suzaku*, the Heracles figure, Suzaku Tsunetaka, is a former imperial chamberlain from a noble family that has for many generations provided chamberlains. The Suzaku family manor is on the shore of Lake Biwa, and a tradition holds that their family deity, the goddess Benten of Lake Biwa, will grow jealous and punish by death any woman who formally marries into the family. In his earlier adaptations of Greek material, Mishima had ignored the role of the gods, or had transformed the acts of deities into human feelings and actions, but in *Suzaku*, Mishima finally solved the problem of Greek religion in a simple and very successful way—he transformed it into the native, pantheistic, Shinto religion.

In the play Tsunetaka has defied tradition by marrying, but his wife has died, and he now lives with a common-law wife, Orei, who is the family servant. Orei is the mother of Tsunetaka's son, Tsunehiro, but the world believes that the boy is the son of Tsunetaka's deceased, aristocratic wife. Tsunehiro's fiancée Ritsuko insists on marrying Tsunehiro before her beloved sets out to war, but Tsunetaka refuses to allow it. Unlike Heracles, Tsunetaka does not kill his son and wife with his own hands, but allows the war to do the job for him. He sends his son off to die in battle, refusing his brother's offer to intercede and have the young man sent to a safe post, and Tsunetaka loses his common-law wife in an air raid that he alone survives by taking refuge in the nearby Benten Shrine. In the last scene, Ritsuko emerges from the Benten Shrine, wearing Tsunetaka's first wife's bridal robes, declaring that she is the new deity of Lake Biwa, and that she intends to punish Tsunetaka for killing her beloved and destroying his whole family.

In the Greek play Heracles remains close to King Theseus of Athens throughout, and Theseus prevents Heracles from committing suicide, but Tsunetaka's loyalty to the emperor is more self-destructive. Because of this loyalty Tsunetaka sends his son into the navy to die, and Tsunetaka resigns from his position of chamberlain after overstepping his authority and helping to overthrow what he perceives as a disloyal cabinet. These two actions, committed out of supreme loyalty, destroy his own life and his son's life, and in his old age he lives on, without his soul, which he has given to the emperor.

In interviews and articles Mishima elaborated on the many meanings he wanted to convey in this dense play: he wanted to create a play with a Greek structure—two conflicts taking the form of triangles, a man, a woman, and a deity; he wanted to create a clear example of selfless service to the emperor;

he wanted to oppose passive humanism with an activist, anti-humanistic sense of oneness with the emperor; and he wanted this to be his most important work about the dilemmas of the emperor system.[127]

Needless to say, this play gave critics the opportunity to write a great deal. From the early sixties Mishima set out to do with his drama what he had been doing for many years in his fiction writing: violating the taboos and norms of Japanese society. In *The Harp of Joy* he accused the judicial system of surrendering to Japan's intellectual left; in *Madame de Sade* he suggested that murder and extreme sexual depravity could in fact be divine acts; in *Yuya* he argued that lying and deceit are what make life beautiful; and in *The Fall of the House of Suzaku* he resurrected war memories and arcane values that most Japanese had been striving to forget and replace for the past twenty-two years. On the stage Mishima had emerged as Japan's genius *bēte noir*, inducing his countrymen to go to the theatre and live through their worst nightmares, gilding the horror and pain with gorgeous words, sumptuous sets and costumes, structural elegance, and fine acting. This was the spirit of late Edo kabuki in the garb of contemporary *shingeki*.

But Mishima was too complex a man to label or compartmentalize, even for a single season of theatre. At the same time he was producing play after play that slapped conventional morality and social values in the face, Mishima continued to write and stage romantic plays, operas, and ballets. In fact, Mishima's love of the romantic gave the name to his next theatre company. In 1968 the NLT decided to turn toward comedy as its mainstay, and Mishima and Matsuura left, founding a new company called Gekidan Roman Gekijō (The Romantic Theatre Company). They were joined by several of Mishima's favorite actors and directors, including Domoto. In a founder's statement Mishima wrote that "Roman Gekijō will stress drama over literature, and theatricality over drama."[128]

The Romantic Theatre Company, My Friend Hitler, *and "Political Action"—1968*

In postwar Japan, at least until the time of Mishima's death, militant leftist activity intensified at the turn of each decade, and on each occasion Mishima was involved in the action. In 1950 a leftist company, the Haiyū-za, had been unable to recognize the merits of Mishima's bourgeois, but profound and artistic play, *The Lighthouse.* In the early 1960s Mishima was developing his own right-wing political consciousness, and thought he could turn the Bungaku-za from its leftward course, but he badly miscalculated his support. In the late 1960s the radical left was at the center of the struggle, and student groups had seized the reins of leadership. By this time Mishima's fiction, essays, and plays had established him as major leader of Japan's right wing, and he took on the left-wing students in direct debates. In 1968 he founded the Shield Society, a private organization of cadets who engaged in military training with their leader, and dedicated their lives to serving the emperor. In the Shield Society much of Mishima's life came together as a whole: his right-wing politics and reverence for the emperor, his love of martial arts, his love of drama and role playing, his newfound commitment to political action, and the companionship of idealistic, athletic young men. But as his essay *Sun and Steel* (1968) hinted, these were also the young men that he chose to die among.

While Mishima was training with the Shield Society, debating with communist students, and working hard to finish his tetralogy, he was also leading a troupe named the Romantic Theatre Company. Ironically, but perhaps not surprisingly, the first Mishima play produced by the Romantic Theatre Company centers around one of the least romantic heroes Mishima ever created: Adolf Hitler. Mishima intended *My Friend Hitler* (*Waga tomo no Hittora,* 1968), as a companion piece to *Madame de Sade*. In the earlier play there are only women characters, and in the latter only men. Mishima wrote that "*Madame de Sade* takes as its subject one of the great monsters of France's Rococo era, and Hitler is the great monster of Germany's twentieth century Rococo era."[129] Both plays are action-less monologue and dialogue dramas. A major difference between the two plays is that while the Marquis de Sade never appears, Hitler is on stage the entire time in *My Friend Hitler*. Each of the characters meets Hitler separately for an isolated dialogue, and occasionally they converse all together, in a manner similar to Racinian drama.

The play is a series of conversations taking place in 1934, immediately preceding the assassinations of storm trooper commander Ernst Roehm and socialist theoretician and former Nazi leader, Gregor Strasser. Mishima flaunts the orthodox postwar vilification of Hitler by portraying him as a reasonable, middle-of-the-road politician who has to resort to unpleasant methods to rid his country of dangerous extremists on both the right and the left. Mishima went so far as to associate himself with Hitler in a flyer distributed at the opening of the play, as if daring the audience to confront this unrepentant, right-wing, militarist playwright.[130]

Mishima was of course pressed to comment on whether or not he admired Hitler. Mishima replied that he did not, but not for the reasons that the rest of the world loathes Hitler. Mishima wrote, "Hitler was a political genius, but no hero. He lacked the necessary beauty and radiance of a hero. He had absolutely none of this. He was as dark as the twentieth century itself."[131] In the play, Hitler is a brutal pragmatist, and the one person who remains important to him, and who survives, is the indispensable industrialist Krupp. The character who Mishima felt closest to in the play was Roehm, the storm trooper commander. "I put more of my own feelings into Roehm than any other character. He is infused with an almost Japanese love of sentiment."[132] In the play, Roehm believes in the sanctity of his friendship with Hitler until the moment he is killed by his good friend. Mishima's identification with Roehm is not surprising, for he is the one idealistic and romantic character in the play. Mishima was writing the play in the fall of 1968, at just the same time he founded his Shield Society, a paramilitary group of young men who shared characteristics with Roehm's idealized storm troopers: "a community of warriors, their oak-like arms locked, beautiful and manly."[133]

My Friend Hitler had such a powerful effect on the actors that, without planning it, they gave Nazi salutes during the opening night curtain call, and continued the practice to the end of the run.[134] Critics noted that, like *Madame de Sade,* it was an elegantly structured, tightly written play. Nevertheless, it did not win the acclaim of *Madame de Sade,* and Japanese critics think it is unlikely to be performed abroad because Hitler is even more of a taboo subject in the West than in Japan.[135]

Cambodia and Kabuki: Two Epic Dramas, and the Curtain Closes

The Romantic Theatre Company followed *Hitler* with a second successful production of *Madame de Sade* in 1969, then set to work on a lavish spectacle to be presented in the Imperial Theatre: *The Terrace of the Leper King (Raiō no Terrasu).* The play is set in twelfth-century Cambodia. The Khmer king, Jayavarman VII, develops symptoms of leprosy and devotes himself wholeheartedly and exclusively to worshiping the female serpent deity and to building the Temple of Bayon at Angkor Tom. The king's primary consort burns herself alive in an attempt to startle the king out of his dual obsession, but to no avail. Work on the temple is completed as the king, blind and rotting with leprosy, finally dies.

Henry Scott-Stokes, who went with Mishima to the opening night show, wrote that Mishima was particularly proud of the dramatic last scene of the play,[136] a conversation between the dying Spirit of the leprous king and an apparition, or reincarnation, of his youthful Body—young, suntanned, handsome, and strong. The Body scoffs at the Spirit as it dies: images in stone are nothing, Body says, the spirit rots away into nothingness, all that truly matters is a living, healthy, active Body.

Mishima had traveled to Cambodia in 1965 and visited Angkor Wat and Angkor Tom. He heard the story about how a king afflicted with leprosy raced against his disease in an attempt to complete a temple at Angkor Tom.[137] Mishima wanted to write a play on the subject soon after returning to Japan, but conditions were not right for staging it until the late 1960s. He wanted the play to have the grandeur and vision of kabuki, but with a careful development of the play's themes and plot.[138] "The main theme is that absolute love, absolute quests, and absolute faith are sure to fail in this world, but that superhuman, or inhuman, immortality can be the result of such absolute endeavors. None of this, however, has anything to do with beauty. The only true beauty is an eternally healthy and beautiful human body, and that is only possible through death and rebirth."[139]

No one who reads *The Terrace of the Leper King* and Mishima's commentary on it can help but think that this play was a precursor to and an explanation of his suicide. Mishima would leave a literary edifice for the world grander than the Temple of Bayon, an edifice that would speak only of a young and vigorous Mishima. Mishima would not have to wait for leprous old age to do him in—he was in no race against time since his edifice was complete. His reincarnation as a healthy new human being would come when he willed it.

But more than a year was to pass between *The Terrace of the Leper King* and Mishima's suicide, and while *Leper King* was on the boards at the Imperial Theatre, Mishima was working on an even grander epic play that was by no means a harbinger of suicide. In the autumn of 1969 Mishima directed his most ambitious kabuki project, a full-length, three-act historical play with *gidayū* narration, adapted from Takizawa Bakin's (1767–1842) mid-nineteenth-century epic adventure story, *The Moon Drawn like a Bow (Chinzetsu Yumiharizuki)*, a work previously thought impossible to put on stage.

The Moon Drawn like a Bow is the happy result of an argument between Mishima and author/playwright Osaragi Jirō (1897–1973), which took place in November 1968. Both men were attending an award-winning production of Chekhov's *Three Sisters*, and both happened to be members of the Board of Directors at the newly established National Theatre. Mishima, rarely one to mince words, criticized two of Osaragi's recent kabuki plays for being too contemporary in language and spirit. Osaragi apparently responded, "If that's the way you feel, why don't you write a better play," and Mishima answered, "I think I will."[140]

The National Theatre, completed in 1967, was a new venue for kabuki. Its missions included promoting the revival of full-length classical plays and encouraging the writing of new kabuki plays. With government support, the leaders of the National Theatre could afford to take risks that Shochiku could not when planning their commercial kabuki productions. As a board member Mishima had no difficulty in persuading the National Theatre to support his project. His play would celebrate the third anniversary of the founding of the theatre.

The Moon Drawn like a Bow is an adventure romance about a great twelfth-century warrior, Minamoto no Tametomo, supporter of Emperor Sutoku. Sutoku and Tametomo are defeated in battle during the Hogen Insurrection (1158). Sutoku dies, and Tametomo is forced into exile on Ōshima Island, leaving his wife, Princess Shiranui, behind. She becomes the leader of a gang of bandits who take refuge in a mountain stronghold and continue to fight a guerilla war against the enemy. Tametomo defeats a ship-borne army that comes to Oshima Island to kill him. After the sea battle Tametomo visits the grave of Emperor Sutoku, where he attempts ritual suicide to atone for his failure in the Hogen War, but Sutoku's ghost appears, stops the suicide, and directs Tametomo to persevere against the tyrannical Heike clan and also orders Tametomo to go to Kyushu. Tametomo reunites briefly with Shiranui in Kyushu, then loses her in a tempest at sea. Finally, after conquering and establishing his son as king of the Ryukyu Islands, Tametomo departs the world riding a white horse over the waves to join his emperor in the land of the dead.

The project was a huge undertaking for Mishima. It took from May to the end of August to write the play because, as always in his kabuki, Mishima was firmly committed to writing a text entirely in classical Japanese, structured around poetic *gidayū* narration. Mishima insisted on directing the play because he knew that without his continual involvement it could never become anything like what he wanted to see. This last experience in the theatre was the longest and most intense in Mishima's whole theatrical career. Because the cast would only be available to rehearse for one week, every other aspect of the play had to be made ready so that each moment of that brief time could be used with maximum efficiency. Mishima recognized that "sixty to seventy percent of the direction of the actors will come from the *gidayū* music,"[141] and he arranged for his text to be set to music as soon as possible by a leading musician from the Bunraku theatre, and then worked with him, planning the actors' movements on stage in time with the music.

Mishima worked on the design of all the sets and helped to plan the machinery necessary for the many spectacular scenes in the play, among them a typhoon that breaks a huge ship in two and sinks it. To accomplish the myriad tasks required to prepare the play for production, Mishima scheduled weekly staff meetings beginning in May for a November production, and long, grueling individual sessions with the *gidayū* musician. When he stepped back from the fray and noticed what he was doing, he observed, "Theatre is a fantasy that explodes and disappears at once, lasting no longer than a burst of fireworks. How is it that this momentary fantasy can compel so many grown men to work so hard together for so long?"[142] When finally it was time to work with the cast for his precious one week of rehearsals all was ready.

Tametomo would be played by the top actor of martial roles in the late 1960s, Matsumoto Koshirō VIII (1910–82), but Princess Shiranui would be played by a nineteen-year-old *onnagata*, Bandō Tamasaburō, whom Mishima had first seen a few years earlier. "His body is like a wisp of gossamer, and when he sways gracefully on the stage he overflows with a lyrical beauty that is fraught with a sense of danger. And what is most important, he has an old fashioned, classical beauty. Kabuki cannot survive on art and technique alone. It needs to have this beauty, this flower."[143] As it turned out Mishima had a fine eye for both beauty and talent on the kabuki stage, and Tamasaburō is now the top kabuki *onnagata* of the twenty-first century and artistic heir to Utaemon.

The cast responded admirably to Mishima's enthusiasm and hard work.

Figure 7. *The Moon Drawn like a Bow*, 1969, with Bandō Tamasaburō, above, as Princess Shiranui and Katsumura Jun as the villian Butōta, who is being tortured in the snow by Princess Shiranui's ladies-in-waiting. Photograph courtesy of Waseda University Tsubouchi Hakase Memorial Theatre Museum.

Mishima was amazed that Koshirō arrived the first day with all of his lines memorized, ready to fine tune his acting and work on the action scenes.[144] This level of preparedness is almost unheard of in kabuki rehearsals. Tamasaburō remembers Mishima as the finest director of kabuki action he has ever worked with in producing a new work.[145] Mishima knew how many people and how much time it takes to move properties, how much time it takes an actor to run from point to point in the cellar under the stage, and so on.[146] Mishima was also attentive to minute physical details in acting. For example, he made Tamasaburō repeat a certain snap of his head twenty times until he did it in just the way Mishima felt expressed the emotion he was striving for.[147] During their one week of rehearsals Mishima and his cast and crew created a play that would dazzle the eyes of its audience. On the day of the final rehearsal Mishima held a dress parade and reception to celebrate the first anniversary of the Shield Society on the roof of the National Theatre.

It had been eleven years since audiences and critics had seen a new Mishima kabuki play, and once again they marveled at his creation. Mishima had pulled out all the stops. His old spirit of playfulness and parody were apparent in many scenes. He even insisted that the huge wave that swept his heroes out to sea be a replica of Hokusai's "great wave."[148] Many of the special effects were intentionally primitive so that audiences could enjoy the mechanics. Ghosts and sorcery amazed one and all. His hero was bright, indefatigable, and tragically flawed. His gorgeous princess, driven to take cruel revenge on the man she thinks murdered her husband, ordered her beautiful lady bandits to kill the villain slowly by sticking long bamboo needles into him while she played her husband's favorite song on her *koto.*

Gunji Masakatsu, kabuki scholar and director, wrote that "it had a tone unlike any of his previous works. He handled the spirit of "display" *(miseba),* so essential to kabuki, excellently. I hadn't thought this novel could be adapted to kabuki, and it is characteristic of Mishima's madness that he dared to try it."[149] Kawatake Shigetoshi, scholar and grandson of the last great Meiji-period kabuki playwright, called the play "an attack on *shin kabuki's* psychological realism, historicism, and intellectualism. It is an attempt to revive the theatricality of kabuki. I applaud his use of *gidayū,* classical language throughout, and the three-act structure."[150] Only those who wanted to see rational, subdued, sensible new kabuki plays were displeased with *The Moon Drawn like a Bow.*

When the accolades subsided and Mishima coolly evaluated the production, he felt that it had been gentler and weaker than his ideal.[151] The Bunraku puppet theatre would perhaps be a better genre for *Moon Drawn like a Bow.* The Bunraku *gidayū* chanters are stronger than their counterparts in kabuki, and women's lines are delivered with a different timbre and in a slightly different idiom. Mishima began writing revisions of his script to adapt it to Bunraku and began working with Bunraku musicians on the music and staging.

In the fall of 1970 Mishima was as active in the theatre as ever. He was working on his Bunraku adaptation of *Bow* and also meeting with Matsuura on his adaptation of *Salome,* scheduled to open in early 1971. Mishima was codirector and designer. Between October 22 and November 23 the Romantic Theatre Company produced *The Rose and the Pirate.* During this run, the Tōbu Department store art gallery ran the five-day "Four Rivers" exhibition that Mishima designed himself. Even in private, Mishima expressed the belief that his work and his actions were his life:

> Not long before he killed himself, Mishima arranged a shelf of objects in his upstairs sitting room at his home in Magome. These were a Greek vase, a small bronze nude of himself, a collection of translations of his books, and a stage model of the last scene of *The Terrace of the Leper King.* One evening he showed this display to some friends. "How do you like it?" he asked them in an ironic tone. "This really sums up my life, don't you think?" And he burst into laughter.[152]

What did that ironic tone and laughter mean? That Mishima was putting his friends on, and that this was all a facade? Or, now that it was too late, Mishima sensed that life could have other meanings than this? There is no way to know for sure. At any rate, it is clear that one quarter of the Mishima that Mishima presented to the world was his work in the theatre. And today, thirty years later, when his body and action are gone, all that remain are his fiction, his essays, and his plays.

Mishima planned his actions of November 25, 1970 with the same meticulousness he had planned the production of *The Moon Drawn like a Bow.* As tragic and as senseless as his suicide seemed to his family, friends, colleagues, and the world at large, it was his last drama, and it was like so many of his plays, melodramatic and sad. His suicide was so compelling that it has, for better or for worse, dominated the discourse on his literature and drama for the last thirty years.

In Japan and around the world thousands of pages have been written by Mishima's friends about their last experiences with him, or where they were and what they thought when they heard the news of the "Mishima Incident." Here are a few short anecdotes to add to those that have found their way into English. Matsuura writes that he was meeting with Mishima to plan *Salome* up until a few days before he died, but his friend betrayed no hint of his intentions.[153] Nagayama called Mishima five days before his suicide and asked Mishima if he would write program copy for an upcoming production of a new play called, *Japanese Knights (Nihon no Kishi).* Mishima laughed and said, "I can't write it because I *am* a Japanese knight."[154]

One week before his suicide Mishima visted Miwa Akihiro in his dressing room. Miwa was the transvestite singer whom Mishima had "discovered" and elevated to national stardom as an actor in film and stage versions of *The Black Lizard*. Mishima came alone and brought two hundred red roses. It was the most lavish stage gift Mishima had ever given Miwa, and in the past Mishima had always visited Miwa's dressing room in the company of friends. Mishima expressed his affection and esteem for Miwa, but to Miwa the visit seemed tense and vaguely portentous. When a week later a friend called Miwa to the television to witness live coverage of the Mishima incident, Miwa thought to himself, "So he's finally done it."[155]

News of Mishima's suicide interrupted a meeting of the Bungaku-za board of directors. Sugimura Haruko screamed and collapsed, weeping.[156] Utaemon heard the news of Mishima's death in his dressing room, and his first reaction was, "How sad. What a waste."[157] Talking with kabuki actors over the last few years, I have found that all share Utaemon's sentiments. Utaemon and others who had worked with Mishima experienced deep personal grief, but all kabuki actors still feel a profound sense of professional loss. No other playwright since World War II has been able to write classical kabuki plays, and perhaps none ever will.

The Aftermath

For some twenty years following his suicide, Mishima as a topic of discussion was anathema in Japanese intellectual circles and in the general national discourse. Foreigners who wanted to talk about Mishima found their inquiries brushed aside by most Japanese. Japanese were closeting memories of Mishima beside the locked closet reserved for memories of World War II. Mishima was dismissed as insane and in no way representative of the new Japan.

Things were different in the world of the theatre. All of the plays Mishima was working on at the time of his death were staged more or less as scheduled. In the twenty years following his death, his best plays were presented every year. In 1980, the tenth anniversary of his death, seven of his plays were produced in Japan. During 1990, the twentieth anniversary year, nine Mishima plays were produced. Finally, the Mishima taboo eased in the country at large, and people began to rediscover his literature. In 1990 Nakamura Kanzaburō XVIII and Bandō Tamasaburō remounted *The Sardine Seller* for the first time in seventeen years, and Mishima found his way back onto the kabuki stage for frequent productions.

In the thirty years since Mishima's suicide, more than half of his sixty-two plays have been performed in Japan. His most frequently performed long *shingeki* plays are *Rokumeikan*, *Madame de Sade*, and *The Black Lizard*, and the most popular one-act plays have been his modern noh plays, especially *Hanjo*, *Sotoba Komachi*, and *Lady Aoi*. Experimental directors have staged them using a variety of approaches, sometimes using classical noh actors, music, and dance—very different from what Mishima originally intended. The five modern noh plays in the Keene anthology have become so well known abroad that they are widely mistaken for classical noh plays. These plays, and *Madame de Sade*, have been performed all around the world, but most of the rest, unfortunately, have remained unknown outside Japan until very recently.

MISHIMA ON STAGE: ABOUT THE ANTHOLOGY

The Selection of the Plays

Mishima on Stage was conceived, and the plays selected, with the purpose of demonstrating the breadth and scope of Mishima's talent as a playwright. All the plays in this anthology are being presented for the first time in English translation. The plays are arranged in chronological order so that they can support a study of Mishima's career as a playwright. All but two of the nine plays exemplify Mishima's devotion to formalism and strict adherence to the language and stage conventions of specific theatrical genres, convictions he held throughout his career as a playwright. In the two exceptions, *Busu* and *The Black Lizard,* Mishima consciously broke his own rules, creating a linguistic hybrid in the former, and a *shingeki*/ kabuki hybrid in the latter.

The selection of plays for this anthology was determined more by the content of plays than by questions of formalism and genre purity. The anthology is intended to demonstrate three additional aspects of Mishima's play writing: first, that Mishima was an accomplished writer of stage comedy; second, that Mishima's kabuki plays are classical masterpieces for the stage and significant works of literature as well; and third, that Mishima's intimate knowledge of many different theatrical genres enabled him to create plays that combined elements from them in ways that no other playwright could imagine doing.

Mishima was a brilliant writer of humor and comedy of every sort: parody, satire, farce, romance. Not only did Mishima produce dazzling comic wordplay, but he also crafted wonderful scenes of physical comedy in his plays. Mishima used humor to serve different purposes in each play. Plays like *The Sardine Seller's Net of Love* are traditional romantic comedies, charming and heartwarming. In other plays, including *The Lighthouse, Hell Screen, Yuya,* and *The Black Lizard,* Mishima used humorous scenes to support serious psychological or philosophical revelations. In *The Sardine Seller* and *Sash Stealing Pond,* Mishima parodied Japan's classical theatrical tradition and poked fun at conventional morality.

Four of the plays in this anthology are kabuki plays. Mishima took his kabuki playwriting very seriously indeed. He invested more time and effort into the writing of relatively short kabuki plays than he did for much longer works of fiction and modern drama. The result was a series of remarkable plays, absolutely unique in the history of postwar kabuki. Mishima is the only playwright to lend his name to a recognized genre of new work in kabuki: "Mishima kabuki." Mishima's kabuki plays are couched in the language of the Edo period but are entirely intelligible to contemporary audiences. On stage they are a rich brocade of music, poetry, dialogue, dance, and imaginative stage effects. These are the hallmarks of Edo-period kabuki, yet Mishima's kabuki plays are entirely up-to-date in their social values, and several parody Edo-period kabuki at the same time they pay homage to it.

Mishima's mastery of so many disparate theatrical genres enabled him to write plays entirely different from the work of any other playwright. One example is the short *shingeki* play, *Steeplechase,* in which the memories of a dead son possess a grieving mother as powerfully as ghosts possess living souls in the classical noh drama. The structure of the four-scene play follows the shamanic ritual structure that fifteenth century playwrights adapted to use in spirit noh plays. The result is an utterly unique fusion of exorcistic ritual and psychological realism—of Zeami and Chekhov.

The Black Lizard, like *Steeplechase,* is a fusion of two disparate theatrical traditions, but the two plays are as different as night and day. *The Black Lizard* is a spectacular and exuberant kabuki in the guise of modern drama. Mishima brought the histrionic acting, multiple disguises, high adventure and tragic romance, and the eye-popping stage sets of kabuki into a play infused with the spirit of the Roaring Twenties and set in the 1960s.

Adaptation from classical drama and fiction was at the core of Mishima's work as a playwright. His fascination with classical Greek theatre and Racine inspired him to present the universal themes of these plays in various forms of contemporary drama. He returned again and again to his favorite play, *Phaedra,* and this anthology contains two very different adaptations of the tragic, incest-driven struggle of wills between Phaedra and Hippolytus—the subdued and subtly expressed *shingeki* play *The Lighthouse,* and the histrionic kabuki tragedy *The Blush on the White Hibiscus Blossom: Lady Fuyo and the True Account of the Ōuchi Clan.*

Mishima's approach to adapting from the Japanese classics varied radically from play to play, and *Mishima on Stage* provides three examples: *Hell Screen, Busu,* and *Yuya. Hell Screen* remains true to the characters, themes, and setting of the original but couches the story in an entirely new idiom and changes the action to conform to classical kabuki dramaturgy. *Busu* preserves the stage action of classical *kyōgen* play and uses many lines from the original text (in English translation), but transposes the action from medieval Japan to present-day New York City. In *Yuya* Mishima retained the essential characters and dilemmas of the classical noh play but radically altered the play's structure and plot, and converted the language, setting, and stage action to suit a realistic *shingeki* play set in contemporary Tokyo.

The Translations

All of the translations in this volume are faithful to Mishima's scripts as published in *Mishima Yukio's Complete Works of Drama (Mishima Yukio Gikyoku Zenshū).* These are the texts as they are meant to be read as literature, and viewers are likely to find that directors have made slight changes in dialogue and stage directions for specific performances. Mishima has been translated more than any other Japanese writer, and the approaches of different translators vary considerably, following the translators' individual convictions, and the standard practices of the time in which the translation was made. The original texts by Mishima used in this anthology vary greatly in their linguistic style, with the language of the kabuki plays almost identical to classical language written in the eighteenth and early nineteenth centuries. The translators of this anthology have made the decision to translate all of Mishima's texts, whether classical or modern Japanese, into modern English. There is no exact English equivalent to classical Japanese or to the language and rhythm of kabuki lyrics in classical Japanese. We have made no attempt to reproduce the meter of Japanese poetry in English. We recognize the importance of enabling readers and audiences to distinguish between poetry and prose in the kabuki texts and have heightened the poetic passages using changes in diction, rhythm, and sometimes in line length.

Mishima was just as concerned with physical performance and the look of the stage as he was with the spoken text, and he wrote careful and sometimes voluminous stage instructions for his plays. The translations in this anthology include all of Mishima's stage instructions. We have added supplementary stage instructions only when recent stagings of the plays have departed significantly from Mishima's version. In these cases we have been careful to indicate which stage instructions are Mishima's and which reflect the work of directors other than Mishima. Mishima had an insider's knowledge of kabuki, and couched his stage instructions for kabuki plays in the specialized vocabulary of kabuki. We have translated almost all kabuki terms into the language of the American stage. Where specialized kabuki vocabulary is unavoidable, we explain it to readers, and we have provided background information for cryptic kabuki terminology. Attentiveness to stage instructions is important, and serves a twofold purpose: to help readers envision plays as Mishima intended them to be performed, and to help designers and directors create stage sets and on-stage action for their own productions of Mishima's plays.

Translators of plays are very aware of the entirely different requirements of translations meant to be read and translations intended for use on stage. Japanese plays, especially historical dramas and classical plays, abound with references to historical personages, geographical locations, and works of Japanese literature that no ordinary English-speaking reader could be expected to recognize. The usual scholarly solution to this problem is to insert a superscript number in the text and to explain the obscure word in a footnote or endnote. This solution is absolutely useless for stage-ready translations. Plays cannot be stopped in mid-dialogue so that the dramaturge can come on-stage to explain arcana to the audience. Some information can be provided in the play program, but directors cannot count on an audience knowing the contents of a play program.

The translators of this anthology have made the choice to translate for the stage. No footnotes will be found in the play texts. Unfamiliar geographical locations that are rich in associations for Japanese audiences but that kill dialogue spoken in English have been given nuanced equivalents. Names of unfamiliar historical personages and literary works have been rendered in such a way that they provide meaning to an English speaking audience about the nature of the person or the work, without destroying the audience's ability to follow the dialogue by reproducing the actual name in Japanese. The translators of this anthology are cognizant of the fact that, for a non-Japanese-speaking audience, listening to a Mishima play being performed in English, every word uttered in the Japanese language is a small dose of poison threatening to kill the play for the audience. We have kept our doses of poison to the absolute minimum.

Staging Mishima's Plays

Mishima was a man of the theatre. He loved viewing and creating live theatre and he wrote all of his plays with the intention of having them performed on stage. He directed only a few of his own plays, and he accepted the powerful role of the director as the "captain of the ship." Theatre directors have very different aims and goals than the playwright's. While it is clear that, for example, Mishima intended his modern noh plays for pure *shingeki* productions, it is just as easy to envisage other approaches to these plays. Since Mishima's death many directors in Japan and abroad have followed the lead of Takechi Tetsuji and have used elements from noh and *kyōgen*, ballet, opera, and modern dance when presenting these plays.

Mishima's *shingeki* plays are the easiest to present in English in the style of psychological realism. Among plays in this anthology, Mishima wrote *The Lighthouse, Steeplechase, Yuya,* and *The Black Lizard* for the Japanese *shingeki* stage, but the latter three contain elements from noh and kabuki that directors may emphasize in various ways if they so choose.

For his kabuki plays (except for *Sash Stealing Pond*) Mishima believed firmly in utilizing the emotional power of *gidayū* music and singing. Although Mishima worked hard to write poetic texts in classical meter for *gidayū* chanters to sing, their power derives less from the semantics of the lyrics than from the powerful vocal style and rhythms used to deliver them. The words of the *gidayū* chanter usually either describe a scene or action, or are lines spoken for a character. Even for most Japanese audience members, much of the meaning of the sung text is obscure. The vocabulary is the most archaic and poetic in the play script, and the singer's vocal acrobatics deform his pronunciation.

Performing kabuki plays in English can seem a daunting prospect, but just as Japanese feel free to adapt Shakespeare to kabuki, or we in the modern world present Greek tragedy using a variety of stage conventions, so can kabuki be freely adapted to Western theatre. The narration in Mishima's kabuki plays presents a particular challenge, but given what we know about the purposes of the narration and audience reception of the narration, various means can be used to provide the equivalent of this important aspect of kabuki plays. One solution is to attempt to replicate the narrator in some manner. In kabuki plays, the narrator, usually seated downstage left, sings to the accompaniment of music provided by the three-stringed *shamisen,* played by a single musician sitting at his side. In adaptations to the non-Japanese stage various alternative approaches may be used for the narration. Many of the narrator's lines are spoken for characters, and these lines can be assigned to the characters themselves. Lyrics that describe actions or scenery may be deleted if the actions and scenery are in any case clear to the audience. It is important to remember that emotionally intense music is being played whenever the narrator is singing in kabuki plays, so directors intending to create an analogous experience for their audiences will probably want to provide musical accompaniment of some sort during certain sections of the plays.

Mishima's kabuki plays are danced as much as they are acted. The movements of all characters are based on *buyō* dance. The characters and the stage scenery are coordinated so that at all times audience members see a beautiful tableau before their eyes. Directors attempting to replicate the audience experience at Mishima's kabuki plays should be conscious of the aesthetic requirements of Mishima's kabuki. Throughout his career Mishima maintained the strong conviction that new kabuki plays should retain the three basic elements of classical kabuki: music, dance, and acting.

Mishima on Stage is an anthology that we translators hope will serve many purposes. It illuminates an important aspect of Mishima's career that has long been ignored outside of Japan, and the plays themselves provide a fascinating glimpse into the mind and the methods of this remarkable writer. The plays are fun to read and should excite, entertain, and challenge audiences outside of Japan as they have audiences in Mishima's homeland for the past fifty years.

NOTES

1. For example, on page x of the introduction in John Nathan's widely read biography, *Mishima: A Biography* (Rutland: Charles E. Tuttle, 1974), the author writes that Mishima wrote eighteen plays although Mishima's complete dramatic works contains sixty-two plays.

2. Ōzasa Yoshio, *Sengo engeki o utsu* (Tokyo: Chuo Kōronsha, 2001), pp. 30–31. Voting in the survey had Mishima tied for best playwright with Inoue Hisashi, but *Madame de Sade* was the outright winner for "best post-war Japanese play."*Madame de Sade* is available in an English translation: Mishima Yukio, *Madame de Sade,* trans. Donald Keene (New York: Grove Press, 1967).

3. This play, when performed in Paris in French, has been mistaken by audiences for a French play. Ōzasa, *Sengo engeki o utsu*, pp. 31–32.

4. Mishima Yukio, "Gikyoku no yūwaku," *Tokyo Shimbun*, September 6–7, 1955, reprinted in *Mishima Yukio hyōron zenshū*, vol. 3 (Tokyo: Shinchōsha, 1989), 630.

5. Mishima Yukio, "Nihon no shosetsuka wa naze gikyoku o kakanai ka," *Engeki*, November 1949; reprinted in *Mishima Yukio hyōron zenshū*, vol. 3, pp. 616–20.

6. Mishima Yukio, lecture to the National Theatre Actor's Training School, November 3, 1970; reproduced in Orita Kōji, "Kabuki," *Mishima Yukio jiten* (Tokyo: Bensei Shuppan, 2000), p. 476.

7. Mishima Yukio, "Boku no Jigoku Hen," *Mainichi Shimbun*, September 10, 1954; reprinted in *Mishima Yukio hyōron zenshū*, vol. 3, p. 869.

8. Dōmoto Masaki, "Noh," *Mishima Yukio jiten*, p. 555.

9. Ibid.

10. Satō Hideaki, "Mishima Yukio jūyonsai no gikyoku," *Asahi Shimbun*, October 18, 2001, p. 14.

11. Ibid.

12. Mishima's entire theatre journal has been published as Mishima Yukio, *Shibai nikki* (Tokyo: Chuo Kōronsha, 1991).

13. Toita Yasuji, "Wakagaki no shinsensa," *Shibai nikki*, pp. 202–5.

14. Nakamura Utaemon, the kabuki actor who took lead roles in five of Mishima's six plays, agrees with this assertion. Nakamura Utaemon, "'Mishima Kabuki' no sekai," *Shibai nikki*, p. 199.

15. Mishima, *Shibai nikki*, p. 21.

16. Ibid., pp. 75–76.

17. Ibid., p. 80.

18. See James Brandon, "Myth and Reality: A Story of Kabuki during American Censorship, 1945–1949," *Asian Theatre Journal*, vol. 23, no. 1 (Spring 2006) and Marlene J. Mayo, "To Be or Not To Be: Kabuki and Cultural Politics in Occupied Japan," in *War, Occupation, and Creativity: Japan and East Asia, 1920–1960*, edited by Marlene J. Mayo, J. Thomas Rimer with H. Eleanor Kerkham (Honolulu: University of Hawaii Press, 2001), pp. 269–309, for an in-depth analysis of American censorship policy and practice during the occupation.

19. J. Thomas Rimer, *Toward a Modern Japanese Theatre Kishida Kunio* (Princeton: Princeton University Press, 1974), p. 118.

20. Ōzasa Yoshio, *Nihon gendai engekishi Showa sengohen*, vol. 1 (Tokyo: Hakusuisha, 1998), 577.

21. Ibid., p. 578.

22. Dōmoto Masaki, *Gekijin Mishima Yukio* (Tokyo: Gekishobō, 1994), p. 129.

23. Ōzasa, *Nihon gendai engekishi Showa sengohen*, vol. 1, p. 578.

24. Ibid., p. 579.

25. Dōmoto, *Gekijin Mishima Yukio*, p. 129.

26. Ibid., p. 142.

27. Ibid., pp. 144–45.

28. Ibid., p. 143.

29. Ibid., p. 148–49.

30. Ibid., p. 147.

31. Ibid., p. 149.

32. Ibid., p. 150.

33. Mishima Yukio, "Tōdai no enshutsu ni tsuite," in Haiyū-za Tōdai Program, February 1950; reprinted in *Mishima Yukio hyōron zenshū*, vol. 3, p. 740.

34. Ibid.

35. Mishima Yukio, "Kishida Kyōko-san," *Fujin Kōron*, December 1952; reprinted in *Mishima Yukio hyōron zenshū*, vol. 3, p. 673.

36. Ōzasa, *Nihon gendai engekishi Showa sengohen*, vol. 1, p. 840.

37. Dōmoto, *Gekijin Mishima Yukio*, pp. 167–68.

38. Plot summary based on Mishima Yukio, "Kantan," trans. Donald Keene in *Five Modern Nō Plays* (New York: Knopf, 1957), pp. 81–144.

39. Mishima Yukio, "Sotoba Komachi," trans. Donald Keene in *Five Modern Nō Plays*, p. 31.

40. Mishima Yukio, "Gikyoku o kakitagaru shōsetsuka," *Engeki Kai*, September 18, 1949; reprinted in *Mishima Yukio hyōron zenshū*, vol. 3, p. 611.

41. "Passion and form come together to make theatre . . ." from Mishima Yukio, "Engeki no honshitsu," *Kawade shobō engeki kōza 1*, December 1953; reprinted in *Mishima Yukio hyōron zenshū*, vol. 3, p. 620. "But naturalism, proletarian literature . . . strangling a policeman to death" from Mishima, "Gikyoku o kakitagaru shōsetsuka"; reprinted in *Mishima Yukio hyōron zenshū*, vol. 3, p. 615.

42. Mishima, "Gikyoku o kakitagaru shōsetsuka," p. 615.

43. Mishima Yukio, "Nakamura Shikan ron," *Gekijō*, February 1949; reprinted in *Mishima Yukio hyōron zenshū*, vol. 3, p. 845.

44. Ibid.

45. Ibid., pp. 844–845.

46. Ibid., p. 845.

47. Ibid.

48. Mishima Yukio, "Utaemon no koto," Kabuki-za Program, April 1951; reprinted in *Mishima Yukio hyōron zenshū*, vol. 3, p. 861.

49. Mishima Yukio, "Nakamura Shikan ron"; reprinted in *Mishima Yukio hyōron zenshū*, vol. 3, p. 845.

50. Nakamura Utaemon, "'Mishima Kabuki' no sekai," *Shibai nikki*, p. 187.

51. Mishima Yukio, "Odori," *Mainichi Shimbun*, 1963; reprinted in Mishima Yukio, *Shibai no biyaku* (Tokyo: Kakogawa Haruki Jimusho, 1997), pp. 47–48.

52. Dōmoto Masaki, "Buyō," *Mishima Yukio jiten*, p. 583.

53. Ibid.

54. Nagayama Takeomi, interview by author, January 27, 2002.

55. Nagayama Takeomi, interview by author, January 27, 2002.

56. Kanamori Kazuko, ed., *Kabuki-za hyakunen shi* (Tokyo: Shochiku Kabuki-za, 1998), p. 196.

57. Nagayama Takeomi, *Kabuki gojūnen watakushi no rirekisho* (Tokyo: Nihon Keizai Shimbunsha, 1995), p. 163.

58. Ibid.

59. Ibid.

60. Mishima Yukio, "Takemotobon 'Jigoku Hen,'" Kabuki-za Program, December 1953; reprinted in *Mishima Yukio hyōron zenshū*, vol. 3, p. 864.

61. Ibid.

62. Mishima Yukio, "Boku no 'Jigoku Hen'"; reprinted in *Mishima Yukio hyōron zenshū*, vol. 3, p. 869.

63. Mishima, "Boku no 'Jigoku Hen'"; reprinted in *Mishima Yukio hyōron zenshū*,

vol. 3, p. 870, and "Takemotobon 'Jigoku Hen'"; reprinted in *Mishima Yukio hyōron zenshū*, vol. 3, p. 861.

64. Nagayama Takeomi, interview with author, January 27, 2002.

65. Nagayama Takeomi, *Kabuki gojūnen watakushi no rirekisho*, p. 164.

66. Ibid.

67. Nakamura, "'Mishima Kabuki' no sekai," *Shibai nikki*, p. 188.

68. Ibid.

69. Mishima, "Takemotobon 'Jigoku Hen'"; reprinted in *Mishima Yukio hyōron zenshū*, vol. 3, pp. 864–65.

70. Mishima Yukio, "Iwashiuri ni tsuite," Kabuki-za Program, November 1954; reprinted in *Mishima Yukio hyōron zenshū*, vol. 3, p. 869.

71. Ibid.

72. Toita Yasuji, "Shinsen na iwashi," *Engekikai gekihyō*, reprinted in Ogawa Akio, "Mishima Yukio kabuki sakuhin jōen kiroku to nenpyō," *Kabuki*, no. 12, April 1971, p. 39.

73. Akiyama Yasusaburō from *Mainichi Shimbun*, reprinted in Ogawa, *Kabuki*, no. 12, p. 39.

74. Mishima Yukio, "'Iwashiuri koi no hikiami' ni tsuite," *Fujin Shobō*, January 1956; reprinted in *Mishima Yukio hyōron zenshū*, vol. 3, p. 871.

75. Ibid.

76. Nakamura, "'Mishima Kabuki' no sekai," *Shibai nikki*, p. 191.

77. Mishima Yukio, "'Fuyo no tsuyu Ōuchi jikki' ni tsuite," Kabuki-za Program, November 1955; reprinted in *Mishima Yukio hyōron zenshū*, vol. 3, p. 873.

78. Ibid.

79. Ibid., p. 874.

80. Nakamura, "'Mishima Kabuki' no sekai," *Shibai nikki*, p. 194.

81. Ogawa Akiko, "Mishima Yukio sakuhin jōen kiroku to nempyō," *Kabuki*, no. 12, April 1971, p. 42.

82. Toita Yasuji, from *Engekikai;* reprinted in Ogawa, *Kabuki*, no. 12, p. 42.

83. Akiyama Yasusaburō, from *Mainichi Shimbun;* reprinted in Ogawa, *Kabuki*, no. 12, p. 43.

84. Nakamura, "'Mishima Kabuki' no sekai," *Shibai nikki*, p. 194.

85. Nagayama Takeomi, interview by author, January 27, 2002. Nagayama said that he told Mishima over the phone that Utaemon had gone into a funk when Nagayama went into Utaemon's dressing room and criticized his acting in the play. When Mishima heard the story he burst out laughing and said it was the funniest story he had heard in a long time.

86. Mishima Yukio, "Chikamatsu bayari shikan," *Tokyo Shimbun*, April 7, 8, 1958; reprinted in *Mishima Yukio hyōron zenshū*, vol. 3, p. 649.

87. Gunji Masakatsu notes that the mother defends new, hedonistic moral values, while her daughter, at least briefly, supports old-fashioned samurai morality, and that this is unprecedented in traditional kabuki. Gunji Masakatsu, "Mishima Kabuki," Kabuki-za Program, April 1973; reprinted in *Obitori no Ike, Michiyuki Yuki no Furusato, Kanjinchō* Kokuritsu Gekijō jōen shiryō shū no. 392 (Tokyo: Kokuritsu Gekijō Chōsa Yōseibu Geinō Chōsa Shitsu, 1998), p. 6.

88. Ōki Yutaka, excerpted from *Gekihyō*, in Ogawa, *Kabuki*, no. 12, p. 43.

89. Nagayama Takeomi, interview by author, January 27, 2002.

90. Mishima Yukio, "Sakusha no kotoba," Kabuki-za Program, December 1958,

reprinted in *Mishima hyōron zenshū,* vol. 3, p. 878.

91. Kanzai Kiyoshi, quoted in Nobuko Pugarelli, *"The Aesthetics of Destruction: A Study of Six Representative Modern Plays by Mishima Yukio,"* Ph.D. diss., University of Hawaii, 1984. See Imamura Chōjun, "Yoru no Himawari," *Mishima Yukio jiten,* p. 396, for a summary of critical response to the play.

92. Mishima Yukio, "Takechi ban 'Aya no Tsuzumi' ni tuite," Enkei Gekijō Program, December 1955, reprinted in *Mishima Yukio hyōron zenshū,* vol. 3, pp. 753–54.

93. Takechi Tetsuji, *Mishima Yukio: Shi to sono kabuki kan* (Tokyo: Tōshobō, 1971), pp. 41–42.

94. Imamura Chūjun, "Rokumeikan," *Mishima Yukio jiten,* p. 412.

95. Ōzasa Yoshio, *Joyū Sugimura Haruko* (Tokyo: Shūeisha, 1995), p. 193.

96. Ibid.

97. Mishima Yukio, "A small scar on the left kneecap," *"My Friend Hitler" and Other Plays of Yukio Mishima,* trans Hiroaki Sato (New York: Columbia University, 2002), p. 59.

98. Ibid., p. 58.

99. Imamura, "Rokumeikan," *Mishima Yukio jiten,* p. 414.

100. Ibid., p. 415.

101. Ōzasa Yoshio, *Joyū Sugimura Haruko* (Tokyo: Shūeisha, 1995), pp. 202–3.

102. Pugarelli, *"The Aesthetics of Destruction,"* p. 88.

103. Ibid., p. 92.

104. Donald Keene, *On Familiar Terms* (Tokyo: Kodansha International, 1994), p. 202.

105. Dōmoto Masaki, *Mishima Yukio no engeki maku kire no shiso* (Tokyo: Geki Shobō, 1977), p. 137.

106. Mishima Yukio, "Kuro tokage ni tsuite," *Seibu seikatsu,* 1962; reprinted in Mishima, *Shibai no biyaku,* p. 207.

107. Mishima Yukio, "Kuro tokage," in Toyoko Gekijō Program, April 1968; reprinted in *Mishima Yukio hyōron zenshū,* vol. 3, p. 823.

108. Mizutani Yaeko, *Mizutani Yaeko: Joyū ichidai* (Tokyo: Nihon Tosho Sentaa, 1997), pp. 253–54.

109. Mishima, "Kuro tokage," reprinted in *Mishima Yukio hyōron zenshū,* vol. 3, p. 823.

110. Mishima, "Kuro tokage ni tsuite," reprinted in Mishima, *Shibai no biyaku,* p. 207.

111. Bandō Tamasaburō believes that plays like *The Black Lizard* represent the "real Mishima," who was a romantic at heart. But because he recognized that in the world of serious literature romantic melodramas garnered no respect whatsoever, he rarely allowed himself to write the kind of work he felt most at home with. Bandō Tamasaburō, interview by author, February 13, 2002.

112. Ōzasa Yoshio, *Joyū Sugimura Haruko* (Tokyo: Shūeisha, 1995), p. 215. The play was entitled *Chicken Soup with Barley.*

113. Ibid., p. 216.

114. Ibid.

115. Andō Takeshi, *Mishima Yukio Nichiroku;* reprinted in *Mishima Yukio jiten,* pp. 508–9.

116. Inui Ichirō, *Shibai no michi: Bungakuza to tomo ni rokujōnen* (Tokyo: Maruzen,

1999), p. 237.

117. Henry Scott-Stokes, *The Life and Death of Yukio Mishima* (New York: Farrar, Straus and Giroux, 1974), p. 210.

118. Ōzasa, *Joyū Sugimura Haruko,* p. 199.

119. Ibid.

120. Ibid., p. 258.

121. Ōzasa Yoshio, interview by author, November 22, 2001.

122. Mishima Yukio, "NLT no mirai," *NLT spot,* July 1964; reprinted in *Mishima Yukio hyōron zenshū,* vol. 3, p. 726; and Mishima Yukio, "NLT no kao," NLT Gekidan Program, May 1964; reprinted in *Mishima Yukio hyōron zenshū,* vol. 3, pp. 696–98.

123. Minamoto Gorō, "Yorokobi no koto," *Mishima Yukio jiten,* p. 398.

124. Mishima, *Madame de Sade,* trans. Donald Keene, pp. 107–8.

125. Ibid., p. 104.

126. Ibid., p. 83.

127. Mishima Yukio, "Watashi no bungaku o kataru," *Mishima Yukio jiten,* p. 196.

128. Mishima Yukio, "Gekidan Roman Gekijō no miraizu," *Mishima Yukio jiten,* p. 626.

129. Mishima Yukio, "Sakuhin haikei—Waga tomo no Hittora," *Tokyo Shimbun,* December 27, 1968; reprinted in *Mishima Yukio jiten,* p. 422.

130. Stokes, *The Life and Death of Yukio Mishima,* p. 212.

131. Mishima Yukio, "Hittora to iu jimbutsu ga—inyōsha chū," *Mishima Yukio jiten,* p. 422.

132. Ibid.

133. Mishima, *"My Friend Hitler,"* trans. Hiroaki Sato, p. 128.

134. Matsumoto Michisuke, "Waga tomo Hittora," *Mishima Yukio jiten,* p. 424.

135. Ibid., p. 425.

136. Stokes, *The Life and Death of Yukio Mishima,* p. 213.

137. The Leper King's race with death to build the Temple of Bayon is a popular but untrue story, according to Sato, in Mishima, *"My Friend Hitler,"* trans. Hiroaki Sato, p. 162.

138. Ono Yūji, "Raiō no terasu," *Mishima Yukio jiten,* p. 402.

139. Ibid.

140. Orita Kōji, "Chinzetsu yumiharizuki," *Mishima Yukio jiten,* p. 235.

141. Mishima Yukio, "Yumiharizuki no gekika to enshutsu," National Theatre Program, November 1969; reprinted in *Mishima Yukio hyōron zenshū,* vol. 3, p. 902.

142. Mishima Yukio, "Chinzetsu yumiharizuki no enshutsu," *Mainichi Shimbun,* November 7, 1969; reprinted in *Mishima Yukio hyōron zenshū,* vol. 3, p. 904.

143. Mishima Yukio, "Tamasaburō no koto," National Theatre Program, August 1970; reprinted in *Mishima Yukio hyōron zenshū,* vol. 3, p. 907.

144. Mishima, "Chinzetsu yumiharizuki no enshutsu"; reprinted in *Mishima Yukio hyōron zenshū,* vol. 3, p. 904.

145. Bandō Tamasaburō, interview with author, February 13, 2002.

146. Ibid.

147. Andō, *Mishima Yukio Nichiroku*; reprinted in *Mishima Yukio jiten,* p. 71.

148. Mishima, "Yumiharizuki no gekika to enshutsu"; reprinted in *Mishima Yukio hyōron zenshū,* vol. 3, p. 902.

149. Ogawa, *Kabuki* no. 12, p. 44.

150. Ibid.

151. Takechi, *Mishima Yukio: Shi to sono kabuki kan*, pp. 11–16, 69–73.

152. Stokes, *The Life and Death of Yukio Mishima*, p. 216.

153. Heshiki Naoko, "Matsuura Takeo," *Mishima Yukio jiten*, p. 602.

154. Nagayama, *Kabuki gojūnen watakushi no rirekisho*, p. 76.

155. Miwa Akihiro, *Miwa Akihiro no Ichiban Utsukushii Mono*, ETV Documentary, 2003.

156. Inui, *Shibai no michi*, pp. 237–38.

157. Nakamura, "'Mishima Kabuki' no sekai," *Shibai nikki*, p. 199.

The Lighthouse
(Tōdai)

Published in 1949, First Staged in 1949
Translated by Laurence Kominz

INTRODUCTION

The Lighthouse was Mishima's second play to be published and performed. A company of young actors that did new works presented *The Lighthouse* in November of 1949, and in early 1950 Mishima directed the play himself at the prestigious Haiyū-za for his debut as a stage director.

The Lighthouse is a *shingeki* play that brings the incest theme of Racine's *Phaedra* to the modern Japanese stage. Twenty-five-year-old Noboru has returned home from the war to find his recently widowed father, Yūkichi, remarried to the attractive, thirty-year-old divorcee, Isako. Isako and her stepson have concealed their passion for each other until the moment that this play takes place: during a family vacation to the semitropical resort island of Ōshima, south of Tokyo. Noboru's nineteen-year-old sister, Masako, begins the drama as an innocent teenager, but during the course of the play she is forced to confront her brother's incestuous passion, and the very same evening she also falls victim to sex abuse at a party with her friends. Masako successfully meets these two challenges and at the end of the play enters a very painful adult world.

Mishima wrote *The Lighthouse* immediately after returning from his third vacation trip to Ōshima Island in March 1949. In program notes to the first production of the play, he stated that he wrote sketches of some of the guests at the hotel where he stayed, and used them to create the play's characters. The play had been "a joy to write."[1]

Mishima intended *The Lighthouse* to be interpreted and directed in two very different ways. In effect there is a "light *Lighthouse* and a "dark *Lighthouse*." He acknowledged and even applauded the light version in his first program notes.[2] This is the interpretation that has been used in the frequent productions done in high schools and colleges. In the "light version" of the play, Yūkichi, though foolish and insensitive, is a loving father who is blind to his family members' difficulties because he is so intent on reliving his youth: paying court to his beautiful young wife, singing *chansons*, and dancing the jitterbug with his daughter. He is essentially a benign and silly figure. Although Noboru ends the play hiding under his covers and crying, it is possible to play the scene with a light touch, conveying a sense that Noboru will grow out of his difficulties, and go on to live a normal, healthy life.

The light version is easy to perceive, direct, and act, and its charm and accessibility were the reasons that *The Lighthouse* was performed more often during Mishima's lifetime than any other play, and was a special favorite for high school and college productions.[3] Part of the appeal of the "light *Lighthouse*" is the lively and charming sibling rivalry between Noboru and Masako featured in the first quarter of the play. Mishima may well have created Masako in tribute to his own beloved sister whom he had tended daily during her fatal illness in 1945. Masako is intelligent, witty, beautiful, idealistic, and strong-willed. While the play does not end happily for her, she emerges as its strongest, most admirable character.

The "dark *Lighthouse*" is much more interesting. It is dominated by suppressed carnal passions. Yūkichi is no longer an innocent, bumbling romantic. The picture of Noboru in the study that comes to obsess Isako soon after her marriage is not there by accident. Yūkichi left it there on purpose to create a rivalry between himself and Noboru that will force the guilt-ridden Isako to demonstrate her love for Yūkichi more ardently, thus stimulating Yūkichi's ebbing libido. Brother and sister suppress sexual desire for each other under a facade of teasing and childish play. The ending of this dark version is bleak indeed. Noboru has been prevented by his sister from revealing the truth of his love to his father, and lies weeping on his bed, buried under the covers. Masako rails in self-pity against her loss of innocence. She has seen the cruelty of sexual desire at work, and now she must bear sole responsibility for preventing incestuous carnal passions from destroying her family. This ending is far from a rosy "youth coming of age" story. Youth is "a self-wounding, violent struggle with one's flesh which causes passions to steam. Sweat and tears aren't pure, they are excretions of the flesh."[4] In the "dark *Lighthouse*" we witness the incestuous obsessions that led to murder and suicide in *Phaedra*, burning just as intensely in the hearts of contemporary upper middle class Japanese. These passions can still destroy families and individuals, but perhaps in not so dramatic a fashion as in the classical age.

It is clear that Mishima had hopes of directing a dark version of *The Lighthouse* at the Haiyu-za in 1950, but his terrible relationship with his cast doomed the effort. When veteran director Aoyama Sugisaku stepped in to rescue the production, all that Aoyama perceived was the "light *Lighthouse*." Mishima criticized Aoyama's work in his program notes, and then turned to the rival Bungaku-za theatre company to produce his next play.[5]

NOTES

1. Mishima Yukio, "Sakusha no kotoba (Tōdai)," Kansai Jikken Gekijō Program, November 1949; reprinted in *Mishima hyōron zenshū*, vol. 3 (Tokyo: Shinchōsha, 1994), p. 739.

2. Ibid.

3. *The Lighthouse* was the second most frequently performed one-act play dur-

ing Mishima's lifetime by professional companies (five productions). The most frequently performed one-act play by professional companies was *The Damask Drum* (eight productions).

4. Dōmoto Masaki, *Gekijin Mishima Yukio* (Tokyo: Gekishobō, 1994), p. 141.

5. See Introduction, pages 12–14 for a detailed account of Mishima's experience directing *The Lighthouse* at Haiyū-za in 1950.

THE CHARACTERS

Kurokawa Yūkichi (55), an electrical goods manufacturer
Kurokawa Isako (30), Yūkichi's second wife
Kurokawa Noboru (25), Yūkichi's only son by his first marriage, an economics major at a university
Kurokawa Masako (19), Noboru's younger sister, a mission school student, Yūkichi's daughter by his first wife
Chiba Junko (20), Masako's friend

SETTING

A second-floor room in a hotel on the island resort of Ōshima, 300 miles south of Tokyo. Mid-April, from 11 p.m. to past midnight.

A hotel room that could be anywhere. There are two single beds side-by-side at stage left. The heads of the beds are against the upstage wall of the room set, leaving plenty of open stage space downstage of the beds. A small table, also touching the back wall, is between the two beds. The beds should be an obstacle to movement by the actors. The color of the walls should be garish enough to destroy any sense of color harmony in the room. The set should be an ironic antithesis to the simple psychological processes associated with the typical "bedroom drama."

From stage left a door opens into the hall. To the right of the beds is a chest of drawers with a suitcase in front of it. Above the beds is an oil painting of a landscape. To the left of the beds are a vanity and a chair. At stage right a glass door is partly open, and the railing of the balcony is visible outside the glass. In front of the glass door is a small table covered with a white table cloth, and two chairs, one facing the audience, one leaning against the side of the glass door. A nondescript chandelier shines brightly. The view from the balcony includes a distant vista to stage right, and nearer at hand the lights from neighboring guest rooms are seen, brightly lit.

When the curtain rises, MASAKO, *wearing a long, cobalt-blue skirt is half lying on the bed to stage right. She has placed thirteen playing cards on the bedspread and is reading her fortune in the cards. The beds have been made ready for sleep, but only the pillows are out. The bedspreads are still on the beds.* NOBORU *is on the balcony, gazing at the nighttime view of the island. He is in a black student uniform with gold buttons.*

NOBORU: *(With his back to the room)* I'm not at all sleepy. I wonder why?

MASAKO: *(Returning to her cards)* Of course you're not. You didn't sleep at all last night on the boat, and then after we got here you slept all afternoon. . . . If you really want to sleep so much, do what Dad does—drink down five bottles of beer in a row. What a strange old guy Dad is. He drinks before meals, then gargles with beer when he's done, then drinks down the beer he's been gargling. I'm surprised he hasn't taken to using beer to wash his face. *(She looks at* NOBORU.*)* Noboru, why didn't you drink anything this evening?

NOBORU: I just didn't feel like drinking.

MASAKO: *(Turning back to her cards)* Why not?

NOBORU: I just didn't feel like it.

MASAKO: Well, you get what you deserve, and now you can't sleep. But if you don't get a good night's sleep you won't be able to climb Mount Mihara tomorrow.

NOBORU: Mother did drink this evening, didn't she?

MASAKO: Yes, just a little. That's why the two of them are fast asleep now.

NOBORU *comes in from the balcony. He looks around the room, somewhat restlessly.*

NOBORU: Do you know where my binoculars are?

MASAKO: Your "war crimes" binoculars? They're in the suitcase. (NOBORU *goes to the suitcase, then looks back.)*

NOBORU: What's that you just said?

MASAKO: War crimes. After all, they are a parting gift from the navy, aren't they?

NOBORU: Yeah. *(He rummages around in the suitcase, pulls out a pair of naval officer's binoculars, and goes back out onto the balcony.)*

MASAKO: *(Without looking at him)* What are you looking at?

NOBORU: The lighthouse.

MASAKO: *(Looking outside)* You can see it fine from here. And even if you look through binoculars, at night what's there to see but the light? *(Growing more curious)* What are you looking at? *(She stands up childishly and goes out to join her brother.)* Show me too. Come on, let me see.

NOBORU: What a pain you are. Wait a bit, okay?

MASAKO: No, let me see. Let me see.

NOBORU: *(Hands over the binoculars)* You can see heaven through these, so take a good, long look. *(He sits down on a chair and lights up a cigarette.)* It's because those binoculars have seen so many men dying.

MASAKO: You liar. You can't see anything. *(But she continues to look through the binoculars.)* Just the lighthouse. All I can see is the light in the lighthouse. . . . . Oh look, it's gone dark. . . . Now it's on again. . . . But it doesn't seem as bright as it does from the ocean. Oh, I can see a little window in the lighthouse. It's dim, but you can just see it . . . What a cute window in the lighthouse.

NOBORU: If you keep talking so loudly out there, all the men in the hotel will be staring at you tomorrow. It's great publicity.

MASAKO: Publicity for what?

NOBORU: Publicity asking if anyone wants a bride who's a little strange in the head.

MASAKO: You're weird. In that case, if you married me we'd be just right for each other, wouldn't we. . . . Look! The light's still on in Chiba-san's room. *(She lowers the binoculars.)* You know, it looks like Junko and her friends are still up partying.

She comes inside and puts the binoculars down on the dressing table. She jumps back onto the bed.

NOBORU: All that guys like that ever think about is how they can party all night spending just one hundred yen each, or where they can travel if they spend just one thousand yen. When they're done they just collapse and sleep like logs, so satisfied that they're having fun while they're young. And the girls—they're stingy, and what little they do spend is all on clothes. They're all like paper lanterns for a festival, swinging in the breeze, with no idea that tomorrow they'll be burned up.

MASAKO: If that's what makes them happy, it's okay with me.

NOBORU: You're just like them, Masako. You think just like they do. But I'm different. I can't live if I don't think about what will happen tomorrow.

MASAKO: Even if you know tomorrow will be a bad day?

NOBORU: Yes, because the day after tomorrow might turn out to be a good day.

MASAKO: *(Changing the subject slightly)* What are you talking about? Tomorrow we climb Mount Mihara, and the day after tomorrow we take the boat back to Tokyo. We'll never get anywhere if you keep talking like an inaccurate weather report.

NOBORU: *(Teasing her a little)* Masa-bo, what you just said is only a plan. Plans can change, you know.

MASAKO: Yeah, tomorrow's plan would change if someone did something like jump into the crater of Mount Mihara.

NOBORU: Hooray! Then the whole world would change.

MASAKO: Would you be happy no matter who it is that jumps in? If it doesn't matter who, then I might as well be the one. Everyone keeps saying that I have to get married, I have to get married. You're all such pains.

NOBORU: A girl who hates the idea of getting married is sitting there hoping the cards will foretell good fortune in love. A charming sight. *(He goes to the far side of her bed.)* What do the cards say? Will you be lucky in love?

MASAKO: (*Somewhat put off*) Stop that, would you. (*She mixes the cards and begins to re-sort them. Her brother sits down on the stage right bed.*) I know what you're thinking. You just said I'm the same as Junko, but I'm not. I don't want to get married and I don't want a boyfriend. I want to think that I'm still a cute little child. I don't want to have to struggle to rush into the world of adults. I can see that the adult world is all wrong. Always. Since I know that the adult world is all wrong, I don't want to be a part of it. I don't care what anyone else thinks.

NOBORU: I can see that you've been influenced by your teacher, that pretty nun at your mission school . . . what was her name again? But staying a virgin all of your life? Give up that idea, it doesn't suit you. When you've had five lovers, then you can talk to me about how tough adult life is.

MASAKO: Oh, yeah? The same goes for you.

NOBORU: . . .

MASAKO *gets off the bed, shuffles into her slippers, and goes to the desk where she puts the cards in their box. She leans against the sliding lattice door and gazes outside.*

MASAKO: What's the name of that lighthouse?

NOBORU: The Ōshima Lighthouse.

MASAKO: You liar. It's got to have a different name than that.

NOBORU: When we arrived this morning the porter said something about it. I think it was the name of the cape.

MASAKO: I remember. It was the "Early.". . . something . . .

NOBORU: "Early Wind Cape."

MASAKO: They say that beyond that cape the Japan Current is really strong.

NOBORU: The sea is wonderful. When I left officers training school and went to my first assignment in Taiwan, the sea there was so beautiful. It seemed like it was my domain. I'd talk with my navy friends about how, after the war, we'd divide that stretch of sea up and parcel it out among us in four square-mile lots. . . . But of course mother died the day after I was sent there. In Taiwan I didn't hear about it until after the war was over. And father didn't tell anyone that he'd remarried. Not until after I was demobilized.

MASAKO: I didn't do anything wrong.

NOBORU: I know. It's nobody's fault.

MASAKO: How about making it someone's fault? That would make you feel better, wouldn't it?

NOBORU: What?

MASAKO: You're a weakling, Noboru. When the war ended you went back to the same university and turned back into the same weakling of a college student.

NOBORU: Calling me a weakling . . . isn't that going too far?

MASAKO: Maybe it's going too far. But I think you're going too far to come back the same weakling of an older brother that left for the war. . . . When we were kids I'd steal candy from you and you never said anything, never got angry.

NOBORU: You must have stuffed yourself silly.

MASAKO: No, I'd feel guilty and put it back. Later on you'd eat it just as if nothing had happened.

For a while both are silent.

MASAKO: I'm going to tell you something. But I'm sure it will make you angry.

NOBORU: Go ahead and tell me. You're still a child and your feelings are too precious to keep locked inside you. Masa-bo, your feelings are so small they'd fit inside a tiny locket. With a little lid on it, and initials cheaply engraved. With a poorly made crucifix hanging from it.

MASAKO: *(Very awkwardly, but in a burst of speech)* I know why you were standing out there on the balcony so long. You want to know what's going on in there. In Isako-san's room. It's filthy of you. I can't stand you doing it.

NOBORU: You idiot! *(He's very disturbed, but presently is able to suppress and conceal his feelings.)* What a stupid thing to say. . . . What did you just call her? . . . Did you say "Isako-san?"

MASAKO: What? You didn't know? When mother and I are together and no one else is with us, I call her "Isako-san," and she calls me "Masako-chan." She says that it makes her feel more comfortable and she's really happy that I agreed to call her that. She told me she can't stand being called "mother" because it makes her feel like she's suddenly gotten old. I'm only eleven years younger than she is and I call her "Isako-san." Don't you think it's unnatural to be so formal and call her "mother," when you're just five years younger than she is?

NOBORU: Don't be stupid!

There is a soft knock on the door.

MASAKO: Speak of the devil. Come in.

ISAKO *enters. She is wearing Japanese clothing that suits her age, a little garish, but in good taste. She quietly pushes open the door and enters the room.*

MASAKO: *(Cheerfully)* Oh, you aren't asleep yet? And you didn't change into your nightgown.

ISAKO: I just don't feel sleepy somehow. Don't you two feel the same?

MASAKO: How about father?

ISAKO: Sleeping like a log. Every five minutes he lets out a savage snore. It was so funny I lay there counting them. I thought it would make me sleepy. But it didn't work. As I lay counting them I got to thinking that if I fell asleep, I'd start snoring in just the same way.

MASAKO: How awful. *(She laughs.* NOBORU *hardly laughs at all.* ISAKO *perceives the mood in the room, but acts cheerful nonetheless. She sits down in the chair at stage right and gives a small yawn.)*

ISAKO: My, what's this? When I sat in this chair I suddenly felt sleepy and yawned.

MASAKO: That sort of thing happens when you can't sleep.

ISAKO: I don't think I have enough energy to climb Mount Mihara tomorrow. I feel that if I do climb Mount Mihara I won't ever come back to the island again. If there was some smoke coming out of it, it would be interesting, but the volcano's dormant, the camellias are finished blooming, and I can see cherry blossoms just as well in Tokyo. Coming to Ōshima seems pointless. Mr. Yamaguchi's uncle praised the place so highly, I guess we finally gave in to his enthusiasm.

MASAKO: I wonder if Mr. Yamaguchi's uncle gets political donations from Ōshima Island? . . . But you know . . . when Noboru and I took a walk this evening, the singing of the birds was completely different than in Tokyo. It seemed like the singing of free and happy birds that spend all day long gazing at the sea. Don't you think so, Noboru?

NOBORU: Yes. *(As if compelled to speak)* The wind was nice too. Because it comes straight off the ocean.

ISAKO: I can hear the sound of waves from here, I think. Maybe not. Can you hear the waves?

MASAKO: I can't hear waves at all.

ISAKO: You do express yourself directly, don't you. Oh, that's right. I came to borrow a book because I can't get to sleep. Masako-chan, did you bring any novels with you?

MASAKO: Yes, I brought two or three. They're in my case.

ISAKO: Can I borrow one?

ISAKO *and* MASAKO *go to the bureau at stage left.* NOBORU *is left alone in his chair at stage right.* ISAKO *sits on the edge of the bed to the right and watches* MASAKO *sift through the contents of the case.*

MASAKO: Here they are. How's this?

ISAKO: *(Reading the cover)* Jacobsen, *If There Were Roses Here*. . . . No, I've read it already.

MASAKO: Okay . . . how about this one?

ISAKO: Marcel Proust, *Confessions of a Girl . . . (She leafs through the pages.)* I see . . . don't you have any silly romance novels?

MASAKO: *(Looking through the contents of the case)* Here's something. If you read this it will work like magic. You'll start to yawn and feel sleepy.

ISAKO: What is it?

MASAKO: *(Handing it to her)* It's my brother's school text. *(She sits down beside* ISAKO.*)* He's a real grade grubber to bring something like this on a trip.

Because there's nothing written on the cover, ISAKO *turns it over and with apparent difficulty reads the gold printing on the book's spine.*

ISAKO: *Some Issues in Modern Economic History*, by Ōtomo Mamoru, Professor of Economics. *(She smiles.)* This book seems interesting.

MASAKO: I haven't read it yet, but I don't think any book could be more interesting. I tried looking at it once, but couldn't understand anything in it. I thought I might try it again and maybe this time I'd be able to follow it a little. One needs a few thrills in life, after all.

ISAKO: *(Leafing through the pages)* There are a lot of notes and comments written in here.

MASAKO: Probably just doodling and scribbling.

ISAKO: *(Looking at a single page)* You're right. It's scribbling. In pencil—tiny letters.

MASAKO: *(Bending her head over the page to read it)* What's written here? *(She reads innocently in a loud voice.)* "Isako, Isako, Isako, Isako, Isako, Isako, Isa . . ."

MASAKO *reads the word "Isako," written more than ten times in a row, with child-like innocence, counting the words as she reads, but when she realizes the implications of what she is doing, she suddenly shuts her mouth and turns to stare at her brother.* ISAKO, *spellbound in surprise and agitation, stares fixedly at the page, unable to utter a word.*

NOBORU, *who had been sitting silently stage right, lost in thought, stands up in fright when he hears "Isako, Isako" being repeated again and again, and runs to seize the book from* ISAKO's *hand.* MASAKO *sees him doing this and snatches the book from* ISAKO *before* NOBORU *can reach her.* ISAKO *seems not to understand what is going on, and for a moment looks up at* MASAKO *in shock.*

NOBORU: Hey, Masako!

Laughing to cover his embarrassment he tries to grab MASAKO. MASAKO, *holding the book tightly, kicks off her slippers and jumps to the next bed, escaping his grasp.* NOBORU *jumps from bed to bed in pursuit. He chases her around the room, finally catching her at stage right.* MASAKO *holds the book tight and won't let go of it.*

NOBORU: Hey! Give it back! If you don't give it back . . .!

MASAKO *bursts out laughing, thinking it's all a joke, but as* NOBORU *gets more violent in his attempt to seize the book from her, she suddenly gets angry.*

MASAKO: That hurts! What're you doing? I'm not giving it back. You weren't reading it anyway. You selfish pig! Oh, you look funny. You're all red with anger. How brave of you to bully a girl like me. That's why I've been calling you a war criminal.

NOBORU: You barbarian!

ISAKO: Both of you stop it this instant! You're disgraceful! I'm sure you've woken the people sleeping downstairs. What if they complain about it? Masako-chan, give him back his book and pick up your slippers. You, too, Noboru. I'm amazed at you. *(Speaking with a tired voice)* You're like little children.

MASAKO *does not obediently give the book back to her brother. Instead she flings it down on the desk at stage right, and goes stage left to look for her slippers.* NOBORU *does not touch the book on the table, but sits in the downstage chair. Just as* ISAKO *is about to sit on the edge of the bed on the left, she and* NOBORU *briefly look at each other. She immediately stands and joins* MASAKO *who is hunting for her slippers.*

ISAKO: There it is. And the other one is over there.

MASAKO: *(Laughing in amusement as she picks them up)* What, it's over there. ....Yuck. *(She takes two slippers, one in each hand, holding them between thumb and forefinger.)* Look, I caught two fish.

ISAKO: *(Smiling faintly in spite of herself)* You little fool.

MASAKO *puts on her slippers.* ISAKO *brings a chair over from the dressing table, and the three sit uncomfortably around the table that has the textbook on it.*

MASAKO: Darn. I'm even less sleepy than before.

ISAKO: Shall we three stay up all night like this?

NOBORU: *(Remaining focused on the book)* Like spending a sleepless night guarding a treasure.

MASAKO: But if a ninja sneaked in, we'd all be fast asleep, under a ninja spell.

ISAKO: *(In an intentionally matter-of-fact way)* If we fall asleep like this, we'll all catch colds.

NOBORU: Mother, you're worrying needlessly.

ISAKO: *(Very clearly)* It's not needless worrying.

MASAKO: *(Looking at the deck of cards on the table)* Oh, I know what we can do. Let's play cards.

ISAKO: *(Hiding her anxiety)* Yes, let's.

Just as MASAKO *opens the box and takes out the cards there is a knock at the door.*

MASAKO: That must be our drunken ninja. *(She goes to open the door. It is* JUNKO.*)* Oh, Junko. *(Looking back into the room, eyes sparkling with laughter)* It isn't the ninja.

JUNKO: *(Standing in the doorway)* Oh, are you here, Mrs. Kurokawa? I'm sorry for intruding. Masako, you lied to us and now everyone's angry with you.

MASAKO: What?

JUNKO: We invited you to a party in our room, but you said you'd be going to bed early and couldn't come.

MASAKO: I did go to bed early, but I couldn't get to sleep.

JUNKO: Come on over and join us. We saw that the light was on in your room, but we didn't know what was going on.

MASAKO: Are you doing anything fun?

JUNKO: Nothing special.

MASAKO: Mother, have you ever heard of a game called "nothing special?"

JUNKO: I'll pinch you.

MASAKO: Ow. It seems like I'm getting hurt a lot today.

JUNKO: Have you been fighting with your brother? *(She looks flirtatiously at* NOBORU.*)*

ISAKO: I'm impressed. That look would travel a thousand miles.

JUNKO: I want to fight with your brother too.

MASAKO: Noboru, you've got a new partner to fight with. *(*NOBORU *smiles vaguely.)*

JUNKO: *(To* NOBORU*)* Will you come over to our room?

MASAKO: I'll go if Noboru goes too.

NOBORU: You go by yourself. I'm sleepy.

ISAKO: *(In a small voice)* With all those young men there, I'm worried about Masako going by herself.

NOBORU: *(In a small voice)* She'll be all right. She's a tough woman.

MASAKO: *(Catches the import of* ISAKO *and* NOBORU's *whispered exchange, and flings out her words defiantly to play the tough woman and cover her wounded pride)* All right. That's fine. I'll go by myself.

JUNKO: *(Disappointedly)* You'll come? That's great. How about you, Noboru?

MASAKO: (*Not noticing the contradiction between* JUNKO's *words and her tone)* He and I are still angry with each other.

JUNKO: In that case, Mrs. Kurokawa, I'll borrow Masako for a bit.
ISAKO. Please send her back as soon as possible.
JUNKO: I promise to, *if* her brother comes to get her.

The two exit.

NOBORU: Now there's a bad girl for you.
ISAKO: These days lots of girls are like that. I just can't understand girls anymore.
NOBORU: I can't either, anymore.
ISAKO: For you it's not "anymore." For you it's "not yet."
NOBORU: *(Laughing faintly)* Mother, you don't know me at all. I feel like everything has ended for me. But still, I feel a new tomorrow might come at any moment. (*There is a silence of mutual understanding.* ISAKO *makes no move to get out of her chair.* NOBORU *suddenly seems ill at ease.)* Let's play cards. Just the two of us.
ISAKO: All right.

There is a long silence. NOBORU *stands uneasily. He gives a big, unconvincing yawn.*

NOBORU: That's strange. I was lying when I told Junko I was sleepy, but now I really am sleepy. Maybe telling lies is the best way to get sleepy. Mother, don't you want to go to bed? *(Evasively)* Excuse me for lying down here while you're sitting up.

He takes his uniform jacket off a hook, and flops down on top of the bedspread on the bed on the right, covering himself with his jacket. He lies on his back and closes his eyes for a moment, then opens them. He clasps his hands and puts them behind his head. ISAKO *nonchalantly picks up the economics text book and leafs through the pages.* NOBORU *nervously pulls some cigarettes out of his pocket. He smokes, still lying on his back.*

ISAKO: Have you gone to sleep?
NOBORU: No, not yet.
ISAKO: I'd like to have you do something for me before you go to sleep.
NOBORU: What? *(Guessing what she might say, but ignoring it, he speaks too brightly)* Are you going to tell me to brush my teeth before I go to bed?
ISAKO: It's nothing special, but it's hard to say when you're far away.
NOBORU: Go ahead and shout then. No one's around to hear you.
ISAKO: In that case, it's all right if I tell you in a loud voice. I wouldn't be embarrassed even if anyone did hear me. . . . I've a favor to ask of you. It's about your writing in this book. Please erase it. *(Coolly)* It is in pencil, after all, and should be easy to erase. *(A pause.* ISAKO *smiles.)* It's funny

isn't it, to make such a big deal over something this trivial. After all, it's just meaningless doodling, isn't it? Still, since it can be erased, it should be.

A pause.

NOBORU: I don't want to.

ISAKO: *(In a stronger voice)* Why not? I'm your mother now. You shouldn't be so disobedient to your mother.

NOBORU: Yes, a mother does have the legal right to instruct her children, I suppose. Any mother would give this kind of advice to a child. If a child's been bad, a parent has the legal right to discipline him. I learned that in my civil law seminar.

ISAKO: *(Fearfully)* I've never heard you talk like this before. You've never sounded so full of despair. I don't know what to say. *(But with apparent confidence, she continues.)* I wonder if I should tell you something that might hurt you?

NOBORU: Well now . . . I don't know whether you should or not.

ISAKO: There are times when from the outside, someone sees something insignificant and thinks it more important than it really is. This careless misunderstanding can wind up hurting everyone involved.

NOBORU: You're going to a lot of trouble over nothing. *(He laughs bitterly.)*

ISAKO: I know what you're thinking. You think it's fascinating that I'm upset about something so trivial. You think it's funny that I'm upset, but that writing makes it look like you're in love with someone. Of course, the name Isako could be some other woman's name. *(She shudders uncontrollably, then speaks as though chasing something.)* It's not an uncommon name. Not uncommon at all. You find the name Isako everywhere.

NOBORU: *(Sits up halfway, and leans on his pillow)* That's right. But I only know one Isako.

ISAKO: *(Smiling despite herself)* That's beside the point. I'm talking about someone else reading it. Do you follow me? What if by some chance your father should happen to read this? He would suffer terribly from that day on. I can tell you that for certain.

NOBORU: *(In apparent jealousy)* For certain . . .

ISAKO: *(Sharply)* Do you understand? I'm not saying that he would worry about me. No. He would suffer because of how he would think you feel.

NOBORU: *(With despair in his voice)* So my purpose in life has to be to save other people from suffering. An existence a little like oil in an engine. *(With rising emotion)* But if I myself suffer, it doesn't matter to you.

ISAKO: *(Attempting to induce* NOBORU *to speak his mind)* What is it that makes you suffer?

NOBORU: *(Looking away from her)* I don't have enough time to worry about trivial things.

ISAKO: *(Persistently)* Then, you're saying that the absence of suffering is a form of suffering, right?

NOBORU: *(Slipping off the bed)* That's a cowardly thing to say, especially when you know exactly what I'm talking about.

ISAKO: *(Growing fearful—poised to run away if necessary)* What is it that I know? There's no way I can know. I don't know anything at all. *(Letting her words carry her away)* I suffer so, because I don't know anything.

NOBORU: *(His eyes shining)* What?

ISAKO: *(Conscious of the importance of each word she utters)* Perhaps I didn't express myself clearly. Will you let me try again? *(Not noticing the rising pitch in her voice)* My request is small. It's almost silly. *(She tries to laugh, but fails.)* Please bring me an eraser. Won't that solve our problem?

NOBORU: *(Noboru sits on the bed on the left, with one leg up on the bed. He smiles arrogantly and childishly.)* I left all my erasers in Tokyo.

ISAKO: You're different tonight. A totally different person.

NOBORU: There's nothing different about me. It's just that I feel a little nervous because I'm about to tell you what I've concealed from you for the last two years.

ISAKO: Two years ago . . . that would be about the time you got back from Taiwan. The time that we first met each other.

NOBORU: Masako or Father could come in here at any moment, so this is my first and last chance to tell you. You know what I'm talking about. You know that when a rare opportunity presents itself, you have to take advantage of it.

ISAKO: *(Coming to herself)* Last chance? What do you mean? Remember our legal relationship. We are mother and child. We live under the same roof.

NOBORU: Right. And it's that same roof that has killed any chance I might have had.

ISAKO: *(In a frighteningly innocent voice)* Are you going to do something that will hurt me?

NOBORU: I've been telling you all along that I'm not going to do anything. I'm just going to talk. I'll tell you quickly how I have suffered during these two years.

ISAKO: *(In amazement, speaking as if searching within herself)* You've suffered . . . But everyone says they are suffering . . . But they live normal lives, nevertheless. There was a time in my life too when I believed in suffering. These days everyone uses the word "suffer" in excuses they make for themselves. They use it like they use a rail pass every day to get through the wicket at a train station. You don't have to hold it out like a ticket to get it punched. You just flash it and go on through. The less carefully you look, the more quickly things get done.

NOBORU: Well I've got something to tell you. My pass has expired. My *two-*

year pass. I can't breeze through the wicket anymore.

ISAKO: Your pass may have expired after two years, but understand this, mine is good forever.

NOBORU: *(Impatiently)* Come on, Isako-san.

ISAKO: Oh, you're calling me by my name now, are you?

NOBORU: Please be quiet and listen to what I have to say. If you don't like what you hear, just shut your eyes and listen. . . . When I came back to Japan from the war, I felt as though I had entered a very strange world. The house I grew up in had been destroyed in the fire bombing. My mother, who was paralyzed and bedridden, had died. My father had been purged from public service, but was doing well for himself nevertheless. He joined a friend's telephone equipment manufacturing company, and bought a new house where he was living happily. Somehow I didn't want to go to the new house, and when I arrived there I was strangely sad. My father and sister were out. The only person there I knew from before was the old serving lady. She kept crying all the time she was showing me around the new house. She told me nothing about anyone in the family. *(Pause)* That's when it happened, remember? I bumped into you, right there in the hall. You were dressed to go out. I was stunned by the sight. I had been abroad so long that I felt I was seeing an attractive, young Japanese woman for the first time in my life. To be honest, at that moment I felt I was an animal. I felt like a warrior, the moment he goes through a great gate into a castle. You're wearing the same kimono now that you were wearing then.

ISAKO *wishes she were anywhere but here at this moment, and looks down at her kimono.*

The serving lady introduced you in a tearful voice. She could barely bring herself to say, "This is your new mother."

ISAKO: *(Quietly)* I have never felt as sordid as I did at that moment.

NOBORU: You blushed bright red. That first day I didn't understand the meaning of what had taken place. Everything seemed a blur to me then. Just like a blow doesn't hurt at the moment it lands. On the warship I even saw a man stand up and walk toward me right after his arm had been blown off. . . . But, as day after day passed . . .

ISAKO: *(Shaking)* Don't say it. I could sense it myself.

NOBORU: *(Looking away)* I knew my life was over.

ISAKO: *(Being drawn into the conversation)* My first marriage was a love marriage, and it turned out to be a failure. Then the prospect of marrying your father was raised, and I agreed, thinking I could live my life peacefully, married to him. Your father was very kind. He let me bring both my happy and unhappy memories with me. It was as if they were grasses transplanted into his garden, and he allowed me to let them grow there freely. I felt as if I were a girl who had left home to marry, been divorced, and returned to the knee of my doting father. My real father died long ago. . . . My only worry was you. Your picture was on the desk in his study. I'd stare at the picture whenever I cleaned the study. Sometimes for a very long time . . . . sitting in your father's chair.

NOBORU: . . .

ISAKO: I asked myself . . . examined myself . . . Could I become the mother of a grown man? But, he would probably get married soon after returning to Japan. I'd only have to play the role of mother for a very short time. That was how I tried to reassure myself. But despite this I never felt confident that I could be a mother to you. After awhile, just the sight of your picture would fill me with anxiety. It became a threat to the peaceful life I had worked so hard to create for myself. It filled me with dread. I came to hate it . . . and after awhile I began to hope that you would never return.

NOBORU: And after I came home you continued to hate me, didn't you.

ISAKO: Yes, but for selfish reasons. I hated you to protect myself.

NOBORU: What about now?

ISAKO: I don't know. I don't understand anything anymore. All I know is that it's impossible for me to lead the calm, peaceful life I had hoped for.

NOBORU: To me it seems you're leading a peaceful enough life.

ISAKO: Even you think so!

NOBORU: Yes, human beings can perform astonishing tricks, can't they? *(Pause . . . then speaking as if suddenly remembering something important)* Then what happened . . . to your confidence that you could be a mother to me?

ISAKO: *(As if making a passionate confession)* I couldn't do it. I knew that even before I met you . . . and I was certain after I met you. That's right . . . I knew that I could never be a mother to you.

NOBORU: *(Overwhelmed with joy)* Isako-san!

ISAKO: *(In great fear)* No, call me Mother!

NOBORU: How can you ask me to say that anymore . . .

ISAKO: *(Intensely)* I will not make your father unhappy. Your father is a good person, a very good person.

NOBORU: Who said that he's a bad person?

ISAKO: We did. Both of us. With our words the two of us have been kicking him like a dog.

NOBORU: If only we really could!

ISAKO: *(In pain)* You are treating him like a dog, you know.

A heavy and painful silence

NOBORU: It's a disease called cowardice that's making us see such fearful delusions. We're the ones holding ourselves back, no one else is. Everyone is too afraid of temporary names and temporary identities. Just now Masako called me weak-willed. That's helped me make up my mind. Starting tomorrow I'm going to be a strong person. The two of us will talk with father tomorrow and tell him our real feelings.

ISAKO: *(Terribly afraid)* I can't do that.

NOBORU: If you don't talk with him, I will.

ISAKO: Are you insane? Are you trying to intimidate me or is this some kind of blackmail? *(She looks hard at* NOBORU.*)* No, you aren't brave enough to do it. I'm safe.

NOBORU: Why do you think so?

ISAKO: Because like me, you are incapable of causing your father unhappiness.

NOBORU:*(In despair)* I see. You knew this about me from the beginning, didn't you? Since you knew, you could suffer safely on my account. And that's not all. You could convert your dissatisfaction with my father into safe and easy suffering, and hide your true feelings from yourself. What do I mean to you? You probably intended to keep my father and me like a couple of pet dogs. And you've been kicking us two dogs, one after the other, haven't you? And on the surface you lead such a peaceful existence—you're such a chaste wife.

ISAKO: Tell me more! Keep talking! I want to be safe and secure. And I want to be a bad woman.

NOBORU: *(Maliciously)* Don't you feel secure enough already? You've been kicking three dogs around, if you include your first husband.

ISAKO: *(Angrily)* How dare you say that! I love all three of you. All three of you.

NOBORU: That was a revealing slip of the tongue, wasn't it? You just admitted that you love me, and that's what I've been saying all along.

ISAKO: Please forgive me. I'm the one who has brought unhappiness to us all.

NOBORU: That's right. To each of us. . . . But why do you ask me to forgive you? Isn't it your right to exercise the power to make people unhappy?. . . But listen, I am going to strengthen my resolve. I pledge myself to become a strong-willed man. Please help me in this resolve. I need your support.

ISAKO: *(After a long pause)* No, it's too late.

NOBORU: What's too late?

ISAKO: I understand the situation completely. Let's just leave everything as it is, all right? Please, don't destroy everything. I beg you, please allow me to continue with the quiet life I've been leading. Don't upset it. I don't know why, but somehow immersing myself in trivial, daily activities actually dries up my pain. Please let me lead a peaceful, trivial existence.

NOBORU: And when do I get to have a peaceful existence?

ISAKO: I don't know . . . but . . . sometime in the future you're sure to lead a peaceful life. Even though we're only five years different in age, you still don't have the sort of past that tries to pull you back like a magnet. You know, it's happy memories, not unhappy ones, that make people cowardly. You should think of me as someone living in a different country. I'm sure that over time you'll come to understand this. And after some time has passed I think you'll see the truth in what I'm telling you now. If you really love me, you'll listen to what I'm saying, won't you? You'll do what I'm asking you to do.

NOBORU: Isn't that what a woman always says to a man when she has stopped loving him . . . "If you *really* loved me, you would . . ."

ISAKO: *(Distractedly)* I wonder what's happened with Masako-chan?

NOBORU: *(Upset with her)* Isako-san!

ISAKO: *(Walking out to the balcony)* Chiba-san's room was the second from the corner, right? On the first floor. I wonder what's going on? It's completely dark. All the lights are out. I wonder where Masako-chan is? Noboru, what do you think she's up to?

NOBORU *stands, slouching forward, with a worried air.*

ISAKO: *(Pleading with* NOBORU*)* Noboru, this is awful. Chiba's room was the second from the corner, wasn't it? Right?

NOBORU *walks straight over to* ISAKO *and stands beside her.*

NOBORU: That's right. It's that dark room over there.

ISAKO: The room's completely dark!

NOBORU *turns to face* ISAKO *and suddenly tries to embrace her.* ISAKO *pulls away and runs to the mirror. Just then there is an urgent knocking on the door.* ISAKO *appeals to* NOBORU *with her eyes, then sits down in a chair.*

ISAKO: Come in.

MASAKO *enters and hurries to* ISAKO's *side. Her manner is exaggeratedly cheerful, as though she is trying to cover her shock and dismay.*

ISAKO: *(In a chatty, high-pitched voice)* Thank goodness you're back! What on earth have you been doing all this time? I've been so worried. We just noticed that Chiba's room is pitch black. You're face is as white as a sheet. Masako, what happened?

MASAKO: Your face is as white as a sheet too.

ISAKO: *(Hesitatingly)* I'm sure it is. It's . . . it's because I was so worried about you. I was wondering what was going on.

While ISAKO *is speaking the above lines,* MASAKO *glances at the two beds.* MASAKO *sinks into a chair as she speaks.*

MASAKO: What a relief it is to be back. I was so scared.
ISAKO: So, what happened?
MASAKO: I've never hidden anything from you before, have I Mother? So, I'll tell you. But I'm so embarrassed.
ISAKO: Really? Something terrible must have happened.
MASAKO: *(Speaking excitedly)* Those people are all crazy. There were six people in Junko's room. When I got there they were playing cards. Then someone said, "Let's play 'One Hundred Tales.'" I'd never heard of that game before. We all sat around the table, boy-girl, boy-girl. Everyone else was giggling like they knew what was going on, but no one told me anything. They put a little candle on the table and lit it. While I was wondering what was going to happen next, Junko got up and turned out the lights in the room.
ISAKO: My goodness.
MASAKO: Then one of the boys began to tell a really scary ghost story. I tried to leave the room as soon as Junko turned the light off, but the two boys next to me grabbed ahold of me, and wouldn't let go. Junko called me a scaredy-cat, and laughed at me. I was angry at being called a coward, so I decided to stay and put up with whatever happened. *(A little bit confused)* Where was I? Oh, that's right. One of the boys began to tell a ghost story. But before that, one of them told me that I would have to observe the rules of the game to the letter. He said, "I'm sure you all know the rules, but in case anyone doesn't . . . ." I could tell that he was looking at me, and he gave me a leering smile.
ISAKO: What sort of rules were they?
MASAKO: I'm ashamed to tell you. . . . It's like this. If a girl starts to scream, the boy next her has to stop her from screaming.
ISAKO: Stop her from screaming?
MASAKO: It's awful. In fact, what they have to do is kiss the girls on the mouth to stop them from screaming. That's the only way I can describe it.
ISAKO: My goodness.
MASAKO: I hate this kind of thing, and I told everyone that I was going to leave. But the two boys next to me held me down. They said that if I so much as made a peep I'd get kissed, so I had to be totally silent.
ISAKO: What awful people they are.
MASAKO: And then the ghost stories began. I was scared right from the start. Even now, when I think of the stories, they give me chills. And then a girl named Takako gave a little shriek. At that moment the boy

on her left . . . (MASAKO *grimaces*) . . . it was disgusting. He grabbed her tightly and kissed her.

ISAKO *and* NOBORU *unconsciously look at each other, their eyes meeting.*

It was a long kiss. The storyteller went right on with his ghost story. Then the girl on my left gave a little shriek. And again, a really long kiss. It took all my strength to keep from screaming. I bit my lip hard. Both my arms were being held down by the boys, so I couldn't put my hands to my ears and shut out the story. But you know what, Mother, I was really surprised. It didn't seem to me that the other girls were really scared by the story. They were really happy to be kissed. It was so strange . . . and one of the girls is a year younger than me too. They were just pretending to be scared. And when they'd shriek the boys would make fun of them. About the time I figured I was doing all right, suddenly the story came to a really scary place . . . I thought I'd faint, and before I knew it, I screamed. Then the boy on my left . . .

ISAKO: Masako-chan!

MASAKO: I didn't know what was happening. It was like in a bad dream when you fall into a deep hole . . . I didn't know what was going on. *(Her eyes are shining, though she doesn't realize it.)* I don't know how many seconds it lasted. I had no idea. It was terrible. I panicked and slapped the boy's face. Then, with all my strength, I tore myself from his grasp and ran away. I could hear everyone laughing behind me. I was lucky that the door wasn't locked.

ISAKO: What terrible people they are.

NOBORU: *(Sarcastically)* There are many terrible people in this world.

ISAKO: *(Ignoring him)* Masako, don't have anything to do with Junko and her friends anymore. (MASAKO *nods in assent.)* I feel responsible. More than anything, this was an oversight on my part. I should never have let a young girl go out by herself this late at night. I'm sorry, Masako. I shouldn't have let you go.

MASAKO: It wasn't your fault, Mother. I went there all on my own. *(A little sadly)* And I ran out of Junko's room on my own too. *(Aggressively)* There's no reason at all for you to apologize. *(Looking around)* I wonder what time it is?

NOBORU: *(Looking at his wrist watch)* A little past midnight.

ISAKO: We should be going to bed.

MASAKO: It's no good. Now my eyes are open and I'm alert . . . not at all sleepy. . . . It's strange . . . maybe it's because of the ghost stories, but I'm still scared. . . . No, it's not that I'm scared, it's more like . . . I wonder why? Somehow, I feel sad. Mother, please, would you stay with me a little while longer. Just a little while.

ISAKO: Of course I will.

The three sit down around the table. They seem tired and distracted.

ISAKO: *(Picks up the deck of cards)* Shall we play cards?
MASAKO: *(Laughing weakly)* I don't have enough energy for cards.
NOBORU: You should go to bed soon. *(Somewhat harshly)* You're sure to have good dreams tonight since you've just had your very first kiss.
ISAKO: Noboru!
MASAKO: How inconsiderate can you be? You wouldn't care in the least if I threw myself into the Mount Mihara crater.
NOBORU: Why talk about it as if you have some reason to do it?
MASAKO: Well, have you got any reason to throw yourself into it?
NOBORU: (*Pretending he didn't hear her question)* You're quite the eternal virgin. Covered with shame because of a single kiss, the nineteen year-old virgin jumps into a volcanic crater and commits suicide. Wow, a relic from a museum.
ISAKO: Don't get angry at him. Your brother doesn't really mean any harm.
MASAKO: *(Looking up at* ISAKO *in a childlike manner)* Mother, I know you're sleepy, but could you come over here with me for a bit.

The door opens.

MASAKO: I'm scared! *(She clings to* ISAKO.*)*

YŪKICHI *enters. He is wearing a cotton sleeping kimono and slippers. He carries a bottle of whiskey in his left hand.*

YŪKICHI: Well, well. Everyone's here, I see.
MASAKO: *(Her mood suddenly changing)* You're mean to scare me like that. I thought you were a ghost. But what are you doing? Do badgers carry bottles of whiskey instead of sake, these days? What do you think, mother?
ISAKO: We need another chair.
NOBORU: It's all right. I'll sit on the bed.
MASAKO: No you don't. That's *my* bed.
NOBORU: You decided all by yourself whose bed was whose.
YŪKICHI: Oh no, not another brother-sister fight.
ISAKO: It's more tiring for us to watch than it is for them to argue.
YŪKICHI: How long was I asleep, anyway?
MASAKO: Twenty-six hours. It was ten PM yesterday that you went to bed. Yes, I'm sure of it.
YŪKICHI: You can't trick me that easily. My record for sleeping is eighteen hours.

ISAKO: I was really worried about you that time.
NOBORU: More of mother's needless worrying.
YŪKICHI: So here's the group that can't get to sleep. Your naps have taken revenge on you. Well, I woke up completely sober. I don't think I'll be able to get to sleep unless I drink some more.
MASAKO: You're going to start drinking again now? Yuck!
YŪKICHI: What a useless daughter you are. It's about time you learned how to be a big drinker yourself.
MASAKO: Disgusting. Please spare me.
YŪKICHI: *(To Masako)* What were the three of you doing all night, anyway?
MASAKO: *(Casually)* We had an interesting evening of cards and ghost stories, didn't we, mother?
ISAKO: *(Awkwardly)* We were just getting tired of it all when you came in.
YŪKICHI: Is that right? Who was telling the ghost stories?
MASAKO: *(Smoothly)* Noboru was.
YŪKICHI: *(To Noboru)* I didn't know that you tell ghost stories.
NOBORU: *(Awkwardly)* Uh, they're nothing special, but . . .
YŪKICHI: Ghost stories on a spring night. I'm afraid you'll all catch cold. *(He looks out through glass door.)* But what a calm night it is. There's no wind . . . very spring-like.
ISAKO: It feels like May on this island, doesn't it?
YŪKICHI: Let's drink. Masako. The copper cup was in your bag, wasn't it? Bring it out.

MASAKO *goes to get the cup.*

YŪKICHI: *(To* ISAKO*)* If you're tired, you can go to bed. In our room.
ISAKO: I don't want to. If I do that, I'll just keep thinking of the ghost stories.
NOBORU: Those ghost stories sure were potent, weren't they?
ISAKO: *(In an unexpectedly bold voice)* Of course I can't sleep. You're just awful.
YŪKICHI: Of course, ghost stories only scare people when they're young.

MASAKO *returns with the cup.*

MASAKO: Okay, we've got four glasses.
YŪKICHI: Uh, oh. Put away that book or we might spill something on it.

MASAKO *puts the book on her lap and sits down.* NOBORU *and* ISAKO'*s eyes follow her actions.*

YŪKICHI: The only one who drank with me at dinner was Mother. Why don't you all join me now? Let's drink a toast.

ISAKO: Masako shouldn't drink.
MASAKO: *(Defiantly)* No, I'll drink this time. For sure.
YŪKICHI: That was a major declaration. Noboru, you'll join us, won't you?
NOBORU: Somehow...tonight...I'm not in the mood for drinking.
YŪKICHI: I guess that's because when you drink you end up crying. One of my old school friends was a crying drinker. A strange fellow. He drank because he enjoyed crying so much.
MASAKO: Noboru's just the opposite, though.
NOBORU: What?
MASAKO: One time you told me you wouldn't drink when something made you sad enough to cry, because if you *did* drink you would start crying.
NOBORU: You idiot!
YŪKICHI: Come on now you two, no more fighting.
NOBORU: *(Glaring at* MASAKO*)* Bitch. . . . *(To his father)* All right, I'll drink with you, all night long if you want.
YŪKICHI: In that case let's have a toast in celebration of my company's recent accomplishments. We just sold seventy thousand kitchen heaters to Thailand and fifty thousand irons to Shanghai.

All raise their glasses in a toast. YŪKICHI *drinks enthusiastically,* NOBORU *with caution.* ISAKO *and* MASAKO *stick to one glass each.*

NOBORU: When you drink, you can't help thinking how enjoyable life is, can you?
YŪKICHI: You're probing for your father's philosophy of life aren't you? . . . Well, I suppose . . . you can say that life is enjoyable. Of course, I've had to pull a few tricks, and I've had to doctor some accounts now and then. You don't want to be a slave to the account book.
NOBORU: What if someone discovers you've doctored the accounts?
YŪKICHI: *(Drawing his finger across his throat)* You're fired. You have to look for another company.
NOBORU: Can you go through so many companies in a lifetime?
YŪKICHI: An almost infinite number.
NOBORU: I feel that there is only one place for me.
YŪKICHI: *(Changing the subject somewhat)* A banker. I think you'll make a fine banker. I'll help you get a position with Toyo Bank after you graduate.
ISAKO: *(Changing the subject again)* Yūkichi, you haven't sung any chansons yet today, have you?
YŪKICHI: I'll sing if we make it a duet.
ISAKO: But it might disturb the people next door.
YŪKICHI: I wonder if they could hear us. You couldn't hear my snoring from this room, could you?
MASAKO: I heard you. I thought there was a hippopotamus right beside me.

Figure 8. *The Lighthouse*, in 1950, Haiyū-za. From left, Matsumoto Kappei as Yūkichi, Kishi Teruko as Isako, Seki Hiroko as Masako, and Naruse Masahiko as Noboru. Photograph courtesy of the Haiyū-za and the Mishima Yukio Literary Museum.

YŪKICHI: Wonderful, wonderful! We'll start with a chanson by a hippopotamus.

MASAKO: *(To* ISAKO*)* I feel sorry for you, always having to sing duets with a hippopotamus.

YŪKICHI: They say that nightingales and hippopotami make great companions.

NOBORU: Pretty distant companions, I'd say.

YŪKICHI: You've always got to have the last word, don't you. Join us, and make it a trio.

NOBORU: Unfortunately, the only foreign language I know is German.

YŪKICHI: That explains why you always stink of German romanticism.

He begins to sing in a low voice, either Parlez moi d'Amour *or* L'invitation au Voyage *would suit. He has a surprisingly beautiful voice.* ISAKO *joins in part way through the song, singing in harmony.*

NOBORU: *(Pretending to be drunk)* Father, there's something I would like to talk with you about. *(The chanson ends abruptly.)*

ISAKO: *(Sharply)* That was rude of you.

YŪKICHI: It's perfectly all right. Tell me what's on your mind.

MASAKO: Father, let's dance together.

YŪKICHI: I'm very much in demand tonight, aren't I.

MASAKO: You know the song "Five Minutes More," don't you?

NOBORU: Masako! I've got something important to discuss with father.

ISAKO: *(In confusion)* I don't think your father knows any jazz tunes.

YŪKICHI: *(Calmly)* I know a few. The way business is going these days, I have to entertain salesmen from abroad. Of course I know songs like "Five Minutes More."

MASAKO: You know the words then. Let's sing our own accompaniment as we dance. It's a jitterbug. *(She stands up and puts the book on the chair.)*

YŪKICHI: Good, good. We'll go dance over there, where there's some space.

YŪKICHI *and* MASAKO *go downstage center, in front of the beds.* YŪKICHI *sings,* "Give me five minutes more, only five minutes more! Let me stay, Let me stay in your arms!" *etc. and dances a remarkable and strangely graceful and natural jitterbug with* MASAKO. MASAKO *bursts out laughing several times while they dance. For example, when* YŪKICHI *is wondering whether or not to rest his face against hers he makes a funny, puckered face and this makes her laugh.*

When MASAKO *joins her father and they walk to the open space,* NOBORU *walks after her immediately, as if intending to stop her.* ISAKO *stops him and gets him to sit back down in his chair. The two exchange painful glances for a moment. While father and daughter dance, both* NOBORU *and* ISAKO *struggle with their impatience and irritation.*

Finally YŪKICHI *and* MASAKO *return, hand in hand, to where they had been sitting.* MASAKO *puts the book back on her lap.* ISAKO *greets them as they return with a few words of praise.* YŪKICHI *drinks several more glasses, becoming more and more loquacious as he drinks. He notices the book that has been resting on* MASAKO's *lap.*

YŪKICHI: What's that book?
MASAKO: It's Noboru's book.
YŪKICHI: Let me have a look at it, okay?
MASAKO: *(Handing it to him nonchalantly)* All right.
YŪKICHI: Hmm. I'm impressed with you, Noboru. Bringing a school text like this along on a vacation trip. *Some Issues in Modern Economic History.* By Ōtomo Mamoru, Professor of Economics, is it? *(He leafs through it.)*
ISAKO: *(Suddenly)* Oh, I'm drunk already! And I only drank one or two glasses.
YŪKICHI: *(Taking his eyes off the book)* But your face isn't at all red. *(He continues leafing through the pages.)* This book is very well written. I never applied myself to my studies like you do.
ISAKO: Noboru, your father is impressed with you. Aren't you going to say anything to him. . . . Oh, I shouldn't have said that, should I?
NOBORU: *(Staring hard into* ISAKO's *eyes)* It's okay for me to tell him, right? It's really all right for me to tell him, okay?
YŪKICHI: What's going on? It's gotten strange here all of a sudden.
ISAKO: *(Painfully)* Noboru, you'd better pull yourself together.
NOBORU: I'm entirely together as you can see. I'm not at all drunk.
YŪKICHI: Only drunk people say that. In fact it's common for drunks to talk like that. . . . But you're very pale. It's no good if alcohol makes you sick.
NOBORU: I'm not the sort of weakling who has to get drunk to say what I really mean. What I'm going to tell you now I could also tell you when I'm completely sober. That we drank tonight was just a matter of chance.
YŪKICHI: *(Half teasing* NOBORU*)* What are you up to, glaring at your father with that deathly pale face?
ISAKO: Noboru, stop it.
NOBORU: Be quiet. I don't need to listen to you anymore. Father, I want to show you something that will interest you.
YŪKICHI: What is this, all of a sudden?
NOBORU: It's in that book.

He reaches out and starts leafing through the pages in the book his father is holding. MASAKO *has been sitting and watching, so still that she doesn't bat an eyelash. Suddenly, with lightning speed, she snatches the book from their hands.*

MASAKO: You're drunk! You're crazy!

NOBORU: Masako!

MASAKO: I can't watch this. Noboru, you're acting like you're crazy. And it's not just you. Everyone's gone half-crazy. I'm watching you do crazy things, but you all seem to think they're perfectly normal. And you think you understand each other!

There is a long silence.

ISAKO: *(Standing up in a daze, exhausted)* I'm so sleepy. I wonder why? I can't even sit up any more. Darling, I wonder if I drank too much tonight? . . . I think I'll go to bed. Can you help me back to the other room? . . . What's wrong with me? I can't take a single step by myself. It suddenly seems as if my room is terribly far away.

YŪKICHI: There you go again. What a burden of a mother you are. . . . All right, everybody. I'm going to put mother to bed, and then I'm going to go to sleep too . . . . Tomorrow we should all sleep in, because after we get up we're going to climb Mount Mihara. Masako, you'll have to look after your brother.

YŪKICHI *holds the whiskey bottle in his left hand, and with his right arm he helps* ISAKO *out of the door. They exit to their room.*

NOBORU: Masako!

MASAKO: *(Not at all afraid of him)* What?

NOBORU: Right now I feel as if I could kill you. Do you understand? If I killed you I'd have no regrets at all. . . . And you know what, right now I think you're prettier than you've ever been before.

MASAKO: *(Smiling)* You're still drunk, aren't you. You should go to bed now. The pajamas are in the bureau.

MASAKO *sits down in front of the dressing table and begins combing her hair.* NOBORU *takes two sets of pajamas from the bureau. He puts one on his bed and throws the other on his sister's bed. He sits for awhile in a daze on the stage left bed. A fairly long time passes.* NOBORU *suddenly has a fit of coughing. He hurriedly burrows deep into the covers, still dressed in his school uniform. He covers himself completely, even his head, in the quilt. After a short time the sound of sobbing is heard from under the covers.*

MASAKO *finishes combing her hair, and lights the lamp on the table at the head of her bed. She goes to the switch by the door and turns off the chandelier. She goes to her bed, pulls the top cover down, and sits on the bed. She unfastens the top of her dress, and sits, staring out the glass door.*

MASAKO: *(Half to herself)* Hey, look over there. . . . I can see the lighthouse. . . . The light just went on. *(Pause)* Now it's dark again. *(Pause)* Now it's light again. *(To* NOBORU, *in a harsh voice)* Stop it, would you! That crying. A man shouldn't cry like that. It's disgusting, really. Climbing into bed with your uniform on. I can't believe you're the same person who served in the navy.

. . . I won't let myself sleep. I mustn't sleep at all, you know. I'm the only one who can't sleep. . . . You know, I'm just like that lighthouse. I'm the only one who has to be bright. . . . And thanks to me, you all can voyage without getting lost. . . . Because of all of you, I have to stay up all night alone.

. . . Why does it have to be this way? *(In an accusatory tone of voice)* Why? . . . I hate this! I can't stand it any more!

CURTAIN

Hell Screen

(Jigoku Hen)

(a kabuki play)

Published in 1953, First Staged in 1953
Adapted from a Short Story by Akutagawa Ryūnosuke
Translated by Laurence Kominz

INTRODUCTION

Hell Screen, Mishima's first kabuki play, is based on a famous story of the same name by Akutagawa Ryūnosuke (1892–1927), Japan's revered master of the modern short story. The idea for the adaptation was presented to Mishima by representatives of the Shochiku Corporation in the spring of 1953, and Mishima eagerly accepted this first commission as a kabuki playwright.

Hell Screen is the story of a battle of wills between a cruel minister of state, Lord Horikawa, and the painter Yoshihide, a headstrong genius from whom Horikawa has commissioned a major painting depicting the many realms of hell. Yoshihide and his daughter, Tsuyukusa, a lady-in-waiting at the minister's mansion, fall victim to Yoshihide's pride and stupidity and to Lord Horikawa's sadistic brutality. In the play's climactic finale, the minister forces the artist to witness his daughter being roasted alive in a carriage that has been set on fire, and to paint the scene.

For Mishima, *Hell Screen* was an opportunity to put to the test notions he had been developing about the creation of original, classic kabuki plays. It is not his finest kabuki play, but it clearly demonstrates the strengths and weaknesses of Mishima's dramaturgy and illuminates approaches to characterization and play structure that would excite and challenge directors and actors throughout Mishima's career. Mishima was particularly committed to writing lyrical narration for the play in the form of classical *gidayūbushi* (also called *takemoto*). *Gidayūbushi* is vocal and instrumental (three-stringed *shamisen)* music used in all *bunraku* puppet plays and in many kabuki plays. "Kabuki, especially when accompanied by *gidayūbushi*, has the artistic means to express emotions as violent as storms. In fact, it may be the most expressive dramatic medium in the world. So, I wanted by all means to write this play as a drama for *takemoto* accompaniment,"[1] Mishima wrote. Mishima was the only postwar playwright capable of writing *gidayūbushi* lyrics, and this makes his kabuki plays unique. Mishima relied on *gidayūbushi* to govern the music and physical movement of *Hell Screen*, but he found it difficult to strike the proper balance among *gidayū* recitation, dialogue, and physical action.

Writing a kabuki play entirely in the classical language was a difficult task, requiring "the pedantry of a fallen scholar delving into the arcana of Edo Period merchant class life. To recreate the literature of that era is a strange and unhealthy effort. There were times I thought it would make me ill."[2] Mishima was eager to impress the Shochiku management and the kabuki actors he so admired with his literary knowledge and his skill as a writer. He included numerous allusions to classical literature in his text, including two poems from the *Kokin Wakashū* anthology. More than anything it was his ability to write long stretches of original text in classical meter that amazed everyone.[3]

At this stage in his career, Mishima also felt that the three unities should be used in new kabuki plays.[4] The result is a very tight play, presenting events that take place in just a few hours time. To compress the action, Mishima converted an important torture scene in Yoshihide's studio into a recitation of their victimization by two of his disciples, and Mishima also had to change the ending of the story. In Akutagawa's version Yoshihide completes the screen a few weeks after the carriage burning incident, presents Horikawa with the finished masterpiece, and promptly hangs himself to atone for his daughter's death and to join her spirit in the afterworld. In the play the curtain closes on Yoshihide painting like a man possessed, and the evil minister laughing in sadistic glee as Tsuyukusa perishes in the fire. In his last line the narrator simply states, "It is a remarkable event, never to be forgotten."

Mishima made several important additions to the story. He wanted clearer reasons for the minister to harbor murderous intent toward Tsuyukusa, so he has a retainer of the minister inform the audience that she has rejected the minister's amorous advances. Mishima also gave the minister a wife, Lady Aoi, and added the wife's jealousy and suspicions to her husband's frustration. Mishima created two new humorous villains, one who tells of witnessing Tsuyukusa's rejection of her master's advances, and another whose own marriage proposal is curtly rebuffed by the girl. The names of the two villains contain puns on the Japanese words "cow" and "horse," and the two men are transformed into hellish versions of these two animals in the final scene of the play.

Mishima's use of the three unities and his addition of three new characters did not strengthen the play. The three unities forced too much information to be conveyed in the static form of conversations about past events. The only clear evidence of the wife's jealousy comes to us in the form of gossip by a gardener instead of direct interaction between Lady Aoi and Tsuyukusa. Similarly, it is only through talk and not action that the audience learns of Yoshihide's cruel treatment of his disciples and of Horikawa's infatuation with Tsuyukusa.

Mishima made few changes in the three main characters. Tsuyukusa, whose name ("dayflower" / "dew on the grass") suggests delicate ephemeral beauty, is somewhat more headstrong than in the original story. She rebuffs Lord Horikawa's sexual advances and curtly refuses a marriage proposal by a high-ranking buffoon. She is absolutely devoted to her father, despite his cruelty, stupidity, and overweening pride. Her father has his faults, but he is the only person in the world who cares at all about her wellbeing. In the fashion of kabuki heroines, Tsuyukusa unhesitatingly sacrifices her own life to save her father's. This strong-willed but physically vulnerable heroine was just the sort of role that Mishima's favorite *onnagata,* Nakamura Utaemon, excelled in, and he did a fine job with Tsuyukusa.

Mishima himself was most interested in the two leading male roles, and their battle of wills and wits. Of Horikawa Mishima wrote, "His character is unclear in the beginning, following the pattern of the original folk tale, and he even appears as a good person some of the time, but when he laughs excitedly during the carriage burning scene his brutality is exposed. I think of him as a Japanese de Sade or Cesare Borgia. To take a gorgeous young woman and burn her in a carriage strikes me as similar to the cruel sports of the emperors during Rome's period of decadence."[5] Mishima stated that "Yoshihide is myself, an artist. Identifying with him was easy."[6]

Hell Screen was acclaimed in 1953 because of its use of traditional music, lyrical narration, classical meter, and other artistic qualities. The horrific last scene always leaves audiences spellbound. For *onnagata* playing Tsuyukusa, this scene was painful to do. Utaemon found it physically difficult. The smoke used in the scene, and being surrounded by so much false fire made him feel as if he were in fact burning. His fans enquired anxiously about his health and physical safety while he was in the play.[7]

For Bandō Tamasaburō, who played Tsuyukusa in 1978, the role was psychologically painful. To Tamasaburō there is insufficient psychological justification for the exaggerated brutality of the two male leads, and he finds the play difficult because the characters talk "at each other rather than with each other," and are never able to communicate "heart to heart."[8] Tamasaburō considers these sorts of characters typical of many Mishima plays.[9] In *Hell Screen* only two characters love each other—Yoshihide and Tsuyukusa—and even they cannot understand each other at all. Tamasaburō is also disturbed by the ambiguous conclusion to the play. The curtain closes as Yoshihide energetically paints the ghastly hell scene. He does not show his sense of remorse and responsibility as in Akutagawa's story. Tamasaburō feels that in this way Mishima treats his audiences much as the characters treat each other in the play.[10]

Hell Screen was a wonderful first effort in kabuki for Mishima. He impressed actors, producers, and his audience with his genius as a kabuki playwright. Utaemon enjoyed acting in *Hell Screen* more than he had in any modern play to that point.[11] With Utaemon eager to work further with

Mishima, Mishima's career as a kabuki playwright was assured. Mishima's convictions that new kabuki plays should be couched in classical Japanese, and should interweave poetry, music, and dance, in the style of Edo Period kabuki, were vindicated in *Hell Screen.*

NOTES

1. Mishima Yukio, "Takemotobon Jigoku Hen," Kabuki-za Program, November 1953, reprinted in *Mishima hyôron zenshû,* vol. 3 (Tokyo: Shinchôsha, 1994), p. 864.
2. Mishima Yukio, "Boku no Jigoku Hen," *Mainichi Shimbun,* September 10, 1954; reprinted in *Mishima hyôron zenshû,* vol. 3, p. 870.
3. Nakamura Utaemon, "Mishima Kabuki no sekai," in Mishima Yukio, *Shibai nikki* (Tokyo: Chuo Kôronsha, 1991), p. 188.
4. Mishima, "Takemotobon Jigoku Hen"; reprinted in *Mishima hyôron zenshû,* vol. 3, p. 863.
5. Ibid., p. 864.
6. Ibid.
7. Nakamura, "Mishima Kabuki no sekai," pp. 188–89.
8. Bandô Tamasaburô interview, February 13, 2002.
9. Ibid.
10. Ibid.
11. Nakamura, "Mishima Kabuki no sekai," pp. 188–89.

THE CHARACTERS

Lord Horikawa, Grand Minister of State
Ushisuke (the name contains the word "cow"), an official and retainer to Lord Horikawa
Umanosuke (the name contains the word "horse"), an official and retainer to Lord Horikawa
Yoshihide, a painter
Fudeo, Yoshihide's senior apprentice
Hanawaka, one of Yoshihide's junior apprentices
Servants to Lord Horikawa
Lady Aoi, Lord Horikawa's wife
Tsuyukusa ("Dew on the Grass"/"Dayflower"), Yoshihide's daughter, currently in service as a junior lady-in-waiting at the Horikawa mansion
Fuyuhagi ("Winter Bush Clover"), senior lady-in-waiting to Lady Aoi
Honoho, lady-in-waiting to the Horikawa family
Hatata, lady-in-waiting to the Horikawa family
Motohi, lady-in-waiting to the Horikawa family
Kawara, lady-in-waiting to the Horikawa family
Hojishi, lady-in-waiting to the Horikawa family

SETTING

SCENE ONE: The Horikawa Mansion in Kyoto
SCENE TWO: The mansion's inner garden

SCENE ONE: THE HORIKAWA MANSION IN KYOTO

Stately music plays as the curtain opens revealing the stage set for scene one. The set for the Horikawa mansion is a platform that runs the full width of the stage. The mansion verandah is five steps above stage level. There are separate rooms, enclosed by sliding, paper-covered doors, at stage right and stage left. The interior walls of the mansion are covered in gold leaf. There is a bell-shaped arched entranceway in the center of the back wall with a black lacquered arch beam and a colorful divided curtain hanging from the top of the arch. A high railing runs the whole length of the verandah, except in the center, where there are steps down to the stage, representing the ground outside the mansion. Initially the entire front of the mansion is concealed by a bamboo screen which is rolled down. A maple tree, in autumnal tints, stands at stage left. Colorful branches of maple hang down from the top of the proscenium. Four servants are sweeping in front of the mansion. Lighter music plays from the geza *as the servants begin to speak.*

FIRST SERVANT: There are many noblemen in the vast Imperial Capital, but I've never served one as arrogant and autocratic as Minister Horikawa.

SECOND SERVANT: You're right. And he looks so formidable that they say when he encountered a midnight parade of goblins, the whole bunch turned tail and ran away. He even chastised the vindictive ghost of the banished Minister Tōru and the ghost ran off, terrified.

THIRD SERVANT: And what about her ladyship? It's not right to talk about her as if she were a common woman, but she's got a chronic complaint, and it's jealousy. And it doesn't help her illness that the painter Yoshihide's beautiful daughter has been taken into service as a junior lady-in-waiting.

FOURTH SERVANT: And speaking of the daughter, her father, Yoshihide, was ordered by Lord Horikawa to paint a six-panel hell screen showing all the realms of hell. His lordship is in a foul mood because Yoshihide still hasn't finished it, though it was supposed to be done months ago.

FIRST SERVANT: Yoshihide's renown reverberates through the Imperial Capital like a parade of rolling carriages, and no one takes such pride in his artistic skill or fame as he does.

SECOND SERVANT: If today or tomorrow he doesn't send a good progress report to his lordship . . .

FIRST SERVANT: . . . Then I'm afraid . . .

ALL FOUR SERVANTS: . . . Terrible things are in store.

The gidayū *musicians begin to play.*

NARRATOR: At this moment two of the minister's retainers enter, with stern expressions on their faces.

USHISUKE *enters from stage right. He wears a brocade vest and trousers* (kamishimo), *and his face is painted red, indicating that he is a petty villain. He is accompanied by* UMANOSUKE, *who is similarly made-up and attired.*

USHISUKE: Who do you menials think you are, blabbing away like that about your betters? Away with you! Away with you at once!
NARRATOR: They are startled and confused, and run off. Ushisuke looks around warily.

The SERVANTS *run off, two to stage right, two to stage left. The two characters who have just entered wait until the* SERVANTS *have exited, then speak seriously together.*

USHISUKE: You know, Umanosuke, that it has been some time since my wife passed away. The life of a lonely widower seems endless. Fortunately a new junior lady-in-waiting has just joined the household. Her name is Tsuyukusa. She's Yoshihide's treasured daughter. I'm so in love with her! Her fair skin, whiter than snow . . . why she's like the beautiful concubine Yang Kuei-fei who captured the heart of the Chinese emperor. How I'd like to be the ruler who leads her into the garden of earthly delights.
UMANOSUKE: It's remarkable that she's Yoshihide's daughter—like a vulture siring a nightingale. But Lord Ushisuke, you are an assistant to his lordship, a lofty post. Why don't you speak with the lord's wife and arrange for the girl to be released from service so that she can be yours?
USHISUKE: I can't buy her out of service like some post-station prostitute. Even if her ladyship were to consent, the lord himself is the real problem. If I were to lay a hand on Tsuyukusa, my head would go kerplop. Then where would I be? A chopped off head can't embrace a woman!
UMANOSUKE: If that's what you're worried about you'll be fine. The girl is an upstart who doesn't know her place. His lordship is strongly attracted to her, but if he shows her any more favor than he already has, he'll really look like a fool. One way or the other, eventually he will have to release Tsuyukusa from service.
USHISUKE: Tell me what Tsuyukusa has done to offend his lordship.
UMANOSUKE: Her behavior splatters his lordship's good name with mud. I don't think he'll put up with her much longer.
USHISUKE: Tell me more!
UMANOSUKE: Don't rush me. *(He looks around to see if anyone is listening*

to their conversation.) This is what happened. Late last night I had some business to finish up at my post. As I was passing through the palace hallway, I heard a scuffle. It was dark and little moonlight entered the building. Two people were arguing. I hid behind the sliding door and listened. I thought an intruder had broken in, and then suddenly I heard a woman's voice. She seemed very upset.

USHISUKE: And . . .

NARRATOR: *(for* UMANOSUKE) Without pausing to think, I kicked open the door . . .

UMANOSUKE: . . . And ran right into the woman. She was none other than . . .

USHISUKE: Tsuyukusa?

UMANOSUKE: Yes, Tsuyukusa, the junior lady-in-waiting. The moonlight revealed her robes in disarray. And her black hair, in wild tangles, was vivid before my eyes.

USHISUKE: Wow! What an erotic scene.

UMANOSUKE: She ran off at once, but I recognized the silhouette of someone standing a little way off. It was, of course . . .

USHISUKE: His lordship! *(Forgetting the situation, he says this in a loud voice.)*

UMANOSUKE: Not so loud. *(He looks around again, and then speaks in a low voice.)* Yes, it was his lordship.

USHISUKE: Yes, I suspected as much all along. She's a defiant girl to resist her master like that.

UMANOSUKE: He's not the sort of master who will bother chasing after a rebellious servant girl.

USHISUKE: And an opportunity will soon arise for a different gallant gentleman.

NARRATOR: Ushisuke is now full of hope.
He follows his friend's scheme
Like a cart following a horse,
Leading him down the road to meet his destiny.
At that moment a voice is heard at the gate.

VOICE: Her ladyship has returned home!

USHISUKE: That was an announcement of her ladyship's return.

UMANOSUKE: She went on a maple-viewing excursion today. Tsuyukusa is sure to be with her.

USHISUKE: In that case let's go out . . .

UMANOSUKE: . . . And welcome them home.

The two sit and observe the entrance of the ladies.

NARRATOR: Inspired by Chinese poems proclaiming that autumn leaves
Surpass the flowers of March
The lord's wife, Lady Aoi, has gone out maple viewing,

Taking with her the young Tsuyukusa, herself a flower in bud.
Now they return bearing branches dyed in Chinese vermillion
The fragrance of the colored leaves still clinging to their sleeves.

TSUYUKUSA *enters on the* hanamichi *runway, carrying a lantern and a branch of colored maple leaves. She is followed by Lady* AOI, FUYUHAGI *[an old woman with white hair], and all five ladies-in-waiting. Each woman carries a spray of maple leaves. They line up on the* hanamichi. *They speak to musical accompaniment from the* geza.

TSUYUKUSA: The moonlight shines on the laurel, and autumn is resplendent with colored foliage. We went forth amid branches sparkling in the evening moonlight.

AOI: On the road back, we left behind the mountain temples with their tolling bells and came to city streets teeming with carriages. Time has passed and now the chrysanthemums of the Ninth Month festival vie in splendor with the autumn leaves.

FUYUHAGI: Even withered trees, splendidly decorated with frost, take on autumnal radiance. Frost, indeed, is the mother of autumn's color.

HONOHO: Their beautiful companions include the seven autumn grasses, pampas plumes, autumn pinks, maidenflowers . . .

HATATA: . . . Bush clover, asters, bellflowers; their sashes tied diagonally like folded love letters early in the morning.

MOTOHI: If you are sending love letters, attach them to asters or bellflowers, and hope they'll bring happiness.

KAWARA: Peeping through the fence entangled in bush clover, is the pampas plume beckoning the blushing maidenflower?

HOJISHI: For the maidenflower who serves her lord, sad thoughts accumulate during the long night.

AOI: Autumn is . . .

ALL WOMEN: . . . A time of love and tears.

All of the women move from the hanamichi *to the main stage.*

NARRATOR: Ushisuke hurries out ostentatiously.

USHISUKE: Welcome back, your ladyship. I realize that it is a bit sudden, but I have a petition for you to consider. I've written it out for you. Here it is.

AOI: Well, if it isn't Ushisuke and Umanosuke. My goodness, that certainly is a long petition. Come over here and tell me what it is that you request.

USHISUKE *and* AOI *go to stage left and engage in a private discussion.*

USHISUKE: My request, in a nutshell, is none other than this. Please release the junior lady-in-waiting Tsuyukusa from your service so that I may take her as my wife.

AOI: There should be no difficulty with that. I am her master now, and of course it is fine with me. However, there is Tsuyukusa's father, and you cannot marry without his consent. And if you are a worthy son-in-law in his eyes, then, most importantly, you have to learn how the girl herself feels about it.

USHISUKE: Before she accepts my proposal I have something important to tell her. Now then, Lady Tsuyukusa, in the whole wide world there is no finer prospective husband than I. And why, you may ask. I will tell you. My distant ancestor was blessed with the favor of Emperor Kammu and was allowed to serve as sweeper of the Imperial garden. He was given the title, "Dust-Sweeping Man."

Later, in the reign of Emperor Nintoku, His Imperial Highness had occasion to observe the common people enthusiastically cooking at their stoves. The smoke rising from the hearths provided inspiration for a famous painting. My ancestor at that time traveled the country cleaning stoves and was called, "Stove-Cleaning Man." I am his descendant in the sixteenth generation.

It was thirty-one generations ago that another ancestor washed the Regent Shōtoku Taishi's back and was designated Lord of the Bath. Be glad that you have been chosen by me, Ushisuke, to be the bride in a family that goes back sixty-six generations. I too am honored to propose to you. I assume it goes without saying that you accept my offer of marriage.

AOI: Well now, Tsuyukusa, what is your answer?

TSUYUKUSA: Yes, ma'am. How should I put it . . . in fact, he disgusts me.

USHISUKE: What? That was a 'yes,' wasn't it? You did agree, didn't you?

TSUYUKUSA: You can ask me any way you want . . .

USHISUKE: Yes . . .

TSUYUKUSA: But my refusal of your disgusting proposal stays a refusal.

AOI: Come now, Tsuyukusa, for you to refuse this fine offer must mean you are in love with some other man. It couldn't be my husband, could—I mean, tell me the name of the young lord you favor.

TSUYUKUSA: I am not in love with any young lord.

AOI: It is natural for women to tell lies when under duress, but I am a woman too, and I can see through you. Tell me his name.

TSUYUKUSA: But . . .

AOI: Out with it.

TSUYUKUSA: But . . .

AOI: Out with it, out with it, out with it, I say! Answer me, or else!

TSUYUKUSA: The only man I love is my father.

USHISUKE: Don't try to play the fool with me. From the beginning of time no one has done something as silly as take her father for her husband.

Since things have reached this pass, *(He signals* AOI *with his eyes)* your ladyship . . .

AOI: Yes, though I pity the poor child, we must beat her until she tells the truth. Fuyuhagi, prepare to chastise her.

FUYUHAGI: Yes, my lady. *(She holds her breath in apprehension.)*

NARRATOR: As she approaches Tsuyukusa, a voice is heard from inside the mansion.

HORIKAWA: Stop the punishment!

AOI: Why that is the voice . . .

ALL: Of his lordship.

During the following narration the blinds at the front of the mansion are rolled up, revealing Lord HORIKAWA, *sitting inside. His face is white and painted in light blue stripes,* kuge-aku *makeup that indicates he is an evil minister of state. He is wearing a long embroidered coat with a stiff, high collar, and is resting on an armrest.*

NARRATOR: Inside the room sits the powerful and impressive Lord Horikawa, appearing relaxed and at ease. His wife turns to face him.

HORIKAWA: What Tsuyukusa just said may sound like a lie, but it is not. The feelings of the painter, Yoshihide, for his daughter, and her love for him are examples of parent-child affection rarely seen in our world. Accept the truth of this love and forgive her any wrong she may have committed.

AOI: That Yoshihide is a wicked man, but they do say that his love for his daughter is quite remarkable. So much so that I heard if a man so much as exchanges a few words with his precious daughter, Yoshihide assembles a gang of ruffians to go and beat the fellow up. But I've also heard, my lord, that Yoshihide has petitioned you again and again to give his daughter leave to return home to him. Since you are so moved by their love for each other I find it most surprising that you continually refuse to grant his request.

HORIKAWA: Your question is a reasonable one. That proud and haughty man may have a fine reputation, but his own assistants have given him the nickname Chiraeiju, the name of the terrible Chinese goblin. It would be a mistake on my part to allow the girl to return to such a depraved father. When the time is right, I will allow her to return.

NARRATOR: He speaks with benevolence, his words both kind and just.

HORIKAWA: Now let's banish all these tensions from the palace. Bring sake for all! Sake for all! Let's dispel these gloomy feelings from the palace.

NARRATOR: The ladies-in-waiting assent to his command. As autumn leaves flutter into sake cups, Ushinosuke scowls and withdraws into an inner room with his companion.

USHISUKE *and* UMANOSUKE *exit stage right. Lady* AOI, TSUYUKUSA, FUYUHAGI, *and the ladies-in-waiting go up to join Lord* HORIKAWA, *and the drinking party commences.*

AOI: My lord, you seem somewhat out of sorts today. You should drink sake and restore your spirits.

HORIKAWA: There's nothing wrong with *me*. Tsuyukusa, it's all because of you.

TSUYUKUSA: What?

HORIKAWA: It's because of you that Yoshihide, that difficult father of yours, is delaying the project.

AOI: My lord, what do you mean?

HORIKAWA: *(To musical accompaniment)* A few months ago Yoshihide led me to believe that he would finish the hell screen that I had ordered by the Fourth Month, but the Fifth and Sixth months have passed and he hasn't completed it. He has not replied to the messages I've sent urging him to honor his word. It is disgraceful behavior to ignore one's superiors and I cannot let it go unchecked. But I so much want to see that screen. If one is to have a hell screen, no artist can do a better job than Yoshihide. You can see why I am at my wit's end.

TSUYUKUSA: This is all my father's fault. I will send him a letter right away urging him to promptly complete the hell screen, so please forgive him for his rudeness.

HORIKAWA: Paintings are the responsibility of the artist. I won't have the painter's daughter acting as intermediary or sending messages on my behalf. That's not your business. I have ordered Yoshihide to appear before me today and explain his malfeasance himself.

TSUYUKUSA: What? My father is coming here today?

AOI: If Yoshihide continues to act so irresponsibly and insists on delaying the project, then what will you do?

HORIKAWA: I will have him executed.

TSUYUKUSA: Oh, no! *(She collapses, weeping.)*

HORIKAWA: So, whether or not he is to be executed will depend on how deeply you love and respect your father. *(He speaks with intensity.)* Now it is time for you to act so that you do not have reason to grieve later on.

TSUYUKUSA: So, when my father comes before your lordship . . .

HORIKAWA: You are to be with him.

TSUYUKUSA: In that case I must consult with him before he meets you so I can persuade him to comply with your commands.

HORIKAWA: If I do wind up having to execute him, I wonder what would be the best way to signal my decision? *(He catches sight of the maple tree stage left.)* Yes, that's it. If I hand your father a cup of sake with a crimson maple leaf floating in it, that will be the sign that he is to die.

TSUYUKUSA: That means a single maple leaf . . .
HORIKAWA: Yes, just as the famous poem says, "Fashioned by the wind on a mountain stream, / This weir is made of autumn leaves resisting the river's flow." Whether or not your maple leaf remains or is washed downstream to destruction depends entirely upon how strong is the weir of love for your father.
AOI: We set aside today to go out maple viewing but . . .
FUYUHAGI: . . . The presence of a single maple leaf from a single bough . . .
HONOHO: . . . Will be the terrible test for Tsuyukusa.
HATATA: Truly, frightening things . . .
ALL LADIES: . . . Are in store.
HORIKAWA: Let's go inside and resume the feast there. Tsuyukusa,
TSUYUKUSA: Yes, sir?
HORIKAWA: You must be sure to join your father.
NARRATOR: There seems to be hidden meaning in his words. And he goes into the inner chamber.

HORIKAWA *exits upstage center, followed by everyone except* TSUYUKUSA.

NARRATOR: One woman remains, alone and despondent.
Her father's life seems as impermanent
As her own name, "Dew on the Grass."
Why must maple leaves wither and die?
If in this world there were no maple leaves . . .
TSUYUKUSA: . . . Would my father's life still be in danger?
NARRATOR: Beaten madly by the wind, maple leaves fall rustling to the ground.
Such is the impermanence of the lives of trees and grasses.
The falling leaves are one with her falling tears,
But it is the single remaining leaf she holds so dear.
Just at this moment, who should enter with the swirling leaves,
But Yoshihide's two apprentices, Fudeo and Hanawaka.

FUDEO *and* HANAWAKA *enter from stage right, accompanied by clappers.*

FUDEO: Lady Tsuyukusa!
TSUYUKUSA: Are you Fudeo and Hanawaka? What are you doing here?
FUDEO: We fled our master in fear for our lives, but we came here in secret to tell you what happened.
TSUYUKUSA: You broke into His Lordship's mansion just to talk to me? *(She goes down from the mansion onto the main stage.)*
FUDEO: Yes, please listen to what I have to say. *(Music from the* geza *accompanies his monologue.)* Yoshihide has many apprentices, but I am the one

who sees to his personal needs. Until now I gladly performed each and every task he assigned me, and devoted my life to serving him. During the Fourth Month I helped the master as he worked painstakingly on the hell screen. Sometimes I had to play a character wearing a sword, or wear other, strange costumes. I put up with it because it was in service to my master, but when he had to draw sinners being punished in hell, he took out chains that he had kept hidden in the house. He had me strip naked and . . .

NARRATOR: . . . He chained me up, binding my hands behind my back. Then he beat me with muddy rice stalks, saying, "Take that! And that!" All I could move was my head. I was like a sake cask that had been tipped over on its side, and I thought I would go crazy with the pain. I was covered in blood from the chains digging into my naked flesh. The master was steely calm throughout. As I lay immobilized his brush never stopped moving. Then, from a group vats standing in a corner of the room a snake came slithering out.

FUDEO: I was startled, and so terrified it would bite me that I cried out. Finally the master took the chains off me, but I can't be his apprentice any more, I just can't.

NARRATOR: Thus he finishes his story. Hanawaka continues breathlessly.

HANAWAKA: *(In an excited voice)* I went through the same sorts of things as Fudeo did. I was already half dead from the work the master had made me do the for the hell screen sketches, but he told me to come back to work again that night. When I went into the master's studio and looked up, suddenly, from out of nowhere . . .

NARRATOR: I was attacked by a great horned owl. I waved my sleeves at it to drive it away, but it tore at me with its terrible beak. When I stood up I had to drive it off, but if I crouched down it came after me, and it chased me all around the room. It was as if a bird-demon had descended from the heights, and it tore ferociously at my eyes.

HANAWAKA: Finally I was able to escape, but though my hair stood on end and I was shaking with fright, the master sat watching my torture, paper spread out in front of him, licking the tip of his brush, preparing to draw. Seeing him work like that, so cool and collected—why I simply can't study under him any more.

FUDEO: Now that we've told you, we've got to run away faster than boats running before a storm. But please don't tell the master . . .

NARRATOR: . . . What you heard from us. And the two make their escape.

They exit stage right.

NARRATOR: Now Yoshihide enters, the greatest artist of the age,
He who embodies the proverb that says,
"The gods and Buddhas protect the demons of hell."

With his little craftsman's cap on his head,
He looks like a monkey imitating a man,
Far different from the fearsome figure of the stories.
When he sees his daughter
His haughty expression crumbles with emotion.

YOSHIHIDE *enters along the* hanamichi *and goes onto the main stage.*

YOSHIHIDE: Daughter!
TSUYUKUSA: Father!
YOSHIHIDE: How I've wanted to meet you!
TSUYUKUSA: How I've wanted to be with you!
NARRATOR: They embrace, and their words dissolve into tears.
YOSHIHIDE: His lordship has summoned me to the palace, but I'm so worried because of a dream I had last night. A voice called to me from above my pillow, crying, "Descend into the abyss! Come to fiery hell where sinners and criminals burn in flames!" A figure appeared to lead me into the nether world and in an uncanny voice it said, "Come quickly, for your daughter awaits you in hell." I was so startled that I woke up at once, but after that I couldn't get back to sleep no matter how hard I tried. I've been terribly worried about you ever since.
TSUYUKUSA: Father, that dream just shows that you're worried about the hell screen even when you sleep. Vindication of your work is appearing in your dreams. As an artist you should be proud of that.
YOSHIHIDE: Your words make me feel much better. But tell me about the petition that I submitted months ago. Has his lordship granted you leave to come home?
TSUYUKUSA: No. I don't know when he'll give me leave to go home.
YOSHIHIDE: I hope it's soon. I haven't seen you for a long time and you've grown into an even finer young lady than you were before.
TSUYUKUSA: Oh father, it's embarrassing when you look at me like that.
YOSHIHIDE: The days and months pass so swiftly. Why it has already been seventeen years . . .
NARRATOR: . . . You were not yet weaned when the woman . . .
YOSHIHIDE: . . . Who was your mother and my wife departed this world.
NARRATOR: But today I can see a perfect image of her before me,
Just as if she were alive, when I look at your face.
I, your father, raised you, from when you were in swaddling clothes.
You were like a precious jewel in my hand.
When I look back at the joys and cares of those years,
I know that I, your father, was both father and mother to you.
TSUYUKUSA: My debt to you is greater than the mountains and seas and I'll never forget it.
YOSHIHIDE: You're being too formal, talking about your debt to me. You

Figure 9. *Hell Screen*, in 1978, Shimbashi Enbujō, with Bandō Tamasaburō as Tsuyukusa and Nakamura Kichiemon II as Yoshihide. Photograph courtesy of the Mishima Yukio Literary Museum. Photograph by Yoshida Chiaki.

know that when I take up my brush I become totally absorbed in my work. I spend my nights alone and the night wind chills my old bones. Then I remember how I sent you off to work in this palace and I'm so jealous of the lord whom you now serve.

TSUYUKUSA: Be careful what you say, father. We are in his lordship's palace.

NARRATOR: The old man's complaints go on and on to no avail.
Tsuyukusa changes the subject.

TSUYUKUSA: Father, today's summons by Lord Horikawa is different from any previous summons. His lordship is extremely angry at the delay in the hell screen. Today he won't forgive you if you tell him about any further delays. He is usually frightening, but is even more so today, and if you answer him back with your usual excuses and beating around the bush, he might even order you killed. If that were to happen I could not live in this world without you.

NARRATOR: She is about to tell him that the signal for death
Will be a red maple leaf in his sake,
But she keeps that awful secret deep inside.
She thinks that even without telling him,
He knows how much is at stake.
Yoshihide's expression changes,
Revealing his pride and disdain.

YOSHIHIDE: Don't be so upset. It was thoughtless of Lord Horikawa to tell you about this business. I don't have to follow his every whim. I am very different from you. Does he think me the sort of father who can be induced to speed up his brushwork because of the tears of women and children?

Listen to what I am about to tell you. Political power is political power and art is art. Even if the Grand Minister of State wields power throughout the realm, the person who rules the six-panel screen is I, Yoshihide. I may not carry two swords, but I exercise authority in my own domain. This is a truth that you must understand.

The riffraff never stop their useless chatter. They call me a Chinese goblin. They call me a braggart who hasn't any skill. But they're just like the proverbial frog and cricket arguing over who has the better voice. Their words are just as foolish and meaningless as the cries of frogs and crickets.

NARRATOR: Tsuyukusa weeps softly as her father rants on, his pride and voice as big as the long, long nose of a goblin.

TSUYUKUSA: Father, everything you say is true. But if you love your daughter, please, when you appear before his lordship, give him an answer that pleases him, I beg of you.

NARRATOR: She beseeches him with hands pressed together in supplication.

Seeing her like this, Yoshihide's mood softens despite himself. But just at this moment Lord Horikawa makes his entrance.

HORIKAWA *enters alone through the curtained arch up stage center.*

HORIKAWA: Well, Yoshihide. It's been a long time, hasn't it?
YOSHIHIDE: *(Bowing deeply, hands pressed to the floor)* Your lordship. It is a pleasure to see you looking so splendid. I am deeply honored.
HORIKAWA: Well I don't feel at all splendid, and the reason is that screen, of course. Your repeated delays now add up to a half year. It is impossible to grant you any further extension. Tell me here and now the exact day you will finish it.
YOSHIHIDE: Yes, sir. I am working day and night on the screen, giving it my fullest concentration. I am happy to report that it is nearly completed.
HORIKAWA: You say that it's nearly finished? Well done, Yoshihide. I am very happy to hear that.
TSUYUKUSA: Father, how could you have teased me so cruelly? There I was, begging you with clasped hands to complete the screen, and in fact you've almost finished it. You should have told me that from the start.
YOSHIHIDE: Daughter, don't speak out of turn. My lord, please allow me to be more specific. I have almost finished painting the screen, but there is just one scene that I am completely incapable of drawing.
HORIKAWA: What's that you say?
YOSHIHIDE: Let me tell you about the scene I cannot draw. In one of my six panel screens I typically draw over one thousand individual figures. My painting is as life-like as if you were seeing real people with your own eyes. To do this I draw from life. It is my family's artistic heritage that we do not draw what we haven't seen. If I try to draw what I haven't seen, the result is a poor imitation of life, with no feeling in it. It is something I have vowed never to do. So you understand . . .
NARRATOR: . . . "why there is a scene I cannot draw?" he declares. The minister bursts out laughing.
HORIKAWA: *(Laughs)* What you are saying is that if you don't see hell, you can't paint a hell screen? Are you asking me to give you leave to visit hell so you can witness the scenes you need for the screen?
YOSHIHIDE: One can witness hell in this world too. The great fire in the city last year was just like the raging flames in the hell of fire. I used that fire to sketch my "writhing Fudo" scene.
HORIKAWA: I see where you get your flames, but how do you manage to draw demons tormenting sinners in hell?
YOSHIHIDE: With my own eyes I can see naked men bound in chains. I have drawn a bird of prey attacking a youth. I have seen visions, both in real life and in dreams, of innumerable, hellish tortures that appear before me. I have seen the heads of real oxen and horses, and normal faces

and arms can be multiplied. All of this can be used to create demons.

HORIKAWA: If you can create demons, what is it that you cannot draw?

YOSHIHIDE: It is the scene in the very middle of the screen, of a gorgeously decorated, rattan-sided nobleman's carriage falling into hell from the sky above.

HORIKAWA: A rattan-sided carriage?

YOSHIHIDE: Yes, I cannot draw that carriage.

HORIKAWA: Why on earth not? Those sorts of carriages travel the streets of the capital every day.

YOSHIHIDE: I will tell you why I cannot draw it. *(To musical accompaniment)* I cannot draw it because it is like no carriage that I have ever seen in this world. Inside it is a beautiful lady of the upper aristocracy. Her long, black hair is consumed in flames and her face is half obscured by smoke. Her brows are drawn together and she gazes upward. The viewer looks up at the carriage falling from in the sky. The lady clutches at the blinds, trying to pull them off so she can use them to brush away showers of sparks that are falling like rain. Fierce raptors, driven wild by the flames, beat their wings and fly about the carriage.

What I am unable to draw is the beautiful lady in the rattan-sided carriage enveloped in flames.

HORIKAWA: And what would it take for you to be able to execute this scene?

YOSHIHIDE: A great lord, with power unrivalled in the land, exercising his authority to arrange for a rattan-sided carriage with a high-ranking lady-in-waiting in it to be set on fire before my eyes.

NARRATOR: Tsuyukusa is shocked at her father's
Straightforward expression of wickedness and perversity.
But as might be expected of a great minister of state,
Lord Horikawa conceals his astonishment with silence.
At length he speaks.

HORIKAWA: I see . . . an aristocratic lady in a carriage falling into the raging fires of hell. A brilliantly conceived scene—absolutely unique. Even though you are the finest artist in the realm, it must have taxed your creative powers. However, it would tarnish the reputation of your grand lord were he to throw an innocent woman into a fire. How about burning a doll in place of the woman in the carriage?

NARRATOR: The humanity of this suggestion,
Suits the grave responsibility of his office,
But Yoshihide loudly rejects the proposal.

YOSHIHIDE: Burning an empty carriage, or a carriage with a dummy in it is not what I require. I could do that easily enough in my own garden.

HORIKAWA: So, you absolutely require a living woman . . .

YOSHIHIDE: Your lordship has any number of women in your employ. Given your power and prestige, to set one of them on fire should be an easy matter.

HORIKAWA: And what if I refuse your request?

YOSHIHIDE: Then the hell screen you have ordered will never be finished. Not even in one hundred years.

HORIKAWA: Never finished? Not even in one hundred years?

YOSHIHIDE: I am already an old man, and I said "one hundred years" to emphasize my point. In a few years' time I'll die and go to Buddha's paradise, but never, for many ages to come, will there be a painter in this land with the ability to paint a hell screen like this one. I said "one hundred years," when I probably should have said, "for all eternity."

NARRATOR: His words are fearless and filled with foolish pride.
The great lord immediately falls into a rage.

HORIKAWA: It is a ridiculous request. I won't put up with your insults any longer. I have no further need of you. Finish the screen or not as you please. Nothing will make me ask for it now.

YOSHIHIDE: It is in your lordship's power to commission a screen just as it is your lordship's power to burn a carriage. I will indeed present you the screen you ordered, but future generations will laugh at the both of us if that screen has an empty, white, unpainted place right in the middle.

HORIKAWA: Ladies, bring sake to the insolent Yoshihide who so loves to ridicule his superiors.

NARRATOR: Tsuyukusa is stunned when she hears Lord Horikawa mention sake.

TSUYUKUSA: Father, please, what are you doing? His lordship is very angry with you. Please apologize humbly for what you have said to him. Please, I beg of you . . .

NARRATOR: . . . "With my hands clasped in supplication."
She pleads with him but he pays her no heed,
And sits gazing up at the sky with a nonchalant expression on his face.

The ladies-in-waiting enter, bringing sake cups and pitchers. They pour sake first for Lord HORIKAWA. *At Lord* HORIKAWA'S *signal, one of the ladies goes to stage left and plucks a single red leaf from a branch of maple and puts it into the sake cup.*

HORIKAWA: Yoshihide, have a cup of sake. Tsuyukusa, take this cup to your father.

TSUYUKUSA: Yes, sir.

She goes up to the lord's dais, takes the cup from him, and goes back down onto stage level. She sees the maple leaf floating in the sake. Clappers beat as both HORIKAWA *and* TSUYUKUSA *pose dramatically.*

TSUYUKUSA: There is a maple leaf floating in this sake cup. *(Speaking with strong feeling)* I will drink this sake myself!

HORIKAWA: By refusing to give that sake to your father and drinking it yourself, what you are telling me is . . .

TSUYUKUSA: . . . Yes, to put me in that rattan-sided carriage and set it afire!

NARRATOR: Yoshihide is stunned.

YOSHIHIDE: Have you gone mad!? *(He clings to her.)*

HORIKAWA: I see. Tsuyukusa, your filial love is most commendable, but aren't you really hoping that I will spare the both of you? Tell me, Tsuyukusa, what is your true intention.

TSUYUKUSA: My lord, it is difficult . . .

HORIKAWA: Answer me plainly.

TSUYUKUSA: In that case, my lord, may I be so bold as to ask you to provide the second verse to this famous poem: "A parent yearns to protect a child setting out on a distant journey . . ."

HORIKAWA: ". . . Oh barrier guard, do not shut the gate and keep my heart from going along." I see. You intend to sacrifice yourself for your father.

From his high seat HORIKAWA *looks down at* TSUYUKUSA, *but she refuses to look into his eyes, gazing downward all the while.* HORIKAWA *and* TSUYUKUSA *pose dramatically.* HORIKAWA *speaks in an increasingly angry voice.*

HORIKAWA: I accept Tsuyukusa's request. She will be put in a carriage and it will be set on fire. Yoshihide, you should be overjoyed. Your desire, too, has been granted! Servants, bring in the carriage!

SERVANTS: *(Lined up stage right)* Yes, sir.

TSUYUKUSA *begins to walk upstage, but* YOSHIHIDE *clings to her* hakama *skirt and stops her.*

YOSHIHIDE: My daughter, where are you going?

HORIKAWA: She has to dress as an aristocratic lady of the highest rank, as you requested. Tsuyukusa, hurry now!

NARRATOR: So his lordship commands. Yoshihide is mad with grief.

TSUYUKUSA *pulls herself free from her father and exits up-stage.* YOSHIHIDE *follows her part way, climbing up the steps into the interior of the palace.*

YOSHIHIDE: Your lordship's action is even more despicable than the great tyrant of China. It's too cruel of you. How can you be so heartless? I have no idea why my daughter told you she would ride in that carriage, but now that she's gone this far, it's all up to you, my lord. Please stop her, I beg of you!

NARRATOR: He shouts and weeps loudly.
Lord Horikawa gives orders to his servants,
Who have pulled the rattan-sided carriage into position.

Numerous SERVANTS *pull a lacquered, rattan-sided carriage on stage.*

HORIKAWA: Get the decrepit old man away from me!

SERVANTS *surround* YOSHIHIDE *and drag him down out of the mansion onto the main stage level. He struggles with them there in a* tachimawari *fight scene accompanied by music and percussion. He is finally dragged downstage left.*

NARRATOR: Tsuyukusa enters solemnly,
Dressed in the splendid twelve-layered robes of a noblewoman,
Her life now as fleeting as her name, "Dew on the Grass."
She passes before Lord Horikawa, who is as solid as cedar . . .
A door opens to a room where Lady Aoi and Fuyuhagi
Sit weeping, grieving at this parting from the girl.

TSUYUKUSA *enters dressed in the* jūnihitoe *twelve-layered robes of a noblewoman. She goes to* HORIKAWA *and bows to him. The paper-covered lattice door of the room at stage left opens, revealing* AOI *and* FUYUHAGI, *who are sitting inside.*

TSUYUKUSA: Lady Fuyuhagi. (FUYUHAGI *approaches her.)* I know it is a worthless object, but please give this mirror to her ladyship as a remembrance of me. I used it to prepare myself for my journey to the nether world. I give it to her in thanks for all she has done for me.

FUYUHAGI *takes the mirror and gives it to* AOI.

NARRATOR: She calmly descends the steps.

TSUYUKUSA: Father.

YOSHIHIDE: Daughter, how can you possibly go through with this?

NARRATOR: His daughter answers not a word.
All has been decided by fate,
And this calms her heart for the final chapter.
She enters the carriage of the flames of love.
Again and again she looks back at her father,
Her only parting words are her tears.
They gaze into each other's eyes,
Which speak more words in parting,
Than can be counted in a thousand sutra scrolls.

Father and daughter perform a dramatic parting. HORIKAWA *descends from the palace onto the main stage.*

HORIKAWA: Pull the carriage forth!
SERVANTS: Yes, sir!
NARRATOR: Yoshihide runs out to try to halt the carriage,
But Lord Horikawa blocks his way . . .

TSUYUKUSA *enters the carriage.* YOSHIHIDE *breaks free from the guards who are restraining him, rushes toward the carriage, and confronts* HORIKAWA. *The sticks signaling the end of the scene begin to sound.*

NARRATOR: . . . And directs the carriage on its journey to hell.

HORIKAWA *and* YOSHIHIDE *pose dramatically as the curtain closes. The curtain remains closed briefly while percussion is played. It is then opened to reveal a blue* asagimaku *drop curtain.*

SCENE TWO: THE MANSION'S INNER GARDEN

NARRATOR: *(singing in a majestic style, reminiscent of* noh *chant)*
The forbidden pool lies behind the stones.
If one does not gaze upon it,
One will never know of the evil black dragon lurking there.
Such are the depths of Lord Horikawa's heart,
Now revealed deep within his garden.
What shines brightly on the carriage about to burn,
Is not the Buddha's benevolent moon,
But torches carried by all the servants.
Their smoke drives flocks of crows soaring into the sky.

After this sung prelude the blue drop curtain falls. At stage left, in the place of honor, HORIKAWA *sits on a dais covered in rush mats. He wears his golden crown of state and a purple overrobe. Seated beside him, to his left and right, respectively, are* AOI *and* FUYUHAGI. *The five ladies-in-waiting are lined up behind* AOI, HORIKAWA, *and* FUYUHAGI. *A sake drinking party is in progress on this dais. In the middle of the main stage the lacquered, rattan-sided carriage sits in the middle of a sparse stand of bamboo. At stage right* YOSHIHIDE *sits slumped forward, hanging his head. Brushes, and inkstone, paper, and water to rinse his brushes have been placed before him. A large number of* SERVANTS *stand behind* YOSHIHIDE *illuminating the area with torches.*

HORIKAWA: Set fire to the carriage!
NARRATOR: Servants shout, 'Yes, sir!,' and they approach the carriage,

Figure 10. *Hell Screen*, in 1953, Kabuki-za, with Nakamura Utaemon VI as Tsuyukusa and Matsumoto Koshirō VIII as Yoshihide. Photograph courtesy of the Mishima Yukio Literary Museum. Photo by Yoshida Chiaki.

Each with a torch in his hand. The carriage window opens suddenly.

The carriage window opens suddenly, and TSUYUKUSA *reveals her face in the frame of the window.*

TSUYUKUSA: Father!
YOSHIHIDE: Yes!
TSUYUKUSA: Farewell!
YOSHIHIDE: Wait, don't close the window yet! They say that the karmic bonds of parent and child last just one brief incarnation, but that the love for a child can shackle a parent for three lifetimes. That window shackles me. I'll go with you . . .
NARRATOR: He tries to rush to her, but the guards stop him.
The window separating the world of light
From the world of ghosts slams shut.
By the carriage, flames are already licking at the axle guards.
The ladies-in-waiting suddenly scream.

The ladies-in-waiting scream, hide their faces in the sleeves, and collapse in terror.

NARRATOR: Lady Aoi and Fuyuhagi gaze fearfully
At the scene from behind their sleeves,
But the Grand Minister, true to form,
Sits in regal splendor, a smile on his face.

The flames around the carriage gradually grow larger.

NARRATOR: Yoshihide, not surprisingly, is half insane with grief.
He rolls around on the ground weeping and shouting
With a voice that suggests tortured sinners in hell.
Truly this is no different from the hell of flames.
Just at this moment Ushisuke and Umanosuke enter,
Intent on avenging the humiliation of being jilted by Tsuyukusa.

USHISUKE *and* UMANOSUKE *enter from stage right. The flames rage more strongly.*

USHISUKE: Look, his lordship is engaging in magnificent sport.
UMANOSUKE: A beautiful noblewoman is inside the carriage.
USHISUKE: Her white flesh is sizzling and growing tender.
UMANOSUKE: What a delicious aroma.
USHISUKE: Look, the despicable Yoshihide is crawling about on all fours like a dog. I see nothing of his usual haughty pride.

UMANOSUKE: How right you are. Let's kick him around. It will make a merry dance, with the crackling fire as both percussion and backdrop.

NARRATOR: They kick him with their filthy, shod feet.
But a dull sword suddenly stolen
Allows the old man to vent his anger,
And he slices both men through their chests.

USHISUKE *and* UMANOSUKE *kick* YOSHIHIDE *with their shod feet. Waiting for his chance,* YOSHIHIDE *draws* USHISUKE'S *sword from its sheath and in the same motion he inflicts mortal wounds on both men. They fall and writhe in agony.*

NARRATOR: On his knees, hands on the ground, he bows before Lord Horikawa.

YOSHIHIDE: Your Lordship, I have struck down your retainers because they cruelly slandered me. I offer you my life in atonement for this crime.

HORIKAWA: I understand what you are up to. You committed a capital offense in the hopes of following your daughter in death. That's too convenient for you. Too convenient by far. And it's a pretty low way to die for a Chinese goblin like yourself, with a reputation for evil known throughout the land. How can someone as weak-kneed as a woman or a child expect to paint a hell screen?

Those two men brought their deaths upon themselves. You are guilty of no crime whatsoever. Servants, the hot-tempered Yoshihide may turn that blade on himself. Take it from him, and throw the sword and the bodies of the two men into the fire! Quickly!

NARRATOR: Lord Horikawa gives the order, and the two bodies, still breathing,
Are thrown into flames that lick their bloody wounds.
Such are the vicissitudes of life.
At length, the shafts of the carriage burst into flame.

The SERVANTS *throw the two men and the sword into the fire. The two men writhe in agony in the flames, and clutch at the carriage shafts.*

HORIKAWA: Yoshihide, look at the scene. *(He speaks to musical accompaniment.)* There are the carriage and the court lady that you wanted, burning in the hell of flames. There, engulfed in the roaring winds of hell, Ushisuke and Umanosuke are pulling the carriage. They're really a bull-headed and a horse-headed demon, and they add that all-important touch of reality to your design. Before your eyes is an unparalleled scene. What are you doing sitting there with your arms folded? Take up your brush! Get to work!

NARRATOR: "Take up your brush, get to work," the Minister shouts.

Yoshihide's white hair blows
In the hellish wind, fanned by the flames.
Slowly his eyes begin to sparkle and come to life.
Unconsciously, unknowingly, he takes the brush in hand.
A phantasmic strength surges through his whole body.
His pride as an artist drives him to exhaust his physical powers.
Lord Horikawa's admiration is boundless.

AOI *takes a long look at the expression on her husband's face. She speaks rhythmically.*

AOI: Now that you have thrown Tsuyukusa into the flames,
For the first time, I understand your true feelings.
I, Aoi, have been deceived.
How dare she leave me a keepsake—that despicable woman.
NARRATOR: "How low of her," she says, and from her kimono
Removes the mirror with its blue lapis frame.
It flashes brightly in the fire light, illuminating a ferocious expression,
Like a jealous demoness striking a rival in love.
The white-haired Fuyuhagi is like a hell hag from the crypt.
Lord Horikawa, wearing his golden crown and purple robe,
Is Great King Emma, Sovereign of the Ten Rulers of Hades.
It is truly a scene from hell visible in the living world.

AOI *holds up the mirror to reflect the firelight.* HORIKAWA *postures like Emma, King of Hell, and the three strike dramatic poses together.*

NARRATOR: Yoshihide suddenly slaps his thigh.
YOSHIHIDE: The design for the full hell screen
Is now finished in my mind.
There is no question that it will be
The greatest masterpiece of all time.
HORIKAWA: Yes, and among the eight realms of hell, into the hell of flames have fallen . . .
YOSHIHIDE: . . . Murderers, drunkards, thieves, together with their friends—profaners, abusers, and adulterers.
HORIKAWA: The flames leap . . .
YOSHIHIDE: . . . Five hundred leagues into the air,
HORIKAWA: The flames spread . . .
YOSHIHIDE: . . . Two hundred leagues all around.
NARRATOR: Swords of fire flay the sinners,
Their bodies bathed in bubbling, molten iron.
HORIKAWA: They suffer these tortures . . .
YOSHIHIDE: . . . For billions of years.

HORIKAWA: What painted the hell screen were brushes,
YOSHIHIDE: Bristles made of the fur of badgers, winter stags, and summer deer.
HORIKAWA: What painted the flames . . .
YOSHIHIDE: . . . Was red ochre pigment imported from Borneo, ground to dust,
NARRATOR: Gold paint, silver paint, covered in ash from the living fire.
Engulfed in a sea of flames five hundred leagues wide
The rattan-sided carriage collapses with a crash.
Inside the girl is on the verge of death.
At the moment she dies she takes a last look at her father.
Yoshihide, gazing back, bids no farewell, displays no anguish.
He continues to calmly draw, his delusions unchanged.

The carriage sides fall down, fully revealing the body of TSUYUKUSA *inside.* YOSHIHIDE *hesitates for a moment, but then resumes his sketching. Presently he and* HORIKAWA *look at each other.*

HORIKAWA: Yes, you have done well.

There is the first strike of the clappers signaling the end of the play.

HORIKAWA: Mu, ha, ha, ha, ha, ha, ha. *(He laughs long, loud, and villainously, to the rhythm of the clappers in a pattern called "seven laughs" used by the evil minister Shihei in* Tenmangu Netane no Gokū.*)*
NARRATOR: It is a remarkable event, never to be forgotten.

All characters pose dramatically as the curtain closes.

CURTAIN

Figure 11. *Hell Screen*, in 1978, Shimbashi Enbujō, with Bandō Tamasaburō as Tsuyukusa. Photograph courtesy of the Mishima Yukio Literary Museum. Photograph by Yoshida Chiaki.

The Sardine Seller's Net of Love

(Iwashiuri Koi no Hikiami)

(a kabuki play)

First Published in 1954, First Performed in 1954

Translated by Laurence Kominz

INTRODUCTION

The Sardine Seller's Net of Love, Mishima's second kabuki play, is by far his most successful, and is the most frequently performed of his kabuki plays. It is also his finest work of parody in any theatrical genre. The play is more than just a parody of classical kabuki, it is also a warm-hearted romantic comedy that leaves audiences glowing. The text is a tour-de-force of word play couched in classical Japanese. Mishima fuses sophisticated word play with physical comedy so apparent to all that audiences understand everything taking place on stage.

After *Hell Screen,* in 1953, Shochiku left Mishima's choice of material for his kabuki plays entirely up to the author. In 1953, thanks in part to a successful revival of the 1698 hit play *The Courtesan and Mount Asama (Keisei Asamagatake),* Mishima was discovering the joys of Genroku kabuki and its "cheerful, refreshing, generous, bright, dialogue-based plays."[1] The Genroku Era, from the 1680s to the 1720s, was when the first great actors and playwrights created kabuki as a dramatic art, and plays from that era reflect the exuberance and optimism of a great art in its first flowering.

For *The Sardine Seller* Mishima borrowed ideas from two medieval tales *(otogizōshi),* one of which contained a parody of *The Tale of the Heike* in which all of the protagonists are animals and fish. The overall story was an original creation done in homage to Genroku kabuki, with its disguises, parodies, and playful love affairs. Genroku plays proceed at a more rapid pace than later kabuki, and Mishima wrote a play that moved quickly from scene to scene.[2]

The story of the play is charming and improbable. Sarugenji, a sardine peddler and son of a fish wholesaler, falls in love with Hotarubi, a high-ranking courtesan, and with the help of his father disguises himself as a feudal lord so he can visit a woman normally reserved only for the wealthiest patrons. While he is partying with Hotarubi, Sarugenji recites the "Fish Battle of Ichinotani," a "fish *jōruri*" tour-de-force that only a genius like Mishima would even think of attempting to write in this day and age. Presently the inebriated sardine seller dozes off, his head resting on his beloved's lap, but in his sleep he begins to intone the sardine seller's spiel. When awakened and questioned by Hotarubi, Sarugenji maintains his false persona by referring to classic poems. Finally, convinced that the young man is indeed a feudal lord, Hotarubi collapses in tears. She reveals that she is really a princess, and that she fell in love with a sardine seller when, from her castle tower, she heard him call out his spiel in a beautiful voice. She was later kidnapped and sold to a Kyoto brothel, but has never forsaken her first, true love. Princess and fish monger reveal their true identities and are united in love.

The plot and the characters of *The Sardine Seller* form perfect parodies of their Genroku counterparts in romances set within the context of feudal lords' succession disputes—plays called *oiemono. Oiemono* are the iconic plays of Genroku era *kamigata* (Osaka and Kyoto) kabuki. The attitude of the parodist toward the material he parodies is ambivalent. He loves the original but feels that he can make the work more entertaining by using a parodic approach,[3] and this is precisely what Mishima did in *The Sardine Seller.* Mishima wrote that the language and stage conventions of Edo period kabuki were superior to their modern counterparts so should be maintained, but he also wrote that the weakness of Edo period kabuki for modern audiences lay in its characters and their motivations. In particular their intense concern with hidebound and petty rules of honor and decorum failed to resonate with modern audiences.[4] Mishima's solution was to create sympathetic characters within a plot that parodied the tried and true stock conventions of Genroku kabuki story telling.

Every feature of the plot and characters of *The Sardine Seller* is the exact opposite of the archetypical *oiemono* play created by Chikamatsu. The male hero of the Genroku *oiemono* is a young heir to a feudal domain who falls in love with a courtesan (or two), squanders his family fortune on lavish parties in the pleasure district, and so is disowned by his parents, rendering him penniless. He now has to sneak into the pleasure district, clothed in rags (or a paper kimono), to meet his beloved. He is often forced to work as a peddler or other menial just to survive. This role type is known *yatsushi.* Sarugenji is the exact opposite of a *yatsushi.* He is a menial peddler to begin with and his parental intervention takes the form of a father who suddenly showers him with money so he can disguise himself sumptuously as a feudal lord and go to meet for the first time the woman he loves. In the classic *yatsushi oiemono,* a loyal family retainer rescues the prodigal young heir, and the young wastrel then redeems his beloved, who is always a prostitute of humble origins. The two then become feudal lord and lord's consort. In Mishima's play the prostitute, Hotarubi, is in fact a princess, and when a loyal retainer intervenes on behalf of her parents to escort her home and return her to her privileged status, she rebuffs him, and sets out with her new husband to begin her new life as a lowly peddler.

Though the language and stage action of *The Sardine Seller* make it feel like a classical play, no Edo period play ever parodied *oiemono* in this way. Modern audiences are utterly charmed by the conclusion to the play. They know that it is incongruous, and in fact ridiculously improbable. But modern audiences like to see love conquer all, and citizens of Japan's post-war, egalitarian society enjoy plays that disavow the rigid Edo period class structure.

From the first scene Mishima creates the "ludicrous environment" essential to comedy, using slapstick, punning, hyperbolic statements seriously made, and easily seen-through disguises."[5] To cite just one shtick as an example of the ludicrous environment he creates, toward the end of the first scene Sarugenji mounts a horse for the first time in his life. Struggling to mount it, he finds himself facing backwards. He says,

> What's this? It's a headless horse! Even poor little sardines have heads. *(He looks behind him.)* It's like a poem with the prelude stuck on the wrong end. *(He struggles to turn around and face forward, finally succeeding.)*

Ignorance this impossible is utterly delightful.

The response to *Sardine Seller* in 1954 was unanimous popular and critical acclaim. It is an "unpretentious, charming, stylish, elegant, and large-hearted play that summons loud laughter,"[6] wrote kabuki critic, Toita Yasuji. For Mishima the play had been a joy to write, and the actors could sense his upbeat mood from the first read through of the script. Fans and kabuki producers were suddenly urging him to give up fiction and become a full-time playwright.

Utaemon and Nakamura Kanzaburō XVII were thrilled with *The Sardine Seller*. Utaemon felt that there was a "new breath of fresh air in kabuki," and he was eager to work with Mishima on whatever ideas the young writer could come up with.[7]

Utaemon and Kanzaburō XVII performed *The Sardine Seller* five times together between 1954 and 1973. After 1973, seventeen years passed before Kanzaburō's son, Kankurō (now Kanzaburō XVIII), decided to revive the play to celebrate the twentieth anniversary of Mishima's death. Kankurō had never seen his father perform *The Sardine Seller*,[8] but his collaborator in the endeavor, Bandō Tamasaburō, who would play Hotarubi, had played a minor courtesan in 1973 and remembered much of the staging.[9] Together the two actors crafted a version that was a great success. Later, an old film of an Utaemon/Kanzaburō XVII production was found and they learned that their version was remarkably similar to the earlier one.[10] This is a tribute to Tamasaburō's memory, and to an acting style that Kanzaburō XVIII inherited from his father, but it also indicates that Mishima's spoken text and stage directions communicate intimately with kabuki actors, and provide strong guidelines for presenting the play. Kanzaburō XVIII has added some of his own touches, notably a section of ad-libbed metadramatic byplay with the *gidayū* chanter prior to the "battle of the fishes" recitation.[11] Tamasaburō recognizes that their approach is lighter and clearer than the Utaemon/ Kanzaburō XVII version because they have responded to audiences over the years as they have presented the play. Tamasaburō believes that in the fifties and sixties audiences who had experienced World War II enjoyed darker interpretations of the play, but more contemporary audiences "prefer their decadence, pure and unclouded."[12] Tamasaburō is convinced that *The Sardine Seller* affords a glimpse of the "true Mishima." He was really a romantic at heart, but as an intellectual writer, was embarrassed to reveal it, and overlaid his romanticism with other values and beliefs. Only in kabuki could he write unabashed comedy and romance and receive great praise for his work.[13]

Tamasaburō and Kanzaburō XVIII have performed *The Sardine Seller* regularly since 1990, and it is now one of their favorite plays, and a great favorite of audiences all over Japan.

NOTES

1. Mishima Yukio, "Iwashiuri ni tsuite," Kabuki-za Program, November, 1954, reprinted in *Mishima hyōron zenshū*, vol. 3 (Tokyo: Shinchō, 1994), p. 869.
2. Ibid.
3. Margaret Rose, *Parody: Ancient, Modern, and Postmodern* (Cambridge: Cambridge University Press, 1993), p. 46.
4. Mishima, "Iwashiuri ni tsuite"; reprinted in *Mishima hyōron zenshū*, vol. 3, p. 870.
5. Neil Schaeffer, *The Art of Laughter* (New York: Columbia University Press, 1981), p. 160.
6. Toita Yasuji, "Shinsen na iwashi," *Engekikai Gekihyō*, December 1954, p. 42.
7. Nakamura Utaemon, "Mishima Kabuki no sekai," in Mishima Yukio, *Shibai nikki* (Tokyo: Chuo Kōronsha, 1991), p. 191.
8. Nakamura Kanzaburō XVIII, interview with author, January 21, 2002.
9. Bandō Tamasaburō, interview with author, February 13, 2002.
10. Nakamura Kanzaburō XVIII, interview with author, January 21, 2002.
11. Ibid.
12. Bandō Tamasaburō, interview with author, February 13, 2002.
13. Ibid.

THE CHARACTERS

Sarugenji, a sardine vendor
Ebina Namidabutsu, his father, a former fish wholesaler, now in retirement
Bakurō Rokurozaemon, a packhorse driver and horse trader

The master of the Gojō Higashinotōin house of assignation

A gardener, really Yabukuma Jirōta, a retainer of the lord of Tankaku Castle

Samurai vassals, really fish mongers

Usugumo, a courtesan

Harusame, a courtesan

Nishikigi, a courtesan

Taki no I, a courtesan

Rangiku, a courtesan

Hotarubi ("Flickering Firefly"), a courtesan, originally daughter of the lord of Tankaku Castle

Tombo ("Dragonfly"), an apprentice courtesan *(kamuro)* in the service of Hotarubi

SETTING

SCENE ONE: The Gojō (Fifth Avenue) Bridge in Kyoto

SCENE TWO: The House of Assignation at Fifth Avenue and Higashinotōin, Kyoto

SCENE ONE: THE GOJŌ (FIFTH AVENUE) BRIDGE IN KYOTO

Cheerful, rhythmic music plays as the curtain opens, revealing the stage set. Fifth Avenue Bridge is at the center, with the willows of Yanagigawara visible in the distance beyond the end of the bridge. ROKUROZAEMON *enters from stage left, leading a horse, and from stage right a palanquin enters. They enter simultaneously and move to the rhythmic clapping of the* tsuke. *The two have a difficult time passing each other.* EBINA *noisily alights from the palanquin.*

EBINA: Here now, horse trader, what do you mean by this? Your horse is blocking traffic on the biggest bridge in the Imperial Capital. What *are* you doing?

ROKUROZAEMON: Oh, you're Ebina Namidabutsu, aren't you? You must be the father of the famous sardine seller, Sarugenji.

EBINA: I see you must be one of Sarugenji's friends. I'm so glad I ran into you. *(He pays the palanquin bearers and sends them away. He pats the horse as he speaks.)* My, what a fine chestnut you've got here. He looks like a three-year old.

ROKUROZAEMON: I've heard that you are retired and wearing priest's robes now, but once you were a renowned sardine vendor, and before that a samurai from the East Country. That's why you have such a good eye for horses. This horse used to be in the stables of a feudal lord, but he injured his hoof and has come down in the world. Somehow I just can't find a buyer for him.

EBINA: I see, I see. That explains why he was too proud to give way in the street. Anyway, I passed on my sardine selling trade to that boy of mine, and I came around to find out how his business is going. Has Sarugenji been doing well?

ROKUROZAEMON: Doing well? Well...

EBINA: What are you trying to say?

ROKUROZAEMON: Well, what I mean is... Oh, but, look, look! *(He stares intently at the* hanamichi *curtain.)* It's Sarugenji himself. What excellent timing. I'm sorry, I've got some important business to attend to. I hope we can meet again sometime soon. *(He exits stage left, leading the horse.)*

EBINA: What a busy fellow he is.

Geza *music begins to play.* SARUGENJI *enters from the* hanamichi *curtain, walking as if in a daze. He calls out his sales pitch in a weak, monotous voice.* EBINA, *on the mains stage, shows his anger at the weak voice.*

SARUGENJI: I'm Sarugenji from Ako Inlet in the Province of Ise. Buy my sardines.

He repeats this spiel several times, and enters onto the main stage, where he bumps into his father.

SARUGENJI: Oh, hello Dad.

EBINA: What do you mean, "hello Dad?" What a pathetic voice. With a voice like that your sardines will rot. Do you mean to sell red-eyed sardines? Why you scoundrel! *(He beats his son with his closed fan.)*

SARUGENJI: Please forgive me, please forgive me! There's a good reason why I'm like this.

EBINA: Nothing should ever interfere with selling your sardines.

SARUGENJI: Please, just listen to what I have to say. (*Music accompanies his monologue.)* It happened in early autumn.. It was twilight, and I was selling off the last of my sardines here at the Fifth Avenue Bridge. Suddenly a wicker palanquin went past. Just at that moment a strong breeze blew from the river, and the palanquin's brocade blinds flew open. I caught a glimpse of the lady inside, and with that one look, fell hopelessly in love. Now I yearn for her day and night. Because I'm in despair, my voice has disappeared.

EBINA: I see. So lovesickness is the cause.

SARUGENJI: Yes . . . I feel so ashamed.

EBINA: What a pitiful son you are . . . nothing at all like your father. But, it is just as I always taught you. Our guide on the path of love is none other than poetry. After all, as it says in the great book, the purpose of poetry is to "move invisible gods and demons and make sweet the ties between men and women." Even though I am getting on in years, I, Ebina, will assist you, my son, with your love poems. I am with you, heart and soul.

SARUGENJI: Oh, father, I'm so grateful! Buddha be praised! Buddha be praised!

He presses his hands together reverently in thanks to his father. There is humorous business as, hands pressed together, he pursues EBINA, *who backs up in a circle, as* SARUGENJI *circles after him. Presently* SARUGENJI *once again falls into a state of depression. He speaks emotionally.*

SARUGENJI: But the woman I love is so far above me in station, she's dwelling above the clouds. I am just a humble sardine vendor. No, I'm afraid mine is a hopeless love.

EBINA: It might not be an impossible love. What is the name of the woman?

SARUGENJI: I asked about her and found out who she is. She is called Hotarubi and lives in Gojō Higashinotōin.

EBINA: Hotarubi? Hotarubi is a courtesan.

SARUGENJI: Huh?

EBINA: She is called Hotarubi, after the firefly, because she sparkles when night falls. She's a courtesan of great renown, known throughout the city. She truly dwells above the clouds. It must be because I'm such an upright man that I have a son who causes me so much grief.

SARUGENJI: So, does that mean she's a prostitute?

EBINA: Look, there are prostitutes and then there are prostitutes. She does not take customers lower than men of baronial rank. Hmm. I wonder if I can come up with a good plan? *(He ponders as* SARUGENJI *fidgets about in a state of agitation.)* Hey. When you fidget about like that I can't think clearly.

ROKUROZAEMON *reenters from stage left, slowly leading the horse.* EBINA *sees this and slaps his thigh.*

EBINA: Yes, I've got it! It's a great plan.

SARUGENJI: You've got it? *(He joyfully slaps* EBINA *on the back and sets* EBINA *coughing.* SARUGENJI *starts rubbing* EBINA'S *back to assist him, but* SARUGENJI'S *awkward administrations are ineffectual, and* EBINA *continues to cough.)*

ROKUROZAEMON: It's that old fellow I talked with before.

ROKUROZAEMON *ties the horse to a tree, hurriedly takes out a small towel, dips it in the river, and puts it in* EBINA'S *mouth. He then pushes forcefully on* EBINA'S *back as if trying to suppress convulsions.* EBINA *gets angry.*

EBINA: Hey, what're you doing?! Stop that! Stop it, I'm telling you! Using Kamo River water to cure a cough—you may think it's a miracle drug, but it will never work.

SARUGENJI: Father, while you were scolding him, your cough went away.

EBINA: You're right. My cough is gone. Why, aren't you the same horse trader I was talking with a little while ago?

SARUGENJI: Aren't you Rokurōzaemon?

EBINA: He told me that his chestnut horse had been in the service of a feudal lord and that's given me an idea. Now then, Sarugenji, your most effective strategy is to impersonate a feudal lord. The lords of the nearby provinces—Hatagawa, Hatakeyama, Isshiki, Akamatsu, Doi, and Sasaki—are too well known for it to work. Among the eastern barons, Danjō of Utsunomiya has not yet visited Kyoto. Furthermore, I've heard that he will soon make his first trip here. We're very lucky in our timing. You must impersonate the Lord of Utsunomiya.

ROKUROZAEMON: And for your horse, use this swift-footed steed.

EBINA: I, Ebina, will lead him.

SARUGENJI: Rokurōzaemon, you shall play my chief retainer.

EBINA: And for the attendants and servants to accompany the lead actors . . .

SARUGENJI: Yes, we're fortunate to have fellow fishmongers. We'll have each of our comrades play roles . . . as soldiers, servants and so on.

EBINA: Speed is of the essence. My son, you are now Lord Utsunomiya.

SARUGENJI: Bring me my horse!

The geza *orchestra plays a lively tune.* ROKUROZAEMON *leads out the horse.* SARUGENJI *has difficulty mounting it. He finally manages to mount, but finds himself facing backwards.*

SARUGENJI: What's this? It's a headless horse! Even poor little sardines have heads. *(He looks behind him.)* It's like a poem with the prelude stuck on the wrong end. *(He struggles to turn around and face forward, finally succeeding.* ROKUROZAEMON *takes the horse by the bit.)*

ROKUROZAEMON: Why you look like a feudal lord . . .

EBINA: . . . In all his splendor. (ROKUROZAEMON *and* EBINA *look at each other. They are amused but pretend to be impressed with* SARUGENJI.*)*

SARUGENJI: The grasses and flowers on the Kamo River bank soon wither to autumnal brown.

ROKUROZAEMON: At a time like this, firefly hunting is such a pleasure.

EBINA: Now make way . . . *(He opens his fan and signals for a change in the stage set.)* . . . for my sardine-flower lord!

The stage revolves.

Figure 12. *The Sardine Seller's Net of Love*, 1973, at the Kabuki-za. From left, Ichikawa Omezō as Rokurozaemon, Nakamura Kanzaburō XVII as Sarugenji (on horse), and Jitsukawa Enjaku as Ebina. Photograph courtesy of Waseda University Tsubouchi Hakase Memorial Theatre Museum.

SCENE TWO: THE HOUSE OF ASSIGNATION AT FIFTH AVENUE AND HIGASHINOTŌIN, KYOTO

A building with a raised inner room. The back wall consists of sliding doors (fusuma) *gorgeously decorated with paintings of flowers and birds. The area in front of the garden is planted with numerous chrysanthemums. The five courtesans sit surrounding* HOTARUBI'S *apprentice* (kamuro), *a young girl named* TOMBO (DRAGONFLY).

USUGUMO: Tell us, Tombo, is that beautiful lapis jar a gift for Hotarubi?
HARUSAME: I don't know what's inside it, but it must be something quite splendid . . .
ALL: . . . Mustn't it?
TOMBO: Why don't you try guessing what's inside?
TAKINOI: It's sure to be something delicious.
RANGIKU: In that case I wonder if it's candied persimmons.
TOMBO: No, it's not.
USUGUMO: Oh Rangiku, you just said that because candied persimmons are your favorite treat. Of course you're wrong.
NISHIKIGI: In that case, maybe if we say something we hate we'll get it right. Harusame, what do you think?
HARUSAME: What I hate the most is exactly what all of us hate.
NISHIKIGI: And what's that?
HARUSAME: Shall I try guessing what's inside?
TAKINOI: I wonder if you'll guess what it is?
HARUSAME: What I hate the most is . . . of course . . . men.
USUGUMO: *(Even though she actually likes men)* I agree with you. I hate men. Just hearing the word "man" makes my head begin to hurt.
NISHIKIGI: Usugumo, you really do have it bad. I agree. Whenever I hear the word "man," I hate it so much that my body begins to shake violently.
RANGIKU: Does that mean it's not candied persimmons in this jar, *(She puts her sleeve lovingly over the jar.)* but a hateful, hateful handsome man who'll come out like oil from an oil jar?
TOMBO: You're wrong again.
USUGUMO: Since we don't know, let's open it up.
TOMBO: All right, all right. *(She opens the jar and many beautiful painted shells pour out. Each has a classical poem written on the inside.)*
USUGUMO: Look at all these shells. I wonder if Hotarubi is hinting that all of us courtesans assembled here are like a group of seashells. Her friends will abandon her for this.
HOTARUBI: *(From inside the sliding doors)* I'm not comparing you to the shells.
USUGUMO: That voice . . .
ALL: . . . . belongs to Hotarubi-san.

Music plays as HOTARUBI *emerges upstage center from a sliding door.*

HOTARUBI: Usugumo-san, these shells are used in a game that's played for fun. Classic poems are written inside these beautifully decorated shells, see? *(She picks up a shell.)* Verses from old poems are written here, and players enjoy themselves by competing in matching first and last verses of the poem.

USUGUMO: We've had feudal lords and other high-ranking customers, but we've never played the shell matching game. I've heard that it is about the only thing that princesses have to do to while away their boredom. It seems like an interesting game. Girls, shall we imitate princesses, and try playing it this evening?

ALL: That's a fine idea.

TOMBO *spreads the shells out over a wide area.*

HOTARUBI: All right, let's begin. *(She reads the first verse of a poem written in a shell.)* "Even though I see you in my dreams, morning after morning you are nowhere to be seen."

USUGUMO: Let's see . . . what was the second verse . . .

ALL: Which shell is it on? *(They hunt among the shells.)*

HOTARUBI: There it is. The last verse is, "If only I could depart my own body."

USUGUMO: Oh, what a depressing poem that is.

HOTARUBI: All right, next I'll read the last verse first: "As the wind blows and blows, they scatter in disarray."

When she reads this a gardener appears in the garden. Sweeping with his broom, he looks carefully at the women inside. All of the women are busily engaged in searching for the shell with the matching first verse. HOTARUBI *suddenly looks into the garden, and her eyes meet those of the gardener. She senses something strange about him, and she stands up, but he quickly exits.*

HOTARUBI: What a strange gardener. *(She sits down.)* Harusame-san . . . I've never seen that servant before. Who is he?

HARUSAME: *(Engrossed in the shell game)* Hmm. It seems like this could be the first verse: "I wonder who that unknown servant is, in the spring rain?" I wonder if this is the matching shell?

HOTARUBI: Yes, I'm quite bewildered. Nishikigi-san, that servant . . .

NISHIKIGI: What servant?

HOTARUBI: *(Looking around)* My goodness, he's gone.

NISHIKIGI: Come now, Hotarubi. You started out playing the shell identifying game, but have you switched to trying to identify your lover's servant?

HOTARUBI: No, not at all.

USUGUMO: This shell matching game is so upper crust. It's not the right game for courtesans. Let's play a game that's more fun.

The MASTER *of the establishment enters from stage right.*

MASTER: Now, now, this is no time to be arguing. You've heard that Lord Utsunomiya is coming to visit Kyoto from the East Country. Well, he's already entered the city and they say he'll pay a ceremonial call on the court this morning. He'll be here soon.. There is a lot to do to get this room ready for him. Go to your own rooms and prepare yourselves. Let's show him how beautiful the finest courtesans in Kyoto can be.

All of the ladies except for HOTARUBI *stand and exit through the sliding doors upstage center.*

MASTER: There now, Hotarubi. Don't let the girls' thoughtless comments upset you, all right?

HOTARUBI: You're always so concerned about how I feel. I'm so happy that you care.

HOTARUBI *too exits through the sliding doors upstage center. The* MASTER *of the establishment remains alone in the room.*

MASTER: My, my, good and bad fortune are so completely beyond our control.

As he ponders the situation, music begins. EBINA *enters along the* hanamichi, *and stops at the seven-three spot.*

EBINA: I haven't been to this neighborhood since I took religious vows, but somehow my legs seem to remember the way all by themselves. *(He strikes his legs with his closed fan.)* Hey, legs! Stop walking so happily. You mustn't resist the progress of age.

Music begins again. EBINA *goes onto the main stage. He knocks on the outer gate. The* MASTER *descends and opens the gate.*

MASTER: My goodness, if it isn't Mr. "Hail to the Buddha" Ebina. What an unexpected visit. Please come in, come in.

They both ascend to the main level of the establishment. After EBINA *enters through the gate and onto the raised stage, a stage assistant removes the gate.*

EBINA: My apologies for having been out of touch for so long.

MASTER: It has been a long time, and your visit is so unexpected. I thought that weasels never took the same path twice. Where is it that you are going now? Surely you must have taken a wrong turn somewhere and lost your way?

EBINA: Please don't talk like that. You can see that I have taken religious vows, and it would be much worse were I to forget my obligations to the Buddha and the Kannon. One can never do as one pleases in this floating world.

MASTER: At least you're not using your age as an excuse. Always the witty one, aren't you, Ebina?

EBINA: Not at all. Today I'm here as a sort of forerunner for a festival carriage. Recently I went to the East country on business. While I was there Lord Utsunomiya approached me with a personal request. He told me that during his upcoming trip to Kyoto he wanted to visit this establishment and meet the renowned Hotarubi. He asked me to arrange everything for him. I just heard that he has already gone to make his formal calls this morning. He'll probably be coming here very soon. I wanted to warn you to prepare for his visit, so I put these old legs in motion and came here to give you some advance warning.

MASTER: Thank you for taking the trouble to come all the way over here, but everything is in readiness for his lordship's visit. So, please put yourself at ease on that score.

EBINA: I'm so relieved to hear you say that. Since all is ready this afternoon, after so long a time apart . . .

MASTER: . . . Let us burn incense to the Bodhisattva, sitting side by side,

EBINA: And intone the Amida Buddha's sutra.

A voice shouts from beyond the hanamichi.

VOICE: Make way for Lord Utsunomiya!

MASTER: My goodness, his lordship is already here.

EBINA: I think we had better go out . . .

MASTER . . . and greet him.

The two descend to the main stage level and sit there. Music plays. ROKUROZAEMON *enters, dressed as a senior samurai advisor. He leads numerous lesser retainers. After them enters* SARUGENJI, *seated astride the horse and splendidly attired. He is impersonating Lord Utsunomiya. The horse stops at the seven-three spot.*

ROKUROZAEMON: This is the establishment at Fifth Avenue and Higashinotōin.

SARUGENJI: *(wobbling slightly in his saddle)* Kyoto looks just as prosperous as I thought it would.

The music resumes. SARUGENJI *enters the main stage, dismounts, and together with his "senior advisor" enters the establishment.*

MASTER: *(Clapping his hands to emphasize his commands)* His lordship has arrived! Go to the storehouse and get our finest sake cup! The lacquer one, with crickets and autumn grasses on it. Tell the courtesans to come out at once! And bring the sake and dishes that were prepared for his retainers. Quickly, quickly!

Inside a voice answers, "Yes, sir!" Lower ranking samurai retainers lead the horse, exiting stage right. From the up-stage sliding painted paper doors the girl apprentice TOMBO *enters, carrying a lacquer tray with the cricket sake cup on it. She is followed by the courtesans,* USUGUMO, HARUSAME, NISHIKIGI, TAKI NO I, *and* RANGIKU. *They sit.* SARUGENJI *stares at them, all agog at their beauty. [As performed by Kanzaburō XVIII* SARUGENJI *staggers from girl to girl, enraptured by each one. When he sits down, he struggles clumsily to remove his swords from his sash and place them by his side.]* EBINA *taps the floor with his fan to warn him to pull himself together. The* MASTER *has* TOMBO *take the cricket sake cup to Lord Utsunomiya.*

MASTER: My good Lord Utsunomiya. I am so grateful that you have come from so far away to grace our establishment. To begin, please partake of sake served in our finest cup. Now, is there anyone among my ladies that you had particularly in mind? I would be pleased to present her to you.

SARUGENJI *fiddles nervously with his sake cup.*

SARUGENJI: I have long heard of Hotarubi, a courtesan so famous that her name is well known even in the far-off East Country. Which of you is Hotarubi? Since you are all so remarkably beautiful, I can't tell which of you she is.

USUGUMO: Sir, I am that Hotarubi.

SARUGENJI: So, you are Hotarubi? *(He is about to offer her sake, but* EBINA *immediately signals with his eyes for* SARUGENJI *to stop.)*

HARUSAME: No, it is I who am Hotarubi. (EBINA *signals that she is not* HOTARUBI *either.)*

MASTER: Now then, stop your teasing. *(He rebukes the two.)* Your lordship, Hotarubi is not yet with us.

SARUGENJI: *(Emphatically)* What? Hotarubi isn't here?

HOTARUBI: *(From behind the up-stage center sliding doors)* I'm here and will join you right now.

HOTARUBI *enters to music. All the other courtesans look jealous.*

SARUGENJI: Aaah. You are the real one for sure!

He is about to stand up to approach her, but EBINA *and* ROKUROZAEMON *signal him not to stand.*

HOTARUBI: I am happy to share a drink with you.

SARUGENJI *is struck dumb with rapture.* HOTARUBI *receives a cup of sake from* TOMBO, *but he just stares at* HOTARUBI, *stupified. [As Kanzaburō XVIII plays it,* SARUGENJI *knocks* TOMBO *out of the way before she is able to pour* sake *for* HOTARUBI, *and pours for her himself.]* HOTARUBI *drinks the sake and offers her cup to* SARUGENJI.

USUGUMO: Truly you barons from the East . . .
HARUSAME: . . . don't let your eyes stray to other pretty flowers.
NISHIKIGI: You rush to pledge your troth with sake.
TAKI NO I: How jealous . . .
ALL: . . . we all are!
USUGUMO: But you know, one of the rules of this house is that we courtesans have the right to request that a newly arrived guest perform for us all. How lucky that you are a warrior from the East. You must be skilled in martial arts. Come on everybody, why don't we ask him to recount for us a tale of his brave deeds in battle.
HARUSAME: What a fine idea, Usugumo. Yes, a tale of battle . . .
ALL: . . . is our request for you.

SARUGENJI, EBINA, *and the "senior retainer" are in a panic.*

USUGUMO: Attention everybody, attention! A tale of battle . . .
ALL: . . . Is about to begin.

Clappers sound to signal the beginning of an independent section of the play. A jōruri *ensemble is revealed at stage left. [When Kanzaburō XVIII performs the play there is much comical pantomime by* SARUGENJI *and the* jōruri *chanter as they attempt to communicate about how to perform the battle narration together. This sort of meta-dramatic conversation between an actor and a musician is almost never done in kabuki plays.] The* shamisen *player begins his prelude.*

SARUGENJI: Well, if that's what you'd like . . .
EBINA: *(Aside)* This will be painful.

EBINA *and* ROKUROZAEMON *slump down and cover their eyes and ears.*

NARRATOR: *(Singing)* He sits in formal position, about to begin the recitation.
SARUGENJI: And so it came to pass, that near the beach at Akashi,

In a splendid full suit of armor, bound with scarlet cords,
Red Snapper Akasuke raised a great war cry.
"You who flee before me are none other than Ohsuke of the Long Fins.
Come back! Return and fight like a fish!"

SARUGENJI *performs dance and pantomime to the following narration.*

NARRATOR: *(Singing)* When summoned thus,
Ohsuke of the Long Fins feared to dishonor his name,
And he turned his head around in the waves.
As he approached, Snapper's soldiers drew their bows to the full,
Shouting, "Shoot him through his fin!"
The two heroes fought bout after bout in the surf
Surrounded by Red Snapper's oyster and clam minions . . .
(Speaking) . . .Who scattered hither and thither in fear.
"Let's grapple again!" shouted Flounder and Snapper,
When a wave threw them both up upon the beach.
(Singing) They fought on and on, covered all over in sand.
Suddenly Flounder shouted, "Take this!,"
And fitting an arrow to his string he pulled and let fly.
The shaft penetrated deep beneath Snapper's fin
And he writhed in agony.
His vassal, Brother Octopus, the Lay Priest,
Cradled Snapper's fish head in his lap and spoke,
(Speaking) If you have last words to say while you yet live,
Entrust them to me, the Octopus Priest."
(Singing) Snapper spoke in tears and stroked his whiskers,
(Speaking) My dear wife knows that this is the fate of a war fish,
But my children are still just roe inside her womb—
I so wanted to see my children alive in this world just one time."
(Singing) Saying this, Snapper tragically expired.
As all the while the salt wind of Akashi . . .
(Speaking) Resounded with cruel clamor of battle.

ALL THE WOMEN: Well done, well done!

USUGUMO: Yes, but what strange names they are: Red Snapper Akasuke, Flounder Ohsuke, and the Lay Priest Octopus. Even among feudal lords and other distinguished patrons, I've never heard names like those before.

SARUGENJI: That battle was my first taste of combat. You were just a little child then, so of course you've heard nothing about it. Now I've fulfilled my side of the house rule, so come, let's share the sake. *(He hands her a sake cup.)*

USUGUMO: I'm happy to drink with you, although I know I'm not the woman you desire.

Figure 13. *The Sardine Seller's Net of Love*, 1990, at the Kabuki-za, with Bandō Tamasaburō as Hotarubi and Nakamura Kanzaburō XVIII as Sarugenji. Photograph courtesy of the Waseda University Tsubouchi Hakase Memorial Theatre Museum.

They exchange cups. SARUGENJI, *beginning to feel the effect of the wine, rests his head on* HOTARUBI'S *lap. The girls signal each other with their eyes, and exit, leaving the two alone.*

HOTARUBI: *(Speaking loudly to* SARUGENJI, *whose head is resting on her lap)* Your lordship, your lordship! It seems you've fallen asleep.

Musical accompaniment from the geza *begins.*

HOTARUBI: I'm embarrassed to admit this, but in this hard life I lead all the men I've met have been like demons. Now I realize that for the first time I'm lucky enough to be with a kind and charming customer and what happens—you ignore me and fall into a drunken sleep. How can you be so heartless?

SARUGENJI *mumbles in his sleep.*

HOTARUBI: My goodness, he seems to be talking in his sleep. I couldn't quite hear what he said, but I think he spoke another woman's name. What a hateful man you are. If you're going to talk in your sleep, at least speak loud enough so I can hear you.

SARUGENJI *groans.*

HOTARUBI: What was that? Oh, you've fallen asleep again, haven't you?

SARUGENJI: *(Though talking in his sleep, speaking vigorously and clearly)* I'm Sarugenji from Ako Inlet in the Province of Ise. Buy my sardines!

HOTARUBI: My goodness, that was strange. The baron shouted some sort of vendor's cry. Something about the Province of Ise. I do hope he does it again so I can figure out what he's saying.

SARUGENJI: *(In his sleep, but in an even bigger voice)* I'm Sarugenji from Ako Inlet in the Province of Ise. Buy my sardines!

HOTARUBI: What? I know that. That's the spiel of a sardine seller. Could that mean that . . .? Now that I think about it, he does seem to smell a bit like sardines. *(She holds her nose.)* What an unexpected aroma his perfume sachet has. Come now, Sardine Lord, I'd like to ask you some questions. Please wake up!

She shakes him awake. SARUGENJI *opens his eyes, sits up, and speaks in a voice heavy with sleep.*

SARUGENJI: I was in heaven while I slept and I'm still in heaven even now that I'm awake. *(He pinches his own cheek.)* I sure hope this isn't a dream.

Figure 14. *The Sardine Seller's Net of Love*, 1954, at the Kabuki-za, with Nakamura Utaemon VI as Hotarubi and Nakamura Kanzaburō XVII as Sarugenji, asleep on her lap. Photograph courtesy of the Waseda University Tsubouchi Hakase Memorial Theatre Museum.

He lies down again on HOTARUBI'S *lap.* HOTARUBI *slaps him and he sits up.*

HOTARUBI: Come on, please wake up. Please! You were talking in your sleep so loudly they can hear it all over the city.
SARUGENJI: *(Alarmed)* What?! Did you say I was talking in my sleep?
HOTARUBI: Yes, and I want to ask you about what you said.
SARUGENJI: *(Trembling)* What do you want to ask me?
HOTARUBI: You're really a sardine seller, aren't you?
SARUGENJI: What? A sardine seller? *(He claps his hand to his mouth.)* Now then, what do you mean by making such an outrageous statement to Utsunomiya no Danjo, renowned baron of the East Country? A sardine seller . . . what might that be? This is the first time I've heard of such a thing since the day they cut my umbilical cord.
HOTARUBI: In that case, let me ask you some questions about what you said in your sleep. First, what do you mean by "Ako Inlet"?
SARUGENJI: Hmm, Ako Inlet . . . yes. I enjoy poetry and it appears that I've recited poetic places in my sleep.
"At Ako Inlet, where girls gather wood for salt fires
If you cast your net again and again they will appear."
I was thinking about that poem when I talked in my sleep.
HOTARUBI: All right. But what does "Sarugenji" mean?
SARUGENJI: Hmm . . . . yes, Sarugenji. Oh, I know. It's from the poem,
"Like the willows at Sarusawa Pond, I'll take a strand of tangled hair,
From my sleeping sweetheart as a keepsake."
Even in my sleep, I said I could love none other than you. But you're subjecting me to such a strict interrogation.
HOTARUBI: I have just one last question for you. *(She can no longer suppress her laughter as she continues.)* In your sleep you said, "buy my sardines." What sort of poetic origin do those words have?
SARUGENJI: Hmm . . . *(He wipes cold sweat from his brow as he mumbles his attempts to put the words into a poem.)* Now then, the words, "buy my sardines," that I said in my sleep . . .
HOTARUBI: Well?
SARUGENJI: Well . . .
HOTARUBI: Well?
SARUGENJI: Well . . .
HOTARUBI: Yes, well! Tell me what they mean!
SARUGENJI: What those words mean . . . yes, that's right! Long ago, the poetess Izumi Shikibu was about to eat a sardine, the fish, called *iwashi.* Just at that moment the courtier Yasumasa arrived. Izumi was embarrassed and hurriedly hid the *iwashi.* When Yasumasa asked her what she had just hidden, she answered with this poem:
"When one thinks of the nation of Japan, surely none of its people

Have failed to visit Iwashimizu Shrine."

How cleverly she concealed her wish for him to ignore the *iwashi* using the name of the shrine. Yasumasa was impressed. His face revealed his sympathy for her and he answered her poem thus,

"Since it is a medicinal fish that warms the body and improves one's looks,

By all means you should partake."

So it was that a fish go-between secured a love that grew even closer over time. I'm so inspired by this happy love affair that I must have spoken about it in my sleep.

HOTARUBI: There could never be a sardine seller who knows poetry as well as you do. I suppose then that you must be the true Lord Utsunomiya Danjō.

SARUGENJI: *(Sighing in relief and rubbing his chest to relax himself)* That's right. I'm Utsunomiya, the genuine article.

HOTARUBI: Then you're not a sardine seller . . . *(She collapses, weeping.)*

SARUGENJI: Why are you crying?

HOTARUBI: Why shouldn't I be crying? I thought you were a sardine seller and it turns out that you are really and truly the baron.

SARUGENJI: But why would that make you cry?

HOTARUBI: I have good reason to feel the way I do, but until now I've told my story to no one but the master of the house.

SARUGENJI: I want to hear your story too. Please tell me.

HOTARUBI: Since you are who you are, I guess I'll tell it to you too.

Jōruri *music begins to play.* HOTARUBI *dances and pantomimes to the accompaniment of the passages delivered by the* jōruri *narration.*

NARRATOR: *(singing)* I will never forget it . . . It was ten long years ago.

HOTARUBI: I was born the daughter of the Lord of Tankaku Castle in the Province of Ki. When I was a young girl I climbed to the highest tower and gazed all around at the scenery.

NARRATOR: Off in the distance, on the high road,
I spied a person carrying some sort of heavy load.
His voice carried beautifully from far away.

HOTARUBI: "Buy sardines! Buy sardines!"

NARRATOR:This is what he cried.
Suddenly my heart was filled with yearning
And it was as if my soul had left my body in pursuit.
I stole out of the castle through a secret passageway
And rushed off in the direction of the voice.

HOTARUBI: But though I hurried on and on it was as though a strong headwind blew against me. I could hear his voice, but he got farther and farther away. I wanted to stop him and tell him of my love, but . . .

NARRATOR: Soon I was in the shadow of the trees
And his voice was drowned out by the cicadas' raucous trill.
I couldn't see anything.

HOTARUBI: Looking about, it was already dusk. I was lost and as I lay crying I heard the honest-sounding voice of a tradesman speaking to me, offering assistance.

NARRATOR: But the kind-seeming traveler was a slave trader,
A demon in human guise. He captured me
And sold me straight off to this brothel.

HOTARUBI: I've managed to live on here for ten long years, and although I've become a high-ranking courtesan, I still recall the sardine seller's loud, clear voice.

NARRATOR: The sardine seller is my one true love.
Day and night I pray to merciful Kannon to lead me to him.
I so want to meet this humble sardine seller
And become his wife. How I long for him.

HOTARUBI: I thought that today the Wheel of Karma had brought me my salvation, but when I learned that you in fact . . .

NARRATOR: . . . Are a samurai lord, I realized that
I am doomed to a terrible fate
No matter how long I live on in this useless, floating world.

HOTARUBI: I have no more to say. My lord, I bid you farewell.

She pulls out the dagger that samurai ladies always carry and attempts to stab herself. [Or, as currently staged, she uses one of SARUGENJI'S *swords that is lying nearby.]* SARUGENJI *is startled, but manages to intervene and physically prevent her from harming herself with the dagger/sword.*

SARUGENJI: Don't be rash, my lady Hotarubi!

HOTARUBI: No, please let me die!

SARUGENJI: I'm telling you not to go through with it because in truth I am your sardine seller! My robes and swords come from a rental shop. I am of humble birth and my name is Sarugenji.

HOTARUBI: No, no please don't try to deceive me again. I would rather die!

SARUGENJI: Oh please, don't panic! Stay calm!

SARUGENJI *himself is in a panic as he shouts the above lines, all the while tussling with* HOTARUBI. *The upstage sliding doors open and* EBINA, ROKUROZAEMON, *and the* MASTER *enter.*

EBINA: Hotarubi, I heard everything. My son, Sarugenji, is indeed a sardine seller. Because he told me that he wanted so much to meet you, our plan was to turn him into a counterfeit baron. He is a fine young man who loves reading poetry and is himself an excellent poet. And now I have heard from the master all about you and who you are.

ROKUROZAEMON: I am dressed as the lord's retainer but really I'm a horse trader. The chestnut mare that I couldn't sell was useful to my friend, so I joined in the plot and became a fake samurai.

HOTARUBI: So, are you really the sardine vendor?

SARUGENJI: Yes. I carry my load like this.

Using his long sword, SARUGENJI *mimes carrying a load of sardines around the room.*

HOTARUBI: Oh merciful Kannon, how can I ever express my thanks. *(She clasps her hands in prayer.)*

SARUGENJI: From today you are my wife.

HOTARUBI: *(Embracing* SARUGENJI*)* Can this be a dream? I'm so happy.

MASTER: But it will cost two hundred pieces of gold to redeem her.

EBINA: This is a real problem.

ROKUROZAEMON: But what can we do . . .

ALL FOUR: . . . to raise the money?

They silently ponder the problem. Presently a lively drum pattern is played in the geza. JIRŌTA, *a samurai retainer from Tankaku Castle, enters from stage right. He was on stage earlier in this act, disguised as a gardener. Now he is dressed in splendid samurai robes. He has captured the fake samurai in* SARUGENJI'S *retinue and tied them one to another, like a string of beads. He leads them on-stage by a rope.*

JIRŌTA: Princess, I am exceedingly delighted to see that you are in good health. I have witnessed everything from my hiding place in the shadows. I have also captured these false samurai. Now I must beg you to return to Tankaku Castle at your earliest possible convenience.

HOTARUBI: *(Speaking like a princess)* Aren't you the gardener who was here earlier?

JIRŌTA: Yes. My true name is Jirōta and I am a retainer of your clan. Your father and mother ordered me to search for you. I disguised myself as a gardener and sneaked into this establishment to spy it out. We can ascertain your identity for certain using this inscription. If it matches the inscription known to be on the miniature Kannon figurine that the princess had in her possession, then you are the true princess.

HOTARUBI: I have the Kannon figurine right here.

She takes a gold brocade packet from her kimono fold and removes a Kannon figurine made of pure gold. She gives it to the MASTER *who hands it to* JIRŌTA. JIRŌTA *compares the inscription on the figurine with the inscription he has brought with him.*

JIRŌTA: Yes, they do indeed match.
HOTARUBI: Since they match, return the figurine to me.

JIRŌTA *hands the figurine back to the* MASTER *who returns it to* HOTARUBI. HOTARUBI *prays to the Kannon once again in thanks, then carefully puts the figurine away.*

HOTARUBI: Jirōta, untie the false samurai.
JIRŌTA: Yes my lady, but why on earth...
HOTARUBI: I ordered you to untie them, so untie them at once!

JIRŌTA *grudgingly unties the false samurai.*

HOTARUBI: Now then, Jirōta, since you have urged me to return to the castle, I assume that you have brought with you the money necessary to pay off my contract. Am I correct?
JIRŌTA: Yes, my lady, I have 250 gold coins here with me.
HOTARUBI: Then be a good fellow and pay 200 gold coins to the master of this establishment.
JIRŌTA: Yes, my lady.

He gives 200 gold coins in a packet to the MASTER.

SARUGENJI: This is wonderful!
HOTARUBI: That's not all. *(She points at* ROKUROZAEMON.*)* Give the remaining fifty gold coins to this horse trader.
JIRŌTA: Why on earth should I do that?
HOTARUBI: Do you mean to challenge your master?
JIRŌTA: No, my lady.
HOTARUBI: Mr. Rokurozaemon, you have just sold your chestnut horse. Bring it here and give it to Jirōta.
ROKUROZAEMON: Oh, thank-you so much! *(He quickly leaves the building and returns, leading the horse.)*
JIRŌTA: My goodness, there's no telling what she'll do next.

HOTARUBI *takes* SARUGENJI'S *hand and the two descend the steps and approach* JIRŌTA.

HOTARUBI: Now then, Jirōta, tell me—are my father and mother both well?
JIRŌTA: Yes, my lady, both are enjoying excellent health.
HOTARUBI: In that case I want you to convey to them what I am about to tell you. I, Hotarubi, am going to marry this sardine seller. It is a wifely commandment that once a woman leaves her parental gate, she must

never again return home. In the future I will go with my honored husband to sell sardines in the Province of Ki. I will call out, "Buy sardines!" beneath Tankaku Castle. Please tell my parents that at that time they should stand high on the castle tower and they can see me.

JIRŌTA: Oh my god! What a calamity—you have turned heaven and earth upside down! Princess! Princess! Please don't go through with this.

JIRŌTA *clutches at* HOTARUBI'S *sleeve, but she shakes free.* HOTARUBI *and* SARUGENJI *walk toward the* hanamichi. JIRŌTA *begins to follow them.*

HOTARUBI: *(to* JIRŌTA*)* Kneel before me and move no further. Kneel I say!

JIRŌTA: Yes, my lady.

HOTARUBI *and* SARUGENJI *walk to the seven-three spot on the* hanamichi.

HOTARUBI: Now then, Lord Genji...no, I should say, "husband, dear" . . .

SARUGENJI: Yes, ma'am. *(He bows abjectly.)*

HOTARUBI: What are you doing, my dear? From today we are sardine-selling husband and wife. Please teach me your sales call.

SARUGENJI: All right. Listen carefully. *(He straightens up and calls out in a clear voice.)* "I'm from Ako Inlet in the Province of Ise! Buy my sardines!"

HOTARUBI: Let me try. How about this? "I'm from Ako Inlet in the Province of Ise! Buy my sardines!" *(They repeat it several times before she gets it right. She turns to face the main stage.)* Come on everybody, why not give it a try?

On the main stage JIRŌTA, *the* MASTER, EBINA, *the false samurai, and* ROKUROZAEMON, *who is holding the horse by a rope at stage right, all raise their voices and cry out.*

ALL: "I'm from Ako Inlet in the Province of Ise! Buy my sardines!"

HOTARUBI: Oh, you all called out so beautifully.

JIRŌTA: All is lost! I must atone for my failure.

He draws his sword and thrusts it towards his abdomen. Everyone except HOTARUBI *is in a state of shock.* EBINA *runs over to* JIRŌTA *and discovers that* JIRŌTA *is uninjured.* EBINA *seizes the sword and inspects it.*

EBINA: Of course it couldn't cut anything. It's as dull and rusty as a red sardine. Now then, daughter-in-law . . .

HOTARUBI: . . . Mr. Ebina. From now on, as husband and wife, we shall spend our evenings at Ako Inlet, matching shells and their poems.

SARUGENJI: The dish accompanying our nuptial sake . . .
ROKUROZAEMON: . . . will be sardines laid side by side, auspiciously leaving the heads and tails on.
MASTER: What good fortune for you to be able to say farewell to the pleasure quarter.
JIRŌTA: This is all too cruel. *(He sighs dejectedly and* EBINA *looks at him.)*
EBINA: Yes, today we have seen the secrets of the magnificent art . . . *(The rapping of* ki *sticks begins, announcing the impending end of the play.)* . . . of buying and selling merchandise.

Drums join the sticks in a lively rhythm as the curtain closes, leaving only SARUGENJI *and* HOTARUBI *still visible at the seven-three spot on the* hanamichi. *The drumming becomes quieter.* HOTARUBI *takes out her Kannon figurine. She unwraps it and prays to it.* SARUGENJI *takes her arm and leads her off, down the* hanamichi. *They exit together.*

CURTAIN

Figure 15. *The Sardine Seller's Net of Love,* 1973, at the Kabuki-za. Sarugenji (Nakamura Kanzaburō XVII) and Hotarubi (Nakamura Utaemon VI) exit together at the end of the play. Photograph courtesy of the Waseda University Tsubouchi Hakase Memorial Theatre Museum.

The Blush on the White Hibiscus Blossom: Lady Fuyo and the True Account of the Ōuchi Clan

(Fuyo no Tsuyu Ōuchi Jikki)

(a kabuki play)

Based on Jean Racine's "Phaedra"
First Published in 1955, First Performed in 1955
Translated by Mark Oshima

INTRODUCTION

Among all the world's plays, Mishima's favorite was Racine's *Phaedra*.[1] He had been planning an adaptation to kabuki for some years, and finally realized his dream in November, 1955, with *The Blush on the White Hibiscus Blossom: Lady Fuyo and the True Account of the Ōuchi Clan (Fuyo no Tsuyu Ōuchi Jikki)*. Mishima reset the play in medieval Japan because he believed that epic tales from native traditions have a more powerful effect on audiences than do translated works about foreign cultures,[2] and of course because kabuki acting requires traditional Japanese dress. He realized that the "structures of kabuki and Racinian drama are as different as oil and water,"[3] and that it would be a difficult challenge to craft a strong kabuki play from his beloved original. In fact, Mishima was working with two original plays—first and foremost Racine's *Phaedra*, and secondarily the play Racine had used has his own source work, Euripides' *Hippolytus*.

Racine's version changes the focus from Hippolytus to his stepmother, Phaedra, second wife of King Theseus of Athens. In Racine's *Phaedra*, Hippolytus, a worshipper of Diana, goddess of the hunt, is ordered by his father to the town of Troezon in the Peloponnesus, where Phaedra fled years ago in an attempt to cool the fiery passion she feels for her stepson. This passion has been set upon her by Venus, who is using Phaedra as a vehicle to ensnare Hippolytus to punish him for refusing to worship her. When messengers arrive at Troezon with information that Theseus is dead, Phaedra's nurse, Oenone, urges her mistress to relieve the agony of her passion for Hippolytus by revealing it to him. Hippolytus is appalled by Phaedra's confession of love and flees from his immoral stepmother. Hippolytus is in love with Aricia, a cousin whom his father has banished as a potential usurper of the throne.

The news of the king's death proves mistaken, and Theseus arrives in Troezon. Phaedra's nurse convinces Phaedra to slander Hippolytus to his father, by accusing the young man of attempting to rape her. Theseus believes the story, flies into a rage, and not only banishes his son without giving him a chance to defend his honor, but also calls on his patron god, Neptune, to kill him. Only when it is too late does Phaedra admit her slander to the king. Hippolytus is killed by Neptune, Phaedra and her nurse commit suicide, and Theseus is left bereft and in anguish.

Mishima's approach to his adaptation was to streamline the story while at the same time making the staging more ornate. He eliminated three central elements from Racine's story: (1) The divine. In both Racine and Euripides, Phaedra's lust for Hippolytus is instilled in her by Venus, and although her body burns with uncontrollable desire, she knows that it comes from outside herself and attempts to fight it using various strategems. For Lady Fuyo there is no external agent for her desire for her stepson, Harumochi. (2) There is no succession dispute in Mishima's version. Unlike Phaedra, Fuyo has no children, and so is not a political enemy of Harumochi. Theseus' ambivalence concerning succession by sons of two different wives is not an issue in Mishima's play. (3) In Mishima's play there is no equivalent to the Aricia character. Racine added Aricia to his version, and Mishima wrote that he preferred the Euripidean version because a Hippolytus in love with a woman other than Phaedra was too commonplace.[4]

The elimination of Aricia made it possible for Mishima to develop his own new theme in *Lady Fuyo*: the pure, masculine realm of battle as opposed to the sordid realm of heterosexual love. Harumochi's sexual purity was the basis for Mishima's wonderful death monologue by Lady Fuyo in which she gazes at the night sky and sees Harumochi among the stars. But Mishima failed to compensate for the absence of an Aricia character in other parts of the play. In Racine, Phaedra's hatred of Hippolytus after he has spurned her only reaches murderous dimensions when she learns that he is not the pure, sexless man she thought, but is deeply in love with another woman

Even more importantly, Aricia's existence allowed Racine to craft a satisfying conclusion to his drama and Mishima was unable to compensate for her absence here. Theseus has regarded Aricia as a deadly rival in the succession dispute, but following Hippolytus' dying wish, Theseus resolves to take her in and love her as a daughter. In this way harmony will be restored to Athens. Mishima's conclusion is much less satisfying for audiences. Yoshitaka tells Fuyo that he will have lies written into the family history, saying that Harumochi died bravely in battle. Fuyo replies that this will allow her the peace of mind necessary to achieve Buddhist salvation, and then she expires. This falsification of the Ōuchi family history gives the play half of its title.

Mishima followed the plot of the original very closely, with the action of the tragedy completed in a single evening. He carefully preserved unity of time, place, and action. Both *Phaedra* and *Lady Fuyo* rely on a string of disastrous coincidences so impeccably timed as to be almost ridiculous. If a messenger enters a moment too soon, or Hippolytus lingers a minute longer with Phaedra, the crucial misunderstandings and mishaps become impossible, and all ends happily. Occasionally Mishima used some very lame excuses for his sudden entrances and exits. For example, before the crucial nurse-lying-to-Yoshitaka scene, Harumochi rushes from Fuyo's room all afluster and even forgets his sword. Why? Because he does not want his father to see him wearing armor. After his stepmother's confession of incestuous lust, no one, not even a prude like Harumochi, could worry this much about wearing armor in the presence of even a very stern father.

The major character in the work is of course Lady Fuyo, played in 1955 by Nakamura Utaemon, Mishima's favorite kabuki actor. "Fuyo" is a kind of hibiscus flower, and "Dew on the Hibiscus" in the title suggests moisture, which in kabuki represents sexual love. The dew also causes the white hibiscus to tinge pink, suggesting the rise of passion in an otherwise chaste woman. Utaemon found Lady Fuyo the most difficult character to play of the four Mishima roles he had done to that time.[5] This was probably because the motivation for Fuyo's feelings and actions were hard to grasp. For example, Lady Fuyo's anger at Harumochi when she meets him for the first time in the play reads in the text as if it is genuine, but we learn later that it is feigned in an attempt to put Harumochi off so that he will not come close enough for Fuyo's lust to burn out of control. At the same time Lady Fuyo, unlike Phaedra who wants Hippolytus to leave her city, insists that Harumochi not go to battle because she loves him and wants to have him safe and nearby. This kind of contradictory action based on the same emotion must have taxed even the resources of a great actor like Utaemon. The roles of Phaedra and Lady Fuyo are the same at their core. Each woman struggles between the opposing forces of conscience and forbidden carnal desire. Each wants to do the right thing but is vulnerable to the terrible and attractive advice of her nurse, who urges entreating, and then destroying, the object of her love. Both Phaedra and Fuyo are absolved, dying by their own hands in atonement for the unjust murder of the men they desired, having finally told the truth to their husbands.

Harumochi is more like Euripides' Hippolytus than Racine's. He is entirely chaste, interested only in hunting and war. He is proper to a fault, thinking only of his father's injunction against wearing armor when attention to his stepmother's feelings might have saved everyone. This overblown sense of propriety induces him to go off and commit ritual suicide, which is understood in kabuki as the ultimate statement of either innocence or responsibility. Racine's Theseus is complex and satisfying. Though initially stupid, insensitive, and rash in his judgments, after he realizes he has foolishly destroyed his son, he is self-recriminatory. His first inclination is to run away and live out his life as an anonymous, penitent beggar, but in the end he realizes he cannot and must not be so weak. He retains his kingship, and makes amends by taking Aricia as his daughter, thus restoring peace to his kingdom. Mishima's Yoshitaka was too thin as initially written, and Ichikawa En'ō, the actor playing Yoshitaka, demanded that Mishima improve the role, which Mishima did.[6] Even so, Yoshitaka is not so satisfying a character as Racine's Theseus. His negative qualities are the same, but his self-realization is ambiguous. All that he does to make amends for the ruin he has wrought is to have lies written in the clan history book.

For *Lady Fuyo,* as *Hell Screen,* Mishima made a point of using the *gidayū* narrator to explain the feelings and motivations of the major characters. This was very important to Mishima, but it was difficult to put into effective use in performance. Emotions and motivations are best demonstrated by action onstage, or spoken by characters themselves, not simply related by a narrator. Traditional kabuki and *bunraku* combined all three approaches for important characters, in a sort of one-two-three punch. When Mishima uses *gidayū* recitation to reinforce emotions demonstrated by his characters, the play effectively conveys powerful emotions, but when *gidayū* assumes the burden alone, it is less successful.

Racinian drama has a small number of characters onstage at any one time, but kabuki is a grand spectacle. Mishima added retainers and ladies-in-waiting necessary to stage his play as kabuki. In one particularly effective scene Fuyo orders her ladies to prevent Harumochi from departing for battle, and they surround him and "battle" him, wielding branches of flowers. It is ironic that Harumochi, who so longs for the purity of samurai battle, is only able to fight with "immoral" women before he dies.

Greek and Racinian drama rarely depicts violent action onstage, using the accounts of messengers to relay dramatic actions like battles, shipwrecks, and in *Phaedra,* the nurse's drowning, and the death of Hippolytus in a chariot crash caused by Neptune. Kabuki too has its occasional messenger scenes, but more often action is depicted onstage, before the eyes of the audience, using dance, music, and spectacle. Mishima favored the Racinian approach in this play, with messengers reporting Theseus' death, Theseus' survival and return, and Harumochi's ritual suicide. The result is that there is less onstage action in this play than in any other kabuki play by Mishima, and this too contributed to its lukewarm reception.

Mishima was dismissive of the ambiguous and negative reviews of *Lady Fuyo,* saying, "the reviewers know nothing."[7] For this play, though, perhaps Mishima knew too much. Mishima wrote that he wanted to preserve certain elements of the original work in his play, for example, that Harumochi, like Hippolytus, is a worshipper of the goddess of the hunt,[8] but nowhere in the play is it stated that Harumochi's hunting has any relationship to any god. Similarly, Lady Fuyo praises her nurse for taking poison rather than dying by beheading, and the audience never understands why Fuyo is impressed. Only those who have read *Phaedra* know that a slower, more painful death by poison represents a stronger sense of remorse and responsibility.

For all of its weaknesses, *Lady Fuyo* is a play of passion, violence, vindication, and absolution. A comparison with *The Lighthouse*, Mishima's other *Phaedra* adaptation, demonstrates Mishima's conviction in the late forties and early fifties, that *shingeki* was antithetical to classical drama, and better used for plays about the repression and suppression of passion, whereas kabuki and *gidayū* were better suited to acts of violence and the direct expression of intense emotions.

NOTES

1. Mishima Yukio, "Gikyoku o kakitagaru shosetsukaki no nooto," *Nihon Engeki*, September 18, 1949; reprinted in *Mishima hyōron zenshū*, vol. 3 (Tokyo: Shinchō, 1994), p. 615.
2. Mishima Yukio, "Fuyo no Tsuyu Ouchi Jikki ni tuite," Kabuki-za program, November 1955; reprinted in *Mishima hyōron zenshū*, vol. 3, p. 874.
3. Ibid., p. 873.
4. Ibid., p. 874.
5. Nakamura Utaemon, "Mishima Kabuki no sekai," in Mishima Yukio, *Shibai nikki* (Tokyo: Chūō Kōronsha, 1991), pp. 194–95.
6. Ibid., p. 195.
7. Ibid., p. 194.
8. Mishima, "Fuyo no Tsuyu Ouchi Jikki ni tuite," p. 874.

THE CHARACTERS

Ōuchi Ukyo-no-tayu YOSHITAKA, lord of the Ōuchi clan
Ōuchi Shinnosuke HARUMOCHI, his son
OBATA no Shirō, an old retainer of Harumochi
A young boy who is Harumochi's sword-bearer
Several samurai retainers
Several ladies-in-waiting
HAZUE, a lady-in-waiting
KARAFUJI, senior lady-in-waiting and former nurse to Lady Fuyo
LADY FUYO, wife of the lord of the Ōuchi clan

SETTING

The private quarters of the mansion of the family ruling the Ōuchi clan in the domain of Suo [part of present-day Yamaguchi prefecture on the southwest end of the main Japanese island of Honshu] in autumn, the seventh month of Tenmon 12 (1543)

The set represents the Kameyama mansion of the Ōuchi clan in the country of Suo. Most of the back of the stage is a high platform, representing the inner quarters of the mansion of the Ōuchi clan. There are stairs to the platform at stage center. Along the back wall are sliding paper doors covered with delicate, Chinese-style ink paintings. The beams of the transom, railings, and stairs are painted to look like elegant, shiny black lacquer. Stage left, there is a room set off by sliding shoji *screens covered with thin paper and with shiny black frames. Stage right, the front end of the platform continues as a narrow veranda that is one of the entrance passages to the room. In the garden is a cotton rose tree* (fuyo)*, covered with white blossoms. [Translator's note: The* fuyo *is a kind of hibiscus and not only gives its name to Lady Fuyo, but is a symbol of her character as well. The* fuyo *has blossoms that are white or pale pink and open in the morning and close at night. Some varieties even have blossoms that begin as white, but gradually grow red. The word* fuyo *is also a literary name for the lotus, which is the flower of the Buddha's paradise.]*

With claps of the ki *wooden clappers, the curtain is pulled open to delicate koto music suggesting the women's quarters of the mansion of a high-ranking samurai lord. As soon as the curtain opens, the* gidayū NARRATOR *and* shamisen *player begin describing the scene in song.*

NARRATOR: This is the mansion of a mighty lord, but the lord is absent; his family left behind in loneliness. The master left for battle early this year. Many months have passed. Autumn has come with no sign of his return. The ancient Lord Rinsei of the Korean kingdom of Kudara was the ancestor of the mighty Ōuchi clan. Now the present lord wields power over seven provinces of Japan.

Harumochi, the son of the lord of the Ōuchi clan, returns from a hunting trip with his retainers. But his heart is filled with darkness greater than the shadows in the grasses where he hunts.

HARUMOCHI *enters along the* hanamichi *runway in hunting costume, carrying a bow and arrows. His senior retainer* OBATA NO SHIRŌ *is also in hunting costume.* ATTENDANTS *follow, carrying deer, rabbits and pheasants and the like.* HARUMOCHI *stops at the* shichi-san *or "seven-three spot" [the point on the* hanamichi *runway three-tenths of the distance from the stage and seven-tenths from the* agemaku *curtain at the back of the hall where actors make their entrance]. His retinue sits respectfully on the* hanamichi.

HARUMOCHI: Distant are the clouds on the peaks of the mountains above our hunting fields, but more distant still is the country of Izumo. Even now, my father is there battling the Amago clan. But due to the severe counsel of Lady Fuyo, my honored stepmother, I wait here uselessly, prevented from joining the battle. What use is it to have been born to the way of a warrior . . .

NARRATOR: *(As the* NARRATOR *speaks for him, the actor accentuates the words by holding out his bow and arrow.)* " . . . When I cannot shoot my arrows at the enemy? My fighting strength is expended in vain against the birds and beasts of the field." Obata no Shirō is moved by his master's plight.

OBATA: Ah my young master, truly you are a warrior fit to command an army. If your late mother were to see you now, how happy she would be. But ever since your father took Lady Fuyo as his wife, fortune has been against my young lord. You must wait until the heavens smile upon you again . . .

NARRATOR: ". . . Now, patience is vital."

HARUMOCHI: I am loath to call Lady Fuyo mother, but still it is sad that she is so ill. Fortunately we have had a good hunt. Let us present these beasts and fowl to her and restore her spirits.

OBATA: Truly, this will be a good deed for your father's sake as well. If Lady Fuyo is well disposed toward you, this may be the time to ask her to intercede with your father, so that you can go to battle . . .

NARRATOR: ". . . That will be your opportunity." These words give courage to Harumochi.

HARUMOCHI: Indeed! Well spoken, Obata. Follow me, men!

NARRATOR: He gives his orders with the ease of a born leader. But this assault is not on the Amago clan, but is to storm the fortress of Lady Fuyo's heart and win her support for him to become a true warrior. Lady Fuyo is impassive, but she is filled with secret emotion. The constant burden has brought on illness. Her face has the marks of nobility and she greets her stepson with the strictest etiquette.

The central sliding screen doors open and LADY FUYO *enters, accompanied by* KARAFUJI, *her nurse when young and now her senior lady-in-waiting, and her other* LADIES-IN-WAITING.

HARUMOCHI: I have just returned to the mansion from hunting. We left as it was just growing light and here are the birds and animals that I shot. Please accept this offering.

NARRATOR: At his words, Lady Fuyo's face only expresses displeasure. She gazes into the distance and does not deign to answer. Harumochi is angered at being slighted so. Sensing his lord's feelings, Obata hastens to speak.

During the above narration, one of the attendants hands a pheasant to KARAFUJI *while other attendants place the deer, rabbits and other animals by the stairs to the platform.* LADY FUYO *ignores them.* HARUMOCHI *is upset at this rejection and looks angrily at* LADY FUYO. *She turns away to avoid his eyes.* OBATA *tugs at* HARUMOCHI'S *sleeve to restrain him.*

OBATA: Harumochi, you must make your request to our lady now.

HARUMOCHI: Mother, I know that I have not pleased you, but I beg you to ask father to allow me to participate in my first battle.

NARRATOR: No sooner does he speak than Lady Fuyo's face reddens, like the changing colors of the delicate hibiscus blossom. She is visibly angered.

LADY FUYO: You wish to go into battle? Truly these are unpleasant words! This is clearly a sign that you wish to kill me with a curse. Wait until I am dead and gone. You will not have long to wait. Then you can go fight the Amago clan. Fight in China, India, wherever you want! That will be the time for your first battle. Do not rush! Do not rush! You must not rush to your death.

HARUMOCHI: I do not know what you mean by saying that I have put a curse on you. Why would I want to put a curse on you?

NARRATOR: As he protests, she looks at him carefully.

LADY FUYO: Then let me speak. *(From this point, elegant* shamisen *music from the* geza, *stage right, accompanies her speech.)* You carry a fearsome bow, loathsome arrows for hunting. You have presented these bloody carcasses as an offering to your mother . . .

NARRATOR: ". . . What is the true meaning of these suspicious actions?"

LADY FUYO *draws the carcass of the pheasant toward her with her fan and gazes at it, delicately shielding her mouth with her sleeve.*

LADY FUYO: From ancient times, the pheasant has been the symbol of a mother. The poets of old wrote of the mother pheasant rushing into a burning field at the cries of her children. You have imagined that this pheasant is me and you have killed without mercy. This bloody sacrifice is a spell to pray for my destruction. Is that not so?

NARRATOR: Harumochi is astonished by her hysterical suspicions. He grasps his bow so tightly that it might break. He is unable to utter a word.

OBATA: Clearly your mother is feeling unwell. Let us withdraw for the time being.

HARUMOCHI: But we cannot leave things like this.

OBATA: Please, my lord! Leave everything to me.

NARRATOR: Obata comforts his master. He is truly the model of a wise retainer. They both brood on what has passed, as they withdraw to the back.

OBATA *restrains* HARUMOCHI *and urges him to go.* HARUMOCHI *exits stage left and* OBATA *exits stage right. The* ATTENDANTS *leave the pheasant where it is, but take the other animals with them as they follow* HARUMOCHI *off stage left.*

NARRATOR: Finally the tension drains from Lady Fuyo and she trembles, gasping for breath.

LADY FUYO: Perhaps because of the coming of autumn, now, even more than usual, I feel the fragility of human life. I know that I am not long for this world. Karafuji, I have something I wish to tell you before I die. My ladies-in-waiting, please give us a few moments of privacy.

LADIES-IN-WAITING: As you wish. *(They leave.)*

NARRATOR: Lady Fuyo looks warily around her. She wishes to be absolutely sure that no one can hear what she has to say.

LADY FUYO: Karafuji, please come close. *(To music from the* geza.*)* What I am about to reveal to you is something that I had long vowed to keep forever secret. Please consider these as nothing more than the delirious words of one suffering a great chill or overcome with a severe fever. What do you think is the cause of my illness?

NARRATOR: At her words, Karafuji hides her tears. She laughs to try to encourage Lady Fuyo, but how hollow is her laughter.

KARAFUJI: My lady, it is obvious to one who serves as close to you as I do. Since our lord left to do battle, every day you have seemed weaker and weaker. May I be so bold as to suggest that you must be longing for your beloved husband. I am certain that the moment he returns victorious, you will recover completely. There is no need to ask the opinion of a physician.

LADY FUYO: Were that the cause of my illness, the cure would be simple. But my affliction is one that will cause me to be abandoned by the greatest physicians and midwives. My illness is none other than this.

NARRATOR: She pulls the pheasant into her lap and embraces it. Karafuji is shocked at the sight.

KARAFUJI: That is the pheasant that Harumochi hunted down, the pheasant that you condemned as a sign that he was plotting to kill you.

LADY FUYO: This pheasant is the mother; the hunter my son . . .

NARRATOR: ". . . The hunter was beckoned by the cry of the pheasant . . ."

LADY FUYO: . . . The shaft plunged deep. This hunting arrow left a great wound.

KARAFUJI: *(Exclaims in shock.)*

LADY FUYO: Even though I did not give birth to this child, this is a love that rejects the way of heaven and the way of man. My illness is caused by Harumochi. Karafuji, can you understand the way I feel.

NARRATOR: The waters of her heart rush together and threaten to overflow all barriers. Karafuji is astonished.

KARAFUJI: My lady, I am surprised at what I hear! When Harumochi wanted to go into battle for the first time, no matter how he begged his father to let him go, you always refused to give your permission. Everyone knows of the deep disharmony between you and your stepson.

LADY FUYO: I could not bear to let him go to war. Ever since this war began

I have been terrified that I would lose him forever. I've done all I can to keep him from going.

KARAFUJI: Not only that, but you have always treated Harumochi with such coldness. I cannot believe that you are in love with the man that you have always kept at such a distance.

LADY FUYO: The only way I could avoid stepping off of the path of virtue was to harden my heart like a demon's and pretend to be an evil stepmother tormenting her hated stepchild . . .

NARRATOR: ". . . Oh, that he would believe me to be his enemy and hate me . . . "

LADY FUYO: . . . Then I could be impaled by the blade of the person I love so passionately. How happy I would be to die so. But all my hopes have been in vain. Try though I do to stop it, the grasses of love grow thicker and thicker . . .

NARRATOR: ". . . The gossamer illusions that float before my eyes have no substance. I shall perish as one pursuing phantasms . . ."

LADY FUYO: . . . To what depths of degradation have I fallen! Now I barely have the strength to go on living.

NARRATOR: Her sleeves and jet-black hair are like the moist wings of a bird in agony. Her passion is driving her to madness and destruction. Karafuji bends her head in thought.

KARAFUJI: Harumochi is now nineteen. His emotions are strong, but he is like a straight and tall tree. He shows no sign of love of women, but only turns his eyes to hunting and to warfare. Truly he is a child bestowed by Bishamon, the god of war. But he cannot stand the slightest deviation from the straight path of morality, even straying by so much as the width of a hair. What can be done?

NARRATOR: Just as Karafuji is lost in thought, the lady-in-waiting Hazue comes stumbling down from the tower of the castle.

The lady-in-waiting HAZUE *comes from the raised passageway stage right. She is dressed comically. [Translator's note: Often in kabuki, there are comic female characters to set off the more beautiful or more tragic characters around them. They are usually in green kimonos, suggesting a rustic character and, instead of being played by* onnagata *actors who specialize in female roles, are usually played by actors who specialize in male roles.]* HAZUE'S *kimono skirts are tucked up and her sleeves are tied back with tasuki cords. She bows respectfully in the passageway.*

HAZUE: Lady Fuyo, something terrible has happened.

LADY FUYO: What do you mean? (HAZUE'S *report is accompanied by lively music from the* gidayū *ensemble.)*

HAZUE: Please hear my tale. *(She goes down to the forestage.)* Since this spring, I have been lovers with Kamon, the samurai keeping watch in the highest tower of the castle . . .

NARRATOR: ". . . We have promised ourselves to each other as husband and wife . . ."

HAZUE: . . . And now, it is the first day of autumn . . .

NARRATOR: ". . . We gazed at the fields of beautiful autumn grasses from the highest tower. The long stalks of pampas grass seemed like beckoning hands celebrating our happiness."

KARAFUJI: Please be serious. I thought something really terrible had happened and instead, we have to hear all about your love affairs.

The actor playing KARAFUJI *takes this opportunity to put the pheasant on the side of the stage.*

HAZUE: No, it's what I saw next that is a great calamity for our house. On the outskirts of the town below our castle, along the river in the valley, we saw scores of soldiers.

KARAFUJI: Is this an army from the enemy come to attack in the absence of our lord?

HAZUE: No, they are our own forces, but the few horses left are all staggering . . .

NARRATOR: ". . . and our few remaining men were all walking wearily on foot, stumbling this way and that. They looked like drunken merrymakers returning from viewing the cherry blossoms in spring . . ."

HAZUE: . . . But strangest of all was the banner at the head of the procession. It was black!

LADY FUYO: Black? The banner was black? Hazue, are you absolutely sure?

HAZUE: Yes, I saw that strange black banner very clearly.

LADY FUYO: That is the black banner passed down in our family from our founding ancestors in the Korean kingdom of Kudara. I have long heard that this banner is used to announce that the lord of the domain has been killed in battle. Does this mean that my lord has been killed in battle? *(Lets out a long cry of shock and anguish.)*

NARRATOR: Lady Fuyo and Karafuji cry out in shock. Hazue is confused by the terrible meaning of her report.

HAZUE: What, our lord has died in battle? You mean he's gotten himself killed? Oh dear, I can't stay here any longer.

NARRATOR: So saying, she runs back to her post.

HAZUE *exits stage right.*

NARRATOR: Lady Fuyo stares emptily in shock. It is as though her existing lament has found a new one to add to it and they are like her heavily brocaded robes, nested one atop another. Karafuji quietly approaches Lady Fuyo with great respect.

KARAFUJI: My lady, I understand the great depth of your grief. However, they say that good fortune and bad fortune are braided together like an intricate cord. Our lord is dead, but this can erase the sinfulness of your secret desire. Now if you were to enjoy the grass by the side of the road as you wish, what crime would this be?

LADY FUYO: Karafuji! How can you even suggest such a thing. Now I must take holy orders as a nun as befits a young widow. How can you make such an indecent suggestion before I have even donned the robes of mourning? Karafuji, control yourself!

KARAFUJI: My lady, *before* you don robes of mourning is precisely when your chance will come. You have been released from your previous bonds and have yet to take on new restraints. This is the only opportunity to reveal your long-hidden desires to Harumochi. Your spirit has been weakened by our sudden loss, but his spirit has been weakened as well. He may now be prepared to accept your love.

LADY FUYO: Please be quiet! Must you continue to make such suggestions? This goes beyond all the boundaries of decency!

NARRATOR: But even as she speaks, her words become hollow as faint hope begins to spring up. Karafuji speaks even more insistently.

KARAFUJI: No, I cannot keep silent. The setting sun is about to wither the hibiscus blossom that is my lady. I must save my lady's life. Take the medicine that I offer and we shall see whether it is poison or a healing drug.

NARRATOR: Karafuji's sincere concern for her mistress is revealed in her every word. But Lady Fuyo is unable to decide what to do. She is like seaweed, floating helplessly on the swell of the waves. Just at this point, Harumochi appears in a handsome set of armor, the shiny lacquered plates of metal held together by bright scarlet braid.

HARUMOCHI *runs out from stage left in armor with bright scarlet braid. He stops and kneels, bowing respectfully to* LADY FUYO.

HARUMOCHI: I have just heard the report of my father's death in battle. Now I must rush to the afterworld for permission to go to war. I have decided to go myself and fight in his memory and will not return until all of the enemy Amago are defeated. I come to say farewell forever.

NARRATOR: His voice is calm and collected as he takes his final leave. Despite herself, Lady Fuyo can only gaze deeply at him. Karafuji decides that the young lord must not be allowed to go.

KARAFUJI: Ladies-in-waiting! Stop the young lord from going to battle.

From the wings, the LADIES-IN-WAITING *reply obediently. Two come from the sliding doors at center and take away the hunting trophy. The other women all carry branches of chrysanthemum blossoms. With a dance-like stylized fight, they*

Figure 16. *The Blush on the White Hibiscus Blossom: Lady Fuyo and the True Account of the Ōuchi Clan*, 1955, at the Kabuki-za. Jitsukawa Enjirō is standing center, as Harumochi, and Nakamura Utaemon VI is above, left, as Lady Fuyo. Harumochi is surrounded by ladies-in-waiting. Photograph courtesy of the Mishima Yukio Literary Museum. Photograph by Yoshida Chiaki.

hold back HARUMOCHI. *At an appropriate moment,* KARAFUJI *steps down from the raised platform and restrains the women, who then all exit.*

NARRATOR: With a flurry of their long kimono skirts, the ladies-in-waiting withdraw. Harumochi breathes deeply in relief.

HARUMOCHI: Mother, why do you stop me from fighting for my father? I intend to avenge his death and set out filled with the courage of a warrior. Now that things have come to this pass, how can you stop me from going to battle? Don't you understand my agony?

NARRATOR: He bitterly laments his situation.

LADY FUYO: There is a very good reason for me to have stopped you. Please wait. Sit and listen to what I have to say. *(Her speech is underscored by emotional music from the* geza.) It would not do to have rumors of disagreements between you and me reach other countries. Before that happens, we must speak truthfully and make our hearts as one. Until today, my every word has been very harsh. But you cannot have guessed what I have kept hidden in the bottom of my heart. I have purposely tried to keep you away.

NARRATOR: ". . . We have been as distant as two shores separated by sandy beaches and the white waves . . ."

LADY FUYO: . . . But each time I have scolded you so severely, I felt as though I was tormenting my own heart.

HARUMOCHI: I bear no ill will toward you, let your heart rest at peace and pray for the repose of my father's soul.

NARRATOR: His words are clear and pure. His heart is already turned away to the battlefield.

HARUMOCHI: I go now to battle. Farewell.

NARRATOR: He stands to leave.

LADY FUYO: Wait! My will to lead the funeral prayers is weak and faltering. I never expected that my husband could be killed in battle. Even now, it is as though he is still alive. His living image stands before me and leads me into confusion. My lord is standing right here.

HARUMOCHI: Mother, keep your spirit strong. I know full well how you must long for my dead father.

LADY FUYO: No, no! I long for my lord, but the lord I long for is not the man who has left on his journey to the distant afterworld. The lord I long for is a strong young tree with bright scarlet blossoms, a figure in bright red armor. You are the living image of the lord I so long for.

HARUMOCHI: I do not understand why you are saying such things now. Mother, do not let grief lead you into confusion.

NARRATOR: The sleeves of his armor are stiff with sharp corners. How she is drawn by the feeling of martial strength in these square sleeves. How adorable the fact that Harumochi's sleeves have never known soft human emotions. "Onto the threads of these scarlet brocade cords, I will

Figure 17. *The Blush on the White Hibiscus Blossom: Lady Fuyo and the True Account of the Ōuchi Clan*, 1955, at the Kabuki-za. Jitsukawa Enjirō, is at left, as Harumochi, and Nakamura Utaemon VI, is at right, as Lady Fuyo. Photograph courtesy of the Mishima Yukio Literary Museum. Photograph by Yoshida Chiaki.

brush the white blossoms of the Fuyo, the hibiscus of my name. Is it the path of morality to scatter the blossoms? Or is it the way of love to leave the flower untouched. Show me whether the omen of the flowers is for good or for ill. What is in your heart? . . . "

LADY FUYO: . . . Love and passion are the eternal way of this world . . .

NARRATOR: ". . . I am a fragile boat that shivers with the tiniest waves. Imagine how overcome I am, with no power to remain living in the face of such powerful waves of fate. I long to follow my lord in death, but my real desire is to die for your sake. Just once, I beg of you, instead of calling me mother, call me your wife." So she laments and entreats him, revealing the truth of her passion.

LADY FUYO *gestures with a branch of white hibiscus blossoms during this passage. But* HARUMOCHI *poses firmly in rejection.*

HARUMOCHI: I believed that you were lost in the confusion of grief. Instead, you talk of an unspeakable passion. This is throwing filth onto the name of my dead father and will bring shame onto the Ōuchi clan until the end of time.

NARRATOR: Lady Fuyo and Karafuji cling to Harumochi in entreaty, but he shoves them angrily aside.

HARUMOCHI: Your touch defiles this armor! I had always heard people say that the hearts of women are immoral, but I never realized how true it is. Now I must not delay even a moment before I rush to the pure place of battle.

NARRATOR: He hurries off to forget the terrible disgrace. The women cling to him, and he pushes them away from him again and again. Just at that moment . . .

He pushes LADY FUYO *and* KARAFUJI *aside and rushes toward the* hanamichi *runway.*

OFF-STAGE VOICE: Our lord has returned from battle!

HARUMOCHI: What? Father is alive?

NARRATOR: He wishes to see his father as soon as possible, but cannot appear before him in the armor that he is not yet permitted to wear. He rushes to change out of his armor. Now Lady Fuyo is overcome with mad confusion.

All are shocked by the announcement. HARUMOCHI *must change and turns to the back of the stage, but* LADY FUYO *clings to him.*

LADY FUYO: Please, I beg you. Now that I have confessed my passion, at least have the kindness to kill me.

NARRATOR: She clings to him and pulls at his sword, which comes away in her hands. Harumochi looks back at her in contempt and goes into the back. Lady Fuyo is about to draw the sword to take her life, but Karafuji restrains her.

On the platform, LADY FUYO *takes* HARUMOCHI'S *short* wakizashi *sword and indicates that she wishes him to kill her with it. But* HARUMOCHI *refuses to listen and exits through the sliding paper doors upstage center, leaving the sword with* LADY FUYO. LADY FUYO *draws the sword and is about to stab herself with it, but* KARAFUJI *stops her.*

KARAFUJI: Stop, stop! Do not act so hastily! *(She takes the sword from her.)*
LADY FUYO: Let go of me, Karafuji. My lord is alive. Do you think that I could ever face him now? Harumochi worships his father. Some day he will tell his father what happened. I cannot go on living. Please let me die.
KARAFUJI: I cannot do that.
NARRATOR: Again Lady Fuyo tries to draw the sword, but Karafuji stops her.
KARAFUJI: I have an idea of what to do. First, now that you have seen how hardhearted Harumochi is, do you have any regrets if you cannot have your love?
LADY FUYO: *(Thinks deeply as though her true feelings are different from her words.)* Why would I have any regrets now?
KARAFUJI: In that case, I will explain the situation to our lord in my own way, before Harumochi sees his father.
LADY FUYO: What?
KARAFUJI: Leave everything to me. Everything will be as it was before and not the slightest stain of scandal will touch the name of my lady. First, you must withdraw into the other room.
NARRATOR: What plan does Karafuji have hidden deep in her heart? In turmoil, the women retreat into the other room.

KARAFUJI *holds* HARUMOCHI'S *sword in one hand and with the other, urges* LADY FUYO *to go into the back.* LADY FUYO *goes into the room stage left, and a little later* KARAFUJI *exits into the same room.*

NARRATOR: Now returns the lord of the clan, Ōuchi Sakyo-no-Tayū Yoshitaka. He has gone in battle against the Amago of Izumo, but now returns in defeat.
OFF-STAGE VOICE: His lordship has returned.

At this announcement, the sliding paper doors at the back of the platform open and instead of the white wall that was there for previous entrances and exits, there is a set piece showing an enormous hall in forced perspective. YOSHITAKA *enters along the* hanamichi *runway with a* YOUNG BOY *carrying his sword and a party of* RETAINERS. *The procession stops on the* hanamichi. *Hanging from his bow, one of the retainers has a black banner from the Korean province of Kudara.*

YOSHITAKA: Heaven was not on our side. We return to put away our spears and arrows for a while. This black banner announcing my death in battle is a mark of atonement to the ancestors of our clan. But I intend to go into battle once more to clear away this bitter shame.

NARRATOR: Though he speaks bravely, his men are weary. Few are they that return, and disordered are their ranks. Karafuji greets the lord with great respect, not daring to raise her face. She speaks formal words of welcome.

After YOSHITAKA *speaks, he and his party proceed to the main stage. He and his sword-bearer stand in the center of the platform while his men line up behind him. Before they move from the* hanamichi, KARAFUJI *enters from the room stage left, now wearing an embroidered formal* uchikake *overrobe. She kneels respectfully at the bottom of the steps to the platform at far stage right.*

KARAFUJI: How auspicious indeed is my lord's safe return to this castle.

YOSHITAKA: Karafuji, is Lady Fuyo well?

KARAFUJI: I do not wish to cast a shadow on your safe return, but my lady's illness has grown more severe and she may not see the morrow.

YOSHITAKA: She is that ill?

KARAFUJI: There is a reason for her indisposition. *(She is about to speak but hesitates.)* May I speak to you alone?

YOSHITAKA: Men, go and rest.

At YOSHITAKA'S *signal, the sword-bearer and other retainers exit.*

NARRATOR: When the others are gone, Karafuji moves forward.

KARAFUJI: The reason for Lady Fuyo's illness is none other than this sword. *(She holds up* HARUMOCHI'S *sword.)*

YOSHITAKA: *(With a grunt of assent, he takes the sword and examines it.)* But this is the sword that I gave to Harumochi!

KARAFUJI: This sword is the only thing left behind when someone slipped secretly into Lady Fuyo's bedchamber and fled, before he could do what he intended. My lady said that she knows the face of the intruder, but were this to be revealed, it would be a terrible thing. She only says that it would be a stain on her name and on the name of my lord. She worries grievously. She wants to keep it secret and longs to die by her own hand. I was only just able to stop her, but now she is confined because she is seriously ill. The original cause of my lady's indisposition is this villain, who took advantage of the absence of your lordship and attempted to consummate his long-held illicit love.

NARRATOR: Hearing this Yoshitaka is furious.

YOSHITAKA: What is the name of that intruder?!

KARAFUJI: It is that sword that speaks the name of the intruder.

YOSHITAKA: It was Harumochi?

KARAFUJI: My lord, you must investigate to determine whether it is Harumochi or not.

NARRATOR: Lord Yoshitaka does not even allow her to finish speaking. His breast simmers with the bitterness of his military defeat. Lady Fuyo is virtuous and beautiful, a woman without equal in all the world. For his son to have tried to steal this flower means that he is a lecherous monster. Yoshitaka is red with anger and his voice is like thunder.

YOSHITAKA *moves decisively. He takes hold of the legs of his* hakama *divided skirt and stands firmly.*

YOSHITAKA: Where is Harumochi? Harumochi, Harumochi!

NARRATOR: Yoshitaka shouts angrily and Karafuji sees that her plan has worked. As she slips into the next room, Harumochi, full of martial vigor, comes to welcome his father home.

YOSHITAKA *stands and shouts stage right.* KARAFUJI *slips away into the stage left room and at the same time,* HARUMOCHI *enters from the sliding doors stage center. He has changed out of his armor and now wears the formal costume of a samurai with brocaded* hakama *and* kataginu *shoulder pieces. As he enters,* HARUMOCHI *and* YOSHITAKA *walk around each other warily.* HARUMOCHI *goes respectfully to far stage right and bows deeply to his father.*

HARUMOCHI: Father, I am overjoyed to see that you are indeed alive.

NARRATOR: Seeing the living face of his father before him, Harumochi is overcome with emotion and tries to hide his tears of joy.

YOSHITAKA: Be silent! Harumochi, I believe that you know this sword.

HARUMOCHI: *(Glancing at it.)* Yes. You gave this sword to me yourself.

YOSHITAKA: Fine. You know this sword well. There must be a good reason for you to have lost such an important sword. Tell me the reason.

NARRATOR: So questioned, Harumochi is at a loss for words and sweats anxiously.

HARUMOCHI: When I returned from hunting and changed my clothes, I carelessly left this sword behind.

NARRATOR: He must conceal the fact that he disobeyed his father's orders by dressing in armor to prepare for battle. But Yoshitaka is furious.

YOSHITAKA: Be silent, Harumochi! I bestowed this sword as the heirloom of a warrior. I did not give you this sword to aid you in a mission of lust.

HARUMOCHI: "Mission of lust?" Father, what do you mean?

YOSHITAKA: If you do not know, I will tell you. You are an evil monster that has brought shame on the Ōuchi clan and defiled his own father's name. You are the villain who broke into the bedchamber of your mother, Lady Fuyo, intending to use this sword to attack her virtue. This sword is proof of your guilt. If you have anything to say for yourself, speak now.

NARRATOR: Thus accused, Harumochi is so shocked that he can only look down and shed bitter tears. From the next room, Lady Fuyo and Karafuji cannot control themselves any longer and look in at the scene, a sight that breaks their hearts.

As HARUMOCHI *looks down, the screens of the stage left room open and the two women look out. At the end of the* NARRATOR'S *passage, the screens slide shut firmly.*

YOSHITAKA: What do you have to say for yourself?

HARUMOCHI: Well . . .

YOSHITAKA: Well . . .

BOTH: Well, well, well . . .

YOSHITAKA: Tell me or else!

NARRATOR: Overcome with love and concern for his wife, Yoshitaka strikes out blindly at Harumochi. (YOSHITAKA *strikes* HARUMOCHI *with his fan and the blows are emphasized by beats of the* tsuke *clappers.)* For a moment, Harumochi is about to explain exactly what happened. But he stops and thinks again. That would disgrace the name of his stepmother. Whether true mother or adopted mother, filial piety is exactly the same. The young, virtuous Harumochi decides that he must keep everything locked up secretly in his heart. This is the only way that everything can be resolved.

HARUMOCHI: Someone has falsely accused me. I, Harumochi will show my innocence to the gods of heaven and earth.

YOSHITAKA: Only a villain would swear his innocence to the gods without presenting any proof. Harumochi, you are banned from my presence forever. I banish you from all seven territories of my domain . . .

NARRATOR: ". . . You must not approach closer than seven leagues from the border." So does Yoshitaka proclaim his severe judgment.

HARUMOCHI: I hear and obey.

NARRATOR: Harumochi's answering voice is choked with tears. He sheds a rain of bitter tears. The shame of a false accusation defiles his warrior's armor. Harumochi resolves to show his innocence, to recover the good name of a man of the bow. Harumochi knows what he must do now and takes his leave. *(During this, the screens open again showing that* LADY FUYO *and* KARAFUJI *in the next room are confused and distressed by this turn of events.)*

NARRATOR: Unable to endure any longer, despite herself, Lady Fuyo stumbles out of the next room.

HARUMOCHI *stops at the seven-three spot on the* hanamichi *runway and shows his intention to commit ritual suicide to prove his innocence. Then he exits along the* hanamichi. *At the same time,* LADY FUYO *comes stumbling out of the room stage left.* KARAFUJI *comes out of the room as well, trying to stop her mistress.*

LADY FUYO: My lord, how I have missed you!

KARAFUJI: My lady, I know how you have longed for our lord, but you must go back to bed! This will make your illness worse. Please consider your health.

YOSHITAKA: How thin your face has become in the time that I have not seen you. Your loneliness and concern have taken their toll on you. Karafuji, I can see the truth of your words in these lines on my dear wife's face.

KARAFUJI *desperately signals to* LADY FUYO *with her eyes.*

LADY FUYO: Yes, everything that she said is true.

YOSHITAKA: If this is true, we must take even greater care with you. The days of autumn are short and already it grows dark. Somebody bring some light!

There are murmurs of assent offstage and two LADIES-IN-WAITING *bring out candles on tall stands.*

NARRATOR: Lady Fuyo knows that if she does not speak, there is no future for her, but her voice is no louder than a whisper.

LADY FUYO: My lord, I beg that you reconsider your punishment of Harumochi and forgive him.

YOSHITAKA: What, forgive Harumochi? He is the villain that slipped in and tried to attack your virtue. This is a strange request indeed. However, Harumochi is still young and rash. I banished him from my presence, but even though I did not tell him, I intend to allow him to go into battle. If he joins the forces of the Mori clan and does great deeds on the battlefield, then naturally this will give me a reason to forgive him.

NARRATOR: The lion is said to throw his child into a deep ravine, to toughen and test him. So is the love of this mighty warrior for his son. Lady Fuyo is overjoyed at his gentle words. Karafuji too is relieved, and the two women let out a sigh. But at this very moment, Obata no Shiro comes rushing in, his face full of horror.

OBATA NO SHIRŌ *comes running along the* hanamichi *runway, his steps emphasized by beats of the* tsuke *clappers.*

OBATA: My lord! Something terrible has happened!

YOSHITAKA: What has caused you to come in such a panic?

OBATA: The young lord, Harumochi, has just stabbed himself in ritual suicide. His last words to me were to tell his father that he is innocent of any wrongdoing. With these words he died.

YOSHITAKA: What? Harumochi is dead?!

NARRATOR: Yoshitaka, Lady Fuyo and Karafuji are all in shock and can only stare at one another in despair. For a time, all are unable to speak. Lady Fuyo takes the sword that has now become a memento of the dead Harumochi and stabs herself in the chest. Everyone is horrified.

YOSHITAKA: Why have you stabbed yourself?

NARRATOR: He speaks, but there is no saving her, as the blade of an impossible love has wounded her. With agonized breaths, Lady Fuyo speaks.

LADY FUYO: My lord, my story is shameful, but please listen. *(The pathos of her speech is emphasized by the bamboo flute and soft background music from the* gidayū shamisen.) I, Fuyo, have turned away from the path of heaven and the ways of earth. Harumochi is as pure and innocent as the day he was born. I fell in love with him. He so attracted me that I could not trust myself. I grew fearful and struggled to keep my distance, but to no avail. When I saw the black banner showing that you had died in battle . . .

NARRATOR: ". . . My feelings of love gushed forth, bursting through all barriers, like the powerful waters of autumn . . ."

LADY FUYO: . . . Even though I knew that I would drown in those waters, I confessed my feelings to Harumochi. But Harumochi is upright and moral and would not listen to my plea . . .

NARRATOR: ". . . I grew afraid that he would appeal to you, my lord, and tell you what happened . . ."

LADY FUYO: . . . Together, Karafuji and I plotted how to prevent you from finding out, but we never expected that Harumochi would commit suicide. My immoral desires brought on this tragedy . . .

NARRATOR: ". . . What evil spirit could have possessed me to have caused such a horrible thing." As she speaks, her words gradually grow weak.

KARAFUJI: No, my mistress is blameless. It is I, Karafuji, who led her on the path of secret love. Everything that I did was to protect my mistress. Harumochi's suicide was the unexpected result of my foolish plans. Please punish me properly.

NARRATOR: She clasps her hands in supplication. Lord Yoshitaka is furious at what he hears. He raises his blade and is about to strike, but suddenly pulls his sword away.

YOSHITAKA: To kill you with this blade would defile my sword. Obata no

Shirō, execute this woman for me!

NARRATOR: Obata no Shirō follows his lord's orders. He takes Karafuji with him and as she goes she turns back toward Lady Fuyo, eyes brimming over with tears of remorse. Shirō raises his sword, but Karafuji, prepared for death, motions for him to stop.

SHIRŌ *pulls* KARAFUJI *down the steps and as they walk down together,* KARAFUJI *pauses for a moment, turns her back, and takes poison.* SHIRŌ *leads her stage right on the main stage floor and has her sit, prepatory to beheading her. But when* SHIRŌ *raises his sword to cut off her head,* KARAFUJI *restrains him.*

KARAFUJI: There is no need for you to execute me. I just took a powerful poison from a foreign land and I have only a few moments to live.

OBATA: How could you cheat the executioner this way!

NARRATOR: Obata gnashes his teeth bitterly. But paying only the faintest attention to him, the two women gaze at one another.

LADY FUYO: *(Crawling forward to the top of the steps and looking down)* Well done, Karafuji!

KARAFUJI: Farewell, my lady.

NARRATOR: But no sooner does Karafuji utter her final words of parting than her breath expires. Lady Fuyo is also on the verge of death. The image of Harumochi is reflected in her tears as though he is saying a final farewell to her from the evening sky.

LADY FUYO *weakly goes halfway down the steps and looks off into the distance.*

LADY FUYO: Look there! Look, there amidst the night stars, is Harumochi! I can just barely make out the forest of stars. On the crest of the mountains there is a faint light in the sky and there is Harumochi. How pure and handsome he looks, urging along his favorite steed. Do you go out hunting again, my young master?

NARRATOR: Lord Yoshitaka is lost in silent thought. All too well, he knows the ways of human emotion. He speaks to Obata with words of wisdom and mercy.

YOSHITAKA: Surely the reason that I have lost my son and wife at the same moment is because of the poverty of my virtue in heaven's eyes. *(Decisively)* Harumochi died the death of a hero in battle. Obata, you must see that this is the way that it is written in the chronicles.

OBATA: My lord, that is of course what I already intended to do. The young master's death will be a heroic act that will grace the name of the Ōuchi clan to the end of time.

LADY FUYO: This will allow me to find salvation in the land of the Buddha.

YOSHITAKA: Take these words of prayer and find peace.
LADY FUYO: My lord, how grateful I am.
NARRATOR: Lady Fuyo dies, like the dew fading from the blossoms of the hibiscus. Soon she will find another life in the lotus blossoms of paradise, leaving sadness in the world she leaves behind.

With the words, "lotus blossoms of paradise," LADY FUYO *clasps her hands in prayer. This pose is emphasized by a stroke of the* ki *wooden clappers. Before this moment,* YOSHITAKA *descends the steps and holds his sword up in preparation to behead her as her second in a ritual suicide. He poses with the sword held in readiness as the curtain is pulled shut to the repeated strokes of the wooden clappers.*

CURTAIN

Steeplechase

(Daishōgai)

For Sugimura Haruko

Published in 1956, First Performed in 1957
Translated by Laurence Kominz

INTRODUCTION

Steeplechase is the first play Mishima wrote for Sugimura Haruko, the leading actress in the Bungaku-za. He intended it to be presented in the Bungaku-za's atelier series,[1] and it was, but not until after Sugimura had enjoyed great success playing Asako in Mishima's hit melodrama *Rokumeikan,* late in 1956. In her memoirs Sugimura discusses *Steeplechase* after *Rokumeikan*, so it is not clear when she first saw the play in print, but when she did she was deeply moved because it had "For Sugimura Haruko" written immediately under the title, and Mishima had never honored an actor or actress in this way before.[2]

Mishima was an active sportsman and bodybuilder during much of his adult life, but *Steeplechase* is one of the few plays that is centered around sports he engaged in himself. He took up horseback riding as a young adult, joining the Palace Riding Club in October, 1949,[3] but he never rode competitively, and gave up the sport in the mid-fifties when he took up bodybuilding and the martial arts. Mishima identified two separate sources for the play—his memories from his school days of the mother of a friend who had died, and the account of a fatal steeplechase accident at an Imperial equestrian tournament.[4]

The first two lines of dialog in *Steeplechase* bear an uncanny resemblance to Chekhov's *The Bear* (1888), but otherwise the two plays are diametrically opposed. Chekhov's work is a romantic farce that mocks a young widow's pretense of grief and mourning. Mishima's is a sensitive portrait of a mother's tragic obsession with the death of her son. Mishima's own description of the play is as follows: "It is a portrayal of human love in which, on a certain day, at a certain time, the heart of a certain woman is attacked, as if by some demonic arrow, and then suddenly the attack is over. More than being a portrait of a woman, it's an excision from a portrait. It appears on the surface to be a psychological drama, but the woman's feelings do not follow the logic of psychology."[5]

The action of the play is simple. A mother, Mrs. Tsugawa, who has recently lost her son in a steeplechase accident, sits at home in the afternoon, obsessed by a picture of his dead body. Her son's riding club friend, Makimura, comes to visit. He prays at her son's altar and tells Mrs. Tsugawa that he will ride in a steeplechase tomorrow. Mrs. Tsugawa is horrified that Makimura is about to compete in the sport that killed her son. They talk and she becomes hysterical. Makimura's girlfriend, Saeko, has been waiting outside, and she joins the pair. Mrs. Tsugawa calms down and converses with the young couple, and then they leave.

While the action of the play is simple the characters' emotions are not. In this respect, *Steeplechase* resembles both classical noh plays and Mishima's modern noh plays. In classical spirit *(mugen)* noh plays, a ghost is the main character *(shite)*, and the mortal characters' *(waki, waki-tsure)* task is to communicate with and assist the ghost. Much of *Steeplechase* is dominated by a character who is never present— Hisashi, Mrs. Tsugawa's recently deceased son. Mrs. Tsugawa's entire being is wrapped up in the horror of the steeplechase accident and in memories of her son. These memories obsess Mrs. Tsugawa as thoroughly as ghosts possess mortals, or other ghosts, in classical noh plays. Unlike the classical noh, Mishima's purpose is not to use the mortal characters to probe the soul of the departed Hisashi, but to use recollections of Hisashi to probe the psyches of his mortal survivors, most importantly Hisashi's mother. Hisashi never appears in the play. His presence is always entirely in the minds and hearts of the living.

Structurally the play resembles a shamanic ritual consisting of "invocation, visitation, exorcism, and banishment" of a dangerous spirit. Mishima was familiar with this ritual pattern that appears in modified form in spirit noh plays. The first scene, with just Mrs. Tsugawa and her maid present, is an "invoking" of the "spirit" using ritual.[6] Mrs. Tsugawa stares endlessly at a picture of Hisashi dying in a pool of blood on the riding ground, and she repeats the word "steeplechase" over and over, as if it were a mantra. The Japanese word *daishōgai*, which is used for "steeplechase," also means "large barrier" or "large obstacle" and so has broad, even religious connotations that the English word "steeplechase" does not. Mrs. Tsugawa gives rational, psychologically sophisticated explanations for her ritualesque activities during the course of her conversation with her maid. It does not occur to Mrs. Tsugawa that she is participating in anything so primitive and barbaric as the invoking of a dead spirit. The ritual structure of the play is a deep structure—on the surface it is a purely psychological realist play.

The "visitation" of the spirit is represented by Makimura coming to call. Makimura looks enough like Hisashi that Mrs. Tsugawa says they could be twins. She startles Makimura early in their conversation when she envisions her son and Makimura as both dead and sharing the same graveyard. She thinks that Hisashi could reappear at any moment in a shadowy spot in the room while Makimura stands in the sunlight. This sort of "doubled existence" occurs in classical noh plays like *Aoi no Ue* and *Futari Shizuka*.[7]

When not absorbed in her personal reverie, Mrs. Tsugawa speaks with Makimura in a motherly way, and her nurturing instincts are further aroused when he tells her he has inherited Hisashi's role of steeplechase jockey for the club. Makimura's decision to ride in the steeplechase summons the most powerful possession by the spirit of Hisashi. Makimura was Hisashi's closest companion, and now Hisashi's spirit enters his mother, and in an hysterical reverie she envisions herself riding in the steeplechase, and envisions Makimura as her lover.

The spirit is "exorcised" by the arrival of Saeko, negating a sexual bond between the two men and between Makimura and Mrs. Tsugawa. In this scene Makimura confirms that he intends to use Hisashi's spirit in a positive and self-serving way, to aid him in achieving victory in tomorrow's steeplechase. This follows a tried and true pattern in Shinto and Buddhist ritual of turning fearful ghosts into helpful spirits. We also learn that Hisashi's spirit means nothing whatsoever to Saeko. In this scene Mrs. Tsugawa discovers that she and the young couple "live in two entirely different countries," with languages and values so different that meaningful communication is all but impossible. Scene Four consists of just two lines, one each by the maid and Mrs. Tsugawa. It represents Mrs. Tsugawa's failed attempt to "banish" the ghost of Hisashi forever.

Within this formal structure deriving from shamanic ritual, an entirely believable encounter takes place over the course of about an hour among four individuals. Their conversations are in the normal daily speech of the upper class in Tokyo in the mid-1950s. Mrs. Tsugawa is hysterical for a few moments, but she and Makimura understand her situation in modern psychological terms. To them, what is happening is the result of grief, stress, and exhaustion, not spirit possession. No character in the play ever mentions ghosts, though Mrs. Tsugawa does say that she feels as if something is possessing her. Unlike Mishima's modern noh plays, which make constant reference to their classical antecedents, *Steeplechase* is of just one place and time: Mrs. Tsugawa's living room on a spring afternoon. *Steeplechase* is a contemporary psychological drama, but it could not have been written by a playwright who did not thoroughly understand the noh drama.

Domoto Masaki, Mishima's friend and scholar of noh who directed several of Mishima's plays in the 1960s, considers *Steeplechase* to be a unique variety of modern noh play.[8] He never directed this play, but he believes that it could profit from the sort of experimental approaches that he and Takechi Tetsuji used when directing modern noh plays . . . the use of noh actors, masks, dance, and music. Domoto recognizes that this is not at all what Mishima had in mind when he wrote the play.[9] Mishima intended *Steeplechase* as a straight *shingeki* production, and that is what it was in 1957, in the able hands of director Matsuura Takeo and actress Sugimura Haruko.

Steeplechase was performed just that one time. Sugimura was so angry and hurt by the events of 1963 that she never performed in another Mishima play for the rest of her career, even though she outlived Mishima by twenty-five years. Because "For Sugimura Haruko" was under the title in the published edition, no other actress would dare to take the part while Sugimura lived, such was her stature as the greatest living *shingeki* actress. So, between 1963 and 1997 the play could not be performed.

NOTES

1. Mishima Yukio, "Sakusha negoto," *Bungaku-za atorie panfuretto,* April 1957; excerpted in *Mishima Yukio jiten,* vol. 3 (Tokyo: Bensei Shuppan, 2000), pp. 216–17.
2. Ozasa Yoshio, *Joyū Sugimura Haruko* (Tokyo: Shūeisha, 1995), pp. 202–3.
3. Satō Ryōichi, ed., *Mishima Yukio Shinchō Nihon bungaku arubamu 20* (Tokyo: Shinchōsha, 1983), p. 32.
4. Mishima, "Sakusha negoto," p. 217.
5. Mishima, "Sakusha negoto," excerpted in Dōmoto Masaki, *Mishima Yukio no engeki maku kire no shisō* (Tokyo: Geki Shobō, 1977), p. 137.
6. Ibid., pp. 97–98. In this work, Dōmoto interprets the first scene of the play as a kind of ritual invocation of a dead spirit, but he does not write of all four scenes as reflective of integrated shamanic ritual structure.
7. Ibid., p. 100.
8. Ibid., pp. 95, 97–100. Dōmoto calls the play a "*bangai* modern noh," meaning a "noh play from outside the standard repertory."
9. Ibid., p. 95.

THE CHARACTERS

Mrs. Mineko Tsugawa, about forty-five years old
Tatsu, her maid, about forty years old
Makimura, a young man about twenty-two years old
Saeko, a young woman about twenty years old

SETTING

A Western style room used for receiving guests, now being used as a living room. Spring sunlight from the garden illuminates the entire room. In one corner of the room the wall has been cut out in the shape of an alcove, and it has a home Buddhist altar inside, with funeral plaques of deceased members of the family.

SCENE 1 (Mrs. Tsugawa, Tatsu)

MAID: Madam, if you carry on like this you will ruin your health. Why not go out once in awhile? It's a lovely spring day. How about taking a walk for half an hour or so, as far as the embankment? It would make you feel so much better.

MRS. TSUGAWA: Don't worry so much about me. You are constantly urging me to go out and I always refuse. But this daily ritual of mine is important to me. If I were to do each and every little thing you suggest—going out for walks and to the theatre—going out just to cheer myself up, a different sort of emptiness would attack me. I'm happier this way . . . sitting every day in the same chair, gazing at that terrible picture. That picture with all of its blood and gore.

Don't you see, Tatsu, if I were to go out on walks or to the theatre, it wouldn't cheer me up at all. Instead, the blood-stained figure in the picture would seem all the more vivid when I come home. But if I keep staring at the picture day and night, eventually my eyes will tire, my sight will blur, and a time will come when that picture with all its blood will look like a painting of pink-tinted clouds in a sunset—peaceful and beautiful. Gazing at the picture is my recreation, and my consolation.

MAID: That's what you say, madam, but it's been three months now. You don't eat your meals properly and you've grown so thin . . . *(She looks at the altar)* Oh, Madam, you have put away your son's funeral photograph.

MRS. TSUGAWA: Yes, when I look at that youthful, healthy, smiling face, I feel it's all a lie. The morning before he went to ride in the Imperial New Year's tournament, he ate red bean rice for good luck, wearing his brand new horse-riding outfit. He left home with such a wonderful smile on his face. To think that my boy . . .

MAID: Madam, you have told me the story so many times . . .

MRS. TSUGAWA: No. I know that most people struggle to escape from terrible memories. I do the opposite. My child left this house with a smile on his face, then three hours later, before my very eyes, his horse missed a jump over a fence. My boy broke his skull, and lay in the dirt of the riding ground in a sea of blood . . .

MAID: Oh, Mrs. Tsugawa!

MRS. TSUGAWA: I'm going to say it. I'm going to say it over and over again until each of these terrible words makes me feel nothing at all. Tatsu, if I can ever get used to saying that awful word, "steeplechase," again, then there won't be a single word in the whole world that I can't say. "Steeplechase, steeplechase, steeplechase . . ." Look, Tatsu, I can say it as many times as I want to. I'm going to keep saying the word until I don't have to look away when it jumps out at me from the newspaper or the dictionary.

MAID: Madam, it is because you are such a strong person that . . .

MRS. TSUGAWA: You too? Stooping to casual flattery?

MAID: No, it's not that. You're so strong but I feel I've spent my whole life running away from whatever scares me. You know I've never married.

MRS. TSUGAWA: But just a few years ago there were so many people who approached you, hoping to arrange a marriage.

MAID: And I was so stubborn I refused them all. I resolved not to marry until the young master got married.

MRS. TSUGAWA: Yes, you always told me that. But Tatsu, now there's nothing to prevent you from marrying.

MAID: But Madam, now I have no desire at all to marry. I've seen what becomes of happiness in the end.

The two lapse into silence. The doorbell rings. MRS. TSUGAWA *motions for her servant to answer the door.* TATSU *exits, then returns.*

MAID: It's Mr. Makimura.

SCENE 2 (Makimura, Mrs. Tsugawa)

The MAID *leads* MAKIMURA *in, then exits.*

MAKIMURA: I've come to see you again.

MRS. TSUGAWA: Come in, do come in. Please sit down. I'm really so happy you've come. These days you are the only one of my son's schoolfriends kind enough to visit. For the first seven days it was such a bustle with everyone coming to call. And then, all of a sudden, they disappeared. Since then, Makimura, it's just been you.

MAKIMURA: (*Smiles without replying*)

MRS. TSUGAWA: You know, it's at a time like this that I can tell who his true friends were. I think your visits make Hisashi happy too. You can't know how much happier having good school friends made him . . . more than some romantic entanglement could have.

MAKIMURA: It makes me so happy to hear you say that.

MRS. TSUGAWA: *(In a different tone, exaggerating her unhappiness)* I haven't gone out at all since the accident. Everyone tries to cheer me up by inviting me to go out and do this and that, but I simply don't feel like going out anywhere. I'm shut up here like a silk worm in a cocoon. When I see you, and you talk about old times, I feel as if I'm coming back to life at last.

MAKIMURA: I understand how you feel.

MRS. TSUGAWA: *(In a terribly insinuating voice)* My, how very kind you are. I'm sure you'll do great things someday. A man should be considerate, not just strong. What a remarkable young man you are to remember that buried in the depths of Tokyo there is a mother who has lost her only son. Especially on a fine spring day like today which would stir romantic feelings in any heart . . .

MAKIMURA: Could I go and pay my respects to Hisashi?

MRS. TSUGAWA: Certainly, by all means. Hisashi would be so . . .

MRS. TSUGAWA *goes with* MAKIMURA *as he offers incense at the Buddhist altar.* MAKIMURA *appears to be making some sort of request as he prays.*

MRS. TSUGAWA: Thank you. *(The two return to their chairs.)* Is everyone in your family well?

MAKIMURA: Excuse me?

MRS. TSUGAWA: Is everyone in your family . . . oh . . . I know you have come to pay your respects to Hisashi and not to chat with me, but I asked if everyone in your family is well.

MAKIMURA: Yes, there hasn't been any change.

MRS. TSUGAWA: That's good. Yes, that is what's most important. Living uneventfully is the supreme happiness.

MAKIMURA: Uh . . . ? *(He smiles vaguely)*

The MAID *brings tea in and then exits.*

MRS. TSUGAWA: Where is your family grave?

MAKIMURA: Aoyama Cemetery.

MRS. TSUGAWA: Why, that's the same as our family. Where is it? Is it in the middle of the cemetery?

MAKIMURA: You go in the main entrance, and it's in the middle of the right side. You know where there's a circular drive? You turn right and go all the way to the end of the road.

MRS. TSUGAWA: Our family's is on the left side. *(As if in a dream)* Two friends together . . . yes . . . I'm so glad we're neighbors!

MAKIMURA: *(Startled)* What was that?

MRS. TSUGAWA: *(Not noticing anything strange in what she just said)* Excuse me?

MAKIMURA: *(Smiles painfully)* . . . It's just . . .

MRS. TSUGAWA: Whenever I see you, you're the picture of health. My Hisashi was like that too. Whenever you and Hisashi had dinner here together it didn't matter how big the steaks were, you two just devoured them. They disappeared right before my eyes, like snow in the sun. You didn't look at all alike, but underneath you and Hisashi were like twins—robust, healthy twins.

I know I should be thankful that Hisashi didn't die from some long and painful disease. I feel that if his ghost were to appear before me, it would pop out from over there, with a healthy, smiling face just like yours. Sunlight and shadow . . . that's right. Mr. Makimura, you're in the sunlight, and I can't help thinking that Hisashi is just hiding in the shadows over there.

MAKIMURA: Sunlight and shadow . . . I suppose so. You probably think that my place in the sunlight is uncertain too. Youth is merely . . .

MRS. TSUGAWA: *(With exaggerated falsity)* No! Not at all! Your place in the sunlight is absolutely certain. That's the kind of person you are. I haven't the slightest doubt.

The two are silent.

MAKIMURA: *(Suddenly)* Actually, even though today is not a ritual occasion, I wanted to come and pay my respects to Hisashi. Tomorrow I'm going to be in a revenge match, though I suppose I'm exaggerating to call it that. Anyway, I think that if Hisashi were still alive, he'd slap me on the back to wish me luck.

MRS. TSUGAWA: My, my, tell me more.

MAKIMURA: *(Hesitantly)* There isn't all that much to say. When it came to riding, I was never a match for Hisashi. But you know that. Hisashi was always chosen to compete for our club in the steeplechase. If he'd kept on like that he'd have gone to the Olympics for sure. But now . . . even though I'm not ready for it, I've been chosen to take Hisashi's place.

MRS. TSUGAWA: Yes . . .

MAKIMURA: And . . . and you see. In the national championship tomorrow, I'm going to ride in the steeplechase for the first time, just as Hisashi used to.

MRS. TSUGAWA: The steeplechase!?

MAKIMURA: Yes, the steeplechase. With one hundred and forty centimeter box fences.

MRS. TSUGAWA: Oh, my, Mr. Makimura, this won't do at all.

MAKIMURA: I'll be all right. I've had all the practice I need. I know I can do it. And my horse will be Tsunefuji, one the finest steeplechase horses ever.

MRS. TSUGAWA: You mustn't do it. Not the steeplechase. Have you kept it secret from your family?

MAKIMURA: No, it's not a secret, but . . .

MRS. TSUGAWA: Does your mother know about it? Does she? Did you trick her into giving you permission? She didn't stop you? . . . Why not? If I were your mother I'd never give you permission! Never! I'd do whatever was necessary to stop you.

MAKIMURA: *(Making a serious lapse of the tongue)* But did you stop Hisashi when he rode in the steeplechase?

MRS. TSUGAWA: Oh! What an awful thing to say! *(She grows suddenly angry.)* It's not just you, then. It's your whole family—they're so confident in you. Hisashi died in the steeplechase, but you all think you'll be just fine!

MAKIMURA: It's not like that. . . . . I don't know what to say. . . . I put it the wrong way. I . . . how can I say this? I didn't want to commit to riding in the steeplechase until I received Hisashi's blessing. And that's why . . .

MRS. TSUGAWA: *(Breaking into tears)* I understand . . . yes, I understand. I'm sorry for breaking down like this. Your dedication to Hisashi's memory, your continuing friendship for him, even after his death. I understand everything. I understand you too well. I'm afraid I made the mistake of treating you like my own son. I'm so worried about your safety that I . . .

MAKIMURA: *(Calming her down and consoling her)* A little while ago you said that Hisashi died in the steeplechase, and you thought I said I would succeed where he failed. But it isn't like that at all.

MRS. TSUGAWA: Tell me more, Makimura. I was very upset when I said that.

MAKIMURA: Well, I . . .

MRS. TSUGAWA: *(Overwrought)* There's not the slightest chance you'll fail. I'm sure you'll succeed! A resounding success! Hisashi's spirit will protect you tomorrow. To fail—don't even dream of that . . . I'm afraid . . . that sea of blood! I don't care if you lie to me or not, just tell me that you're not going to ride in the steeplechase.

MAKIMURA: *(Full of confidence)* No. I never think of failure. And, as I've told you before, what happened to Hisashi wasn't because of any failure on his part. It was an accident, nothing more than remarkably bad luck. It wasn't Hisashi's fault at all. That sort of accident happens just once every ten years in competitive riding. The tiniest little slip, invisible to the human eye, resulted in tragedy. It was beyond human control. Fate—yes, that's what it was—it was an accident caused by fate. I've said this many times. Hisashi was a splendid rider. That's for certain. We're not going to see a rider like Hisashi for a long time. Everyone in the equestrian world thinks that. Mrs. Tsugawa, that won't change.

MRS. TSUGAWA: So, Makimura, you are able to dismiss the accident as merely a bit of bad luck? You make much of the word "fate." But what I think is . . . yes . . . fate is more than conceit invented by human beings. You have a fate of your own, Makimura.

MAKIMURA: *(Good naturedly, but with a hint of doubt)* It's not nice of you, Mrs. Tsugawa, to try to frighten me like this.

MRS. TSUGAWA: I'm not trying to frighten you. It's just that I'm worried about your safety.

MAKIMURA: Thank you for your concern. But if I followed your recommendation, I wouldn't be able to take part in any sports at all. Your life is in danger to some degree in almost every sport.

MRS. TSUGAWA: You talk as if you enjoy flirting with death. I wonder . . . are you trying to be a hero?

MAKIMURA: No, it's not that dramatic. In fact, it's nothing at all remarkable. It would be different if I were to jump off a skyscraper in front of a crowd, but my horse will just be jumping over some log fences less than two meters high. And all I have to do is sit on the horse. I lean forward, raise my hips from the saddle, spur the horse, thrust my fists forward and pull on the reins. That's it. It's nothing special.

MRS. TSUGAWA: But Hisashi died by doing that "nothing special." How can you be so sure that you'll be safe?

MAKIMURA: Death, that nasty fellow, is always lying in wait. Like a bullet in Russian roulette. Where is your guarantee that a person walking along the street won't be hit by a car?

MRS. TSUGAWA: That's true, but . . .

MAKIMURA: *(Triumphantly)* I'm right, aren't I, Mrs. Tsugawa?

MRS. TSUGAWA: *(With displeasure)* No, Makimura, you're not. My fears are not just based on reason, you know. Something larger than me is trying to stop you from riding in the competition. Something has borrowed my voice and is speaking through me. Is this too difficult for you to imagine? I don't want to upset you, but when you walked in from the entryway . . .

MAKIMURA: Yes?

MRS. TSUGAWA: I thought you looked just like Hisashi. I don't know why, but you looked identical. And then, as we were talking, this strange fear grew stronger and stronger. You are here with me now, but I felt somehow that you would soon disappear. Everything seems so impermanent.

MAKIMURA: *(Now somewhat ill at ease, but continuing to oppose her premonition)* It is probably because of all the stress you've been under, Mrs. Tsugawa.

MRS. TSUGAWA: *(Gradually becoming intoxicated by her own words)* No, it is a deeper, more real foreboding. How can I put it into words? You are here now. Soon you will leave. And I have the feeling that once you leave, you will be gone forever. And then suddenly you begin to talk about the steeplechase. Oh, I . . . *(She presses her hand to her forehead and slumps forward.)*

MAKIMURA: *(Stands up)* What happened? Are you all right?

MRS. TSUGAWA: Yes, yes. Thank you. I'm all right now. These days I sometimes have dizzy spells like this. I'll try repeating the same word over and over as I sit here in front of you. Steeplechase, steeplechase . . .

MAKIMURA: *(Drawn into the litany)* Steeplechase, steeplechase . . .

MRS. TSUGAWA: That word has a terrible magic power. For you the word evokes glory, sunlight sparkling off a temple roof. For me it reeks of blood. The sound of that word holds within it death, misfortune, and all the darkness this world can bear. Can you comprehend this, Makimura? You say this word thinking of what it means to you, but when I hear the same word, the image I see is entirely different.

MAKIMURA: Yes, I understand you.

MRS. TSUGAWA: Do you follow me? If you do you should understand that a terrible aura surrounds you. Your blood is staining the sand of the riding ground, your face grows utterly pale, and your head, wrapped in bandages . . .

MAKIMURA *unconsciously presses his hand(s) to his head.*

A few minutes ago I said that you would win the competition tomorrow, but I was lying. I was fighting against a premonition of disaster, and I tried to drive it away with lies.

MAKIMURA: *(Struck with fear)* What?

MRS. TSUGAWA: But then the vision became clearer. Why, when you entered this room, did you appear so insubstantial? And now . . . when you leave, knowing that you will be gone forever . . .

MAKIMURA: Gone forever, you say?

MRS. TSUGAWA: Yes, if you don't withdraw from tomorrow's tournament.

MAKIMURA: *(Seized with fear)* I won't withdraw! Nothing can make me withdraw!

MRS. TSUGAWA: Then you are irretrievably lost.

MAKIMURA: *(Growing upset)* You're terrible. Mrs. Tsugawa, you're heartless. You know I've made up my mind to compete, you should have been kind enough to give me some encouragement. Why can't you help me by reassuring me? . . . I've taken the trouble to visit you, and this is what you do in return . . .

MRS. TSUGAWA: *(Coolly)* I'm telling you, no harm will come to you if you withdraw.

MAKIMURA: *(With fire in his eyes)* Do you think that at this point it is possible to withdraw?

MRS. TSUGAWA: Oh, scold me more! Your face is so handsome when you're angry. If your face were to disappear from my sight, what a loss that would be. Yes, irrevocable . . .

MAKIMURA: *(Uncertainly)* What? Are you making fun of me?

MRS. TSUGAWA: Making fun of you . . . ? I, no, it's no use. What was I saying? Just be silent a bit, would you please. I'm trying to think. About what I've been trying to tell you.

MAKIMURA: I . . . um . . .

MRS. TSUGAWA: Don't say anything. Please. I see something that looks like flames, like a butterfly fluttering its wings too fast. That's what I see . . . *(She closes her eyes)* I feel you're going to a far off place and won't return. I'll be left alone . . . . I wonder why? *(Opens her eyes)* I wonder why? This feeling is so strange. I feel that . . . now that you've come here, if I don't keep you here forever, you will be lost forever. Now—this moment—there's something very special about it, isn't there? You're right there. I'm here. . . . What are you thinking, I wonder? I . . . I feel as if I've just awakened. Precious time is slipping away. The moment you jump over a fence in the steeplechase, you must surely feel this way. The air around me has become like fire, and my body like ice. Yes. Then a terrible jolt. The blue sky begins to spin above me . . . it pierces my forehead . . . violent waves . . . my head is spinning. Now! I've just jumped over the steeplechase fence. My head is reeling . . . and you, Makimura, right in front of me . . .

MAKIMURA: *(Not recognizing this convulsive confession of love, and feeling more and more overpowered,* MAKIMURA *stands and begins to back away. He speaks in a hurried voice.)* I . . . I have a friend whom I've kept waiting. I shouldn't keep her waiting any longer. I'll go call her.

MRS. TSUGAWA: Makimura! *(She stands up.)*

MAKIMURA: I'll be right back. I'm just going to call her in.

MAKIMURA *runs into the garden.* MRS. TSUGAWA *stares after him blankly. She composes herself and sits down, with a sense of defeat.* MAKIMURA *returns from the garden, leading* SAEKO *in.*

SCENE 3 (Mrs. Tsugawa, Makimura, Saeko)

MAKIMURA: Let me introduce you. This is Ukita Saeko. She's a member of the Union Riding Club.

SAEKO: I'm pleased to meet you. My apologies for intruding.

MRS. TSUGAWA: I'm Tsugawa Mineko. I'm pleased to meet you.

MAKIMURA: I told her I'd be staying just a short time, and asked her to wait outside the gate. But I made her wait much longer than I thought.

SAEKO: Please forgive me. The flowers in your garden are so pretty, I let myself in through the side gate. *(To* MAKIMURA*)* You know how forward I can be.

MRS. TSUGAWA: *(Endeavoring to conceal feelings of jealousy and disappointment)* You are Miss Ukita? I wonder if your father is president of Ukita Life Insurance?

SAEKO: Yes, he is.

MRS. TSUGAWA: In that case, your father and my husband must be golfing acquaintances.

SAEKO: My father told me about the accident. *(Looking at the altar)* I'm so sorry for you . . . Would you allow me to pay my respects?

MRS. TSUGAWA: *(Remaining seated)* Please go ahead.

MAKIMURA *joins* SAEKO *at the altar. Both pray for the deceased.*

MAKIMURA: *(To* SAEKO) Mrs. Tsugawa has been telling me that I mustn't compete in tomorrow's steeplechase.

SAEKO: Why on earth not?

MAKIMURA: Because she says it's dangerous. *(Attempting to soothe* MRS. TSUGAWA*)* It's only natural that she should feel that way. I'm very grateful for her concern.

SAEKO: But what's so dangerous about it?

MAKIMURA: After all . . . *(He glances meaningfully at the altar, but* SAEKO *doesn't catch his intent.)*

SAEKO: It'll be easy for you. My goodness, what a coward you are.

MRS. TSUGAWA: *(In amazement)* Do you really mean what you just said?

SAEKO: *(Shocked by her tone of voice)* Yes . . . but . . .

MRS. TSUGAWA: He's going to be jumping in the same steeplechase as Hisashi, you know.

SAEKO: Yes, but Hisashi was just terribly unlucky. That sort of thing almost never happens. *(To Makimura)* You know how crazy I am about steeplechases, don't you?

MRS. TSUGAWA: *(For the first time revealing open enmity)* You can only think the way you do because you are young, healthy, and have never experienced misfortune.

SAEKO: I've fallen from my horse seven times while riding, you know.

MRS. TSUGAWA: But you weren't injured, were you?

SAEKO: No, but . . . *(She looks at Makimura in consternation.)*

MRS. TSUGAWA: True misfortune, you know, occurs very rarely. But once misfortune has paid a visit, the person in question, and those close to that person, must live with misfortune the rest of their lives. We become dwellers in the land of misfortune. And the language of the land of misfortune is incomprehensible in your land. Between your land and mine there is an uncrossable border. You are lucky that you can't cross this boundary, and perhaps it's good that I can't either. I'm satisfied to go on living forever with Hisashi's misfortune, that misfortune that you tell me almost never happens.

MAKIMURA: But that's . . . so sad for you. I don't understand things very well, but I'm afraid that my visit has brought the tragedy back to you. *(Straightforwardly)* Please forgive me if I have said anything wrong.

MRS. TSUGAWA: *(Touched)* How sweet you are!

SAEKO: *(Reacting to the drift of the conversation)* Makimura, shouldn't we be getting ready to leave?

MRS. TSUGAWA: Not at all. Please, relax and stay for a while. *(Claps her hands)* Tatsu! Tatsu! *(Tatsu enters.)* Please bring some sweets for our guests. *(Tatsu exits.)*

SAEKO: Please, you needn't go to such trouble. Really.

MRS. TSUGAWA: I wonder if I might ask you something?

MAKIMURA: What is it?

MRS. TSUGAWA: Not you . . . you. Saeko is your name, isn't it?

SAEKO: Yes.

MRS. TSUGAWA: Are you just Makimura's friend, or are you lovers?

SAEKO: What? My goodness! What a question to be asked the first time you meet someone! You have a lot of nerve.

MRS. TSUGAWA: *(Smiling stiffly)* Please indulge me. I want to learn more about young people. I seem to have aged more than I thought, you see.

That's why I feel I must speak frankly with you, even too frankly at times.

SAEKO: Makimura, you answer Mrs. Tsugawa's question.

MAKIMURA: I'm afraid I can't.

MRS. TSUGAWA: That's all right, you answered my question well enough. Now I'd like to ask you a question, Saeko. I know I seem to be asking the same thing again and again, but are you really not worried about what might happen to Makimura tomorrow?

SAEKO: Not in the least.

MRS. TSUGAWA: *(Intently)* Really?

SAEKO: Yes. There's absolutely nothing to worry about.

MRS. TSUGAWA: Even though you know what happened to Hisashi?

SAEKO: *(Shaking her head)* Yes. Perhaps I shouldn't put it this way, but I don't think there is any connection between the two events.

MRS. TSUGAWA: Are you saying that Hisashi's accident taught us nothing, that it has no meaning at all?

MAKIMURA: No, Hisashi's death does have meaning. I believe that Hisashi was a blessed sacrifice. He has helped me in my mental preparation for the event, and to raise my level of concentration one step higher. I dedicate this match to his memory. My fighting spirit increases, and . . .

MRS. TSUGAWA: *(Sighs)* So, neither of you are in the least worried. Am I right?

SAEKO: I have absolutely no worries.

MAKIMURA: *(Fawningly to* MRS.TSUGAWA*)* So, have you finally given your approval?

MRS. TSUGAWA: Not yet . . . but, I am very impressed. I see now that we really do live in different worlds. You have no fear whatsoever of warnings, forebodings, what the future holds in store. No worries exist for you. *(She laughs as she speaks the following sentence.)* Saeko, you said, "I have absolutely no worries," didn't you?

SAEKO: I don't like it when people make fun of me. Perhaps I am a little stupid, but . . .

MRS. TSUGAWA: That's perfectly all right.

MAKIMURA: What's all right, being a little stupid?

MRS. TSUGAWA: *(In a superior tone)* Don't say any more. You comprehend nothing. It's fine for you to understand nothing of human beings. It's quite enough for you to understand horses. You're just a healthy, energetic child.

MAKIMURA: Now you're being unkind.

MRS. TSUGAWA: *(Gazing at him fixedly)* You understand absolutely nothing.

SAEKO: What you said is right. Makimura is more a horse than a person.

MAKIMURA: Hey, you'll be sorry you said that.

MRS. TSUGAWA: He's a young horse that likes to kick, isn't he.

The three laugh cheerfully for the first time. Tatsu brings in tea and cakes.

SAEKO: *(Looks at her watch)* Oh my, and now that you've gone to all this trouble on our account.
MAKIMURA: Yes, it's time to go. We have to hurry.
MRS. TSUGAWA: Are you going somewhere on a date?
SAEKO: Yes. Nowhere special though. And after all the trouble you've taken. *(She looks at the tea.)*
MRS. TSUGAWA: It's all right. Go ahead and gulp down the tea.
MAKIMURA: Go ahead, show her just how bad your upbringing is.

SAEKO *gulps down her tea standing up. When she finishes she looks at the other two mischievously.*

SAEKO: I must apologize for my unannounced visit.
MRS. TSUGAWA: Please, the two of you, do come by again.
MAKIMURA: Let me add my apologies.
MRS. TSUGAWA: *(Patting him on the back)* I want you to ride your best for me tomorrow.
MAKIMURA: Yes, I'll give it my all.

MAKIMURA *bows his head once more at the altar. While he is praying* TATSU *takes* SAEKO's *shoes from the garden entrance to the main entrance, then guides* SAEKO *to the main entrance. The two guests exit.* MRS. TSUGAWA *and* TATSU *go outside the door to see them off. After a short while they reenter.*

SCENE 4 (Mrs. Tsugawa, Tatsu)

TATSU: Mr. Makimura is going to ride in the steeplechase tomorrow, isn't he?
MRS. TSUGAWA: *(Sits down gloomily in a chair. Time passes. She mutters to herself)* . . . Steeplechase . . . From now on, that word is forbidden in this house.

CURTAIN

Figure 18. *Steeplechase*, in 1957, Bungaku-za. From the left, Sugimura Haruko as Tsugawa Mineko, Taniguchi Kaoru as Saeko, Tashiro Nobuko as Tatsu, and Higuchi Michiya as Makimura. Photograph courtesy of Bungaku-za and the Mishima Yukio Literary Museum

Busu

(an adaptation of the classical *kyōgen* play)

Written in 1957, Published in 1971
(never performed professionally)
Translated by Donald Keene and Laurence Kominz

INTRODUCTION

Busu is a unique play in this anthology in a number of respects. It is the only play that has never been performed on a professional stage, the only play Mishima wrote as an expedient, and the only play he wrote to be performed in English, *not* in Japanese. *Busu* is the only modern *kyōgen* play in Mishima's entire opus.

Kyōgen plays are short-short farcical comedies traditionally performed between noh plays. The stories from most *kyōgen* texts date back to the fifteenth and sixteenth centuries, and play scripts to the seventeenth and eighteenth centuries. *Kyōgen* was Japan's first dialogue drama (though it contains song and dance as well), and like noh and kabuki, professional *kyōgen* is performed by hereditary acting families who have been *kyōgen* actors for many generations.

Despite the fact that Mishima had seen *kyōgen* performed from the time he was in middle school, his interest was always in the more serious noh drama, and his one-act plays adapted from noh (see *Yuya* in this anthology) are among his finest works for the stage. Donald Keene published translations of five of these modern noh plays as a book in 1957. Mishima went to New York that year in hopes of mounting a Broadway production using them. In New York Mishima fell in with two promoters who were likeable enough, but proved in the end to be incompetent. They struggled for some months but failed to find financial backers for a Broadway production of Mishima's modern noh plays.[1] One of the difficulties they encountered was that Broadway producers shied away from staging unrelated one-act plays. The first attempted solution to this problem was to create the semblance of a traditional noh/*kyōgen* production in Japan. It was at this time that the promoters, Keith Botsford and Charles Schultz, asked Mishima to write a modern *kyōgen* play for them. Mishima complied, and *Busu* was the result.

The traditional *kyōgen* play *Busu* is the most popular play in the entire repertory. It has achieved such iconic status that today it is the first classical Japanese text that all school children read—as part of the sixth grade curriculum. The hero of the play is Tarō Kaja, the archetypical clever and capricious servant. The master summons his two servants, Tarō Kaja and Jirō Kaja, and tells them he has to go away for a while on business. He tells the two servants to guard a vat of dangerous poison, called Busu, while he is away. Tarō and Jirō have never heard of Busu before. Busu is so deadly, their master tells them, that if a breeze blowing over it should happen to enter their noses, they will die instantly. After their master has left, Jirō and Tarō grow curious about the poison and Tarō hits on the idea of using their fans to blow the wind away from the poison while they investigate it. The deadly poison turns out to be brown sugar, an expensive delicacy in medieval Japan. The master lied to his servants because he thought they would eat it on the sly while he was out. Tarō and Jirō eat up all the sugar, and then, at Tarō's instigation, destroy several of their master's treasured art objects. When their master returns home, Tarō explains to him that they broke the objects by accident, and then ate the "poison" so that they could kill themselves by way of atonement. He and Jirō "cry" because the poison was ineffective and did not kill them. The two servants have out-tricked their trickster of a master.

Thanks to its popularity and iconic status, the traditional *Busu* has been translated many times into English. The first was Donald Keene's translation, also published in 1957. Mishima's plan for his modern *kyōgen* version was to use most of the English text as it stood in Keene's translation. Mishima would add text in Japanese that would be translated back into English and grafted into Keene's translation of the traditional play. Mishima's text relocated the action of the play to an antique store on Third Avenue in Manhattan. The master became the aristocratic emigre Russian owner of the store, Raspotinov, and Tarō and Jirō became his American employees, Keith and Chiz, named after the two would-be producers of Mishima's Broadway show. Busu is sugar in the original play, but it became expensive caviar in Mishima's version. Mishima set his play in an antique shop so that there would be ornate fans available to Keith and Chiz and they could fan the wind away from the poison in the traditional manner. The antique shop also provided Keith and Chiz with a fine selection of expensive art works to destroy.

In his adaptation Mishima retained all of the physical comedy and farce of the original play, while adding new layers of parody. He poked fun at the aristocratic pretensions of Russian emigres who are forced to associate with the common herd in New York, and at the ignorance of Americans who know nothing of culture or caviar.

Mishima's approach to this adaptation, of grafting his own modern text into a text in classical Japanese, would have resulted in a very choppy, and to Mishima, unsatisfactory text were it to be performed in Japanese. Mishima condemned this sort of linguistic mish-mash when Japanese playwrights used it for the stage. Mishima made a point of writing purely classical Japanese texts for his own new kabuki plays, and purely modern Japanese texts for his modern noh plays. But Mishima wrote *Busu* to be performed in English, not in Japanese, and he realized that there is little difference between classical Japanese and modern Japanese when both are translated into modern English. In the translation for this anthology Donald Keene and I have remained faithful to Mishima's original plan, and even in English there is a difference in style between text that has been translated from classical Japanese and modern Japanese. This becomes part of the unique incongruity and comic appeal of this particular version of *Busu*.

The original play is full of exaggerated physical comedy and slapstick, but it is executed with the precision and grace used in all *kyōgen* performances, which distinguish *kyōgen* as a classic theatre form. Mishima's version could be performed in this way, but had it been performed in New York in 1958, it would likely have been done with more vulgarity and buffoonery. Either way, *Busu* would have wonderfully complemented a production of two modern noh plays.

Even after Mishima tried yet another solution to the one-act play problem, tying together two unrelated noh plays,[2] his Broadway production was destined never to take place. *Busu* was for him the souvenir of a major disappointment, and he never allowed it to be published in his complete works. Finally, a half-year after his suicide, *Busu* was released to the outside world, but it was hardly noticed.

Busu was never meant to be performed in Japanese, and to my knowledge, has never been performed in Japan. Obviously it has never been reviewed, but one scholar has written that "its new characters, its staging, and its use of properties are first rate, affording a glimpse of what might have been possible had Mishima written more modern *kyōgen* plays."[3] *Busu* has a place in this anthology because the play does make an excellent addition to a program featuring one or two of Mishima's modern noh plays, because it demonstrates the breadth of Mishima's work as playwright of comic drama, and because it is the one play that, from the outset, Mishima intended solely for presentation in English.

NOTES

1. See Donald Keene, *On Familiar Terms: A Journey across Cultures* (Tokyo: Kodansha International, 1994), pp. 201–2, for a brief account of Mishima's attempt to produce a Broadway show in New York in 1957.

2. The playlet is called "Long after Love," and is in Mishima Yukio, *Gikyokushû ge* (Tokyo: Shinchôsha, 1990), pp. 894–98.

3. Ono Yûji, "Busu," *Mishima Yukio jiten* (Tokyo: Bensei Shuppan, 2000), p. 314.

THE CHARACTERS

The Master: Duke Raspotinov

He is the stingy, eccentric, middle-aged, unmarried owner of a Third Avenue antique shop. He is a lonely, suspicious hedonist, and he sports a goatee. His clothes are elegant in a refined, nineteenth-century style. His establishment is called "Duke Raspotinov's." He speaks in a grandiloquent, old-fashioned manner, and never, ever smiles. There is something about him that resembles a magician. This quality mesmerizes his customers and he sells his antiques at exorbitant prices. He usually wears gloves, and he uses snuff. There are rarely any customers in his shop, but if any appear they are certain to be extremely wealthy.

Employee A: Keith
Employee B: Chiz

The employees' clothing is left to the discretion of the director. But it would be uninteresting to clothe them in suits. It would be all right to have the master, following his propensity for ostentation, force them to dress as seventeenth-century French court pages– this despite the fact that he is dressing large men as page boys. But if the director does this, program notes will be necessary or the audience will confuse the play for a story set in the seventeenth century.

The director may fly in the face of logic and have the two employees wear fashionable sport shirts, in direct opposition to the style affected by the master.

The director may have the two employees wear sport shirts with "Duke Raspotinov's" emblazoned on front and back in imitation of the Japanese *happi* coat with company logo. I think that this may be the best plan for their dress.

Keith has some knowledge of the world and he knows the value and appeal of fresh caviar.

SETTING

If a realistic approach is used, the set should represent a well-stocked antique store, recognizable as such in a single glance. Stage left is the inside of the show window, with a glass door next to it with "Duke Raspotinov's" written on it, visible in reverse from the inside. There is a shelf at stage front where the jar of *busu* will be placed.

The time is five p.m. The master is going to a cocktail party and plans to return by closing time. He orders his employees to mind the store until then.

SEASON

Director's discretion. (This "Season" entry may be cut since the season is irrelevant to the play.)

RASPOTINOV, KEITH, *and* CHIZ *enter. The two employees sit upstage facing the audience and* RASPOTINOV *stands, facing them from downstage left.*

RASPOTINOV: You understand? Keith, Chiz, you're to take good care of the place while I am out. Duke Raspotinov's antique store is the finest establishment on Third Avenue. We don't have many customers, but all are of the finest quality. The President, foreign royalty, the ten richest people in the world . . . they have all come here, to buy or to sell. Of course, those who sell are of better lineage than those who buy from us. Blood lines are important to an antique dealer. If the times were only what they once were, I myself would be mingling with European royalty. Oh blessed Tsar, may you rest in peace!

Anyway, you are to take good care of the place while I am out. I am going to a cocktail party. The common horde invented cocktail parties, but I find customers at them. It means spending time away from the shop, but I haven't much choice. So, both of you, be sure to mind the store well while I am away.

KEITH: Your orders will be obeyed, master, but you have always taken one of us with you when you go out, and today too . . .

TOGETHER: One of us would like to accompany you.

RASPOTINOV: No, that is out of the question. Today I have something important to leave in your care, and both of you must guard it. Wait here.

TOGETHER: Very good, master.

RASPOTINOV *goes upstage where he picks up the Oriental bucket. He places it downstage center on the shelf, and returns to his former position.*

RASPOTINOV: This is what is known as *busu,* a deadly poison. If even a wind blowing from its direction should strike you, it will mean instant death. Be on your guard.

KEITH: Yes, master.

CHIZ: But if this poison is so deadly that even a breeze passing over it can strike a person dead, how is it that you are able to handle it?

RASPOTINOV: Poison is antique, and antiques are poison. Furthermore, this substance loves its master, and as long as I handle it, there is not the slightest danger. But if either of you so much as approach it, you will suffer instant death. Beware even of being touched by a breeze from its direction.

CHIZ: Yes, master.

RASPOTINOV: Now I shall be leaving.
KEITH: Have a good time
TOGETHER: And come back soon.
RASPOTINOV: Thank you.

RASPOTINOV *exits. The two employees sit at center stage, facing the audience.*

KEITH: He always takes one of us with him. I wonder why today he left both of us to look after the house?
CHIZ: I wonder why?
KEITH: At any rate, it's always lonesome being left here alone, but since we are both here today, we can have a pleasant chat together. Oh!
CHIZ: What's the matter?
KEITH: There was a gust of wind from the *busu*!
CHIZ: How frightening!
KEITH: Let's move a little farther away.
CHIZ: A good idea.

They move upstage right and sit again.

KEITH: Just as you said before, why should the master keep in the house a thing so deadly that even a breath of wind from it will cause instant death?
CHIZ: However much it may love its master, I still don't understand why he keeps it.
KEITH: You know, I'd like to have a look at the *busu*. What do you think it can be?
CHIZ: Have you gone mad? Don't you know that even a breeze from its direction means certain death?
KEITH: Let's approach it fanning from this side. That way we won't get any wind from it.
CHIZ: That's a good idea.

The two men stand, take fans from among the store's stock and, fanning vigorously, approach the bucket.

KEITH: Fan, fan hard!
CHIZ: I'm fanning!
KEITH: I'm going to untie the cord around it now, so fan hard.
CHIZ: Right!
KEITH: I've unfastened it. Now, I'll take off the cover.
CHIZ: Do it quickly!
KEITH: Keep fanning!

CHIZ: I'm fanning!
KEITH: It's off! *(They flee upstage)* Oh, that's a relief!
CHIZ: What's a relief?
KEITH: That thing—it's not an animal or it would jump out.
CHIZ: Perhaps it's only playing dead.
KEITH: I'll have a look.
CHIZ: That's a good idea.

They approach the bucket as before.

KEITH: Fan, fan hard!
CHIZ: I'm fanning!
KEITH: I'm going to go close and look at it, so fan hard!
CHIZ: Right!
KEITH: There's some sort of cold wind bottled up inside. *(He wraps his hands around the bucket.)* Hyaa!
CHIZ: What happened? What happened?
KEITH: Why, it's like a wind from hell. My hands seemed to freeze solid, like sticks!
CHIZ: That *busu* sure seems to be cold stuff, doesn't it?
KEITH: Fan, fan hard!
CHIZ: I'm fanning, I'm fanning!
KEITH: There, I've seen it! I've seen it!
CHIZ: What, you saw it? *(They flee upstage as before.)*
CHIZ: What did you see?
KEITH: Something dark gray that looked good to eat. You know, I think I'd like a taste of that *busu.*
CHIZ: How can you even think of eating something which will kill you if you only catch a whiff of it?
KEITH: I must be bewitched by the *busu.* I can't think of anything but eating it. I'll take a taste.
CHIZ: You mustn't.

He takes KEITH'S *sleeve, and they struggle.*

KEITH: Let me go!
CHIZ: I won't let you go!
KEITH: I tell you, let me go!
CHIZ: I tell you, I won't let you go!

KEITH *frees himself and approaches the bucket.*

KEITH: *(Singing)* Shaking off with sorrow the sleeves of parting, I come up to the side of the *busu.*

He uses his closed fan to scoop out some of the contents. He licks the busu *off his fan.*

CHIZ: Alas, now you're going to die.
KEITH: Oh, I'm dying. I'm dying. *(He falls over.)*
CHIZ: I knew this would happen. Keith! Are you all right? *(He rushes to* KEITH'S *side.)*
KEITH: It's so delicious, I'm dying. *(He gets up.)*
CHIZ: So, what *is* the *busu*?
KEITH: It's caviar.
CHIZ: What? Caviar? What's caviar?
KEITH: You are a hopeless hick, aren't you? It's true, genuine, fresh caviar. It looked like any old antique, but it's really fresh caviar. My grandfather used to be rich, and he once told me that there's nothing in the world as delicious as fresh caviar. Now that I've gotten a better look at it I can see that there's an icebox built into this thing. Oh. There are lemons inside too.
CHIZ: In that case, let me have a little taste too.
KEITH: Let's dig in. Let's have at it. But, it isn't any good if we don't have wine to go with it. The master keeps his secret reserve in the cellar doesn't he? Lend me the duplicate key.
CHIZ: *(Takes it out of his shoe)* Here you are, use this. *(*KEITH *takes the key and exits.)*

*(*CHIZ *tastes the caviar fearfully)* Yes. Now that I've eaten a little . . . yes, it is the most delicious food I've ever tasted. I'll put a little lemon on it. . . . Why, I thought I'd just try a little, but it's the sort of flavor that makes you want to eat more and more.

KEITH *enters, bringing an old wine bottle. The two men pass the bottle back and forth, drinking from it. The two of them eat, using their closed fans to scoop out the caviar.* KEITH, *seeing that* CHIZ *is too busy eating to notice, carries the bucket to stage left. While* KEITH *is eating,* CHIZ *comes up and takes the bucket to stage right so he can have it to himself.*

KEITH: Hey, what're you doing? What do you mean by eating it up all by yourself? Give some to me.
CHIZ: You started eating before me. Give me some more. *(They tussle over the caviar.)*
KEITH: Let's eat it together.
CHIZ: Good idea. *(They put the bucket between them.)*
KEITH: Delicious, isn't it?
CHIZ: Really delicious.
KEITH: The master told us that it was *busu,* to keep us from eating it. That was really most unkind of him. Eat up! Eat up!

CHIZ: It was disagreeable of him to have told us that we would die instantly if we got so much as a whiff of it. Eat up! Eat up!
KEITH: I can't stop eating.
CHIZ: It feels as if our chins are sagging, doesn't it?
KEITH: Eat up! Oh, it's all gone!
CHIZ: Yes, all gone.
KEITH: Well, you can be proud of yourself.
CHIZ: *I* can be proud of myself? It was *you* who first looked at the *busu* and first ate it. I'll tell the master as soon as he gets back.
KEITH: I was only joking.
CHIZ: So, what shall we do for an excuse?
KEITH: That's easy, just tear up that Byzantine banner.
CHIZ: All right. *(He takes the banner and tears it up.)*
KEITH: Bravo! First you looked at the *busu,* then you ate it, and now you've destroyed the master's prized banner. I'll inform him of that as soon as he returns.
CHIZ: I only did it because you told me to. And I shall inform the master of that.
KEITH: I was joking again.
CHIZ: But what shall we do for an excuse?
KEITH: Just smash this Chinese plate.
CHIZ: No, I've had enough.
KEITH: Then, let's smash it together.
CHIZ: All right. *(They pick up the large plate and dash it to the ground.)*
KEITH: Ah–it's in bits and pieces.
CHIZ: Now what excuse will we make?
KEITH: When the master returns, the first thing to do is to burst into tears.
CHIZ: Will tears do any good?
KEITH: They will indeed. He'll be coming back soon. Come over here.
CHIZ: Right.

They hide the wine bottle somewhere in the shop and go upstage and wait. RASPOTINOV *enters through the shop door and speaks.*

RASPOTINOV: I have just returned from the cocktail party. My employees must be waiting anxiously for my return. *(As he moves downstage left.)* Keith, Chiz, I'm back.
KEITH: He's back! Now start weeping! *(They weep.)*
RASPOTINOV: Keith, Chiz! Where are you? What is the matter here? Instead of being glad that I have returned they are both weeping. If something has happened, let me know at once.
KEITH: Chiz, you tell the master.
CHIZ: Keith, you tell the master.
RASPOTINOV: I don't care which of you it is, just tell me quickly.

KEITH: Well, then, this is what happened. I thought that it wouldn't do for me to sleep while on such important duty, but I got sleepier and sleepier. To keep awake I had a wrestling match with Chiz. He is so strong that he knocked me over, and to keep from falling, I clutched at the Byzantine banner, and ripped it—as you can see. *(They weep.)*

RASPOTINOV: What a dreadful thing to happen! *(He examines the shredded banner in amazement and anger.)* How could you tear up my precious banner like this?

KEITH: Then he threw me back and spun me over the stand with the Chinese plate on it, and the plate was smashed to bits. *(They weep.)*

RASPOTINOV: This is awful! *(He examines the remains of the plate in amazement and anger.)* You even smashed my precious Chinese plate. The two of you do not deserve to live.

KEITH: We knew you would feel that way so we ate up the *busu*, hoping to die. Isn't that so, Chiz?

CHIZ: Exactly.

KEITH: *(singing)* One mouthful and still death did not come.

CHIZ: *(singing)* Two mouthfuls and still death did not come.

KEITH: *(singing)* Three mouthfuls, four mouthfuls

CHIZ: *(singing)* Five mouthfuls

KEITH: *(singing)* More than ten mouthfuls *(They get up and begin to dance.)*

KEITH and CHIZ: *(singing)* We ate until there wasn't any left,
But still death came not, strange to tell,
Ah, what a clever head!

They approach the master, singing and fanning, then suddenly strike him on the head with their fans.

RASPOTINOV: What do you mean, "clever head!"

At this moment the wine bottle rolls out. RASPOTINOV *picks it up and looks at it. He looks carefully at the two men, who are seemingly in distress.*

RASPOTINOV: You hooligans! *(They run away, laughing.)* Where do you think you're going? Somebody seize them. I won't let you off!

KEITH and CHIZ: Forgive us, forgive us!

RASPOTINOV *chases them. While the two are running away they throw an antique at him. This takes* RASPOTINOV *by surprise, but he catches it. This gives the two employees the opportunity to put some distance between themselves and* RASPOTINOV. RASPOTINOV *resumes his pursuit. Again an employee throws a valuable antique at* RASPOTINOV. RASPOTINOV *assumes a silly posture in the act of catching it. This gives the two employees the opportunity to escape through the door at stage left. Both* RASPOTINOV'S *hands are full, holding two valuable antiques. He stands unable to move. Beside him stands a Buddha statue in exactly the same position.*

CURTAIN

STAGE NOTES

Properties

1. A jar of *busu:* a large, antique Oriental bucket. The bucket has an ice-box inside. Inside the bucket is kept a large quantity of the master's favorite delicacy–priceless, fresh caviar. Lemons may also be inside.

2. A tapestry: This will later be pulled down and torn up. There should be a price tag affixed to it from the start, exhibiting an exorbitant price, say $50,000. But a real tapestry could not be destroyed just by a sumo wrestling accident, so it has to be some other specialty item made of fabric. It could be a painting on cloth, a banner from the Byzantine empire, or some such item.

3. A china doll or a large, ornamental plate to be smashed during the play. A tag, showing an exorbitant price, should hang from this object.

4. A bottle of wine: The employees drink this wine to go with the caviar. When the master returns, for a moment he thinks that the story the two have told him is true, but when he finds the wine bottle, he discovers the truth and gets angry.

5. Numerous dishes and porcelain ornaments, and at least two fans.

6. A sculpture of Buddha in a contorted pose, or a small sculpture of a demon. This is used only at the closing curtain.

Sash Stealing Pond

(Obi Tori no Ike)

(a kabuki play)

Published in 1958, First Performed in 1958

Translated by Laurence Kominz

INTRODUCTION

Sash Stealing Pond (Obitori no Ike) (full title: *The Pond that Steals Sashes Young Women Like [Musume Gonomi Obitori no Ike]*) was the last one-act play that Mishima wrote for kabuki. After the relatively negative experience with his adaptation of Racine's *Phaedra* to the kabuki stage in 1955, and a mediocre *shimpa* melodrama for Nakamura Utaemon in 1957, Mishima returned to kabuki parody. This time Mishima set out to parody historical drama, specifically the most revered and celebrated act in kabuki—the pursuit of blood revenge. In this he was inspired by, among others, the great Edo Period playwright, Chikamatsu Monzaemon (1653–1724). In a 1958 essay Mishima wrote that he admired Chikamatsu's art, but unlike his contemporaries who held Chikamatsu's domestic tragedies in highest esteem, Mishima preferred the history plays, and he particularly admired Chikamatsu's parody scenes in the history plays.[1] Chikamatsu had parodied the sacred act of blood revenge in several kabuki and puppet plays.[2]

Sash Stealing Pond is an original play, not an adaptation. The only elements of the play that Mishima borrowed from Edo Period literature were the setting, the lead male character, and the name of his wife. An obscure illustrated adventure story[3] by Santo Kyōden (1761–1816) features a thief named Gamamaru (Toad Bandit) who has a magic potion that allows him to breathe under water, and he uses it to drown and rob travellers who pass by Sash Stealing Pond, north of Kyoto. The plot of the story and all other characters were invented by Mishima.[4]

The heroine of the play is Princess Kiku (Utaemon) who is on a quest to take revenge on the man who robbed and murdered her mother. Because Toad Bandit uses Kiku's mother's sash to lure travelers to the pond, Kiku is convinced that he murdered her mother. Toad Bandit had in fact waylaid and raped her mother, but her mother chose to become the bandit's wife. When her mother suddenly appears to put a stop to her daughter's vendetta, Princess Kiku expresses humiliation and revulsion at her mother's depravity. This scene turns conventional kabuki upside down. In traditional kabuki it is common for samurai mothers to reprimand daughters who are engaging in illicit love affairs, but unheard of for a mother to defend hedonistic behavior while her daughter chastises her for departing from the moral strictures of samurai class women.

The audience soon learns that Kiku's assumption of the high moral ground is hypocritical. She is herself deeply in love with the handsome, young family retainer Samanosuke, but their difference in station prevents her from marrying him. The play concludes after all the principal characters agree to keep the liaison between the Toad Bandit and the mother secret from the world so that Princess Kiku and Samanosuke can travel around the country on a sham revenge quest and sleep together as husband and wife when they spend the night at inns.

The women characters are entirely immoral, both by Edo Period standards, and the standards of Japanese society in 1958. One marries her rapist and the other fakes the sacred act of blood revenge to cover up an illicit love affair. Why then, have they been so appealing to critics and audiences? The answer lies in the triumph of true love and the post-war "democratic" repudiation of the feudal social hierarchy. Mishima attacked or called into question conventional morality in many of his serious novels and plays. In *Sash Stealing Pond* he did the same thing in a play that was a parody and a romantic comedy. The difference between *Sash Stealing Pond* and Mishima's noncomic approaches to alternative morality lies in the nature of comedy itself. Traditional stage comedy brings people together and affirms romantic love. In *Sash Stealing Pond* hedonism and immorality unite a mother and daughter, and two pairs of lovers who could never have come together had they followed the dictates of feudal morality. This is very different from a noncomic work like *Forbidden Colors* in which hedonism and immorality condemn characters to emotional and social isolation.

In *Sash Stealing Pond* Mishima dispensed with the three unities and used kabuki spectacle to great effect with swimming and swooping sashes, an actor-swallowing pond, a huge flying kite sent by Samanosuke, and a dramatic *gandōgaeshi* scene change in which the entire set for Scene One rotates upwards, revealing Scene Two. Mishima wrote that stage spectacle was central to the appeal of kabuki, not mere gimmickry.[5]

Mishima's text for *Sash Stealing Pond* is considerably different from his earlier kabuki texts in that while it is written in classical Japanese, it has no sung narration. *Sash Stealing Pond* recalls the great bandit plays by nineteenth-century playwright Kawatake Mokuami (1816–93), but Mishima's bandit hero is a modern creation. Instead of Mokuami's noble bandit fighting against corrupt samurai officials, Toad Bandit, despite his impressive appearance, is a lecherous, henpecked husband who can not even prevail in a fight against a princess, and who has to struggle to maintain his dignity in front of his jealous wife. As pathetic as Toad Bandit is, his henchmen, half-animal and half-human, are even more ridiculous. Samanosuke enters very late in the play. He is a handsome prude, very like Harumochi in *Lady Fuyo.* In the end, however, he surrenders to his love for Kiku and her love for him, and so becomes a sympathetic character in the eyes of the audience that wants to see the daring Kiku get the man she loves.

When it first appeared, audiences and kabuki critics loved *Sash Stealing Pond* for its quirky characters, unexpected plot twists, its playful eroticism and spectacular staging. One critic summed up what many expressed: "It is rare that authors of new works write with the possibilities of staging in mind. It had the feeling of an old ghost story or adventure story. Even though this is play for Mishima, it is play in a good sense. There is a special quality of *esprit* in this ridiculous story."[6]

But *Sash Stealing Pond* has not been produced as often as *The Sardine Seller's Net of Love.* There are no characters in *Sash Stealing Pond* as charming and lovable as the silly, lovelorn sardine vendor and the gorgeous courtesan who falls for a man who smells of fish. In a 1998 production of *Sash Stealing Pond* at the National Theatre, director Orita Kōji took the same liberties with Mishima's text as he would with a traditional text, cutting over a page of material from the henchmen's conversation, and adding more business for Samanosuke at the end of the play because Samanosuke was being performed by a popular, young actor. Kabuki has always been an actor's art, and Mishima recognized that from the outset. Even when he directed his own kabuki plays, he accepted changes such as these when they had to be made.

Mishima clearly stated his approach to writing kabuki plays in his author's notes in the Kabuki-za program of December, 1958, the show that included *Sash Stealing Pond*: "Newly composed kabuki plays should be couched in the idiom of traditional kabuki, and should partake of the beauty, stage mechanics, and all of the acting conventions, just as they are used in traditional kabuki. I believe that within this framework, contemporary themes and modern humor and wit must be interwoven into a new and original work."[7] Mishima followed this prescription to the letter in *Sash Stealing Pond.*

NOTES

1. Mishima Yukio, "Chikamatsu bayari shikan," *Tokyo Shimbun,* April 7 and 8, 1958; reprinted in *Mishima hyôron zenshû,* vol. 3 (Tokyo: Shinchô, 1994), p. 649.

2. See Laurence Kominz, *Avatars of Vengeance: Japanese Drama and the Soga Literary Tradition* (Ann Arbor: The Center for Japanese Studies, The University of Michigan, 1995), pp. 118–30, 140–45 for studies of two kabuki and three puppet plays by Chikamatsu that parody the theme of blood revenge.

3. Mishima Yukio, "Sakusha no kotoba," Kabuki-za Program, December 1958; reprinted in *Mishima hyôron zenshû,* vol. 3, p. 878. The name of the work is *Sakurahime zenden akebono zôshi,* and the chapter it comes from is "Gamamaru no den, Obitori no Ike no ki."

4. Ibid.

5. Ibid.

6. Oki Yutaka, in *Gekihyô,* December 1958, excerpted in Ogawa Akiko, "Mishima Yukio kabuki sakuhin jôen kiroku to nenpyô," *Kabuki* 12 (April 1972), p. 43.

7. Mishima, "Sakusha no kotoba," p. 878.

THE CHARACTERS

The Toad Bandit, a thief
Scheming Crow, Toad's henchman
Eight Owl, Toad's henchman
Fox Fist, Toad's henchman
Bear Liver, Toad's henchman
Silver Badger, Toad's henchman
Yogobei, a silk merchant
Yokuroku ("Six Greeds"), Yogobei's chief clerk
Princess Kiku ("Chrysanthemum")
Samanosuke (Princess Kiku's family retainer)
Owaki, Toad Bandit's wife, really Lady Nowaki, Princess Kiku's mother, in disguise

SETTING

SCENE ONE: Sash Stealing Pond, in the mountains north of Kyoto
SCENE TWO: Toad Bandit's house, nearby

SCENE ONE: SASH STEALING POND, IN THE MOUNTAINS NORTH OF KYOTO

The main stage set depicts a deep mountain valley. In the middle is a large pond, with a blue fabric surface over a trap in the stage, constructed so that actors can jump in and sink beneath the surface. At stage left a vertical sign identifies it as "Sash Stealing Pond." The curtain opens to clappers and a water drum roll from the geza. YAGOBEI *and his clerk enter down the* hanamichi, *accompanied by the drum roll.* YOKUROKU *leads the way, carrying a lantern. They stop at the seven-three spot.*

YOGOBEI: My goodness it's lonely out here in North Saga, isn't it Yokuroku? It's already sunset and we haven't run across so much as a woodcutter.

YOKUROKU: Master, there's nothing to be afraid of. Night after night strange things take place at Sash Stealing Pond, which is somewhere in this area. Rumor has it that a woman's gold brocade sash floats around on the pond's surface. If you take it back to Kyoto and sell it to some rich woman, you're sure to make a fortune.

YOGOBEI: Your name means "greed," and you really do live up to it. You made it sound so lucrative you persuaded me to come all the way out to a desolate place like this.

YOKUROKU: Don't worry, you just have to be patient a little bit longer. The footing's dangerous here. *(He takes his master's hand, and they mime stepping over bad places in the road.)* This is the way.

They enter the main stage, and YOKUROKU *sees the sign standing at stage left.*

YOKUROKU: Oh, look!

YOGOBEI: What is it? What is it? *(He is so scared he begins to run back the way he came.)*

YOKUROKU: It's nothing to be frightened of. I found the sign. Look, there in the moonlight you can see inky black characters reading "Sash Stealing Pond." We've come to the right place.

YOGOBEI: Really? That's wonderful. *(He looks around.)* Well, I see the pond, but I don't see any sashes. I wonder if someone has deceived us about this place?

YOKUROKU: Don't worry, Master. After all, when you've sold silk, you've deceived others, but you've never allowed yourself to be deceived, even once.

YOGOBEI: How can you say that about me? What if someone were to overhear you?

YOKUROKU: The only thing that could hear us out here is that owl.

Suddenly the large drum in the geza *begins a* doro-doro *drum roll, signalling a supernatural occurrence. The two men flee back to the seven-three spot on the* hanamichi, *and covering their heads with their jacket sleeves, they tremble in fear. A golden brocade sash rises up from the middle of the pond, and hovers above it. Its movement makes it look like a great serpent. The two eventually overcome their fear, look up, and see it.*

YOKUROKU: Hey, hey Master, take a look at that! A golden sash is swimming around. Look at it swim!

YOGOBEI: I can see that it is of rare quality. I could get at least one hundred gold coins for that.

YOKUROKU: What? I could probably sell it for two hundred.

YOGOBEI: What, two hundred gold coins? *(He pushes* YOKUROKU *aside and runs to the edge of the pond.)*

Master and servant struggle to get at the sash. Eventually YAGOBEI *manages to grab it. Just as he is about to pull the sash out of the water, instead it pulls him forward and he falls into the pond with a splash, indicated by loud beats of a drum. He disappears and the sash continues swimming around.*

YOKUROKU: Now what? Should I try to save my master or should I take the sash? Should I save him or take it? Save him or take it? Wait a minute . . . my name means greed. Who am I to deny my nature?

He seizes the sash, but it pulls back, and they engage in a humorous fight. The sash coils around his neck like a boa constrictor and pulls him into the pond with a splash. Music invoking an uncanny supernatural occurrence plays in the geza, *and from the pond the* TOAD BANDIT *emerges on a trap lift. His face is painted in red make-up, and he holds two wallets in his teeth.* YAGOBEI *and* YOKUROKU *are on either side of him, clutching his sleeves, but* TOAD BANDIT *brandishes a short sword, and slashing to his left and right, cuts off their arms. He climbs deliberately up onto the embankment and silently calculates the weight of the two wallets. He puts them inside his robe, laughs cruelly and silently, and, as he begins to roll up the sash floating on the pond, he strikes a dramatic pose. As he continues to roll up the sash he looks toward the* hanamichi, *notices that someone is approaching, and puts the sash back into the water. It disappears back into the pond. The* TOAD BANDIT *takes some ointment from a medicine case and rubs it on his ears, eyes, nose, and mouth. Then he once again enters the pond and disappears.*

The music from the geza *changes to a lively tune, and Princess* KIKU *enters on the* hanamichi. *She wears a scarlet brocade over-kimono, and flowered hair ornaments. She carries a traveler's staff and hat. She advances down the* hanamichi *and stops at the seven-three spot.*

KIKU: I am on a perilous journey in the mountains north of the Capital. A woman's legs are frail, but I have come so far from the mansion of our clan. My only support has been my retainer, Samanosuke, but somehow we became separated during our journey. I hope I can find a sign that will guide me on my way.

The doro-doro *drum roll from the* geza *announces a supernatural occurrence.* KIKU *hides her face behind her sleeve in fear, and very cautiously advances to the edge of the main stage. There she sees the gold sash floating on the surface of the pond.*

KIKU: That sash!

She goes onto the main stage. She has difficulty catching hold of the sash, but when she does it pulls her and she struggles with it for a while. Eventually it pulls her into the pond with a splash. Music from the geza *suggests mysterious happenings. The trap rises, lifting the* TOAD BANDIT *up onto the stage. He carries the princess in his arms. He puts her down on the ground beside the pond and looks intently at her face. He laughs silently, rolls up the sash, and puts it in his kimono. The* TOAD BANDIT *turns back to the princess and rubs her back. The princess regains consciousness and screams. She tries to get up and run away but the* TOAD BANDIT *stops her and covers her mouth with his hand. He leads the princess by her hand, and the two go to the seven-three spot on the* hanamichi. *They pose dramatically, then exit down the* hanamichi *to musical accompaniment. The play's set rotates on a vertical axis* (gandōgaeshi), *revealing the next scene. What was the backdrop of scene one swivels down so that it is under the floor of scene two.*

SCENE TWO: TOAD BANDIT'S HOUSE, IN THE MOUNTAINS NORTH OF KYOTO

The set represents a rustic dwelling deep in the mountains. The dwelling has a floor downstage at stage level and a raised platform upstage representing the main room. There is a sunken hearth in the middle of the main room. A second raised room, stage left, is separated from the main room by a shōji *partition. There is a door in the back wall of the main room, and a window in the stage right wall. Outside the brushwood gate at ground level, the set's backdrop depicts a night scene deep in the mountains. Laundry is hung on the branches of forest trees and these trees look even more imposing than other trees in the background. When the scene change is completed* TOAD BANDIT'S *henchmen,* SCHEMING CROW, SIX OWL, FOX FIST, BEAR LIVER, *and* SILVER BADGER, *are seated around a pot hanging over the hearth fire, gazing at the burning coals, awaiting their master's return.*

CROW: That's a great plan our boss the Toad Bandit thought up—luring people to the pond with those stories. As long as greed exists in this floating world, business is sure to thrive. We are very lucky to have him as our boss.

OWL: A thriving business is great, but now we've all got to take turns doing the work that the Boss used to do all by himself. We're still engaged in thievery, but if my father saw me swimming around in the water and pretending to be a toad, he'd be so upset.

FOX: Thanks to the ointment that came from the land of the Southern Barbarians, we can operate in the water just as if it's land. Even under water we can see, hear, and speak with no problem. That makes it easy to pull travelers who grab the sash into the water, strangle them to death, and steal their money.

BEAR: Of course when the Boss thought this plan up, it was summertime. Now that it's autumn he hates getting soaked in that cold water. Tonight he went even though he didn't want to, so I hope he got a good haul.

BADGER: It's our job as his henchmen to have his favorite badger stew ready for him when he gets back. I wonder if the badger we caught today has made a tasty stew? *(He tastes some of the stew in the pot.)* That's a very fine badger.

CROW: Badger stew to warm the body from the inside . . .

OWLS: Then, to warm the body from the outside . . .

FOX: A woman—much better than a badger . . .

BEAR: Though she yearns for the capital night and day . . .

BADGER: She is happy with her wifely duties.

CROW: Well, it's about time for the Boss to be getting back.

The TOAD BANDIT *and* KIKU *enter down the* hanamichi, *stopping at the seven-three spot.*

KIKU: You don't have to hold my hand so tightly. I'll follow you obediently, so just go ahead and show me the way.

TOAD BANDIT: As you wish, my lady. Since you find my ugly hand offensive . . . I know, I'll use this. *(He partially unrolls the sash he has been carrying.)* Hold onto this and follow along, follow along.

KIKU: I'm supposed to hold onto this? (*She takes one end of the sash and looks at it very carefully.)* The more I look at this . . .

TOAD: What?

KIKU: I mean . . . the more I look at it, the more radiantly it shines.

TOAD: Of course it does. Now come along this way.

KIKU: This way? *(She continues to hold onto one end of the sash.)* Is your mansion still a long way off?

TOAD: My "mansion" you ask? All we have to do is climb to the top of this slope, and . . . there it is, right before your eyes.

They proceed to the main stage. TOAD *knocks on the brushwood gate.*

TOAD: I'm back! I'm back!

CROW: Our boss, the Toad Bandit . . .

ALL UNDERLINGS: . . . has returned home.

The underlings open the gate and bow to their leader. TOAD *enters alone, leaving* KIKU *outside the gate.*

CROW: So, how did you do tonight?

TOAD: A big catch . . . very big. An incomparable prize. I've brought back a noble bride.

CROW: She is beautiful to behold. Standing in the moonlight the princess looks just like an angel or a goddess. When I look at her I feel as though I'm melting. What a fine souvenir you've brought back. I'm so lucky.

TOAD: Fool! You think I'll give her to you?

CROW: In that case . . .

ALL UNDERLINGS: Whose bride will she be?

TOAD: Mine of course.
CROW: But Boss, you can't do that.
TOAD: Why can't I?
CROW: Well, when you put it like that . . .
TOAD: Ssssh! *(He silences his henchmen.)*
ALL UNDERLINGS: Yes, sir. *(They bow in obedience.)*
TOAD: I know that a woman's brocade sash should never be exposed to water. But every night we soak it through, and though we hang it out to dry, it's always damp. But this our only way to make a living. Go hang it out to dry.

He hands the rolled up sash to CROW. CROW *bows as he receives it, and takes it outside the gate. Intimidated by the Princess' nobility, he takes a wide berth around her as she stands outside. While he is doing this,* TOAD *sits down by the open hearth and the other henchmen sit in a line on the main stage. Outside the gate* KIKU *addresses* CROW.

KIKU: Are you going to hang the sash to dry it?
CROW: Yes Miss, I'm going to hang it up to dry.

Without thinking KIKU *grabs the sash from* CROW *and uses it to dry her tears.*

KIKU: In that case, allow me to assist you.
CROW: A noble lady shouldn't do such things. I don't need any help.
KIKU: What do you mean? It's like a scene in an old poem—drying a gold brocade sash in the light of the moon. "From a thousand-year old cedar, straight as a spear, deep in the mountains, under a splendid moonlit sky . . . " That's right, raise it high aloft to dry it. That will be best.
CROW: Like this?
KIKU: Higher.
CROW: The sash will become golden halls and jewelled turrets . . . a glorious nest for birds.
KIKU: It would make a fine lodging for a wild goose who's longing for its mate.
CROW: What?
KIKU: Remember that in poetry, the moon and geese always go together.
CROW: This is too much for me. Stop talking about geese and show some sympathy for this Crow. *(He takes her hand.)*
KIKU: How dare you! *(She runs away from him, entering the gate that has been left open.)*
TOAD: What's going on?
KIKU: The crows are in such a frenzy this moonlit night.
TOAD: Then bring your damp wings over to this warm hearth.

KIKU: Your hospitality is especially welcome right now. *(She looks around at the faces of the henchmen.)* You gentlemen all have such horrible faces.
OWL: We were born with these faces . . .
ALL UNDERLINGS: . . . And are stuck with them.
KIKU: Today is the first time I've ever been invited into a bandit's mansion.
OWL: Please be our guest . . .
ALL UNDERLINGS: . . . and come to the hearth.
TOAD: Princess, please enter first.
KIKU: Then I shall enter right away.

To the accompaniment of courtly music KIKU *enters and takes the seat of honor by the hearth.* CROW *enters surreptitiously after her.*

TOAD: The more I look at you the more I can tell that you are a lady of rare high breeding. I'm afraid that this is but a poor mountain dwelling. *(To his henchmen)* Serve her a bowl of soup!

One of the underlings ladles badger stew into a bowl and gives it to KIKU.

KIKU: *(Raises the bowl and looks at the contents)* I wonder what kind of stew this is?
TOAD: Nothing warms the stomach as this fine old recipe does. By all means partake of it.
KIKU: But it is all brown looking . . .
CROW: Of course it is, it's badger stew.
KIKU: What? Badger stew?

She drops the bowl on her knees. TOAD *signals with his eyes to* BEAR *and* FOX, *who wipe off the Princess' lap.*

TOAD: Now then, let's cheer the princess up by showing her the dance we've been practicing.
ALL UNDERLINGS: Yes, sir.

All the henchmen dance to the accompaniment of music from the geza. *As the dance comes to an end* TOAD *speaks.*

TOAD: After dancing comes the all-important toast. Quickly, bring the sake cups we've prepared.
BADGER: As you request, sir. *(He brings sake cups made of deer antlers.)*
KIKU: My, what warlike sake cups. In honor of what will we be drinking sake tonight?
TOAD: I'm sure you can figure it out without my telling you. *(In a huge voice)* It will be our nuptial wine!

KIKU: You don't seem at all like a mountain bandit, and I believe you will make a fine husband. So, I have resolved to give myself to you. I know I'm in no position to complain, but how can we drink sake and become man and wife with that ugly bunch sitting there all in a line? Please make them all go away.
CROW: You're already acting as bossy as a wife.
OWL: Even though she's only been away from the capital for a short time . . .
FOX: . . . These days all the princesses . . .
BEAR: . . . are so pushy,
ALL UNDERLINGS: Aren't they!
TOAD: What are you all chattering about? Begone, begone!
ALL UNDERLINGS: Yes, sir.

They exit through the upstage center door.

TOAD: Finally we are alone, and no one will trouble us.
KIKU: Lord Toad, do you mind if I sit closer to you?
TOAD: Not at all. Please come sit by my side.

She moves from the opposite side of the hearth and sits down right next to him.

KIKU: Here I am.
TOAD: I can't wait any longer. *(He restrains himself from embracing her, instead reaching for the deer antler sake cup.)*
KIKU: Don't be in such a rush. Drinking sake comes first. *(They exchange cups and drink together, engaging in ad-libbed small talk.)* I was terrified when I first saw your face by the lakeside in the moonlight filtering through the trees. But when you led me on my frail legs into these unknown mountain fastnesses, you seemed so strong and dependable that step by step I found myself climbing up the steep path of love. And now that I have arrived at your mansion, I can tell that you will be a fine husband. I am embarrassed to beg this of you, but please accept my devotion and promise never to betray my love.
TOAD: Why should I ever betray your love? This mountain dwelling so far from the flowers of the capital will be your capital now. You will always be by my side, giving your all as a bandit's wife, and I will gain wealth and renown unrivalled even by the great bandit Ishikawa Goemon.
KIKU: It fills me with joy to hear you tell me this.

TOAD *lays his head down in* KIKU'S *lap.* KIKU *looks warily around the room, then pulls a dagger from the kimono fold at her breast.*

KIKU: Murderer of my mother! Prepare to die!

Figure 19. *Sash Stealing Pond*, 1973, at the Kabuki-za. Princess Kiku (Nakamura Shikan) seduces the Toad Bandit (Nakamura Ganjirō II). Photograph courtesy of the Waseda University Tsubouchi Hakase Memorial Theatre Museum.

She tries to stab him, but TOAD *dodges away from the blade and defends himself with a long pipe. A* tachimawari *fight ensues. Finally* KIKU *prevails. She holds* TOAD *down as she speaks. [As staged in 1998, the two pose apart from each other,* TOAD *lying on his back, vulnerable, stage right, and* KIKU *poised to strike, stage left.])*

KIKU: During the Sixth Month my mother, Lady Nowaki, was murdered while returning from a pilgrimage to a temple. Her sash was stolen when she met her cruel end. All this was, no doubt, the work of a bandit. So I set out with our family retainer, Samanosuke, determined to find the whereabouts of my mother's murderer. But we became separated and I wandered around, alone in the mountains. Then I came upon the pond with the gold embroidered sash all spread out on the surface. It was none other than my mother's sash.

I pretended to be in love with you, secretly waiting for you to let down your guard, then seized my opportunity. Toad Bandit, my blood enemy, my hatred for you is boundless! Taste Princess Kiku's steel blade!

They fight again. Voice shouts from inside the room at stage left.

OWAKI (really LADY NOWAKI): Wait! Stay your hand! Your mother is right here.

KIKU: That voice . . .

As KIKU *starts in surprise the stage left lattice door opens and* LADY NOWAKI *enters, but not dressed as a noble lady. She has become the bandit wife* OWAKI. *She sits down.*

KIKU: You are my honored mother.

OWAKI: Sit down. I said, sit down. *(Music from the* geza *accompanies her monologue.)* You have every reason to be surprised. It is true that in the Sixth Month I was attacked in the dark of night by the Toad Bandit. After he defiled me, I made up my mind to die, but when I caught sight of him in the moonlight he seemed such a handsome, strong, reliable man. I had long become accustomed to my widow's robes, but I gave up the robes I had worn and the life I had become accustomed to and became the wife of the Toad Bandit. I took the corpse of some poor person and made it look like my corpse, and so have deceived the whole world. But there is no reason whatsoever for you to seek to avenge me. *(Reverting to common speech)* What do you think, Lord Toad . . . oh, I mean, husband darling . . . don't we enjoy our life together?

TOAD: What's that? Oh yes . . . we enjoy it very much.

OWAKI: But right now I hate that face of yours that's enjoying life so much.

What do you mean by bringing a young woman here and going through a wedding ceremony when you have me here all the time? When I peeked in from the shadows I realized it was my daughter Princess Kiku and it made my stomach hurt to see it. Thanks to her filial devotion nothing terrible took place, and the situation resolved itself, but what would have happened had she been some other girl? This is too much—don't treat me like this. Oh, how you have hurt me. I am so upset with you! *(She weeps loudly.)*

KIKU: I'm the one who has been hurt. Mother, you were my perfect model of virtue, and look what you have become. Really Mother, how could you? *(Music begins to play from the* geza *to accompany her monologue.)* Although you did not cut off your hair and become a nun, you said that a faithful wife does not remarry, but night and day reads the sutras and visits temples praying for her dead husband's salvation. The moral lessons you taught me every day sunk into the fiber of my being. Then you set out on your pilgrimage. After you met a cruel fate my tears flowed unceasingly. Somehow they spurred me on and my lifelong desire became to confront your murderer and avenge your death. Now, after I have struggled across the mountains, what do I find but my mother looking as I never imagined she would.

You were Washio's respected widow. For you, who were once called Lady Nowaki, to be the companion of a bandit even for a moment is utter degradation. Now you screech in a jealous rage in front of your own daughter. How cruel of you, mother, to disappoint me so terribly. You have sunk so low, I just can't take it!

She weeps loudly. Caught between the two weeping women TOAD *is at a loss what to do.*

TOAD: Now, now, it won't do to have mother and daughter crying like this. Why don't you each have a cup of sake to restore your good spirits? *(He first takes a sake bottle and cup to* KIKU.*)* Come now, since I've learned that you are the daughter of my wife, this sake celebrates our bond as parent and child. Cheer up.

He presses her to drink, but KIKU *refuses him, eventually pulling out her dagger and brandishing it at him.*

TOAD: Watch out! That's dangerous. My, my, you get your stubbornness from your mother I guess.

He gives up on KIKU *and goes to* OWAKI, *offering a cup of sake to her.*

TOAD: Here darling wife, how about a little sake before bed? *(He presses her to drink, but she refuses him.)*

OWAKI. This is not the time for drinking sake. (*To* KIKU) Your admonition is just and I recognize that I have done wrong. But please think of Lady Nowaki as dead. I am now Owaki, the wife of the Toad Bandit.

KIKU: What do you mean, "Owaki"? My mother can't have such a lowly name.

OWAKI: Owaki sounds more stylish and up-to-date than Nowaki. I've left my life in the capital, and life here in the mountains is such a pleasure. The cuckoo calls in the summer, and in the autumn I rise from quilts to the cries of birds flying south. The myriad flowers blooming in the fields are more remarkable than twills and embroidered brocades. It is only since I married a bandit that I have come to understand the good life, and I want you to enjoy it as well. Yes, I've just had a good idea. As good luck would have it, there are many young men here in my husband's service. They may not be as good-looking as those fools in the capital, but they're much finer prospects as sons-in-law. Lord Toad, how about introducing my daughter to one of your followers?

TOAD: Well, I don't know . . .

OWAKI: You disagree? Does that mean you're still infatuated with her yourself?

TOAD: No, it's not that.

OWAKI: In that case, please agree to it. Now then, daughter, I'm going to call them in one by one, and it's your job to choose the one who'll be your bridegroom. First of all, yes *(She shouts loudly.)* Scheming Crow!

A voice saying "Yes, ma'am" is heard from inside.

KIKU: Mother, this is so unfair of you!

OWAKI: Unfair? What do you mean unfair? You were so full of filial devotion that you were willing to go through a marriage ceremony with the bandit who abducted your mother in order to avenge her. If you love your mother so much, how dare you disobey her command right now?

KIKU: But I . . .

OWAKI: So, you understand what I am saying. Good. You are the same good girl you have always been.

CROW *presents himself.*

CROW: Did you have some business with me?

OWAKI: How do you find this gentleman?

KIKU: He looks horrible with that beard. And his eyes, as big as metal saucers, are disgusting.

OWAKI: Now that you mention it, he does look a bit like that . . .

CROW: That's a pretty cruel assessment, if you ask me.

Figure 20. *Sash Stealing Pond*, 1973, at the Kabuki-za. From left to right, Jitsukawa Enjaku III as Owaki, Nakamura Ganjirō II as the Toad Bandit, and Nakamura Shikan as Princess Kiku. Photograph courtesy of the Waseda University Tsubouchi Hakase Memorial Theatre Museum.

OWAKI: You can go. Wait over there. Mr. Six Owl, take his place.

OWL: Yes, ma'am. *(He comes forward.)*

OWAKI: How is the next one?

KIKU: The more I look at him the shabbier he seems. He's a man who reminds me of a torn umbrella.

OWAKI: Yes, now that you say so, that's just what he looks like. Go back and sit over there. Mr. Fox Fist, Mr. Bear Liver, and Mr. Silver Badger!

THREE: Yes, ma'am. *(They come forward.)*

KIKU: What I see here . . . yes, yes. It's just as if a fox, bear, and badger were lined up before me.

OWAKI: You're right. In the dim light and from a little distance I can't tell from their faces if they are animals or people. When I compare these fellows to my husband *(She takes a sidelong glance at* TOAD.*)* his good looks make him seem unlike a bandit. It's just like my daughter to recognize that no other man raised in the mountains could surpass the Toad Bandit. Now, whatever are we to do?

Just at this moment a kite rises stage right, just outside the house. It has a picture of a handsome man painted on it. It seems to be attracted to the sash that is drying high in the tree. KIKU *watches this from the window.*

KIKU: Oh wonderful! It's Samanosuke.

OWAKI: Our family retainer Samanosuke? What is he doing here?

KIKU: Just take a look at that kite! *(She goes over to the window.)*

OWAKI: You're right. The face on the kite looks just like him. Has he become so famous that they're selling kites of him in the capital?

KIKU: No, no. It shows that Samanosuke is trying to communicate with us. We agreed that my signal to him would be my mother's sash hung out to dry high up in the branches of a tall tree. The moonlight shining brightly on it makes it all the more vivid. I so want to hear from Samanosuke.

TOAD: Does that mean the kite is a signal that pursuers are coming for me? That was a clever plan.

KIKU: I wouldn't say "pursuers." Samanosuke is alone.

TOAD: That's more like it. Men, go capture Samanosuke and bring him here to me.

ALL UNDERLINGS: As you wish, sir!

TOAD: Off with you!

ALL UNDERLINGS: Yes, sir.

One after another they stand, and, as staged in 1998, they push their way past KIKU, *who ineffectually tries to stop them. They exit down the* hanamichi. *The kite falls to the ground.*

KIKU: I'll be so happy to see Samanosuke again, but it would be terrible if he were injured fighting with the bandits. What should we do, mother? Whatever shall we do? *(She clings to her mother and cries in her lap.)*

OWAKI: Listening to what you say, it seems to me that you are in love with Samanosuke.

KIKU: Yes, I am.

OWAKI: If you are already in love with a man, why didn't you say so from the beginning? Here we're up-to-date in everything we do. I'll set you up with anyone as long as it's not Lord Toad. Put your heart at ease and leave everything to your mother.

KIKU: Mother, will you really do this for me?

OWAKI: Why would I deceive you?

KIKU: Oh, I'm so happy. Mother!

OWAKI: Daughter!

KIKU: I'm so glad you are actually alive!

They embrace each other and weep. TOAD *is exasperated with their behavior.*

TOAD: Now are you weeping tears of happiness? They say that women have more tears than the grains of sand on a beach. I guess it's true. But I've heard this handsome wimp of a samurai from the capital called Samanosuke is still wet behind the ears. I don't think he'll make a good match for a headstrong girl like your daughter.

OWAKI: What, you don't accept the match? Are you still infatuated with Kiku?

TOAD: Not at all. Now that I know you're parent and child I'm speaking as her step-father. Gods and demons never stray from the straight and narrow, you know.

Percussion sounds from the geza. SAMANOSUKE *enters along the* hanamichi. *He has captured all of the* TOAD'S *henchmen, has tied them up with a rope in a big bundle, and leads them in, pulling them by the end of the rope. He stops at the gate to the house.*

SAMANOSUKE: Is anyone home? Is anyone home?

KIKU: That is Samanosuke's voice. *(She runs to the gate, opens it, and flies into his arms.)* Oh how I missed you! I missed you so much!

SAMANOSUKE: You needn't worry any more. Now that we know where your mother's murderer lives, you will soon be able to return to the capital with all of your hopes realized. *(He drags the tied up henchmen inside.)* These louts are your enemy's underlings. I'll dispatch them here and now.

He prepares to decapitate them but KIKU *comes forward and stops him.*

KIKU: Samanosuke wait! You don't have to do that!

SAMANOSUKE: What do you mean?

KIKU: Mother is right here with us.

SAMANOSUKE: What are you saying?

OWAKI: *(formally)* Samanosuke, thank you for your devoted service.

SAMANOSUKE: My goodness, it is Lady Nowaki! I am yours to command. *(He bows deeply.)*

OWAKI: I will never forget how you loyally stayed by Princess Kiku's side and sought out her blood enemy. I am very grateful to you.

SAMANOSUKE: This seems like a dream. I thought you had been cruelly murdered. To see you before me unharmed is such great good fortune that I can't help but shed tears of joy. *(He weeps.)*

I, Samanosuke, have arrived, so you no longer have anything to fear. I will conduct you back to your palace right a away. With all due respect I find it most grievous and astonishing that you have survived so long in this lowly, ramshackle hovel. And over there is a most suspicious looking man. *(He gazes fixedly at* TOAD.*)* It would appear that it is he who abducted you. Come forth, I challenge you to a duel!

He pulls his sword out a few inches and, snapping the sword hilt against the sheath opening, advances toward TOAD.

KIKU: Don't do anything rash, Samanosuke! The Toad Bandit is my mother's husband, so now he is my father.

SAMANOSUKE: What a strange tale you tell me.

TOAD: Now then, my good wife. This young man has turned out to be much more impressive than I thought. He's brave and dependable. With that feat of tying up my useless henchmen and leading them home, why he seems the finest bridegroom in three provinces.

KIKU: We already knew...

KIKU & OWAKI: That he is the finest bridegroom in three provinces.

TOAD: So, since we have settled the marriage issue, there is no need to discuss who my heir will be. I hereby bequeath to you, Samanosuke, the title of Toad Bandit II. You should be overjoyed.

SAMANOSUKE: I'm flabbergasted by this. Princess Kiku, what is going on here?

OWAKI: In all things, the duty of a retainer is to obey his master. Don't you agree?

SAMANOSUKE: Yes, ma'am.

CROW: It's very difficult for us to pay our respects to the Boss' successor all tied up like this.

OWLS: The ropes—please . . .

ALL UNDERLINGS: . . . Untie them for us now.

KIKU: Samanosuke, untie the ropes, would you please?

SAMANOSUKE: Yes, ma'am. *(He unties the ropes.)*

CROW: Now then, honored leader, Toad Bandit II, from this day forward . . .

OWL: We beg . . .

ALL UNDERLINGS: . . . to be favored with your acquaintance. *(They all bow.)*

SAMANOSUKE: I come from a family of retainers to the venerable Washio house. To be called a bandit is intolerable. I refuse to give up my true identity.

CROW: He has no ambition at all,

ALL HENCHMEN: What a goody-goody he is.

TOAD: All of you, begone.

ALL HENCHMEN: Yes, sir. *(They exit.) (This line and the previous line have been added in recent productions.)*

KIKU: Now Samanosuke, please be sympathetic to my situation. I know it seems unfittingly coarse for me, a girl raised in the capital, to speak to you so directly, but this decision to make you heir to an estate, not to mention our ability to take marriage vows together, would be impossible were we to return to the capital. In the capital, master and retainer could never wed. If you only give your consent, you, Toad Bandit II, and I, your wife, can live out our years in this mountain dwelling, enjoying a carefree married life here together, viewing the flowers in spring and the foliage in autumn. Imagine it, Samanosuke, and please agree to be my husband.

SAMANOSUKE: I'm overjoyed that your feelings for me are so strong, but to become a bandit would stain my family's honor. And I don't want to turn you into a rustic mountain wife like her. *(He looks at* OWAKI.*)* If you give up your fine robes and flowered hair ornaments your beauty will eventually fade. You are a woman of the highest class, and romantic love is your glory. If I were to sink so low as to become a bandit I would lower you as well, and to that I cannot consent. Please, won't you be so kind as to listen to this advice from one who loves you.

KIKU: Does this mean we will just return to the capital as we are, the barrier separating master and retainer preventing us from ever meeting as man and wife? *(She weeps.)*

TOAD: The more I listen to this, the more it seems to be the right thing to do.

OWAKI: But what my daughter wishes is right as well.

TOAD: Isn't there any . . .

TOAD & OWAKI: . . . Solution to this? *(They ponder together, inclining their heads in thought.)*

OWAKI: *(Slapping her thigh)* Oh, my daughter, there is something you must never forget. Lady Nowaki has departed this world. I am Owaki and you are Princess Kiku.

Figure 21. *Sash Stealing Pond*, 1973, at the Kabuki-za. From left to right, Jitsukawa Enjaku III as Owaki, Nakamura Shikan as Princess Kiku, Nakamura Ganjirō II as the Toad Bandit, and Nakamura Fukusuke VIII (currently Baigyoku) as Samanosuke. Photograph courtesy of the Mishima Yukio Literary Museum. Photograph by Yoshida Chiaki.

KIKU: And that means that . . . yes! My mother was, in fact . . .
OWAKI: Murdered. And the murderer . . .
KIKU: Yes. Must be somewhere in this wide world.
OWAKI: As long as you are on the road tracking down the murderer,
KIKU: To the outside world we are master and retainer,
OWAKI: But in fact you can live as man and wife.
KIKU: From now on the two of us will pursue my blood enemy, traveling together from inlet to inlet and bay to bay, for many long years until we confront him.
SAMANOSUKE: Yes Princess Kiku, we must not delay. We must push our way through roots of trees and roots of grass, and when we find your mother's murderer, we'll never let him escape.
KIKU: And when that time comes, I, Princess Kiku, although I am a woman, will dispel the rancour my mother's spirit still feels. I will flourish my sword blade in the wind *(She gestures as she talks.)*, slice off his head, and . . .
TOAD: *(Stroking his neck)* All of this somehow makes my neck itch.
KIKU: *(Laughing)* Ho, ho.
OWAKI: Ho, ho.
SAMANOSUKE: Ha, ha.
TOAD: Ha, ha.
ALL: Ha, ha, ha, ha, ha, ha!

A cock crows and the sky lightens.

TOAD: My goodness, it is already dawn. You'd better leave quickly, before you arouse any suspicions.
KIKU: Yes, we'll descend the mountain while the cedar thickets are still enveloped in mist in the dim early morning light.
SAMANOSUKE: Tomorrow we will cross over Mount Kurama and set out for the town of Shiga, on the shore of Lake Biwa.
TOAD: Oh, I just thought of something. *(He hands* SAMANOSUKE *a medicine case.)* This is a magic ointment from the land of the Southern Barbarians. Rub it on your ears, eyes, nose, and mouth and when you are in the water it will seem as though you are on dry land. You'll be able to see, hear, and speak freely. If your enemy is voyaging on a boat, you can pull him into the water and capture him.
SAMANOSUKE: I can't thank you enough for such a splendid gift. Now then, Princess . . . *(He bows before her.)*
KIKU: *(Looking into the eyes of all assembled)* I wonder where my mother's murderer may be?
SAMANOSUKE: *(Gazing around, and into the distance)* I wonder where he has hidden himself away?
OWAKI: The murderer's whereabouts will become harder and harder to

find. You two companions who set forth this morning, be strong in your resolve.

KIKU: Farewell mother.

OWAKI: Your mother is gone, I am just Owaki.

KIKU: In that case, Lady Owaki, Lord Toad . . .

OWAKI: He's your father now, won't you call him "Daddy?"

KIKU: Farewell Daddy.

TOAD: Farewell.

After TOAD *says, "Farewell," the* ki *clappers begin to sound. A lively percussion joins in as the two lovers proceed to the* hanamichi. TOAD, OWAKI, *and the* HENCHMEN *watch them as they depart on their journey, exiting down the* hanamichi. *The curtain closes.*

CURTAIN

Yuya

(a modern noh play)

Published in 1959, First performed in 1967
Translated by Laurence Kominz and Jonah Salz

INTRODUCTION

Mishima's one-act adaptations of classical noh plays to the modern *shingeki* stage are among his best known plays in Japan and abroad. Donald Keene published translations of Mishima's first six modern noh plays in *Five Modern Nō Plays* (1957) and *Death in Midsummer and other stories* (1966),[1] but Mishima wrote three more modern noh plays: *Yuya* (1959), *Yorobōshi* (1960), and *Genji Kuyō* (1962). Mishima had been thinking about writing a modern noh version of *Yuya* since 1955, when he converted the classical noh play *Yuya* into a kabuki dance drama of the same name for his favorite kabuki actor, Nakamura Utaemon.[2] The original *Yuya* was one of Utaemon's favorite noh plays, and it has been a favorite of noh audiences since medieval times.

The story of the classical play is a simple one. Its setting is the late twelfth century in Kyoto. The beautiful Yuya, a dancing girl, is the mistress of the Grand Minister, Taira no Munemori. Yuya's mother, who lives in the East Country, is ill, but Munemori has not allowed Yuya to return home to visit her. The mother's servant, Asagao, comes to Kyoto, bearing a letter from Yuya's mother begging her daughter to return home before she dies. After hearing the letter read, Munemori still refuses to relent. He wants Yuya to entertain his guests at a grand cherry blossom viewing party at Kiyomizu Temple the next day. The day of the blossom banquet arrives and Yuya travels to Kiyomizu Temple in a splendid carriage, as the chorus describes the beautiful sights she passes. At the banquet Yuya dances magnificently, never betraying her sadness and anxiety for her mother. The actor playing Yuya, clothed in a sumptuous, embroidered orange robe, moves sedately around the stage, always keeping his mask tilted slightly downward, preserving a sad, "clouded" expression. Yuya couches one last request to Munemori for a leave of absence in the form of a poem that likens her mother to cherry blossoms beaten to the ground by rain. The poem moves Munemori, and he grants Yuya permission to go to her mother's side. Yuya is happy for the first time—and for the first time in the play the actor tilts his mask upward, creating a joyful expression. The play concludes as Yuya sets out for the East Country to visit her ill mother.

The appeal of the classical noh play lies in the juxtaposition of the anxious and grieving Yuya with the gorgeous scenery of Kyoto bedecked in floral splendor. Her sadness is given immediacy by her mother's letter, which is read in its entirety on stage, and by her own subsequent expressions of grief and worry. The chorus provides the descriptions of the flowery capital. Classical noh plays usually develop only one character fully and the audience/reader is given no clue as to why Munemori is so unkind to his mistress. Munemori exists in the classical version of the play simply as an agent of denial.

For his 1955 kabuki dance drama version of the play, Mishima continued the tradition of focusing on Yuya as the central character, but he developed Munemori somewhat, turning him into something of a Japanese medieval sadistic epicurean, and he also added a Buddhist priest, an entirely new character.[3] At this time Mishima wrote that he wanted to develop the Munemori character even more fully in yet another play.

The spark to Mishima's imagination that led to the essential premise for his modern noh play *Yuya* came when he read performance notes to the classical play in the memoirs of the great twentieth-century classical noh actor, Kita Roppeita (1874–1971). Kita wrote that his school of noh had a secret tradition which held that Yuya in fact wants to go to the East Country to meet her secret lover there, and that the letter from her mother is a fabrication. If the actor keeps this in mind when he plays Yuya, the role will have more allure and beauty, and not be dominated by worry and gloom. Kita wrote that there is nothing in the actual play text to support this interpretation, but that if the actor playing Yuya remained aware of the possibility of a lover in the East Country, it would add another level of beauty to the play: "brilliance hidden within sadness."[4]

In Mishima's play Yuya's secret lover becomes the central truth of the work. Yuya is the kept mistress of business tycoon Munemori, and she fakes her mother's illness as an excuse to go to Hokkaido to visit a young lover serving in the military there. Munemori wants to take Yuya cherry blossom viewing with him to a park that he owns, but Yuya refuses to go, saying she must return to Hokkaido immediately to visit her dying mother. Yuya's friend Asako brings a letter from Yuya's mother that indicates that the mother is about to die. At this point Munemori knows for certain that Yuya's mother is fine, although Yuya and Asako do not know that he knows. Viewers of the play only know that he knows if they are able to decipher a very cryptic on-stage phone conversation between Munemori and his personal assistant early in the play.

Mishima develops two separate dialectical themes during the course of the play: beauty versus death, and trickery and deceit versus truth. During the first half of the play Munemori and Yuya engage in battle of wits and wills, espousing conflicting philosophies of beauty and death. Munemori is here a fully developed epicurean, who believes that the only thing that gives life meaning is the perception and experience of beauty. His beautiful cherry blossoms will last just one more day, and must be viewed immediately. Yuya counters that her mother's life is in danger, and the regret she will feel if she cannot visit her mother before she dies will negate all the beauty in the world. In this section of the play Mishima develops philosophical themes found in the classical play and his earlier kabuki dance drama.

The debate over beauty and death is interrupted by an *ai-kyōgen*, a brand new structural element that Mishima added to his modern noh play. In classical noh plays *ai-kyōgen* are serious or comic interludes performed by *kyōgen*, not noh, actors. Traditional *ai-kyōgen* are used to support and restate the action of the first act of the play, but Mishima uses his to totally undercut the validity of the first half of the play. Munemori's personal assistant, Yamada, escorts Yuya's healthy mother, Masa, into the apartment. Masa admits to Munemori that she colluded with her daughter to give her an excuse to visit her lover in Hokkaido. By the time Masa and Yamada finally leave, darkness is approaching and a heavy rain is falling, dashing all of the blossoms from the trees. It is too late to go flower viewing.

All of Yuya's tears in the first half of the play, all of her profound statements about the value of love and human life have been given the lie. And what about Munemori? If he really wanted so much to see his beautiful Yuya surrounded by his beautiful cherry blossoms he could have told her immediately that he had penetrated her ruse, and taken her off to see the blossoms in the fine weather of mid-day.

In the short remainder of the play after the interlude, Munemori reveals what he has really been about during this entire day. In the last line of the play Munemori tells Yuya that today she, not the cherry blossoms, was his blooming flower. Yuya bloomed by working so hard to deceive him. She lied to Munemori with such conviction that she was able to weep piteously, speak eloquently, and never give in to him. It is this remarkable human ability to construct reality out of a fabric of lies that fascinates Munemori, and Mishima, and everyone who reads or sees the play. The construction of reality out of untruth is born of a uniquely human impulse, the impulse to play, to create worlds of make-believe, and to act in these worlds as if they were real.

In 1967 Dōmoto Masaki was the first man to direct *Yuya,* and he was also the first to set forth the notion that this play is not a flawed, tongue-in-cheek parody of a serious noh play, but an important statement by Mishima about a kind of beauty different from the purely visual and superficial beauty he most often presented in his novels and plays.[5] "To live is to play act,"

Dōmoto wrote, "and when a woman is acting to the limit of her resources, she blooms like a flower. This is the meaning of the last words of the play. Adult love begins after these lines."[6]

This play is about the "flower of deceit," and as much as readers and audience members may deplore lying and deception, Mishima pulls them into his world. The characters most intriguing to us are the ones who lie: Munemori, Yuya, even, to a lesser extent, Asako. The characters of the interlude are flat and somewhat ridiculous. Is it because they, by and large, tell the truth?

If the comic interlude has exposed the entire underpinning of the first part of the play as a pack of lies, what are we to make of the earnest discourse between Munemori and Yuya about beauty, grief, guilt, and death? Their verbal sallies and retreats are like cherry blossoms in bloom. They flower briefly and magnificently. If the winds of revealed deceit blow these blossoms away, they were nevertheless significant and real while they bloomed. The merits of the discourse on beauty, sadness, and guilt, are worth pondering after the play, just as we look back and remember the beauty of cherry blossoms months after they have fallen.

Yuya has been performed infrequently since 1967. Though Japanese have accepted Dōmoto's interpretation of the play as valid, the main theme is hidden from the audience's view until the last few lines of the play, and viewers are left to ponder what it all meant after the curtain has closed. *Yuya* remains, nevertheless, a unique and intriguing play, a fine example of how humor and irony can support serious philosophical themes, and one of the best presentations of the appeal and beauty of lying and deception in Mishima's opus.

NOTES

1. *Five Modern Nô Plays,* trans. Donald Keene (New York: Knopf, 1957), includes the plays "Sotoba Komachi," "The Damask Drum," "Kantan," "Lady Aoi," and "Hanjo"; *Death in Midsummer and Other Stories,* trans. Donald Keene (New York: New Directions, 1966) contains the modern noh play "Dôjôji."

2. Mishima Yukio, "Yuya ni tsuite," Tsubomi-kai Program, February 1955; reprinted in *Mishima hyôron zenshû,* vol. 3 (Tokyo: Shinchô, 1994), p. 873.

3. Ibid.

4. Dômoto Masaki, *Gekijin Mishima Yukio* (Tokyo: Geki Shobô, 1994), p. 224.

5. Ibid.

6. Ibid.

THE CHARACTERS

Munemori, a successful business magnate, about fifty-years old
Yuya, a beautiful twenty-two or twenty-three-year-old woman

Asako, Yuya's friend who lives in the same apartment building. Younger than Yuya, her clothing is also flashier.
Yamada, Munemori's personal secretary, a servile man in his forties
Masa, Yuya's mother. A fiftyish, plump, and seemingly energetic woman in Japanese dress.

SETTING

A room in YUYA*'s luxurious apartment. On the fourth wall, facing the audience, are imaginary glass doors and a balcony. A bed is in the stage left area. Beside the bed is a telephone. The windows at the back of the stage face the apartment building's inner garden; only the next apartment building's windows can be seen. In the center of the stage is a table with chairs. At stage right is a door. There is a three-sided mirror and other items. A large suitcase sits beside the bed. The room is extremely neat, with a mood of imminent departure.*

It is a tranquil Sunday morning in spring, at the peak of the cherry blossom season. YUYA*, in her traveling clothes, is lying atop the bed-covers.* MUNEMORI *sits in the easy chair at stage right, having taken off his jacket. He is smoking a cigar.*

MUNEMORI: So? Shall we leave? From the hilltop you look out on a sea of cherry trees. If we miss the view today, we'll have to wait until next year. Every forecast in every newspaper said that the blossoms will not last another week. And only the unemployed can go cherry-blossom viewing on weekdays. So, this year's blossoms can only be viewed today. Right?

I'll tell you once again: this will be our last chance to see such a magnificent display of cherry-blossoms. This year I'm going to cut down half those trees because I have to expand the zoo and rebuild the aquarium. We no longer live in an age when customers can be lured to my park by cherry trees alone. My train has to carry passengers to the amusement park all year round.

(Looking at his wristwatch.) It's already eleven o'clock. Come now. We planned to leave here by ten. Spring weather is so unpredictable. What if it starts to rain? Well?

You don't understand, do you, Yuya? What I want to show you are not just any cherry trees—*(Pats his chest)*—these are my trees. I want to show you my cherry trees, in full-bloom.

(Stands up, annoyed.) To drive there takes at least two hours. Even if we leave now, we'll arrive at one o'clock at the earliest. And even if we leave immediately, it will take three minutes to get to the lobby by elevator. Then greeting that over polite doorman will take another ten seconds. And if the chauffeur happens to be dozing off in this fine weather, it will take another three minutes to rouse him.

No, I'm not blaming you for keeping the chauffeur waiting or anything like that. I am just explaining to you that, although you may not realize it, at my usual business pace, one split second could mean millions of yen, sometimes even tens of millions of yen. And I am saying that you lack sympathy for that fact.

I suppose, on the other hand, that it is precisely because you do not understand these things that you are who you are. (*He approaches her, and looks down at her face.*) Isn't that so?

As he is about to stroke her hair, the bedside telephone rings. MUNEMORI *picks up the phone.*

Yes, it's me. Right. I see. Hm . . . Right. Right. Yes, very good work. Right. Yes, please do take care of that for me. That's fine. *(He returns the phone.)*

That was my secretary. He is my manager on Sundays. (*He again tries to stroke* YUYA's *hair, but* YUYA *avoids him, sitting up in bed. Her face is pale with sorrow.)*

YUYA: Please, don't be offended. I usually adore it when you stroke my hair. But I can't stand it now. I'm drenched with grief and anxiety to the ends of my hair . . . I feel as though tears might pour even from my hair. And so I'm asking you: please don't touch me. My tears are brimming over. If I move my body even just a little they will overflow. But, I am glad that you thought of taking me with you cherry-blossom viewing . . .

MUNEMORI: You see? You always talk to me this way, even when refusing me. Even when you're angry, you use such gentle words. At a time like this all the other women I've known would scream, "If you want to go so badly, why not take your wife and children!?"

YUYA: (*Sadly, but with a faint smile.*) I suppose there really are women who would speak so bluntly to a man like you.

MUNEMORI: Well? Why are you never blunt with me?

YUYA: Because I'm afraid of you.

YUYA & MUNEMORI: *(He mocks her.)* You're so wonderful . . .

MUNEMORI: (*Laughing.)* See? That won't do.

YUYA: Well then, would it be better if I said, "You, who are so wonderful, and kind . . .?"

MUNEMORI: "I, who am so wonderful and kind, try to force you, so anxious for your mother, to go flower viewing." Even though you could fly to your hometown in Hokkaido in one short hop, I absolutely forbid you to go. You are right. You are correct.

As I've been telling you all along, of course I won't let you go. No matter how sick your mother is, I have my own reasons. I want to be with you as often as possible—every day is precious to me. These days, it doesn't matter to me what people think; I even ignore my own family.

But what I'm trying to do now is offer a compromise. If you accompany me on today's excursion, that will be enough. Tomorrow, I will allow you to return to your mother's side. That's a promise. But instead you're obstinate, and insist on abandoning our flower viewing. You fret and pester me about it, saying that you want to go home today. . . . You should think it over. Or, we should call someone to sit as a mediator and judge this case? Who would not recognize the reasonableness of my position?

YUYA: But do you really think that you can take me with you, with my face so full of sorrow, and still enjoy your flower viewing?

MUNEMORI: I keep telling you—I will be happy.

YUYA: *(Covering her face.)* If you really loved me, you couldn't be happy. You don't really love me.

MUNEMORI: There you go again, talking of love. I am speaking of pleasure. Taking you with me cherry-blossom viewing—that will satisfy me, and I will be happy.

YUYA: But what about my grief? What about my heart? Are you saying that they have nothing to do with it?

MUNEMORI: *(Decisively)* That's right. Your feelings have got absolutely nothing to do with it. You have a beautiful face. And a beautiful body. To accompany a woman like you cherry-blossom viewing—that alone is enough. For pleasure in this earthly life.

YUYA *raises her face to* MUNEMORI, *then, startled, quickly lowers it. Pause.*

MUNEMORI: *(Facing away, extremely gently.)* Well, will you come? *(*YUYA, *facing* MUNEMORI'S *back, her head bowed, does not answer.*) Well, then, I guess you do not care for me.

YUYA: *(Facing* MUNEMORI *again)* You, you also talk of love, don't you? But can't you understand that it is precisely because I care for you that I am pleading with you like this? If I had no worries at all, how happy I would be to drive off on such a splendid spring day to view the blossoms with you! But worried sick about my mother, I am about to collapse with grief. If you drag me against my will to go cherry-blossom viewing, however brilliant the blossoms, they will appear worthless to me. The happier the people are, the more of a contrast they will be to my own unhappiness, and the bright sky will seem like night. And in the end, I'm certain that I will come to hate you. And that is what I am most afraid of. I would rather visit my mother now, as soon as possible, to make certain that she is all right. Then as soon as I return, we can go out on a wonderful excursion to view the blossoms!

MUNEMORI: The blossoms will not wait, Yuya. I keep telling you—the blossoms will not wait.

YUYA: A heavy heart, the trees in full bloom—the pleasure of that flower viewing and this deep grief can never become one . . .

MUNEMORI: Those are things that I will bring together.

YUYA: At a time like this, there are no pleasures that could comfort me.

MUNEMORI: *(Taking* YUYA's *chin.)* Take courage, and turn this sad face towards happiness, Yuya. Your face is like the moon. When struck by the light it is bright, but when stricken by grief, it's shrouded in shadows. Don't be a prisoner of your love, but boldly throw yourself into happiness. Will you? If you do, your youth will allow you to forget a thing like your mother's illness.

YUYA: *(Shaking free and lowering her face)* I can't do it! I can't!!

Just then, there is a knock from the stage right door. YUYA *and* MUNEMORI *do not move. Another strong knock, then a voice is heard.* "It's me, Yuya, Asako." YUYA *starts to rise.* MUNEMORI *gestures for her to wait, then quickly puts on his jacket and opens the door.*

ASAKO: Oh, am I interrupting anything?

MUNEMORI: Come in.

ASAKO: Is it really all right to come in? *(She enters.)* Yuya, here is a letter from your Mother. *(She hands it to* YUYA, *who quickly takes and opens the envelope.)*

MUNEMORI: How long have you been delivering mail for the Post Office?

ASAKO: It's your fault, Mr. Munemori. Yuya's mother fears you like a god. The trains, the amusement parks, the zoos, the banks—she knows you own them all. And she even thinks that with a word from you, they'd censor the mail. So she started sending important letters in care of me.

MUNEMORI: You really know how to flatter me, don't you?

ASAKO: After all, everyone knows that Yuya and I are close friends.

MUNEMORI: Anyway, it's delightful to imagine two such beautiful women sharing each other's secrets. And I suppose Yuya has also proved useful to you with your intrigues?

ASAKO: Oh, Yuya's no good at all. She's useless. She's just too honest. *(During this exchange,* YUYA *has been reading her mother's letter, weeping bitterly.)*

MUNEMORI: Come now, show me the letter.

YUYA *silently hands* MUNEMORI *the letter.* MUNEMORI *takes out his reading glasses and puts them on, turns the letter around and starts to read it, then returns it to* YUYA.

Will you read it to me? Usually I have really important letters read to me by my secretary. Besides, the handwriting is so faint, it's hard to read. So, please read it—I am listening.

YUYA: *(Reading the letter)* "As I wrote you in early March, I feel somehow that I will not be able to greet the cherry-blossoms this spring. Still, the northern snow has begun to melt, little by little. And as the clouds in the sky take on the gentleness of spring, I have come to believe that this omen of spring is but an omen of my death. Like the stubborn icicles under the eaves growing thinner and thinner, I grow weaker, day by day. I want so much to see you once more before I die." *(*YUYA *cries.)*

ASAKO: *(Crying sympathetically, puts a hand on* YUYA's *shoulder.)* Poor thing, poor thing.

YUYA: "I want so much to see you once more before I die. These days, a sort of rainbow often appears in front of my eyes, and dark shadows pass across it. So while I can still see clearly with these eyes, I want to see your face, even for a moment. That is all I want—that is all I have left in this world. Somehow, get permission to leave, and come visit me one last time."

While YUYA, *occasionally wiping away her tears, continues reading the letter,* MUNEMORI *puffs on a cigar, silently staring at her.* ASAKO *gradually notices* MUNEMORI'S *manner, and she glares at him.*

ASAKO: Well, Mr. Munemori? Yuya is weeping like some charming, beautiful doll, isn't she?

MUNEMORI: What are you talking about?

YUYA: "Please come visit me once more,
Please come, before this dying cherry tree falls,
Without blossoming in season.
Please fulfill this old nightingale's hope,
Chilled with snow and about to die
Not having seen this year's cherry blossoms."

MUNEMORI: *(To* ASAKO*)* What are you talking about? *(Amused)* I am listening sympathetically.

ASAKO: No, for you, Yuya is a charming, pretty, sad doll. The beauty of this weeping woman—I wonder what it looks like from a man's perspective? I know what you're thinking: "She's like a cherry tree in the rain"—right? You look happy in that haze of cigar smoke, your gaze changing Yuya into a small, sad, beautiful, sorrowful, doll.

MUNEMORI: Imagine what you wish—I am sympathetic.

YUYA: "Please fulfill this nightingale's hope,
Chilled with snow and about to die."

MUNEMORI: *(After a pause)* Is that all?

ASAKO: *(Taking* YUYA's *arm)* Yuya. Don't worry. Mr. Munemori said that he sympathizes with you. You won't have to go cherry-blossom viewing. You can go home right away.

Figure 22. *Yuya*, 1999, at B-Plan Theater. Sugano Kaoru is at left, as Asako, and Tanaka Mikiko is at right, as Yuya. Photograph courtesy of the Mishima Yukio Literary Museum.

YUYA: *(A faint smile floats to her face.)* Really?
MUNEMORI: No, I am not abandoning our flower viewing.
ASAKO: Mr. Munemori!
MUNEMORI: Once I have decided something, it cannot be changed.

Pause.

YUYA: *(She dries her eyes, then mounts a counterattack.)* Are you saying that we must go, no matter what?
MUNEMORI: Yes, no matter what.
YUYA: Flowers bloom every year; this is not the last spring ever. But if I don't visit my mother now, I may not see her again in this world.
MUNEMORI: This year's blossoms can only be seen this year, Yuya. Today's pleasures will not come again. "Today" only comes once in a lifetime.
YUYA: Oh! Then what is more important to you, a person's life, or a blossom's life?
MUNEMORI: The most important thing for me is this moment. The "today" which is this day. On that point, regrettably, a person's life and a flower's life are equal. And if they are equal, then I prefer something pleasant to something painful, Yuya. After all, even I may die tomorrow.
ASAKO: What? When you're in such good shape?
YUYA: It is my mother who is dying.
MUNEMORI: What has that got to do with blossom viewing? Your mother was so proud of your beauty. Her daughter's beauty was her "career"—she went so far as to say that. That shows tremendous forethought, Yuya. If your mother truly believes that, then when her daughter is at the peak of her beauty, turning strangers' heads as she walks beneath the cherry trees in full-bloom on my land—if her daughter is to be the glory of that once-in-a-lifetime "today," your mother would not mind giving up her own life. In any case, because your mother has such a beautiful daughter, she has been able to live very comfortably, has she not?
YUYA: Oh, what a horrible thing to say!
ASAKO: Mr. Munemori, that's too much!
MUNEMORI: Yes, perhaps I have gone too far. But I—how shall I put it—I regret that you have neglected life's pleasures. The thing called pleasure is like death; it calls us from the ends of the earth. Once you are called by that shining voice, that penetrating sound, in the end you must jump up from your chair and go forth.
YUYA: For you, pleasure is a duty, then?
MUNEMORI: Not a duty. No more than death is a duty. No, not a duty. But he who neglects it will be punished.
YUYA: What kind of punishment?
MUNEMORI: A punishment called "regret." The dark, gloomy monster of regret will appear. I hate it to the depths of my heart. To avoid regret, I

do not mind spending any amount of money.

YUYA: If I don't go to visit my mother on her deathbed, it will be I who suffer regret.

MUNEMORI: Why should you feel regret? No matter how you look at it, it would be my fault. If you blame me, that will be the end of it. If only you would go flower viewing, you and I both, together we will escape that demon, regret.

ASAKO: You will regret that all you had was mere "pleasure."

YUYA: While mine will be an awful regret that will pursue me all of my life.

MUNEMORI: But both our regrets will vanish together. If you come with me submissively, blindly. Do not think, but follow me, silently—and those regrets will leave this earth. And only the image of a woman beautiful in sorrow, that rare image of her flower viewing, will remain in people's memory.

ASAKO: After treating Yuya like a doll, now you just want to paint her into a beautiful picture, don't you?

YUYA: *(Weakly)* I don't want to become some picture.

MUNEMORI: Why do you place such importance on your own emotions? Yuya. That's a kind of disease, you know. You become concerned with all sorts of conflicts between your happiness and sadness, but actually it is those conflicts that people enjoy. Opposites can illuminate each other; things that are incompatible can be fused together. This is what we call beauty. A grieving woman viewing cherry blossoms is more beautiful than a cheerful woman viewing them. Is that not so, Yuya? You are very beautiful. And because of your beauty, you have the power to make two things, two things which are at odds with each other, become one. Going out blossom viewing in your grief—that is the fate that your beauty invites. *(Approaching the telephone)* Well, shall we call down to the lobby? To tell them to rouse that dozing chauffeur?

YUYA: *(Responding quickly)* Wait a moment! I'm begging you, wait a moment! Look! You can view the blossoms from right here.

She gestures as though opening the doors at the edge of the stage to the right and left, and takes two steps forward "onto the balcony." A railing may be used specifically for this scene.

Even from the balcony, you can see so many cherry trees. Come here, you can see so many of them!

MUNEMORI: *(Goes out on the balcony, and stands next to* YUYA.*)* You mean that tiny park's few, pathetic cherry trees? *(Stretches)* Oh, but it does feel good out here. The sun warms you up, and the air is refreshing—far better than arguing in that tiny room.

YUYA: *(Encouragingly)* You're right. Out here I'm sure you will feel refreshed. And now look at those trees. Each branch is filled with blossoms; it's so pretty.

MUNEMORI: Are you talking about those two or three tiny, withered trees, with faded blossoms that look like cotton fluff?

YUYA: But they are beautiful. Bathed in sunshine, they look like silver hair ornaments. Today the park is full of children. A child dressed in yellow. Another dressed in green. Listen, you can hear sounds carried by the wind . . . the squeak-squeak of the swing.

MUNEMORI: The high-arcing swings at my amusement park are much grander. And there are twenty-five of them in all.

YUYA: Look at the children riding the swings—their shoulders are covered in blossoms. And the petals keep falling. The children love it. Even for the child playing all alone, the blossoms will be playmates.

MUNEMORI: You keep repeating, "the child, the child"—it seems as though you have converted—so now you want a child?

YUYA: Look at that little girl; that's me when I was a child. With the needle and thread that she's stolen from the sewing box, she threads each fallen petal one by one. But her hands are slow, and the petals are thin. Before she can finish the flower necklace, the day is over.

MUNEMORI: More importantly, before she can finish that necklace, the petals will rot.

YUYA: On that bench, beneath the cherry trees, there's a pair of young lovers. They sit where the light filtering through the canopy of blossoms softens their cheeks, afraid to embrace lest they just melt away. Hearing the cheerful shouts from the swings, and the bees' heavy buzzing, they gaze forever into each other's eyes, perfectly still.

MUNEMORI: They are young, and on top of that, poor. They sit that way not to be romantic, but because they have no choice.

YUYA: Look! That thing that looked like a flower petal—it's a butterfly! It's landed in the black hair of the man. If his hair were greasy with pomade, the butterfly would soon be repelled. So he must have used only a faint gel, giving off the natural scent of a field of grass.

MUNEMORI: He hasn't got the money to buy even a cheap pomade, so he borrows some of the woman's leftover hair oil, and rubs it in.

YUYA: Look! The woman notices the butterfly—she stretches out her hand—oh! The butterfly flew away. Surely the butterfly must be a female, and just as the face of a woman passing by will cast a slight shadow on even the love-blinded heart of a man, the butterfly paints a single brushstroke of wing powder into the man's thick, black hair.

MUNEMORI: Imagine the future of the man who marries her, jealous even of a butterfly. I know many men like that. They fill the tiny boxes of their lives with the hollowness of unattained aspirations and pathetic trust in their wives' faithfulness, becoming the most ridiculous of cowards.

YUYA: The trees are so beautiful in full bloom. The blossoms fill the shadows, and in the brilliant sunlight, each branch displays its fountain of blossoms, seductive dark branches in their midst.

MUNEMORI: What a pitiful sight. Pathetic, miserable cherry blossoms.

YUYA: *(Looks up at the sky.*) Oh, where did those dark clouds come from so suddenly?

MUNEMORI: *(Looks up at the sky too.)* Damn. I told you so.

YUYA: But the park is still lit by so much sunlight . . . oh, it has shadowed over. The blossoms have suddenly lost their color. They have turned into white flowers of mourning. In the sandbox black dots appear here and there. It's raining. My cherry blossoms—soaked in the rain. *(Still gazing at them, she begins to cry.)*

MUNEMORI: Why are you crying? Hm?

YUYA: My cherry blossoms are . . . My cherry blossoms are . . .

MUNEMORI: *(Pause)* Do you really want to go home so badly? *(Pause)* It's already begun to rain—but surely it's only a passing shower. . . . Well, it's all right I guess. If you want to go home, hurry up and get ready to leave.

YUYA *and* MUNEMORI *return to the room. The balcony handrail is put away.*

ASAKO: *(Hugging* YUYA*)* Yuya, it's turned out all right, hasn't it? It's turned out all right. You can go home! I really wondered if you'd be able to. Everything's all right now.

YUYA: I am so happy. I never wanted to leave without getting the proper permission. You understand. I never wanted to escape down a back alley, to have to sneak home.

ASAKO: That's what's meant by a woman having self respect, Yuya. It's the right way to do things. Now I'll help you pack your things for the trip.

Just then, a knock from the stage right door.

MUNEMORI: Come in.

The door opens, and MR.YAMADA, *the secretary, enters.*

YAMADA: Sir, I've brought her along.

MUNEMORI: You've done well. Tell her to come in.

YAMADA: Come on inside. We've come all this way so there's no need to struggle now. Come in, please.

Pulled by the hand by YAMADA, YUYA'S *mother,* MASA, *enters.* YUYA *and* ASAKO *are shocked and speechless.*

MUNEMORI: *(Gently)* Well, Yuya. Greet your mother, who is on her deathbed.

YUYA: *(Angrily)* Mother! You're . . .

MASA: I know. You must be really angry with me, but there was nothing I could do. *(She points at* YAMADA.) His secretary came all the way to Hokkaido and found out that I was in perfect health. And without letting me get a word in edgewise, he took me on a plane and dragged me all the way here.

YUYA: *(To* MUNEMORI*)* Why has my mother been telling such lies? I have absolutely no idea. And she's made me so worried.

MUNEMORI: *(To* MASA*)* So, please relax and tell us everything. I am not so vindictive by nature as to summon you here to attack Yuya, or anything so petty.

MASA: Yuya, I am going to tell him everything.

YUYA: Go ahead, spin whatever lies you want to.

MASA: You needn't speak so recklessly, Yuya. Even if it's painful for you now, at a time like this it's better to expose all, the whole truth. In any case, the President sees through everything. Gentlemen do not like lies. They prefer the truth. This is something that I can say from my long experience. But a gentleman, once he's grabbed hold of the truth, is soon bored . . . *(to* MUNEMORI*)* I meant no harm. I never intended to fool you or lead you astray.

MUNEMORI: Excuses are not necessary. Just tell the truth.

MASA: I wrote the letters because my daughter begged me to. She told me that she has an old lover, named Kaoru, whom she wants to visit no matter what it takes.

YUYA: Mother! So, you've been bribed, have you?

MASA: *(Ignoring* YUYA*)* Kaoru works for the Self-Defense Forces, so he cannot easily come to Tokyo. If I became sick, then Yuya could say she'd returned home to Hokkaido to take care of me. Yuya, of course, never intended to stay in Hokkaido. She would handle everything quietly, and when she returned to Tokyo, would continue to receive your patronage. *(Looking over the room)* After all, no one could easily give up a life like this.

ASAKO: Yuya, don't give in. Could a real mother betray her daughter in such a filthy way?

YUYA: *(Contemplating for a moment, she appears to wake up.)* This woman is not my true mother.

MUNEMORI: Are you still saying that your real mother is back in Hokkaido, gravely ill?

MASA: Whatever else you say, I am still the mother who bore this child.

YAMADA: *(Deliberately removes a document in his briefcase)* Well, according to this family register, Masa is not, in fact, Yuya's birth mother. Her birth mother passed away before Yuya was fifteen years old.

MUNEMORI: All right, I see. Then who is Kaoru?

YAMADA: There really is a Kaoru and he is stationed at the Chitose Army Base. According to the reports of the private detective agency, this Kaoru has even boasted to his friends in his unit that his girlfriend in Tokyo is a wealthy man's mistress. He told his friends that she is saving up money for their marriage expenses.

ASAKO: Munemori, you're really something, aren't you? You've got your hand in things all over Japan, don't you?

YAMADA: Yes, it's true. It goes without saying.

All are silent for a moment.

MUNEMORI: Well, now I wonder if everyone could please leave? I would like to take some time to relish the truth of this affair.

YAMADA: *(Coaxing* MASA*)* All right, you've done your part. I think it would be best to leave now.

MASA: Everyone, please excuse the disturbance I've caused. *(Both exit.)*

ASAKO: Yuya, let's go now, and talk things over in my room; after that, you can go on your trip. *(She rises first.)*

YUYA: *(Rises slowly, follows* ASAKO, *then turns back, and speaks gloomily.)* Good-bye.

ASAKO: Come on. *(She goes out the door.)*

MUNEMORI: *(Pause)* Yuya.

YUYA: . . .

MUNEMORI: You know, you don't have to leave.

YUYA: *(Slowly beginning to smile.)* Oh? *(She shuts the door behind her.)* Oh.

MUNEMORI: Come lie down on that bed, just as you were before. (YUYA *does as she's told.)* That's right. And now, put on the same sorrowful expression as before.

YUYA: *(Idly gazing at the balcony)* The rain is getting worse.

MUNEMORI: *(Takes off his jacket, and lights a fresh cigar.)* So it seems. It looks as though it was not just a passing shower.

YUYA: It's getting worse and worse. The room's grown dark. Shall we put on some lights?

MUNEMORI: It's fine just as it is, just as it is.

YUYA: I'm sure all the children have left the park. That pair of young lovers is gone too. And that little girl threading petals is gone. The puddles that have formed there are full of dirty, fallen blossoms. And I'm sure that those branches, heavy with blossoms, are stooping and shaking, struck by the rain.

MUNEMORI: Shall we be quiet for a little while?

YUYA: Yes. *(Pause.* YUYA *takes off her jacket, and edges over to stand beside* MUNEMORI.*)* May I say just one thing?

MUNEMORI: Go ahead.

YUYA: You believed me more than that lying old woman, didn't you?
MUNEMORI: You shouldn't ask such foolish questions.
YUYA: . . . I don't have to travel anywhere anymore.
MUNEMORI: You might as well stay here.
YUYA: Yes, I'll stay here.
MUNEMORI: But can't you make your face look sadder, the way it was before?
YUYA: But how can I make a sad face when I'm happy?
MUNEMORI: What are you so happy about? What, Yuya?
YUYA: Everything's been settled.
MUNEMORI: Yes, and your mother has fully recovered.
YUYA: Yes, there's nothing left to worry about. Just being with you makes me happy.
(Pause. The room grows increasingly dark.) The rain is terrible, isn't it? It's a shame we couldn't go blossom viewing today.
MUNEMORI: *(Gently unwraps* YUYA's *arm from his neck, then continues holding her hand, gazing at her face from a slight distance.)* But I had a fine blossom viewing today. A truly splendid blossom viewing.

CURTAIN

The Black Lizard

(Kuro Tokage)

Based on the Original Novel by Edogawa Rampo
Published in 1961, First Performed in 1962
Translated by Mark Oshima

INTRODUCTION

Thanks to its several popular film and stage versions, *The Black Lizard* is probably Mishima's best-known play in Japan. It is based on a novel of the same name by Edogawa Rampo, the father of the Japanese detective novel, and master of pulp fiction in the prewar era—a style called *eroguro* ("erotic and grotesque"). Rampo's novel *The Black Lizard* made a strong impression on Mishima when he read it as a youth, and Mishima had long planned to adapt the story to the stage. He wrote a ballet libretto version some years before the *shingeki* play.

The original novel is a battle of wits between a woman gang leader and master jewel thief who calls herself "Black Lizard," and Japan's premiere private detective, Akechi Kogorō, a favorite hero who appears in many of Rampo's detective stories for both adults and children. *The Black Lizard* is one of Rampo's most erotic novels. Black Lizard's chief henchman, Amamiya, is a young gangster who is obsessed with her beauty. Their sado-masochistic relationship runs throughout the novel. Black Lizard is obsessed with "eternal beauty," and in her secret "Museum of Terror" she displays the finest gems in the world and corpses of beautiful humans in dynamic poses, treated so that they will last forever. Soon after the novel begins Black Lizard sets elaborate plans into operation in her attempt to steal the biggest diamond in Japan, currently in the possession of a wealthy Osaka jewelry storeowner. Her strategy requires her to often operate in disguise, sometimes as a man. Black Lizard kidnaps the jeweler's beautiful daughter, Sanae, and gains the diamond as ransom, but when she is betrayed by the jeweler and Akechi, she resolves to add Sanae to her collection of corpses. The story reaches its climax in a suspense-filled series of encounters and dramatic changes in fortune inside the Museum of Terror.

For his adaptation of the novel to the stage Mishima wrote a text that centered on a developing love affair between Akechi and Black Lizard. Their love is only hinted at in Rampo's novel. In Mishima's play Akechi is obsessed with the allure and beauty of crime, and Black Lizard, for the first time in her life, encounters a man who can see past her physical beauty and understand the beauty of her soul. Black Lizard falls in love, but her love leaves her vulnerable, and destroys her in the end. Akechi, for his part, never loves Black Lizard as anything more than the perfect criminal, so is never endangered by tender feelings for her. Mishima visited Rampo to discuss the changes he intended to make, and Rampo was enthusiastic about the new version, saying that this love affair was the one element his novel lacked.[1]

Rampo's novel is set equally in Osaka and Tokyo in the 1920s, but Mishima's producer convinced him to set the play primarily in Tokyo, in the 1960s.[2] Tokyo Tower was recently completed and the pride of Japan, and the producer was eager to have a scene set in the tower observatory. Despite these changes that were forced on Mishima from the outside, he nevertheless strove to preserve the decadent spirit of Roaring Twenties in his text: "The play should be like a gorgeous decorator cake. But when you look carefully at the cake, it is crawling with maggots."[3]

Mishima's dramaturgy in *The Black Lizard* is radically different from his other plays. Normally Mishima was careful to remain true to the language and stage conventions of the genre he was working in, but in *The Black Lizard* he created a *shingeki*/kabuki hybrid. Mishima wrote that in some ways *The Black Lizard* was a forerunner to the *angura* ("underground" *avant garde)* plays of the mid to late sixties,[4] most of which were hybrids of various performance genres. In *The Black Lizard* Mishima ignored the three unities: the action of the play spans several weeks and there are three acts and thirteen scenes, many requiring spectacular staging. The play's technical and scenic requirements were as sophisticated as the most complex kabuki plays. Mishima used other formal aspects of kabuki, including delivery of lines by several actors in formal succession (*wari zerifu* and *watari zerifu*) and long, histrionic monologues meant to express the deepest feelings of the character. Mishima wrote that "this kind of formal, stylized approach to dialogue and monologue rescues the narrative. If presented naturally, the narrative would be too irrational. I tried to strengthen the aestheticism of the original work."[5] Mishima had written that the fusion of aesthetic beauty and cruelty is the essence of kabuki, and he achieved the same fusion in this play.[6]

Mishima envisioned the title role being performed "in the style of the great French actresses of the nineteenth century,"[7] and to his delight Mizutani Yaeko played Black Lizard in the first production in 1962. The leading actress of *shimpa* had a grandeur and presence unlike any *shingeki* actress of the day. In 1968, in the second major production during Mishima's lifetime, transvestite singer/actor Maruyama Akihiro (now named Miwa

Akihiro) played his first major stage role as *The Black Lizard*. Mishima and Matsuura decided to entrust the title role to him, despite his lack of stage experience, and their trust in the young singer was vindicated. Although this production had a lighter, campier feel to it, Mishima was pleased with the result,[8] and supported the effort to make a film version starring Maruyama. Mishima played one of Black Lizard's handsome preserved corpses in the 1969 film.

Since Mishima's death, Miwa Akihiro and kabuki *onnagata* Bandō Tamasaburō have worked most often with *The Black Lizard*. They have both performed in and directed the play. Tamasaburō often acts in *shingeki* and *shimpa*, and he played the title role in *The Black Lizard* in 1984 and 1986, and in 1990 directed Matsuzaka Keiko in the role. All three shows were large-scale Shochiku productions. Tamasaburō has played the leading lady in many of Mishima's great plays, including *Rokumeikan*, *Madame de Sade*, *Hanjo*, and three Mishima kabuki plays. Among the Mishima *shingeki* plays he has done, Tamasaburō enjoys *The Black Lizard* the most, and also believes it to be the most enjoyable Mishima *shingeki* play for audiences.[9] Unlike many Mishima plays, in which the characters talk "at each other," instead of "with each other," with the result that heart-to-heart communication and empathy is impossible, Black Lizard tells Akechi how she truly feels, and he understands her soul.[10] Tamasaburō also believes that *The Black Lizard* is Mishima's clearest expression of the tragedy inherent in the hopeless search for enduring beauty.[11]

When he acts and directs the leading role, Tamasaburō feels that it is crucial to create empathy for Black Lizard by foregrounding the pain and humiliation experienced by an older woman in love with a younger man, and the hopelessness of her love for Akechi, who can only love crime and can never love a woman. Tamasaburō feels it is important to counteract this dark side of the leading character with a light, witty, kitschy, black humor approach to the play as a whole.[12] Tamasaburō believes that Mishima's romantic and tragicomic kabuki plays and *The Black Lizard* represent "the real Mishima," but that too much of the time he felt compelled by his pride and ambition to don the mask of the intellectual writer or the right-wing political activist.[13]

In several essays he wrote about the play, Mishima emphasized that both the play's story and staging were all about finding an important truth in the midst of lies and deception—a theme he had begun to explore in the modern noh play *Yuya*. As *The Black Lizard* unfolds on stage, the hero and heroine repeatedly engage in acts of trickery, deception, and disguise in their desperate battle of wits and wills. Criminal and detective are one in the means they employ to prevail, and each comes to respect the other for the remarkable ingenuity, intensity, and humor of the deceptions they practice. Mutual deceit leads to mutual respect, and even to love.

In 1962 Mishima wrote, "The play should be a thing with substance. There should be the feeling that behind eight hundred lies, a shining truth can be seen."[14] Six years later, casting Maruyama in the title role—a man playing a woman—added another lie. Mishima wrote that "Maruyama Akihiro's role was to tell multiple layers of lies, but a single action by the actor/character could suddenly reveal the truth."[15]

Critics have not taken the play as seriously as Mishima himself did in his essays. They recognize the play's structure as a masterful fusion of kabuki and *shingeki*,[16] but have for the most part dismissed it as a playful melodrama. Producers, directors, and actors for stage and film consider *The Black Lizard* one of Mishima's most appealing plays. It is Mishima at his exotic, erotic, and humorous best. It demonstrates what kind of play Mishima could write when he let down his formalistic defenses and threw purity of genre to the winds.

NOTES

1. Dōmoto Masaki, Mishima Yukio no engeki maku kire no shiso (Tokyo: Geki Shobō, 1977), p. 137.
2. Mishima Yukio, "Kuro Tokage ni tsuite," Seibu seikatsu, 1962; reprinted in Mishima Yukio, Shibai no biyaku (Tokyo: Kakogawa Haruki Jimusho, 1997), p. 206.
3. Mishima,"Kuro Tokage," in Tyoko Gekijō program, April 1968; reprinted in Mishima hyōron zenshū, vol. 3 (Tokyo: Shinchō, 1994), p. 823.
4. Ibid.
5. Mishima, "Kuro Tokage ni tsuite," p. 207.
6. Mishima Yukio, "Nakamura Shikan ron," Gekijō, February 1949; reprinted in Mishima hyōron zenshū, vol. 3, p. 845.
7. Mishima, "Kuro Tokage," p. 823.
8. Ibid.
9. Bandō Tamasaburō, interview with author, February 13, 2002.
10. Ibid.
11. Ibid.
12. Ibid.
13. Ibid.
14. Mishima, "Kuro Tokage ni tsuite," p. 207.
15. Mishima, "Kuro Tokage ni tsuite," Fujin Shohō, June 1968; reprinted in Mishima hyōron zenshū, vol. 3, p. 824.
16. Andō Tsuruo, "Mishima Yukio no kakikae kyōgen," Asahi Shimbun, March 8, 1962; reprinted in Mishima Yukio jiten (Tokyo: Bensei Shuppan, 2000), p. 108.

THE CHARACTERS

(in order of appearance)
Madame Midorikawa, actually Black Lizard

Sanae Iwase
Jun'ichi Amamiya
Bellboy
Shobei Iwase
Kogorō Akechi
Akechi's assistants: Sakai, Kizu, Gifu
Policemen
Iwase's elderly housekeeper, Hina
Deliveryman, Gorō
Bodyguards: Haraguchi, Toyama, Okawa
Yumeko, the Iwase's maid
Mrs. Iwase (voice only)
Laundryman
Maids: Aiko, Iroe
Furniture store men
Dwarves
Sightseers at Tokyo Tower
Wife of the proprietor of a souvenir stand on the observation deck of Tokyo Tower
Taxi driver
Kitamura, a member of Black Lizard's gang
Sailors
Police detectives
Mrs. Iwase
Hayakawa, Sanae's fiance

THE SETTING

Act One

The "K" Hotel on Nakanoshima island in Osaka, early spring. Six scenes in various rooms.

Act Two

Scene 1: The kitchen of the Iwase mansion in the Shibuya district of Tokyo, spring

Scene 2: Alternating between Black Lizard's hideout and Akechi Kogorō's office

Scene 3: The observation deck of Tokyo Tower, the following day

Scene 4: A bridge near the Shibaura district of Tokyo

Act Three

Scene 1: Inside the mysterious ship— Black Lizard's cabin and on deck

Scene 2: An abandoned factory in the port of "S"

Scene 3: The Museum of Terror

ACT ONE

The act is set in rooms 522 and 524 of the "K" hotel on Nakanoshima Island in the center of Osaka. The stage is divided into three rooms. Farthest stage left is room 524. There is a large trunk in the room. The center and stage right rooms represent room 522, which is a lavish suite. The center room is the living room of the suite and is the largest space on stage. The stage right room is the suite bedroom, with twin beds. In the center of the back wall of both the suite living room and room 524, there are doors opening into the hallway of the hotel. There is a large clock above the stage at far stage left, up near the border curtains. At the beginning of the act, the clock indicates "8:00." From stage right to stage left, the three rooms are "room A," [suite bedroom] "room B" [suite living room] and "room C" [neighboring room with large trunk]. As the curtain opens, the clock chimes eight.

SCENE 1

When the curtain opens, only room B is lit. MADAME MIDORIKAWA *sits in an armchair center stage while* SANAE *is leaning against the window on the side of the room closest to room C, looking down at the river. The window faces out at the audience. Both women are in evening dress.*

MADAME MIDORIKAWA: Sanae, my dear, haven't you ever seen a river at night before. After all, this isn't your first visit to Osaka, is it?

SANAE: I was here once before, when I was still in girl's school. We stopped in Osaka on the way back from Kyoto, but it was only for a day.

MADAME MIDORIKAWA: Only that one time?

SANAE: Yes. Oh look! Nakanoshima is an island, isn't it? Is that river down there the Yodo River?

MADAME MIDORIKAWA: Yes, of course it is. You're asking questions just like a little girl. Sanae, you're nineteen already.

SANAE: Madame Midorikawa, you're awful, you even know my age!

MADAME MIDORIKAWA: Of course I know your age. I know everything about you. But surely you are still young enough not to mind people knowing your age.

SANAE: Madame Midorikawa, you know everything about me, but I don't know anything about you.

MADAME MIDORIKAWA: And that, my dear, is the secret to becoming good friends!

SANAE: *(Smiles immediately)* I guess you're right. *(Looks down through the window again)* Look! Even at night, there are boats on the river. There are lights moving down there on the water. There must be people who spend day and night living on those boats.

MADAME MIDORIKAWA: Sanae, not everyone can live like you, the daughter of a rich jeweler, staying in an expensive hotel suite.

SANAE. It's not that unusual; after all, you're staying here too.

MADAME MIDORIKAWA: Yes, I suppose that some people might think that I'm just a little bit wealthy. Oh I'm not all that rich, but I am, of course, a regular customer at your father's jewelry shop. Over the years, I've bought several tiny gems from him. I've been fortunate enough to become a sort of friend of the family . . . Oh, but that's not important. You know, I don't think that I would like to have to stay cooped up in a hotel suite, like you are. But then, I don't think that I would want to live on a boat, either. How can I describe what I want? I want to live in a world where things can always contact other things directly. I want a world where everything kisses other things, without anything coming in between. It's money that separates people and things from one another. It comes between you and me. When everything is so separate, the world is a boring place, don't you think?

SANAE: *(intrigued)* I guess so.

MADAME MIDORIKAWA: In the world I imagine, jewels will soar through the sky together with little birds. Lions will stroll through carpeted hotel lobbies. Beautiful people will always have the special right reserved for them to never, ever grow old. Precious vases in national museums will suddenly be replaced by yellow thermos bottles. The guns of the world will become huge flocks of ravens, darkening the sky everywhere. There will be lightning and fireworks all around. And on the ground below, there will always be festival crowds. The fountain pens of newspaper reporters will let out wild shrieks and spurt out fountains of ink, turning the white breast pockets of journalists' shirts dark blue. And then, when that moment comes, there will be an official proclamation. Yes, there will be a proclamation making me queen. When I am queen, people will be able to enter anyone's house that they want to. All partitions, all walls will become as flaky as piecrust and crumble at a finger's touch. We will wear rings made of pencil erasers and at the same time, the brown leather straps of subway cars will become chains of platinum, studded with diamonds.

SANAE: Oh, how wonderful! Father's jewelry store would go bankrupt. Then I would be free! He wouldn't have to drag me to Osaka to protect me, and he wouldn't have to arrange a meeting with a prospective husband. Then I could marry anyone I want, even if he is penniless.

MADAME MIDORIKAWA: Yes, then you would be free. Not only that, you would be young eternally. You would always be just as beautiful as you are now.

SANAE: Really, Madame Midorikawa?

MADAME MIDORIKAWA: How could I lie to you, my dear. I insist on inviting you into my world of dreams. That is because you are so very young and pretty . . . You play volleyball, don't you? Look at how strong and well proportioned your body is. How wonderful it is to be so slim and healthy. I can see how superb the shape of your breasts is, even through your clothing.

SANAE: *(reddening)* Oh, please don't say things like that!

MADAME MIDORIKAWA: No matter how pretty someone's face is, if they do not have a beautiful body to match, I can never really like them.

SANAE: Madame Midorikawa, you have a beautiful face and body yourself. I think father likes you.

MADAME MIDORIKAWA: You mustn't change the subject! Whenever I see someone with a beautiful face and body, suddenly I feel very lonely. In ten years, in twenty years, what will that person look like? More than anything, I want to keep beautiful people unchanged forever. Maybe when people age, it is not because the body grows old; perhaps it's actually the mind and heart that grow old. I believe that the gradual sickening and decline of a person's heart is reflected in the body. The inner weaknesses of the heart spread out and appear as ugly wrinkles and horrible stains. So if you could take away a person's heart, then maybe . . .

SANAE: But people can't live without hearts!

MADAME MIDORIKAWA: *(bitterly)* That is why this can only happen in my world of dreams. Take a diamond or a sapphire. Have you ever looked deeply into a jewel? Really deeply? A jewel is transparent and clear to its very core. Jewels have no hearts. A diamond is young forever.

SANAE: Excuse me for a moment. *(She is about to pick up the phone.)*

MADAME MIDORIKAWA: Where are you calling?

SANAE: I'm calling the bar. Father would love to hear this.

MADAME MIDORIKAWA: Oh, don't call your father. Let's talk a little longer, just the two of us. I have something to tell you that will make you very happy, but I can't do that if your father is here.

SANAE: All right. *(She obediently puts down the phone.)* What do you mean, you have something to tell me that will make me very happy?

MADAME MIDORIKAWA: I can't tell you yet.

SANAE: Don't leave me in suspense.

MADAME MIDORIKAWA: All in good time, my dear. By the way, who was that man Akechi that your father introduced just before dinner?

SANAE: Haven't you heard of him? I thought everyone knew him. Kogorō Akechi is the most famous private investigator in Japan.

MADAME MIDORIKAWA: Oh, that was Kogorō Akechi! A private investigator? How dreadful! What is your father doing with someone like that?

SANAE: Father is probably chatting and drinking with Akechi down at the bar right now. Lately, father has been so tense that he can't sleep unless he has something to drink first. Then, just before he goes to bed, he always has to have his sleeping pills.

MADAME MIDORIKAWA: What does that have to do with Akechi?

SANAE: I guess I can let you in on the secret since you are an old friend of the family. Lately there have been threatening letters coming every day to our house in Tokyo.

MADAME MIDORIKAWA: Oh how frightening! What kind of letters?

SANAE: They always say exactly the same thing. Every word is etched indelibly on my brain: "Guard your daughter carefully. There is an evil monster looking for a chance to kidnap her."

MADAME MIDORIKAWA: How awful!

SANAE: It doesn't bother me too much. I think it's just someone's idea of a joke. But father is very worried. He didn't want to call the police because he's sure that it would get into the newspapers. So, very secretly, he's asked for Akechi's help. Father and mother were eager for me to come to Osaka for a meeting with a prospective husband because they thought that going to Osaka would take me away from danger for awhile. Akechi came with us. Now, even if I just go out for a little bit of shopping, Akechi always goes with me.

MADAME MIDORIKAWA: If he's as good as they say, you have nothing to worry about.

SANAE: He's also a really nice man.

MADAME MIDORIKAWA: How can any private detective be a "really nice man"? They're horrible people, suspicious and prying, with an ugly look in their eyes. No decent person would want to associate with a private detective.

SANAE: But Akechi isn't like that. Did he look like that to you?

MADAME MIDORIKAWA: You know, that's funny. No, he didn't.

SANAE: You see! *(The two catch each other's eyes and laugh girlishly.)*

MADAME MIDORIKAWA: Did you like the man your father wants you to marry?

SANAE: You must be joking. He has glasses and he talks like a prissy old woman. "Sanae, I understand that you have many athletical abilities." Who talks like that these days?

MADAME MIDORIKAWA: In short, you don't like him.

SANAE: No.

MADAME MIDORIKAWA: I don't want to interfere with your father's business, but I found someone perfect for you. He's a young man with his own company in Tokyo, and he's very attractive. It just so happens that he is staying in this very hotel. I ran into him yesterday and mentioned you to him. At that moment, I thought it would be wonderful just to look at the two of you sitting side by side. You know, he's staying in the room next door. I know what kind of people you like and I'm sure you'll like him. How about it? Would you like to meet him?

SANAE: But I don't want to have two meetings with prospective husbands in one day.

MADAME MIDORIKAWA: I'm not talking about anything so formal. If you like each other, you can become lovers. When we get back to Tokyo, I'll be happy to arrange secret meetings for you any time you want.

SANAE: How can you say that when I haven't even met him yet?

MADAME MIDORIKAWA: That's why I will introduce him to you now. Let me call him.

SANAE: He's next door? Right at this moment?

MADAME MIDORIKAWA: No, I think that he's at the bar right now.

SANAE: Madame Midorikawa, you had this all planned from the start.

MADAME MIDORIKAWA: Yes, but I had to do it because I like you so much. *(She stands and reaches for the phone.)*

SANAE: But if he's at the bar, father will notice.

MADAME MIDORIKAWA: Don't worry, leave everything to me. Hello, connect me with the bar, please. Is this the bar? There should be someone named Amamiya there. Could you please call him to the phone? Yes, he's a young man and he should be drinking by himself. Hello, Jun'ichi? I am visiting in room 522 right now. Can you come up? I'll introduce you to a very pretty young woman. Come right away . . . He already hung up, he must be rushing up here now.

SANAE: Somehow, I'm a little frightened.

MADAME MIDORIKAWA: There's nothing to worry about.

SANAE: I mean that ever since I was a little girl, I've had a kind of sixth sense. I have a feeling that I'm about to enter a more wonderful world than I've ever seen before.

MADAME MIDORIKAWA: Now there's no need to exaggerate. Jun'ichi Amamiya is nice, but he's not going to change the world.

SANAE: All my life I've been treated like a jewel. I've been raised and protected so carefully. But lately I've had dreams of not being bought properly like a valuable jewel, but stolen away.

MADAME MIDORIKAWA: Really?

SANAE: I want to meet someone who has the passion and the nerve to steal me away. I feel like I'm a jewel on a velvet cushion protected by a thick glass case. I'm tired of people peering into the case, their looks of resignation that this treasure is beyond their grasp. Looks of anger, looks of arrogance. Secretly, I've even begun to hope that a daring thief will fall in love with me.

MADAME MIDORIKAWA: Is that how you feel? In that case, Jun'ichi's eyes will steal you away.

SANAE: Really, Madame Midorikawa?

MADAME MIDORIKAWA: Really. *(There is a knock at the door.)* Come in. *(She stands.* JUN'ICHI AMAMIYA *enters. He is dressed neatly in a business suit.)*

MADAME MIDORIKAWA: May I introduce you? Jun'ichi Amamiya, this is Sanae Iwase.

AMAMIYA: How do you do?

SANAE: How do you do?

MADAME MIDORIKAWA: All they can do is to stand and gaze into each other's eyes. That's the way it should be. You don't need any words. As long as the two of you are silent, I will talk for you. *(The two of them sit, facing each other.* MADAME MIDORIKAWA *stands and goes by the window.)* I like beautiful young people best when they are silent. Their words are all too commonplace. Anything they say is sure to ruin their youth, their beauty. You don't need any clothes either. Clothes are for hiding old and ugly bodies from the eyes of others. How beautiful are lips open for love. But the pores of the skin open wide for love are just as beautiful, the silky down by each pore reaching out passionately. If a face blushing shyly is beautiful, the entire body bright red with bashful joy is even more beautiful . . .

It's night. Our time is approaching. Separate from the night of ordinary people looms our night, dizzying and steep, like a sheer cliff. Apart from clusters of families in their comforting night, there stands our night, surrounding it like a terrifying forest. *(As she speaks, she looks down out the window, lights a cigarette with her lighter, then makes a big circle by the window with the flame of the lighter.)* A car is waiting. It will go far away from the bright lights of the hotel lobby. The car is waiting for its beautiful, heavy burden. *(She makes another small circle with the flame of her lighter.)* All the preparations are complete. The driver looks to make sure that there are no mistakes, not even the slightest error. Breathlessly, everyone waits for this vehicle of lies and deception to begin moving. When it moves, it will move smoothly like it's gliding on oil. All that it takes is the lightest touch to start the gears moving. Instantly, in ecstasy, the machinery of illusion and evil will begin moving. Once it begins to move, nothing can stop it. *(She closes her lighter with a snap and puts it away, then turns to the two again.)* Jun'ichi, why don't you show Sanae what you bought yesterday.

AMAMIYA: What do you mean?

MADAME MIDORIKAWA: Don't you remember, that beautiful doll of a girl in a wedding dress that you found at an antique store. The doll that you're so proud of?

AMAMIYA: But it's too big to bring here.

MADAME MIDORIKAWA: You don't have to bring it here. Sanae and I can go to your room to see it, can't we?

SANAE: Well . . .

MADAME MIDORIKAWA: Don't worry, as long as you're with me, I'm sure that everything will be all right. That doll is definitely worth seeing. It looks exactly like a beautiful young girl and the face is very well done. Come to mention it, Sanae, you could even have been the model for this doll.

AMAMIYA: Wait a moment, are you going to come over right now?
MADAME MIDORIKAWA: Of course, is anything wrong with that?
AMAMIYA: I didn't expect any guests, so my room is a mess. I'll tell you what. I'll go straighten up. Then when everything is ready, I'll call you.
MADAME MIDORIKAWA: Fine. Don't keep us waiting long.
AMAMIYA: It will just take a few minutes.

He nods to SANAE *again and leaves the room. Immediately he enters room C at stage left. He puts on the light, quickly puts on a beard and changes his clothes. He takes out a handkerchief and soaks it with ether, then he turns out the lights so that the room is lit only by a single lamp. He hides by the door and conceals the handkerchief behind his back. During this time, in room B . . .*

MADAME MIDORIKAWA: Well, what did you think of him?
SANAE: I've never met anyone like him before.
MADAME MIDORIKAWA: Didn't I tell you so?
SANAE: He seemed so hesitant and reserved, but his eyes . . . his eyes were bold and daring.
MADAME MIDORIKAWA: There is something mysterious about him, but all the same, he's a very successful businessman.
SANAE: I guess I shouldn't have let him do all the talking.
MADAME MIDORIKAWA: But he didn't say anything either. It was I who did all the talking.
SANAE: Oh, Madame Midorikawa, I didn't notice! Did you say something then?
MADAME MIDORIKAWA: I can see that you didn't hear a word I said.
SANAE: I'm so sorry . . .
MADAME MIDORIKAWA: How adorable you are, truly adorable. *(She puts her arm around* SANAE's *neck.)* So adorable that I'd like to strangle you, like this.
SANAE: *(Paying no attention, she brushes* MADAME MIDORIKAWA's *arm away.)* Being the daughter of a rich jeweler, dull meetings with prospective husbands, life in a hotel, all of that is about to disappear. I feel like I have turned into a silver top and I am spinning with wonderful, dizzying speed.
MADAME MIDORIKAWA: When I get involved, that's what always happens.
SANAE: Madame Midorikawa, I have faith in you.
MADAME MIDORIKAWA: Yes, do trust me, my dear. Oh how beautiful your eyes are! Gazing into the eyes of someone who really trusts me always makes me feel deliciously happy. *(The phone rings.* MADAME MIDORIKAWA *picks up the receiver.)* Yes . . . yes . . . We'll be right over. *(To* SANAE*)* Let's go, Sanae, a bright new world is about to open up right before you. *(She urges* SANAE *out of the room.)*

As they leave, the lights go out in room B.

SCENE 2

There is a knock on the door of room C. SANAE *enters. She looks around the dark room, but sees no sign of anyone and hesitates for a moment.* MADAME MIDORIKAWA *enters after her and pulls the door shut behind her.* AMAMIYA *jumps out, pins back* SANAE'*s arms from behind and pushes the handkerchief in her face.* SANAE *loses consciousness.* AMAMIYA *and* MADAME MIDORIKAWA *strip her of her outer clothing, then open the trunk and push* SANAE *inside.* AMAMIYA *helps* MADAME MIDORIKAWA *put on* SANAE'S *clothing. When she is almost finished changing,* AMAMIYA *picks up the phone.*

AMAMIYA: Hello . . . This is Kensaku Yamakawa in room 524. I'm ready to check out. Can you send someone to carry my trunk? Thank you.

Now disguised as Sanae, MADAME MIDORIKAWA *picks up a cloth bundle that had been stashed in the room beforehand and leaves the room. Room C goes dark.*

SCENE 3

MADAME MIDORIKAWA *enters room B. The lights go up in the room. She goes into room A, the bedroom, and closes the door to the living room. She lights the room with only a single table lamp and then rings the bell. After a while, there is a knock on the door of room B. In a disguised voice,* MADAME MIDORIKAWA *calls,* "Come in!" A BELLBOY *comes into room B.*

BELLBOY: Did you ring?

MADAME MIDORIKAWA: *(She opens the door of the bedroom very slightly so that her face is in shadow, but the light from the table lamp in the bedroom illuminates her clothing. She imitates Sanae's voice.)* Yes. My father should be downstairs at the bar. Can you call him and ask if he's ready to go to sleep.

BELLBOY: Yes, very good ma'am.

The BELLBOY *leaves.* MADAME MIDORIKAWA *starts undressing and then changes her mind and takes a negligee out of a dresser. Again she starts undressing, but then pauses and waits for Iwase to come and see her changing into her negligee.*

IWASE: *(Enters drunk, says farewell to* KOGORŌ AKECHI *at the door, laughing heartily.)* Thank you for keeping me company tonight. Most enjoyable. It's all right now, I'll keep an eye on things here. Go ahead and go to bed. Good night. *(He locks the door.)* Sanae, why are you alone here? I thought Madame Midorikawa was with you.

He opens the door to room A, but thinks he sees his daughter undressing and quickly goes back into room B and sits in an armchair.

MADAME MIDORIKAWA: *(Imitating Sanae's voice)* I felt a little sick, so I sent Madame Midorikawa away. I'm going to bed, father, why don't you go to bed too?

IWASE: Now Sanae, you know you shouldn't be all alone here. How many times do I have to tell you that? What if something happens?

MADAME MIDORIKAWA: But that's why I called you.

IWASE: Well that's right, you did, didn't you? *(He stands, pours himself a glass of water and drinks it. Then he pours himself another glass of water and carries it into room A.* MADAME MIDORIKAWA *is already lying in Sanae's bed, her back to him.* IWASE *takes the sleeping pills on the night table with the water and changes into pajamas during the following.)* Are you feeling any better, Sanae?

MADAME MIDORIKAWA: I'm fine. Let me sleep.

IWASE: Ha, ha, ha, you're still such a little girl. You're still mad at me for forcing you to meet that man that you didn't like. *(He gets into bed and stares at the ceiling.)* Go ahead and sleep. If you're tired, you don't have to answer. You know Sanae, no matter how much I love my 130 carat diamond, the Star of Egypt, you are much more precious to me. If someone tries to kidnap you, I know it's not you they want, they must really be after the diamond. So to protect you, father is paying good money, one million yen a month, to Kogorō Akechi. That's right, one million yen. I insist on the best of everything. The best daughter in all Japan . . . the biggest diamond in Japan . . . and the best detective in Japan. The three are a matched set. If any one of these three is missing, I'm not happy. You know, Sanae, jewels always have some kind of worry stuck to them. Worry is what makes jewels beautiful. Ever since those letters started coming, I've had to worry about you. Sanae, those letters made you into a jewel too. *(He yawns.)* Good! Good! Finally I'm sleepy. Now I can get to sleep. But this is the tricky part. If I think I'm sleepy then instead, I'll stay awake. Papa's not sleepy! Papa's not sleepy! There, I think it's working . . . People sleep. But jewels never sleep. Even when the city is asleep and everything is silent, inside their cases, under lock and key in safety deposit boxes, jewels are always awake, their bright eyes staring unblinking. Jewels never sleep and they absolutely never dream. The diamond syndicate guarantees that the value of diamonds will never change. Something that always lives up to its full worth has nothing incomplete. It has no need to dream. Jewels never dream . . . Ah . . . ah . . . *(yawns with great gasps)* Isn't that right, Sanae? Jewels never dream, but worry and anxiety always surround them. This is the incurable illness of gems; a very elegant sickness. The sicker a jewel is, the more valuable it is. The more valuable a jewel is, the sicker it is. But no matter how sick it gets, a diamond can never die. Ah . . . ah . . . That's it, all gems are really diseases. Your father buys and sells diseases. Pure, clear, sparkling diseases. Diseases as transparent as glass. Blue diseases, red diseases, purple diseases . . . Sanae, Papa wants to make more money, a lot more money! One hundred thousand whole grilled fish. One hundred thousand skewers of chicken. You know, they say that in America they even sell babies. Ah . . . ah . . . Two hundred thousand little black babies. Ten million goldfish. Ah . . . ah . . . Thirty million sticks of cotton candy. Ah . . . ah . . . The biggest carnival in the world. Ah . . . ah . . . mine, all mine. Ah . . . ah . . . Ah . . . ah . . . Aaaa . . .

Finally IWASE *falls asleep. Silence.* MADAME MIDORIKAWA *slowly lifts her head and carefully gets up. She appeared to have changed into the negligee, but when she gets up, it becomes clear that she had only draped the negligee over her and is still in Sanae's clothes. She takes the cloth bundle from under the bed and slips out a mannequin head resembling Sanae. She puts the head on the pillow and arranges the bed so that it looks like Sanae is still sleeping there. Then she slips out of room A and leaves the suite through room B.*

SCENE 4

The stage is dark. Only the clock at stage left is lit up. The hands move from 8:45 to 10:00. The lights go up in room B. Suddenly, there is loud knocking at the door. The knocking continues for a while. Finally in room A, IWASE *groggily gets up and goes to room B. He opens the door and yawns.*

AKECHI: *(Enters the room.)* There's been a telegram. Another threatening telegram!

IWASE: What? Oh it's you, Akechi. A telegram? *(Still half-asleep, he takes the telegram.)*

AKECHI: *(Impatiently grabs the telegram back and reads it for Iwase.)* "Be on your guard at midnight tonight."

IWASE: Midnight? . . . tonight? . . .

AKECHI: Finally the letters are beginning to specify the time.

IWASE: Ah . . . ah . . . Damn! It's some kind of bad joke. I was just getting to sleep.

AKECHI: Is your daughter all right?

IWASE: She's fine, she's fine. She's sleeping in the bed next to me. *(He stumbles to room A and peeks in at her and then returns.)* Let's not wake her. She said she wasn't feeling well and now she's sleeping so peacefully.
AKECHI: Are the windows in the bedroom secure?
IWASE: They've been locked since this afternoon. *(As he returns to room A.)* Kogorō, I'm sorry to trouble you, but lock the door and hold on to the key.
AKECHI: No. If you don't mind I'll stay here. Leave the door to the bedroom open. (IWASE *nods and goes back to bed, leaving the door to the bedroom open.)*

AKECHI *walks slowly around room B, then locks the door and puts the key in his left pocket. Finally he sits down and lights a cigarette. He sits watching the bedroom.*

SCENE 5

There is knocking at the door. After a while it stops. AKECHI *gets his pistol from his right pocket and stands ready. Again there is knocking.*

AKECHI: Who is it?
MADAME MIDORIKAWA: It's me.

AKECHI *puts the pistol away. He unlocks the door and returns the key to his left pocket.* MADAME MIDORIKAWA *enters, now dressed in an elegant, brightly colored kimono.*

AKECHI: Ah, Madame Midorikawa.
MADAME MIDORIKAWA: I see that you are here. It must be because of that strange telegram.
AKECHI: How do you know about that?
MADAME MIDORIKAWA: The bellboys in this hotel talk a lot . . . . Is Sanae sleeping?
AKECHI: Yes.
MADAME MIDORIKAWA: And her father too?
AKECHI: Yes.
MADAME MIDORIKAWA: If you are here keeping guard, there is nothing in the world to be afraid of.
AKECHI: Well, something like that.
MADAME MIDORIKAWA: It looks like a very boring job.
AKECHI: Danger only exists in the midst of boredom. It comes like the sudden appearance of words written in invisible ink on the blank paper of tedium. I am waiting for that moment . . . But don't worry about my

work. This really isn't any of your business. Why don't you go on to bed?

MADAME MIDORIKAWA: My, this certainly is a warm reception! I'll have you know that I have known the Iwase family much longer than you have. I'm so worried about Sanae that I couldn't possibly sleep.

AKECHI: In that case, do as you like.

MADAME MIDORIKAWA: Well then, I think that I will keep you company, until the crucial hour of midnight.

AKECHI: I'm honored.

MADAME MIDORIKAWA *sits down across from* AKECHI. *She takes out a cigarette.*

MADAME MIDORIKAWA: Can you give me a light?

AKECHI: Certainly.

He lights her cigarette with a lighter.

MADAME MIDORIKAWA: *(Looking around her.)* Tonight is different from usual. It's as though the night itself is holding its breath, waiting for something to happen. This night is like an intricate piece of parquet woodwork. There is something almost pleasant in the tense sheen of that parquet. A night like this makes my body glow red hot. It makes me feel alive.

AKECHI: When crime approaches, the night becomes a living thing. I've experienced many nights like this. The night starts to have a pulse and a heartbeat, and warms to body temperature . . . In the end, the night itself invites the crime in, and night sleeps together with crime. Sometimes blood flows.

MADAME MIDORIKAWA: You've lived through many of those experiences, I imagine. By now, you and crime must be like the negative and the positive print of a photograph. Your eyes see the same thing the criminal sees. In your heart, you experience the same feelings as the criminal.

AKECHI: I wish that were true.

MADAME MIDORIKAWA: I'm surprised that you don't have more self-confidence.

AKECHI: It would be nice if everything the criminal sees as black, I could see as white. I wish that just like a photograph and its negative, the pattern matched exactly. But it doesn't work that way. Even though I've dealt with lots of cases, always in a crime, there is something that I can't understand. Every time I encounter a crime, I try to imagine that I am the criminal. I believe that if I could reproduce the thoughts of the criminal exactly, then I would know everything and there would be no riddle that I couldn't solve. So I concentrate on imitating the criminal. I

Figure 23. *The Black Lizard*, in 1990, with Matsuzaka Keiko as Madame Midorikawa (the Black Lizard) and Tsukayama Masane as Akechi. Photograph courtesy of the Waseda University Tsubouchi Hakase Memorial Theatre Museum.

try to think like the criminal. I put my soul into trying to do the things the criminal did . . . But just when I think I've succeeded, I realize that somehow I've failed to fully become the criminal. There is something in my heart that gets in the way. . . .

MADAME MIDORIKAWA: It's your decency. The decency that allows you to walk boldly anywhere in society, on the city streets in broad daylight, in a courtroom, on a golf course. That decency gets in your way.

AKECHI: That's a very strong statement. But I don't think that it's that simple. In crime, you have to have certain qualifications. Do you see? Maybe qualifications that even the criminal himself is unaware of.

MADAME MIDORIKAWA: What do you mean by qualifications?

AKECHI: This is what I mean. For example, imagine a woman. She has just received a bouquet of roses from someone. She loves roses. She holds the flowers to her face and smells the fragrance. But suddenly, she notices hidden deep in the petals, a disgusting insect. There is a blazing fire in the fireplace next to her. With a scream, she throws the bouquet into the fire. This kind of woman cannot commit a crime.

MADAME MIDORIKAWA: Why not?

AKECHI: I'll explain in a moment. Now there is a second woman. She loves roses too. Then she sees the insect. She coolly picks the insect out of the flowers and throws it into the fire. Then she enjoys the fragrance of the insect-free flowers. Then there is a third woman. Now this woman doesn't want to kill the insect and she doesn't want to burn the flowers. She has a very tender heart. She is so full of emotion that - now listen carefully here - she goes around behind the man who sent her the flowers and, most tragically, shoves him into the fire . . . In the end, she burns his face to a crisp.

MADAME MIDORIKAWA: Oh my!

AKECHI: You see, the third woman is very tender and sensitive. The first woman can be a bit cruel, but she only acts cruelly by instinct in the face of danger. She throws both the flowers and the insect into the fire and saves herself. All the time, she preserves society and its framework. The second woman can be consciously cruel to some extent, but she is very rational about it. She makes a careful distinction among the importance of an insect, roses, and the moral framework of society. The third woman is so true to her own tender spirit that she doesn't hesitate to uproot and destroy social order and morality . . . But in fact, of the three women, the third actually has the least innate cruelty. But this is the very kind of person who has the qualifications to become a criminal.

MADAME MIDORIKAWA: What a wonderful explanation. I have never met a detective like you before. I have never met a detective who loves crime from the bottom of his heart, a man with a kind of romantic attachment to crime.

AKECHI: Crime is romantic. With all crime, there is a kind of elegance, the rustle of silk decorated with panels of lace. And there is something a little old fashioned about it, a little exaggerated. It's like listening to grandmother's stories.

MADAME MIDORIKAWA: Is that what crime is like? Is that even true of a car thief? Political corruption? The violent crimes committed by a filthy giant of a man?

AKECHI: Yes, I think so. No matter how vulgar and commonplace, every crime has a kind of dream in it. Our modern society is held together by law. This law is made of glass and steel and concrete—hard things, things with no vulnerability or softness at all. Crime, this flower bouquet of lace and silk and blood, comes floating elegantly toward the edifice of law from another world. Any deadly weapon has a kind of elegance that something harmless and mundane, like the poor washing machine, doesn't have. A weapon carries a cloud of tender emotion with it precisely because it isn't utilitarian. Don't you think so?

MADAME MIDORIKAWA: What good would my agreement do you?

AKECHI: For example, take a look at this. *(Takes his pistol from his right pocket)* Don't worry, I'm not going to shoot you. If something appears in the bedroom window, then and only then, this will spit flame. *(Aims at the window)* But look, outside the window, the only thing you can see is the black night sky and the stars. Now this pistol is aimed at the night; the enormous, incalculable night filled with the cold air of early spring. This pistol faces the night in its entirety. But even if I were to fire this pistol, the night won't disappear. It won't fall down like the target figure in a shooting gallery and be replaced by the face of the morning sun. The night will stay there, just the same as before. This pistol is nothing more than a dream, removed from everything normal, and waits for just one thing. It waits for the moment that the night begins to beat with a pulse of its own, the moment it takes on body temperature and starts to emit the smell of an animal. It waits for the moment when the night takes on shape and appears as a human being.

MADAME MIDORIKAWA: And when that person appears, you will shoot him in the name of the law.

AKECHI: No. *(Puts the pistol away)* No, I shoot in the name of dreams. That is where the job of a private investigator is different from that of the police. We punish criminals by attacking dreams with dreams. I strike the dream in a crime using the dream that my reason creates. What else is there for me to live for?

MADAME MIDORIKAWA: That's a very cold reason for living.

AKECHI: Do you mean the coldness of my profession?

MADAME MIDORIKAWA: No, it's more than that. It's an inhuman coldness. I mean, when the law punishes a criminal, people are punishing other people. But you go beyond the realm of dreams and lie in wait there in the distance with your net. I wonder if you can really say that this is a dream attacking a dream. No, you are pretending to be fate itself when you pass judgment. How arrogant you are with your pretty white forehead as beautiful as that of an innocent little boy . . .

AKECHI: Ah, but Madame Midorikawa, how modest the look in your eyes is . . . should I return your praise like this?

MADAME MIDORIKAWA: You can say anything you like. But hidden deep in your cold eyes, I see desires that are still unfulfilled. There I sense the shimmer of a cowardly, hesitant passion. In other words, you are suffering from unrequited love. An unrequited love for crime. Isn't that so?

AKECHI: That's a very poetic way of putting it.

MADAME MIDORIKAWA: The instant that you think that you have won your love, crime has already slipped out of your hands. It disappears in forests of red tape in the police station and the courts.

AKECHI: It may sound conceited, but sometimes I fancy that it is the other way around. Crime is in love with me and it is crime that feels the pain of unrequited love.

MADAME MIDORIKAWA: How childish and selfish this particular pair of lovers is.

AKECHI: Exactly. Childish lovers, their hearts beating with excitement, always only hurting themselves. The result is that this unhappy pair of lovers can only betray each other constantly.

MADAME MIDORIKAWA: I hate to admit it, but I imagine that you are irresistibly attractive to crime.

AKECHI: Really? And am I irresistible to you too?

MADAME MIDORIKAWA: No, the kind of attractiveness that you have is very special. An ordinary woman like myself couldn't possibly feel the charm of that kind of attraction.

AKECHI: Ha, ha, ha . . . I wish there was some way of passing the time while we wait. I can't drink at a time like this . . .

MADAME MIDORIKAWA: There should be a deck of cards around here somewhere. How about a game of cards?

AKECHI: Fine.

MADAME MIDORIKAWA: *(Stands and gets two decks of cards from the shelf. As she brushes by Akechi, she slips the pistol out of his pocket.)* There are two decks here, perfect. *(Carries the two decks back)* Let's play American pinochle.

AKECHI: All right.

MADAME MIDORIKAWA: *(Takes all the Aces, Kings, Queens, Jacks, Tens and Nines from the deck.)* Shall we bet? *(Translator's note: One odd thing about the play is that in the original novel, the bet is over whether the criminal will succeed in kidnapping Sanae or not. In the play it is ambiguous whether this is the bet, or whether it is just over cards. Now it is over cards, but later it seems to be over the success of the crime.)*

AKECHI: I don't mind betting, but you're rich and I'm just a poor private investigator.

MADAME MIDORIKAWA: I will wager all the jewels I own.

AKECHI: Now that's a grand gesture. What should I bet?

MADAME MIDORIKAWA: *(Reaches out and squeezes his hand.)* There is something I would like you to place as a bet.

AKECHI: Please don't ask for the impossible . . .

MADAME MIDORIKAWA: I want . . . *(Gazes into his eyes.)*

AKECHI: Mm?

MADAME MIDORIKAWA: I want you to bet your profession as private detective.

AKECHI: *(He gazes steadily at her in return. Silence. Finally, lightly)* All right, you're on.

MADAME MIDORIKAWA: Oh, how wonderful! *(Enthusiastically)* Look, the ace, ten, king, queen jack and nine. Six cards each, four suits and two decks makes forty-eight cards. This is the deck we play with. We take twelve cards from here, six cards for you and six cards for me. *(She deals the cards and places the rest in a pile face down. She turns over the top card of the deck.)* And this suit is trump.

Silently the two begin playing. They each take a single card from their hand and place it on the table face down. Then at the proper moment, they turn the cards face up. Depending on the rank and value of the two cards, the winner of each trick is decided. Only cards of the same suit can compete with one another. If two cards of the same rank, same value are played, whichever player played the card first wins the trick.

AKECHI: I win this trick!

MADAME MIDORIKAWA: Do you have a meld?

AKECHI: *(Examines his cards)* Not yet.

The game continues.

MADAME MIDORIKAWA: I win this trick!

AKECHI: How about it?

MADAME MIDORIKAWA: *(Lays out her cards.)* Here! A Normal Marriage.

AKECHI: Oh no! Already down twenty points.

The game continues.

AKECHI: I win this trick!

MADAME MIDORIKAWA: Do you have the cards for a meld?

AKECHI: Maybe . . .

MADAME MIDORIKAWA: You're bluffing.

AKECHI: Voila! A Royal Marriage.

MADAME MIDORIKAWA: That's forty points for you, I'm behind twenty points.

The game continues. AKECHI *looks at his wristwatch.*

AKECHI: *(Suddenly puts down his cards.)* Let's quit.
MADAME MIDORIKAWA: That's not fair. The game's not over yet.
AKECHI: It's almost twelve o'clock. There's only a minute to go.

The clock above the stage at stage left lights up and shows that it is one minute to twelve.

MADAME MIDORIKAWA: Let's go on playing cards, nothing is going to happen.
AKECHI: But in just one minute, something is supposed to happen.
MADAME MIDORIKAWA: You have a lot of faith in the criminal.
AKECHI: That criminal has a reputation to live up to as well.
MADAME MIDORIKAWA: Stop talking like that! Are you trying to frighten me? In the middle of the night, the only sound comes from the plumbing in the nearby rooms. Or, I suppose, there is a faint sound from the picture frames and a soft creaking of the furniture. But with everything unmoving, everything asleep, all sorts of things might be possible. That picture of Mt. Fuji might suddenly change into a picture of a naked woman. The hair tonic in the bathroom might transform into a beautifully colored bottle of poison. The knots in the woodwork might change into staring, bloodshot eyes. Something might happen. I don't know, somehow, I'm beginning to feel very uneasy. Let's keep playing cards.
AKECHI: Shh! It's midnight.

The clock chimes twelve.

MADAME MIDORIKAWA: You see, nothing happened.
AKECHI: I guess I won the wager.
MADAME MIDORIKAWA: I'm not so sure. Anyway, it is clear that just like sticking your bare feet in the freezing water of a mountain stream, our feet have been washed by the flow of time. How does it feel? The cold clear water of time that has been flowing over our bare feet. This hotel room has been caught in its flow as well. This entire hotel will soon be washed away. Steel bridges, boats, parking lots that are brightly lit even deep in the night, people sleeping, the jewels in safety deposit boxes; everything is changed by the swift flow of the water of time. Can't you hear it? Listen to that roaring sound, that is the sound of time! The hour foretold by the criminal approaches. More punctual than the arrival of the procession of a king, it comes along a cleanly swept, purified road.

AKECHI: I don't know, I certainly don't hear anything. Maybe the criminal's watch is broken. I know the feeling when a crime is approaching, and it is totally different. First, the air in the room seems to become very dense. The folds of the curtains seem to freeze like motionless cascades of ice. The crystal pendants of chandeliers clink against each other softly like chattering teeth. At that moment, crime has already invisibly slipped into the room.

MADAME MIDORIKAWA: If there is nothing like that, then we're all right . . . But Kogorō, I'm scared. Maybe all of that has been happening, but we just didn't notice it. Maybe we've become so accustomed to the feeling that we didn't recognize the signs. Maybe the crime has already been committed, but we were too blind to see it.

AKECHI: What do you mean?

MADAME MIDORIKAWA: This is just an instinct, probably just my imagination. But I have a feeling that Sanae may already be gone.

AKECHI: You think that she has been kidnapped?

MADAME MIDORIKAWA: Somehow, I have a horrible feeling that something has happened.

AKECHI: But Sanae is absolutely safe.

MADAME MIDORIKAWA: Yes, I know! I know that Sanae is sleeping next to her father in the bedroom next door. Of course she is! She must be! But still, somehow . . .

AKECHI: What are you trying to say?

MADAME MIDORIKAWA: It's just a feeling . . .

AKECHI *suddenly runs to room A and roughly shakes* IWASE *awake.*

IWASE: *(Drowsily)* What is it? What is it? Why are you waking me so suddenly?

AKECHI: Check your daughter. Is that really your daughter sleeping over there?

IWASE: Of course it's my daughter. Who else could it possibly be? (IWASE *is shocked awake and calls at Sanae's bed.)* Sanae! Sanae!

There is no answer. IWASE *stands and goes to the bed. He tries to shake Sanae awake.* AKECHI *switches on the room lights.*

Ahh!!

IWASE *holds up the puppet head with the face of Sanae. Her negligee is attached to the neck of the head.* AKECHI *and* MADAME MIDORIKAWA *stand uncertainly in the door of room A.* IWASE *roughly pushes them aside and goes into room B. The two follow him.* IWASE *carries the head with him, the negligee dragging along the floor.* IWASE *sinks to his knees in despair and finally drops the head on the floor.* MADAME MIDORIKAWA *picks up the head and gazes deeply at the face.* IWASE *sits down heavily in a chair. Then he jumps up and runs back into room A. He gropes around the bed and throws the blankets in the air searching desperately. He rushes to the bathroom and flings open the door, looks in and slams the door shut again. He pulls open the drawers of the dresser and searches through the contents. He is overcome with fury and stands in the doorway between room A and room B.*

Akechi! What are you going to do about this?! I hired you to protect my daughter and now she's gone. And you're supposed to be the best detective in Japan? Don't make me laugh. Is this what I get for one million yen a month?

AKECHI: You say one million yen, but when you deduct salaries for my assistants and investigative expenses, what I get is really not all that much.

MADAME MIDORIKAWA: *(Bursts out laughing.)* Very business-like, indeed. But even I could stand guard over a doll's head like this, and it wouldn't cost nearly as much. Isn't that right, Mr. Iwase?

IWASE: Exactly! *(Notices* MADAME MIDORIKAWA *for the first time.)* You're here too?

MADAME MIDORIKAWA: Yes. In this room there are three human beings *(Points to the doll's head),* and one of these.

IWASE: How can you be so calm? My daughter is gone and we're all talking like we're sitting in a coffee shop somewhere.

MADAME MIDORIKAWA: But why not? There is no dead body. There's no blood. Aside from the fact that Sanae has vanished, everything is normal.

AKECHI: At least this situation is normal for me. Finally I can breathe easily.

IWASE: Either the two of you are crazy or I've gone completely mad.

MADAME MIDORIKAWA: *(Cradles the doll's head and gazes at it.)* The criminal is much, much cleverer than we imagined. Look at how he slipped by us with this childish trick. A mere doll has three grown adults running around in confusion.

AKECHI: *(Not taking his eyes off of Madame Midorikawa)* You're putting your fingerprints all over that crucial bit of evidence.

MADAME MIDORIKAWA: *(Looks at her own fingers)* My fingerprints? But you didn't tell me not to touch it.

AKECHI: I'm lenient with beautiful fingerprints.

MADAME MIDORIKAWA: As a detective, you're hopeless. *(She puts the head on a table.)*

IWASE: *(As though suddenly waking)* What are you two talking about?! This is no time for chatter like that. Sanae has disappeared, my adorable Sanae. *(Weeps.)* I can't go on living.

MADAME MIDORIKAWA: There's no need to exaggerate.

AKECHI: You were about to say that at least he still has his jewels, weren't you?

MADAME MIDORIKAWA: Ah, you've seen through me. You understand my feelings very well.

AKECHI: That's not terribly comforting to Iwase just at this moment.

IWASE: *(Embracing the head.)* Sanae! Sanae! Be alive. You are the dream of my life. You are my greatest treasure. When I was fifteen, I worked in a rock quarry out in Ibaragi. Once, in a chunk of metamorphic rock, I found a sparkling green stone. I slipped it into my pocket and secretly took it to the town office to be assessed. The assessor in the town office pretended to know what he was talking about and insisted that it was an emerald. All the way home, I felt like I was in a dream. It was the time of the village festival and there were market stalls everywhere. There were stalls with pinwheels and goldfish and cotton candy and grilled fish. At night, all of these stalls glittered like a row of jewelry boxes. When I walked through the festival streets I thought, if I ever get rich, I hope I have an adorable daughter. I want to take her by the hand and go to the festival. Then I would buy up the entire place for her. This was the first page of the story of my success. Sanae! Oh, my Sanae! You were the dream daughter that I wanted to take to the festival. Stay alive! Stay alive for papa!

MADAME MIDORIKAWA: *(Pretends to cry.)* This is so sad I feel like crying myself.

AKECHI: False tears are not worthy of you. You are too honest for that.

MADAME MIDORIKAWA: But don't you feel sorry for him?

AKECHI: I'll feel sympathy when the situation calls for it. But in this case, I don't think there is any particular reason for sorrow. That is what my sense of reason tells me.

IWASE: See, that is the kind of man Akechi is, a man without blood or tears. Madame Midorikawa, have you ever seen such a miserable excuse for a human being? I thought I was a good judge of people, but how blind I was. I was taken in by a crook. Listen Akechi, you won't feel so amused when I have you thrown in jail together with the kidnapper. I should have called the police in the first place. After all, they're free. I thought I could get the job done better if I paid a lot of money. That's the weak point of being a jeweler. I thought money could buy me anything. I never realized that you had to deal with jewels and people so differently. I'm calling the police.

He goes toward the phone.

AKECHI: Calm down and wait a moment. *(Stops* IWASE.*)*

IWASE: You have no right to stop me, you fraud!

AKECHI: Making a fuss now will not help to capture the criminal. I believe that Sanae was abducted at least two hours ago. In any case, it was long before the telegram came. That telegram was not warning us about a crime that was about to happen. It was intended to make a crime that had already been committed look like it was still about to happen. It was meant to make us focus on this room at midnight. While we were waiting, the kidnapper has probably long since made his escape.

MADAME MIDORIKAWA: *(Bursts out laughing.)* So for two hours, the great detective has been playing guard to a doll's head.

As she laughs, for the first time, IWASE *begins to regard her suspiciously. Long silence. Suddenly* IWASE *stands, pushes* AKECHI *aside and goes to the phone. Just at this moment, the phone rings noisily.* IWASE *picks up the receiver.*

IWASE: Yes, yes! What? Akechi, it's for you.

AKECHI: What? *(Stands and takes the receiver from IWASE.)* Yes? . . . Yes . . . I see.

In ten minutes? That's too long, be here in five. Got it? I won't wait longer than five minutes.

IWASE: *(Sarcastically)* If your business is finished, perhaps you would be kind enough to call the police while you are at it.

AKECHI: There is no need to call the police yet. Give me a moment to think.

IWASE: What is there to think of besides Sanae's safety? What a disgrace! And you told me in such confidence that you could guarantee my daughter's safety.

MADAME MIDORIKAWA: Shobei, you are just wasting your breath. Akechi is busy thinking about the wager that he just lost.

IWASE: Wager?

MADAME MIDORIKAWA: I bet all my jewels, he bet his profession as detective. It looks like he lost and now has to face going out of business.

AKECHI: No, actually I was concerned because, Madame Midorikawa, I was feeling sorry for you.

MADAME MIDORIKAWA: And why might that be?

AKECHI: *(Slowly)* Because I did not lose the wager. Madame Midorikawa, you are the one who has lost.

MADAME MIDORIKAWA: You're just a sore loser.

AKECHI: Do you really think so?

MADAME MIDORIKAWA: Of course you are just bluffing. Why don't you do something to capture the criminal?

AKECHI: But why do you think that I have let the criminal escape. I have the criminal in my hands right now.

MADAME MIDORIKAWA: Are you dreaming? Dreaming with those beautiful, clear eyes of yours?

AKECHI: Yes, I've finally caught my dream. But it's a very complicated dream, so I don't know quite where to start. Ah, that's it. Madame Midorikawa, I know where your friend Kensaku Yamakawa went after he left this hotel.

MADAME MIDORIKAWA: What?

AKECHI: Of course, this was all just in my dream. I wonder why Mr. Yamakawa bought a ticket all the way to Nagoya, but got off the train part way. He got on the nine-twenty train, but got off at the next stop. Then, and this was a lot of work, mind you, he took his trunk, loaded it into a car and came right back to Osaka where he is now staying at the "M" Hotel. He has a first-class room there because you are scheduled to join him there tomorrow. Now just what could it be that Mr. Yamakawa has in his heavy trunk? I'm sure that you know very well, don't you?

MADAME MIDORIKAWA: . . .

AKECHI: If you will forgive me, I know too. My three assistants are fine, loyal young men and are geniuses at tailing people. Until just a moment ago, I was waiting anxiously for their call. To be perfectly honest, it was quite a job to hide my concern . . . Well Madame Midorikawa, I will be happy to accept all your jewels. Then I will be able to eat without having to worry about Mr. Iwase's paycheck.

MADAME MIDORIKAWA: Then Yamakawa . . . Yamakawa is . . .

AKECHI: The bearded gentleman? I'm afraid that he got clean away.

IWASE: You mean you've captured the criminal?

AKECHI: The real criminal is right here.

IWASE: But there are only the two of us here.

AKECHI: Have you forgotten, there is one beautiful woman here. May I introduce you to Black Lizard, a very rare female gang boss and the person responsible for kidnapping Sanae?

MADAME MIDORIKAWA: Is this some kind of bad joke? Shobei, do something about this! Akechi's jokes have gone too far, someone might think that this is true.

AKECHI: You can say anything you like. *(There is a knock at the door.* AKECHI *unlocks the door and leaves the key in the lock.)* Go ahead and try to explain since we have a proper witness.

Akechi's THREE ASSISTANTS *appear with a semi-conscious* SANAE *dressed in a robe, supported by one of them. Two* PLAINCLOTHED POLICEMAN *enter as well.*

IWASE: Sanae! *(Embraces her)* Thank goodness! It's like a dream! *(Seats her in a chair.)* Thank goodness! Thank goodness! Akechi, you are a real crook. Starting next month, I'm raising your salary to a million and a half.

AKECHI: Thank you. We can discuss that later when we have time . . . Officer, I'm handing this woman over to you. She is responsible for this kidnapping.

The policemen approach MADAME MIDORIKAWA.

MADAME MIDORIKAWA: Kogorō, feel your right pocket.
AKECHI: What!
MADAME MIDORIKAWA: *(Aims the pistol at them.)* I borrowed this a little while ago because I suspected there was a chance that things might turn out like this. Please raise your hands everyone. Hands up in the air just like you're doing your morning exercises. *(All raise their hands.)*

MADAME MIDORIKAWA *slips quickly to the door and, not taking her eyes off of them, reaches back and takes the key out of the door with her free left hand.*

MADAME MIDORIKAWA: Kogorō, this is your second mistake. Look!

Dangles the key in front of his face. She opens the door and takes one step back into the hallway.

MADAME MIDORIKAWA: Oh and Sanae, I really feel sorry for you, but you will just have to accept your bad luck in being born the daughter of the richest jeweler in Japan. And you are very beautiful. Too beautiful for your own good. I love jewels, but now I want your body even more than jewels. I won't give up. Kogorō, I'll be back soon for Sanae. *(She gradually retreats through the door until only her bare forearm and the gun are visible. There is a tattoo of a black lizard on her forearm.)* Look at this tattoo, it is my mark. I don't need fingerprints. Remember this adorable black lizard.

The arm disappears and the door shuts. There is the sound of the door being locked from the outside. All in the room start rushing about and AKECHI *runs for the phone.*

AKECHI: Hello, hello, this is Akechi. Akechi! This is an emergency. Guard all of the hotel exits! It's Madame Midorikawa . . . Madame Midorikawa!! She is going to try to leave the hotel. Stop her! She's a dangerous criminal. Whatever you have to do, don't let her out of the hotel. Alert the manager and all the staff. Oh, and by the way, send a bellboy to Shobei Iwase's room immediately with a spare key. This is an emergency!.

The lights go down gradually in room B and by AKECHI'S *final words, blackout.*

Figure 24. *The Black Lizard*, in 1968, with Miwa Akihiro as the Black Lizard and Amachi Shigeru as Akechi. The Black Lizard reveals her tattoo and makes her escape in Act One. Toyoko Gekijō. Photograph courtesy of the Waseda University Tsubouchi Hakase Memorial Theatre Museum.

SCENE 6

At the same time the lights go out in room B, the lights gradually go up in room C. In the center of the room there is a young man in a suit with a soft felt hat holding an overcoat. It is actually BLACK LIZARD *disguised as a man. She poses handsomely and peeks at the mirror out of the corner of her eye.*

MADAME MIDORIKAWA: There, now I can escape. No one will ever know that it is me. Of course, that is because there is no real me! *(To the mirror)* You good-looking man in the mirror, do you think that Kogorō Akechi is attractive? There are a lot of men around, but he is the first one that I have ever met that is right for me. Maybe this is love. But if this is love, which me is in love with Kogorō Akechi? Why don't you answer? It's just as well. Tomorrow a different me will ask a different mirror the same question. Well, adieu.

She takes off her hat and salutes in farewell to the figure in the mirror. Then she quickly opens the door and disappears.

CURTAIN

ACT TWO

Note on the setting: The set for the first scene represents the kitchen of the Iwase mansion. At the end of the first scene, the set splits in the middle and the two halves revolve. The half of the set on stage left represents Akechi Kogorō's *office and the half on stage right represents* Black Lizard's *hideout. Then these two sets are pulled into the wings to reveal the setting for the third scene, which represents Tokyo Tower. Finally, this set descends and the stage becomes the pier for scene four.*

SCENE 1: THE KITCHEN OF THE IWASE MANSION

Two weeks after the first act. It is now the beginning of the cherry blossom season.

The kitchen of the Iwase mansion in the wealthy Sarugaku neighborhood of Shibuya in Tokyo. All the windows are covered with iron bars. There is a door stage left leading to a hallway. Stage right, there is a door leading off to the room where the food is prepared. The kitchen is enormous and all its fittings big and lavish. Near the stage left door, there is an intercom speaker. When the curtain opens, off stage right there is the sound of several large dogs barking. At the door to the stage right food-

preparation area, the old housekeeper HINA *and handyman* GORŌ *are talking. At center stage, the bodyguards* HARAGUCHI, TOYAMA *and* OKAWA *are sitting with their backs to the audience, eating vigorously in silence.*

HINA: And then we need some pork *(Lowers her voice)* . . . the cheapest cuts you can find . . . Oh, I guess about three kilograms.
GORŌ: *(Jotting this in his notebook.)* Uh huh, three kilograms . . . What, three kilograms?
HINA: Yes, that's three kilograms! *(Looks pointedly at the three bodyguards eating.)* Take a look for yourself. That's why.

The maid YUMEKO *comes bustling in from stage left.*

YUMEKO: Oh, is it lunchtime? *(Looks at what they are eating)* You poor little things, you have almost nothing but rice. *(To* HARAGUCHI) Haraguchi, just leave everything to me.
HARAGUCHI: Gee . . .
YUMEKO: How about some corned beef. *(Pulls out three cans of corned beef from a cupboard and quickly opens them.) (To* HARAGUCHI) Here, one can for each of you.
HARAGUCHI: Gee, thanks . . .
HINA: *(Whispering to* GORŌ) Look at her. She doesn't think twice before happily giving away all the master's expensive imported food.

MRS. IWASE'S *voice squawks from the speaker of the intercom.*

MRS. IWASE'S VOICE: Yumeko! Yumeko! Come back here. How can I do anything if you keep running off! You know how busy we are.
YUMEKO: *(Into the intercom)* Yes, yes. *(Switches off the intercom.)* They keep saying it's a free country now, but for poor folks like me, there sure isn't any freedom or peace yet. *(Runs off stage left.)*
GORŌ: *(Looking at his notebook.)* So that's twenty eggs, three kilos of pork, and . . . let's see . . . a kilo of scrap meat for the dogs. Is that all?
HINA: Yes, I think that's all we need today. Thank you for your trouble.
GORŌ: Don't mention it. *(He is about to go, but hesitates.)* Hina, is everything all right around here? It's been two weeks since all those headlines about the kidnapping attempt at the K Hotel in Osaka.
HINA: Now that you mention it, you're right. And in those two weeks, even the season has changed. It was still chilly back then, but now, the cherry blossoms are starting to appear.
GORŌ: Black Lizard has been quiet for an awfully long time.
HINA: No matter how clever Black Lizard is, even she can't make a move when the house is protected like this. Look! All the windows are covered with iron bars. There are big watchdogs in the garden. There are guards

at the front and back gate, and they change shifts regularly twenty-four hours a day. And inside the house *(she silently motions with her eyes to the men busily eating),* we have these three fine bodyguards.

GORŌ: Even people like me who come here all the time have to follow the security rules. They say there's no exception, not even for us. *(Pulls an ID card from his pocket.)* We have to show these ID cards at the gate every time we go in or out.

HINA: Let me see. *(Looks at Gorō's ID card.)* My, look at this picture! You look just like a wanted criminal!

GORŌ: No, I don't! . . . But come to think of it, how's the daughter of the house? We haven't seen her at all lately.

HINA: *(Half in tears.)* The poor little girl! She's so young and now it's like she's under house arrest. It's a wonder she hasn't gone crazy having to endure this day after day.

GORŌ: It's been like this ever since the kidnapping?

HINA: Yes, we got Miss Sanae back after Black Lizard tried to kidnap her in Osaka, and she was closely guarded all the way home. Miss Sanae is in her own home, but for her, it must feel like being in prison. She's almost like a different person. It's so sad that sometimes I can't bring myself to look at the poor thing. She used to be so cheerful and lively, but these days she hardly ever says anything and she just ignores her food. Oh, I can understand perfectly how she feels. After all, she can't even take a step out into the garden without all those darn bodyguards.

GORŌ: I thought the famous detective Akechi was supposed to solve everything. What does he think he's doing?

HINA: Akechi and the police say that they are doing everything they can to track down Black Lizard. But as busy as he is, Akechi always finds the time to come here and check on things once a day.

GORŌ: How long do you think it will go on like this?

HINA: Who knows?

The watchdogs start barking again.

LAUNDRYMAN: *(Enters from stage right.)* Down! Be quiet! Stop barking! Hello, hello, it's me the laundryman.

HINA: Sorry for all the trouble. There's not much today, just this little bit. *(Hands him an enormous bag of laundry.)*

LAUNDRYMAN: No trouble at all. *(Starts listing it in his notebook.)*

GORŌ: What a job it is taking care of things here.

HINA: It's almost as though it's some kind of punishment. I have a feeling that fate won't let us alone. I feel like something terrible is going to happen. It has that smell about it. . . . The master here is a remarkable man. He's made his fortune all by himself. But still, with any family, no matter how prosperous, things can change. Even a tiny little incident can set off a decline in a family's fortune that goes fast, just like a ball rolling down a hill. I saw this happen once with a family that I was sent to work for by our housekeepers group. It was the family of a very important politician. His wife was a fine, hard-working woman. But one day she was grinding some sesame seeds in a bowl for a vegetable dressing, when suddenly her youngest son threw one of his father's dress gloves into the bowl as a joke. What a shock! In an instant, the nice vegetable dressing she was making turned into glove salad. She was furious. She washed the glove very carefully and hung it out to dry. But then, the wind blew the glove right onto the head of the gardener, who happened to be walking underneath. The gardener jerked his head to avoid the glove, twisted his neck, had a stroke and died. . . . After that, there was nothing but trouble for that family; sickness, losing the election, bankruptcy. Finally, everyone in the family ended up being scattered to I don't know where.

GORŌ: *(Fascinated)* Wow! . . . Oh, look at the time. I'm going to have to be going. Pleased I could be of service, Ma'am.

LAUNDRYMAN: Thanks for your patronage.

HINA: We expect you for tomorrow's groceries as well. Thanks for all your trouble.

BODYGUARD HARAGUCHI: *(Finally finished eating.)*You know all kinds of interesting stories, Hina, don't you?

HINA: I don't have time to bother with your type. Go play with Yumeko.

BODYGUARD TOYAMA: Grandma, you're jealous!

BODYGUARD OKAWA: I'm full. . . . Hey, remember the thing I was telling you about before lunch?

BODYGUARD TOYAMA: You're still talking about that?

BODYGUARD OKAWA: Yeah. That camera I'm supposed to carry is too big and heavy to lug around everywhere, so I tried to get that coffee shop across the street to keep it for me. Then you know what happened, the master of the coffee shop came out from the back . . .

BODYGUARD TOYAMA: We've heard this story a thousand times.

BODYGUARD HARAGUCHI: By the way, Hina, how come this rich girl is depending on us to protect her, but doesn't seem to be impressed at all with how strong we are?

HINA: That's because your strength can be bought for money.

BODYGUARD HARAGUCHI: Yeah, but, you won't find good bodyguards like us just anywhere. Kendo, fourth rank, Judo, fifth rank, Karate, third rank. In all that's . . . uh, twelve ranks. We even know boxing. Even so, the whole time we've been here, only the kids across the street pay any attention to us.

HINA: You bodyguards were just born at the wrong time. If you lived in the Edo period, you could have been samurai bodyguards.

BODYGUARD TOYAMA: That's what I always thought. Then I would have been someone really important.

HINA: Shall I tell you why you'll never amount to much of anything?

BODYGUARD HARAGUCHI: You're always such a know-it-all. Tell us, if you're so smart.

HINA: It's because you think you are serving a really good cause with your hard-earned muscular strength. Most things that people consider good can't actually exist in the real world, but if they can, exist they have to have something a little bit dirty in them somewhere. That's your problem. You're always fighting in the name of a good that is actually dirty. There will always be something a little shady about your work. But that Akechi is different. He is fighting for the kind of good and justice that can never actually exist in this world.

BODYGUARD HARAGUCHI: What do you mean? Akechi is getting paid too.

HINA: Even if a jewel has a price, that has nothing to do with the real value of the jewel itself.

BODYGUARD OKAWA: . . . so, like I was saying, I tried to get them to keep that heavy camera at the coffee shop. They started complaining that they couldn't take responsibility for something so valuable. Then, you know what happened, from the back of the store . . .

BODYGUARD TOYAMA: Yeah, yeah, the master of the coffee shop appeared.

BODYGUARD OKAWA: How did you know that? You're really smart!

From stage left, there is the sound of a piano.

HINA: My, my, miracles do happen! The only person here who plays the piano is . . .

BODYGUARD HARAGUCHI: . . . Is Miss Sanae, right?

HINA: Goodness gracious! It's the first time she's played the piano since coming back from Osaka. She must be feeling especially good today. *(Listens carefully)* How well she plays! She plays just as wonderfully as ever.

The three listen intently to the piano. Suddenly the stage left door opens and the maids YUMEKO, AIKO, *and* IROE *appear.*

YUMEKO: Listen to that! She's playing the piano!

HINA: Yes, we hear it. Why do you suppose she's feeling so much better today?

AIKO: It must be that nice spring breeze today. Everybody is feeling better. Everyone except the missus, that is. She's just as hysterical as ever.

IROE: At least the master is in a good mood. Finally they delivered all the new furniture he had made especially for the guestroom.

YUMEKO: The furniture he ordered this time is really something. I've never seen chairs and tables that fancy before.
BODYGUARD HARAGUCHI: What does all that furniture have to do with the piano?
YUMEKO: The master thought that if he got some beautiful new furniture for the guestroom it would cheer Sanae up. He set his mind on getting new furniture for Sanae, and you know how stubborn the master is when he decides he wants something. Ever since then, he's been arguing with the missus over that furniture. These days the missus constantly complains that she has migraine headaches and she never leaves her room. We don't have a moment's peace. She wants ice. She wants someone to massage her feet. Finally, she fell asleep and we went to the guestroom to peek at the furniture. There was the master, all smiles, and finally Miss Sanae came out of her room.
HINA: You mean, her jail cell.
YUMEKO: Oh, don't say that. You may think that it's a jail cell, but to me, it is like a hotel suite. I'd be happy to be shut up in there.
HINA: Anyway, what happened next?
YUMEKO: The master led Sanae from her room and showed her all the new furniture. "Look at this armchair!" "How about this sofa!"
AIKO: We joined in too and admired the new furniture.
IROE: He said, "This sofa is covered with genuine Nishijin brocade. Just look at this! If you made a necktie from a scrap of this material, it would cost you at least two thousand yen."
HINA: That's our master, all right. The first thing he thinks of is how much something costs.
YUMEKO: Miss Sanae looked at all the furniture and tried sitting on the chairs and the sofa. For the first time in ages, she smiled.
BODYGUARD HARAGUCHI: That furniture must be really something if it cheered Miss Sanae up.
YUMEKO: What do you know about good furniture?
AIKO: Then she went to the piano for the first time in so long.
HINA: And she started playing! What a miracle!
IROE: The master listened to her playing and just smiled and smiled. You know how Miss Sanae is everything to him. They're father and daughter, but they almost seemed like a couple of lovers.

All listen to the piano again. Suddenly there is a voice from the intercom speaker.

IWASE'S VOICE: I have to go to the office on some urgent business.
YUMEKO: It's the master.
IWASE: While I'm gone, Haraguchi, Toyama and Okawa, I want the three of you to keep guard in the hallway. Stay right in front of the door to the

guestroom. Don't go into the room because it will disturb Sanae. Don't leave your post for even a second.

THE THREE BODYGUARDS: OK.

They exit stage left. The piano music continues.

YUMEKO: We have to go see the master off.

HINA: As long as there are guards in the hallway, there's absolutely nothing to worry about. The guestroom is all the way at the end of the hall, all the windows are barred and there are watchdogs out in the garden. It's impossible for anyone to get to Miss Sanae.

IROE: Of course everything's all right! With all this security, even a germ would have trouble slipping through.

HINA: This is no time for silly jokes. Get to work and see the master off.

They all exit stage left in a great confusion. The sound of the piano continues. HINA *listens intently to the music. Then she looks around carefully, picks up the receiver of the phone on the table and dials.*

HINA: *(Speaking on the phone.)* The beautiful sky turns purple at sunset. The monkeys set candles on the back of the ox and their breath has the smell of red meat. A silk automobile. The prime minister's cabinet is made up of dwarves. A woman is born from the neck of a man, a lobster is born from the ear of a woman. People burn in the middle of the mountains. The ocean burns in the middle of a crowd of people. Um . . . The pomegranate hat has shattered like glass. Um . . . um . . . that's all.

Hangs up the phone. The piano music still continues. The sound of a car leaving off stage left. After a few moments, the THREE MAIDS *return.*

AIKO: Those bodyguards look so funny, standing so stiffly in the middle of the hall like that.

YUMEKO: I think that Haraguchi is really good looking.

IROE: I think there's something wrong with your eyes.

HINA: Ever since those bodyguards came, the servants around this place have been absolutely useless. *(About this time, the piano music stops.)*

YUMEKO: But Hina, you're actually the newest person here. You have no idea what things were like here before. It used to be that as long as we kept up appearances, we could get away with anything. In the back of the house, we've always done whatever we wanted. The mistress has never come into the kitchen, not even once. The kitchen is our castle. Here, together with the meat and vegetables and seasonings, we cook up gossip about men. Who are you to try to stop us now?

HINA: You can say anything you like. It's just that I'm old fashioned and

I like a well-ordered kitchen. If a household has a disorderly kitchen, then something terrible is sure to happen in that house. Look at this household here. You can see why such awful things have happened. In a proper kitchen, from top to bottom, everything has its place. The salt is in the salt cellar. The sugar is in the sugar bowl. In a house where the kitchen has all the plates and glasses neatly arranged, there's no confusion of healthy appetite and lust, and tragedies never happen. A kitchen like that is like a fresh spring breeze. But this kitchen looks like it's been hit by a storm. At this rate, you could even toss diamonds and rubies from the master's jewelry shop into the stew and never even notice.

YUMEKO: Shh! Listen! The piano seems to have stopped.

Everyone is silent.

HINA: You're right. I hope nothing has happened.

AIKO: Don't scare us like that. I'll go take a look.

She goes out stage left. Everyone waits. She comes back shortly.

AIKO: I can't do anything with those bodyguards. They say that they've been ordered not to let anyone into the guestroom, so they won't let me in. Probably Miss Sanae is just taking a nap inside.

Everyone is quiet.

YUMEKO: I'll go take a look.

She leaves. After a few moments, YUMEKO *screams. There is the sound of the* BODYGUARDS *shouting in confusion and then entering the guestroom.* AIKO *and* IROE *rush out of the room. There are the drunken shouts of a* STRANGER. YUMEKO *shouts,* "Mrs. Iwase! Mrs. Iwase!"

IROE: *(Enters running.)* Hina, something terrible has happened! Miss Sanae has disappeared!

HINA: What?

IROE: There's no way that she could have left that room, but we can't find her anywhere. Instead, somehow, a strange bearded man snuck into the room. He's stinking drunk and sleeping on the new sofa. He smells and he's filthy. He vomited all over that beautiful brocade and now he's snoring away and lying with his muddy feet on the sofa. The mistress is in hysterics.

The intercom speaker squawks.

MRS. IWASE'S VOICE: *(Hysterically)* Get that filthy sofa out of my house immediately! Do you hear me! I want the brocade on that sofa replaced right away. Call the furniture maker and have them pick it up this very instant!

HINA: I'll call the furniture people for you.

IROE: Would you? Oh thank you, Hina. *(Leaves.)*

HINA picks up the phone receiver, but pauses and reconsiders and then puts it down again. She looks carefully stage left. IROE comes rushing in.

IROE: What did the furniture people say?

HINA: They said that they'd be here right away. Fortunately, there is a truck with some men in the neighborhood, so they'll call the truck and have it come here right away.

IROE: Thank goodness! If they don't come soon, I don't think there will be any way to calm the mistress down.

HINA: Oh Iroe, would you go to the guards at the back gate and tell them that the furniture people are coming? The last thing we need now is for them to be stopped by the guards.

IROE: All right. *(Puts on slippers and starts to go.)*

HINA: *(Stops her.)* Tell them that there are four men coming from the furniture makers. That's four men.

IROE: Okay, okay.

She leaves through the kitchen door stage right.

YUMEKO: *(Comes in from stage left.)* Where's Iroe?

HINA: She just went out to the back gate.

YUMEKO: As soon as she gets back, tell her to come immediately. The mistress is going crazy. We need all the help we can get to calm her down.

HINA: Yes, yes.

YUMEKO *leaves. At the same time,* IROE *comes in from stage right.*

IROE: I told the men at the gate to let the furniture people in immediately.

HINA: Thank you. The mistress is calling for you.

IROE: Oh dear, oh dear. (*About to rush off stage left.*)

HINA: Iroe, Iroe! What happened to that drunk with the beard?

IROE: Haraguchi and Toyama took him out the front and are going to take him to the police.

HINA: What's happening! What's happening! Poor Miss Sanae! Oh, poor, poor Miss Sanae! How could she vanish just like smoke?

IROE *goes rushing off stage left. After a few moments, the* FOUR MEN *from the furniture maker appear from stage right.*

FURNITURE MAN A: Excuse me. We're from the Yamamoto Furniture Store.

HINA *suddenly becomes cool and efficient. The* FOUR FURNITURE MEN *enter through the kitchen door stage right.* HINA *signals them with her eyes and silently directs them stage left. The* FURNITURE MEN *exit stage left.*

HINA: *(Phoning.)* Yellow lion, yellow lion. The beard of the night and the tail of morning.

She hangs up the phone. After a few moments, the FOUR FURNITURE MEN *reappear solemnly carrying the muddy, vomit-covered sofa.* HINA *goes out with them through the kitchen door stage right. The stage is now empty. Silence.*

YUMEKO: *(Enters from stage left.)* Where did Hina go?
AIKO: *(Enters from stage left.)* How could she leave the kitchen unguarded like this. She's always bossing us around, but look at her!
YUMEKO: I just don't know what is going on any more.
AIKO: Where is Kogorō Akechi?

There is the sound of the front bell and also a voice from the intercom speaker.

MRS. IWASE'S VOICE: Where is everyone? That's the front door. That must be Kogorō Akechi.

The TWO MAIDS *rush off stage left. They forget to cut off the intercom, so the audience can overhear what is going on in the guestroom. There is noise for a while, then the sound of the door to the guestroom opening; there is a confusion of voices.*

MRS. IWASE'S VOICE: But Mr. Akechi . . .
AKECHI'S VOICE: "But"!? Mrs. Iwase, what do you mean by saying that you had the sofa taken away by the furniture people? That's ridiculous! Where did the sofa go? They took it out through the kitchen? I'll go take a look. You should rest here. If you go running around, you'll make yourself sick.

After a few moments, KOGORŌ AKECHI, *his* THREE MEN, *and* YUMEKO *appear from stage left. They look around the kitchen.*

AKECHI: We're too late! *(Sees the phone.)* What's the phone number of the furniture store?
YUMEKO: Here it is. *(Holds out the notebook of phone numbers.)*
AKECHI: *(Dialing rapidly.)* Hello, Yamamoto Furniture? This is the Iwase residence. You picked up a sofa a little while ago, and I want to know

if it has arrived at your place yet. . . . Yes . . . yes . . . What? You haven't sent anyone yet? You're just about to leave?

Everyone is silent. There is the violent barking of one of the watchdogs. Blackout. The set splits in the middle and the two parts revolve to form the two stage sets, right and left, for the next scene.

SCENE 2: AKECHI'S OFFICE AND BLACK LIZARD'S HIDEOUT

At stage left is Akechi's office, with a bare desk, shelves and file cabinets, etc. No one is present at the beginning of the scene. At stage right is Black Lizard's hideout, a small, dark room with no windows. BLACK LIZARD *is relaxing on a lavish chair, wearing a dressing gown and smoking leisurely. There are* TWO DWARVES *at her feet. A clean-shaven* AMAMIYA *is standing attentively by her. The set revolves into place with all four in position. It is the afternoon of the day after scene 1.*

(A) Black Lizard's Hideout

BLACK LIZARD: Call Hina.
AMAMIYA: Yes, ma'am.

He calls off stage right, and HINA *appears, still dressed as the housekeeper in the previous scene.*

HINA: Did you call me?
BLACK LIZARD: Hina, you were truly magnificent. You infiltrated the Iwase mansion long before things started, suffered through long months of unbearable indignities and grueling labor, and finally made possible the success of yesterday's operation. You are the real star of yesterday's mission. It was only possible because of your action behind the scenes, always moving things in the right direction.
HINA: It was the least I could do to serve you.
BLACK LIZARD: In view of your achievements, I am making you a member of the Order of Reptiles. And in honor of your years of service, I bestow upon you the distinguished name of Blue Tortoise.
HINA: Thank you, master. I will never forget this great honor.
BLACK LIZARD: Your coded messages were both elegant and to the point. As a reward, I give you this flawless five-carat sapphire.

She signals to AMAMIYA *with her eyes. The* DWARVES *pull out a small box and hand it to* BLACK LIZARD. *She opens it and gives it to* HINA.

HINA: I don't deserve such a beautiful thing, how can I ever thank you?
BLACK LIZARD: The only thanks I want from you, Blue Tortoise, is even

more loyal service in the future.

HINA: Of course, as ever, your wish is my command. I would like to give this sapphire to my nephew. Since he is my only relation, he is very dear to me. He wants to open his own rice cracker shop on the outskirts of the city.

BLACK LIZARD: You should be able to sell this sapphire for a nice sum. It is a fine thing for a beautiful sapphire to turn into rice crackers. That is all, Blue Tortoise.

HINA: Thank you. *(She leaves.)*

BLACK LIZARD: Call in the men who masqueraded as furniture men.

AMAMIYA: Yes, ma'am.

He goes to call them. He comes back with the FOUR FURNITURE MEN *from the previous scene.*

BLACK LIZARD: You played a shining role in the success of this operation. You are models of courage, determination, and quick action. But your success was possible only because everything was prepared and set out for you. I would, of course, like to make you all members of the Order of Reptiles, but I think that it is still a little too soon. However, you should strive even harder in the future so that you can receive that honor as quickly as possible. As your reward for yesterday's valorous service, I will present to each of you a beautiful piece of turquoise.

She signals with her eyes to the DWARVES. *The* DWARVES *hold out a box with turquoise in it.* BLACK LIZARD *hands a stone to each of the* FURNITURE MEN. *They each bow as they receive their stone.*

BLACK LIZARD: That is all.

The four bow very respectfully and withdraw.

BLACK LIZARD: Now we're done with the awards. I hope that Sanae is locked up securely.

AMAMIYA: There's no way that she can escape. She doesn't have any appetite and doesn't say a word. Other than that, though, she seems healthy enough.

BLACK LIZARD: When you see Sanae, you must always wear your beard and be dressed as one of the sailors. I trust that you have been careful to follow my orders.

AMAMIYA: Of course I have, but I thought that it would be all right not to wear the disguise when I'm with you.

BLACK LIZARD: You want to show your pretty face, don't you? Well, that's all right. I am very forgiving of people's vanity.

AMAMIYA: How long will it be before you let me become a member of the Order of Reptiles?

BLACK LIZARD: How can you say such a thing after your miserable failure in Osaka?

AMAMIYA: I can never apologize enough for that.

BLACK LIZARD: But this time, things went beautifully. A trick should be as daring, and childish and as silly as possible. The only way to fool adults is with the cleverness of a small child. A criminal genius always has the pure simplicity of a child. That is so, isn't it?

AMAMIYA: I guess so. . .

BLACK LIZARD: I wasn't talking to you. *(To the* DWARVES.) What do you think? *(Laughs raucously.)* Oh, but I forgot. You're not children, you are fully grown adults. I'm different. I have a child's cunning and cruelty. No ordinary adult could ever have anything of the sort. Crime is like a wonderful box of toys. Inside the box, a model car lies upside down, and the dolls lie with their eyes closed just like dead bodies. A house of wooden blocks falls apart. Wild animals look around for an opportunity to strike. No sane member of society would ever be able to guess what's in my heart. But Akechi might. Akechi. Akechi is the one and only man I'm not sure of . . .

The lights go down on Black Lizard's hideout.

(B) Kogorō's Akechi Office

When the lights go up, AKECHI *is in the center and his three subordinates* SAKAI, KIZU, *and* GIFU *are seated.*

AKECHI: *(Speaks into the receiver of the telephone on his desk.)* What? So it's come, just as we expected. What does the letter from the kidnapper say? It's all right, you can read it over the phone. I'll have one of my men take it down in shorthand. Sakai! *(Hands the receiver to* SAKAI.*)*

SAKAI: *(Takes the receiver.)* This is Sakai. Please, go right ahead. *(Holds the receiver to his ear and starts to jot in shorthand.)*

AKECHI: *(To* KIZU *and* GIFU.*)* A ransom request has come. They probably want The Star of Egypt. Have you two ever seen that diamond?

KIZU AND GIFU: No.

AKECHI: It's only been exhibited publicly once, some time ago at a jewelry show at the Daikyo Department Store, and that is probably when the criminal saw it. That show was really something. There were guards carrying pistols beside the case with the Star of Egypt, every day until the end of the exhibition. The people who came to see it had to look at it from very far away. There's no other diamond like that in Japan. It's one hundred and thirty carats, and absolutely perfect. There's not even a tiny hairline flaw. It was found in South Africa and is a brilliant cut. Once it was owned by the Egyptian kings, but it's gone from hand to hand until finally it ended up with Shobei Iwase. Its current value is estimated at 150 million yen . . . Hey, have you finished that transcript yet?

SAKAI: Yes . . . yes, I got it all here. *(Hands receiver to* AKECHI.*)*

AKECHI: *(Takes the receiver.)* This is Akechi. We have the transcript here. After we analyze it, I'll think of how to deal with the situation. I'll call you back later. *(Hangs up the phone. To* SAKAI.*)* What does it say?

SAKAI: *(Reads)* "I am deeply sorry for having caused you concern. Your daughter is now safely in my hands. She is in a place where the police will never find her. If you would like to buy your daughter back from me—if you are indeed willing to buy her back—I will negotiate the exchange with the item listed below. Purchase price: item, one Star of India, presently in the possession of Shobei Iwase."

AKECHI: See, what did I tell you?

SAKAI: "Date of payment: Tomorrow, April 4th, 6 p.m.. Place of payment: The observation deck of Tokyo Tower. Method of payment: Shobei Iwase must go alone to the observation deck of Tokyo Tower at the aforementioned time with the object for payment. If there is any deviation from these conditions, or if the police are informed, or if any attempts are made to arrest me after the transaction is completed, compensation for these acts will be taken through the death of your daughter. If you follow all these conditions precisely, your daughter will be returned to your house tomorrow evening. I am sure that you will agree to my humble request. No answer is necessary. If you do not appear at the appointed time and place tomorrow, this business deal will be considered null and void and appropriate measures will be taken. April 3d, from Black Lizard to Shobei Iwase."

AKECHI: Hmm, I see, *(Long silence. Finally he picks up the phone.)* Hello, hello. Shobei Iwase? I've read the ransom note. I need to know what you intend to do. Uh-huh . . . uh-huh . . . uh-huh . . . uh-huh . . . you're willing to give it up? That would be a real shame. I don't think there is any need to give up something as valuable as that. You can ignore the note. What? Uh-huh . . . uh-huh . . . uh-huh . . . If you're that determined, then I won't stop you. One strategy is to pretend that we've fallen into the criminal's trap and hand over the diamond. From the standpoint of my techniques, that would come in handy. But Shobei, there is absolutely nothing to worry about. I promise that you will be reunited with your daughter and your diamond. Uh-huh . . . uh-huh . . . Yes, we will give her a few moments of satisfaction, that's all.

AKECHI'S *office goes dark.*

(C) Black Lizard's Hideout

When the lights go up, BLACK LIZARD, AMAMIYA *and the* DWARVES *are standing in the same positions as the end of scene A.*

BLACK LIZARD: *(To the* DWARVES*)* Spray me with perfume. In a room without windows the air gets stuffy so quickly.

The DWARVES *spray perfume on* BLACK LIZARD *with an atomizer.*

AMAMIYA: That fragrance reminds me of that time, the happiest moment in my life . . .

BLACK LIZARD: It was a night in May and you were sitting on a park bench all alone. A handsome young man with nothing on his mind except the intention to die.

AMAMIYA: There was nothing left in the world for me. I had no money, I was all alone. I was sitting on that park bench that night, wondering how I could die. But then a beautiful car stopped in front of me and you stepped out of it. You walked around for a while, then finally you stopped and looked at me. You were dressed all in black. I had never seen anything so beautiful. And then, gradually I smelled that perfume.

BLACK LIZARD: You were so beautiful that night. Probably there never was and there never will be another moment when you will be as beautiful as you were that night. You were wearing a pure white sweater, and as you looked up, the streetlights illuminated your face. All around, there was the suffocating smell of greenery. You were the picture of agonized youth. Your glistening hair and the pure gaze in your eyes had the fragility of a watercolor painting, all because of the shadow of death within you. At that instant, I decided that I wanted this beautiful youth as my doll.

AMAMIYA: You smiled at me, and from that moment, I was your slave. You sat by me on my bench. We exchanged two or three words . . . I thought I was in a dream. Before I knew what was happening, I kissed you. Then you laughed and wiped my lips with your handkerchief. After that, I was completely in a daze.

BLACK LIZARD: That handkerchief was soaked with chloroform. Your romantic handkerchief never existed. The real handkerchief was like the curtain in a theater going down slowly to hide your happiest moment on this earth . . . My men carried you to my hideout. That night, you should have become a doll . . . But . . . you know what happened. How you carried on when you regained consciousness. The shouting, the screaming, all those tears . . .

AMAMIYA: Don't remind me of that . . .

BLACK LIZARD: All of your beauty shattered and melted away. You were so beautiful when you intended to die, but then, when you decided with

Figure 25. *The Black Lizard*, in 1968, with Miwa Akihiro as the Black Lizard and Nakayama Hisashi as Amamiya. Toyoko Gekijō. Photograph courtesy of the Waseda University Tsubouchi Hakase Memorial Theatre Museum.

all your heart that you wanted to live, how ugly you became . . . I did not save your life out of kindness. I was merely startled when you promised to be my slave forever if I saved your life. I simply couldn't believe it. And in a moment of weakness, I agreed.

AMAMIYA: But I've been a good slave to you, haven't I? I haven't betrayed you once.

BLACK LIZARD: You've never betrayed me, but you fumble everything you do.

But I suppose that's all right. Among all my followers, you are the only one I ever considered beautiful, even for an instant . . . But if you ever betray me, if you ever go against me in the slightest way, then you will truly become an unmoving doll.

The DWARVES *hide in terror under the chair.*

AMAMIYA: *(As though struck by a bolt of electricity.)* I understand.

The lights go down on Black Lizard's hideout.

(D) Kogorō's Akechi Office

When the lights come up, AKECHI *is standing with his back to the audience and gazing out the window at the sunset. His three men are sitting at their desks working.*

AKECHI: So the sun has gone down today without any major incident. The sun has set on this city; this city riddled with numberless crimes as though being eaten by termites. Murder, armed robbery, kidnapping, rape . . . reduced to words, they don't seem like all that much, but each crime is full of someone's intelligence and effort, anger and jealousy, desire and passion. Each crime is the self-expression of a human being that has strayed into the path of madness, an expression into which the criminal has poured his whole being. How can anyone understand a crime? You can't understand a crime when you look at it only from the point-of-view of the victim, that is, my client. The client can think only of his own interests. I am the one who must face the essential nature of crime and bathe in the pure essence of the flames of crime. I can see the entirety of crime. It is like the biggest factory in the world, working unceasingly day and night. When I see that sunset out there, it looks like the light of the flames in the giant furnace of the factory of crime . . . I wonder what Black Lizard is doing now?

SAKAI: Black Lizard is crazy. That kind of romantic crime went out of date years ago. All around us are crimes like political corruption and assassination. Who's crazy enough to plan of a masquerade ball crime in this day and age? If you ask me, that woman is in love with her own beauty.

AKECHI: That's precisely why this crime has aroused my interest. These days, even major crimes are the sort that could take place in the apartment next door. Even the cruelest crime seems pretty small in stature. The clothes that crime wears today have the same measurements as our own clothes. Black Lizard will have none of that. In an age when even women wear blue jeans, she still believes that crime, at least, should wear a glittering evening gown with a train five meters long . . . In some ways, I agree with her.

KIZU: We know that there's no one more prone to boredom than you. Black Lizard has saved you from being bored to death, hasn't she?

AKECHI: You could say that. To be perfectly honest, I hope that this case is not solved and that it will not fade away as though it never existed. I have a feeling that when this case is over, my spirit to live will weaken, like a balloon when the air leaks out of it. The thing that scares me the most is that when it's all finished and I'm just sitting around aimlessly, I might end up getting married. I've said this a thousand times before, but there is no profession less suited to marriage than that of private detective. That's why I've worked so hard all these years to avoid getting married.

His three subordinates look at each other and hide their laughter.

AKECHI: What are you all laughing about? Go ahead and tell me. Gifu, what is it?

GIFU: I can't tell you. I mean, it's just something the three of us were talking about this morning, but . . .

AKECHI: Go ahead and tell me. When have I ever gotten angry about something unrelated to work?

GIFU: Well, I'll tell you then . . . no, I can't.

AKECHI: Then you tell me, Sakai, what's this all about?

SAKAI: We were just thinking that it seems almost as though you are in love with Black Lizard.

AKECHI: Hmm . . . really? Well I guess that there is something of that. *(All burst out laughing.)* But when I fall in love, I don't hold hands. The only thing I can do is to push and push my partner to the point of destruction. There probably is no purer, no crueler lover than I. My tenderness is the tenderness that invites destruction . . . . This is the true model of all forms of love. Anyway, why don't you all go and get something to eat? I still have some work to do here.

Lights go down on Akechi's office.

(E) Black Lizard's Hideout.

BLACK LIZARD: There's no need to be so frightened. After all, you are free to feel whatever you want.

AMAMIYA: What do you mean by that?

BLACK LIZARD: You are free to feel any way you want about what I am about to say. I am in love with Kogorō Akechi. How would you feel if I said that?

AMAMIYA: *(Turns pale with jealousy.)*

BLACK LIZARD: Don't worry, I was just saying that to test you. If I said this and you were so jealous that you killed Akechi, that would not amount to betrayal. Rather, that might finally be enough to make you a member of the Order of Reptiles . . . It's not betrayal; it's an entirely different matter.

AMAMIYA: You can't really be in love with Akechi!!

BLACK LIZARD: Why not? I'm a woman, and I can fall in love with anyone I want. *(Enjoying his torment.)* Beginning the night I first met him in the hotel in Osaka, Akechi started to appear in my dreams. Conceited, as phony as an actor, that sarcastic man. In the middle of the night that man's face appears before me, and it's a real nuisance. I've never before been troubled by a man's face appearing in my thoughts, not even once! Akechi pretends to know everything. That know-it-all face, his forehead, his lips. *(She stamps angrily and the* DWARVES *cower in terror.)* . . . He stands in front of my dreams and keeps me from seeing anything. He takes on the outlines of my dreams! Everywhere I go, he keeps changing into the shape of my dreams*! (To* AMAMIYA*)* Get out! Get out! I want to be alone. There are things I have to think about. *(To the* DWARVES*)* You two, leave as well. Let me be here alone.

AMAMIYA *and the* DWARVES *leave.*

(F) Akechi's Office and Black Lizard's Hideout

Stage lights illuminate Akechi's office. AKECHI *is sitting alone at his desk lost in thought. It is dark outside the window.*

AKECHI: Just like the darkness that fills this room...

BLACK LIZARD: . . . his shadow envelops me. If he tries to capture me . . .

AKECHI: . . . she will run and escape, to the farthest reaches of the night, like the red tail light of a train . . .

BLACK LIZARD: . . . his light will remain forever in my eyes. Should I pursue him by pretending to let him pursue me?

AKECHI: Or should I pretend to pursue her and let myself be pursued?

BLACK LIZARD: I don't even know myself. But nocturnal animals who love the night know well the scent of human beings.

AKECHI: Human beings know the scent of animals well.

BLACK LIZARD: Inside me something remains, like the bootmarks left by someone who has stamped out a campfire in the night while human beings sleep.
AKECHI: How strange that those traces remain within me forever.
BLACK LIZARD: Pages from law books have become my love letters.
AKECHI: A jail cell will be my gift of love.
AKECHI AND BLACK LIZARD: But in the end, I will be the winner.

The stage grows dark.

SCENE 3: THE OBSERVATION DECK OF TOKYO TOWER

The set represents the glass-enclosed observation deck of Tokyo Tower. By the window, there are a couple of coin-operated telescopes. There is an elevator stage left. In the center is a souvenir stand selling sweets and other souvenirs. It is decorated with branches of artificial cherry blossoms.
Outside the window the sun is just setting.

The elevator opens and a large crowd of sightseers emerges. They gradually move stage right, looking out the window and using the telescopes before going back and exiting stage left.

At the window, BLACK LIZARD *stands uneasily, dressed beautifully in a Japanese kimono. She looks like she is waiting for someone and glances at her watch several times, but always remains very close to the window. The elevator door opens again and a somewhat smaller crowd of sightseers emerges.* SHOBEI IWASE *is among them. As before, the sightseers look out the window, use the telescopes, and gradually disappear stage left. Only* BLACK LIZARD *and* SHOBEI IWASE *remain. For a while, the two stare at each other in silence.*

BLACK LIZARD: Did you bring it?
IWASE: *(Shaking with anger.)* I don't want to even speak to you. Can you guarantee that my daughter is safe?
BLACK LIZARD: She's just fine.

IWASE *roughly thrusts a small box at her.* BLACK LIZARD *opens the box and looks inside. For a few moments, she gazes at the contents of the box in silence.*

BLACK LIZARD: Yes, this is the requested item. I will keep my end of the bargain as well . . . Please leave first. Then I will go.
IWASE: Why don't we get in the elevator together?
BLACK LIZARD: *(Smiling)* I don't think so.
IWASE: You're afraid of being followed. That's it, isn't it? If you're so afraid, what did you think that you were going to do if I tried to harm you?
BLACK LIZARD: *(Pulls a red handkerchief from her* obi *sash.)* All I have to do is wave this little handkerchief by the window. Then my men will

know that I am in danger and poor Sanae will be dead. That is why I have stayed right next to this window all this time. *(Neatly tucks the red handkerchief back into her* obi.)

IWASE: *(Rushes to one of the telescopes, fumbles for change, stuffs it into the machine and looks around wildly.)* Where are they? Where are your men?

BLACK LIZARD: Go ahead and look all you want. Tokyo is a very big city. There are many rooftops out there. There's no shortage of windows either.

IWASE *abandons the telescope and wipes the sweat from his forehead furiously.*

BLACK LIZARD: Now, if you will be so good as to get in the elevator.

IWASE: Will you keep your word?

BLACK LIZARD: I promise that Sanae will be back with you this evening.

IWASE *backs into the elevator. Then he gets in and exits.* BLACK LIZARD *looks around anxiously. It is almost dark outside.* BLACK LIZARD *rushes to the souvenir stand.*

BLACK LIZARD: Please, somebody help me!

The SOUVENIR STAND OPERATOR *and* HIS WIFE *get up from where they have been sitting behind the glass case of the stand.*

SOUVENIR STAND OPERATOR: What can I get for you?

BLACK LIZARD: No, no! I don't need to buy anything, but I have a very difficult request. That man I was just talking to is actually a dangerous criminal. He's blackmailing me, and there's no telling what he will try to do.

THE OPERATOR'S WIFE: *(Brimming with curiosity and enthusiasm)* That sounds just awful!

BLACK LIZARD: Will you help me? I managed to talk him into leaving first, but I know that he is lying in wait at the bottom of the tower. Please, you'll be saving my life! Will you take my place for a short while?

SOUVENIR STAND OPERATOR: I don't think anyone would ever mistake this old bag for a beautiful woman like you.

THE OPERATOR'S WIFE: What are you talking about? I'll do it! I'll do it! Ma'am, I'll be happy to do anything I can, if it will help.

BLACK LIZARD: Thank you. All you have to do is to pretend to be me for a while. Stand there by the telescope and peek through it every once in a while. We can just exchange clothing.

THE OPERATOR'S WIFE: My goodness!

BLACK LIZARD: And then I have a request for your husband. Since I will be disguised as your wife, I would like you to go with me until I get in a taxi. I will thank you properly later, but here, for now; this is all the money I have on me. *(She takes seven one thousand yen notes from her billfold and presses them into the woman's hand.)* Please help me, I beg you!

Husband and wife confer with each other in whispers. BLACK LIZARD *glances around anxiously. Small groups of sightseers appear again from stage left.* THE SOUVENIR STAND OPERATOR *pulls* BLACK LIZARD *into the souvenir stand. He points to a door behind the stand and* BLACK LIZARD *and* THE OPERATOR'S WIFE *disappear into the back. Then he calmly sells sweets and other souvenirs to the sightseers.*

The door opens and BLACK LIZARD *and* THE OPERATOR'S WIFE *appear, having exchanged clothes.* THE SOUVENIR STAND OPERATOR is *astonished at the change in his wife's appearance.* THE OPERATOR'S WIFE *hands a white facemask to* BLACK LIZARD *making it look as though she is protecting herself from a cold.* BLACK LIZARD *puts on the facemask and urges the amazed* SOUVENIR SHOP OPERATOR *to leave the souvenir stand. He locks the glass case and leaves the stand.*

His WIFE *stands by a telescope and he continues to gaze back at her in shock.* BLACK LIZARD *urges him to accompany her to the elevator and they push their way into the crowd that is already waiting there. The elevator arrives, the door opens, the crowd boards and the door closes again. The only person left on stage is* THE OPERATOR'S WIFE *disguised as* Black Lizard.

Blackout.

SCENE 4: A BRIDGE NEAR THE SHIBAURA DISTRICT OF TOKYO

While the set is being changed, there is the sound of a car rushing from stage left to stage right. There is a flash of headlights. In the darkness, one can see a wooden bridge over a small canal. Nearby there is a telephone booth. Under the bridge, near a loading dock a small Japanese-style boat is moored.

When the set is ready there is the sound of a car stopping suddenly stage left. The SOUVENIR STAND OPERATOR, *actually* KOGORO AKECHI *in disguise, appears. He looks around carefully as though searching for someone he has been tailing. Finally he notices the boat at the foot of the bridge. He faces stage left and motions the* TAXI CAB DRIVER *to come over.*

THE TAXI CAB DRIVER *appears.* AKECHI *presses some money into his hand and whispers to him. All with gestures,* AKECHI *mimes picking up a large rock and throwing it into the water. Then he indicates that the* DRIVER *should shout. At the same time,* AKECHI *indicates that the* DRIVER *should shine his headlights on the boat. The* DRIVER *agrees, scratching his head in puzzlement.*

The DRIVER *exits stage left and the headlights go out. There is the sound of a car being moved.*

AKECHI *keeps his eye on the boat. Then he picks up a large stone and hides in the darkness near the bank of the canal.*

TAXI DRIVER'S VOICE: *(Suddenly)* Help! Help! Somebody help me!

As he screams, AKECHI *throws the rock into the canal and there is the sound of a big splash. The paper screen covering the window of the boat slides open and* BLACK LIZARD *peeks out. At that very instant, the car headlights turn on and* BLACK LIZARD *blinks in the sudden brightness and quickly slides the screen shut.*

AKECHI *quietly stands and goes to the telephone booth. He starts to dial . . .*

CURTAIN

ACT THREE

SCENE 1: INSIDE THE MYSTERIOUS SHIP

(A) Black Lizard's Cabin

The floor is covered with a Persian carpet. There is an ornate chandelier, a three-paneled mirror, an enormous wardrobe, a decorative cabinet, a round table and several armchairs. In the center, beside of the wardrobe, is a large sofa. This sofa is in a totally different style from the rest of the furniture. Clearly this is the same sofa that appeared in the first scene of Act II. There are signs that the sofa has been altered and reupholstered in places.

The windows are the round portholes of a ship. The door on stage right leads out to the deck. It is night.

BLACK LIZARD *is in a black satin dress. Her ears, chest and fingers are bedecked with pieces of jewelry studded with large gems.*

When the curtain rises, BLACK LIZARD *is sitting on the stool in front of the mirror. She takes the Star of Egypt from its box, holds it to her chest and looks at her reflection in the mirror.*

BLACK LIZARD: *(Facing the mirror.)* Now I finally have you in my hands. I've waited for you for so long . . . It took so much suffering and danger before I could finally get this cold, dead stone. I had to have you because the only thing that matches my cold flesh is something beautiful and dead—this stone, and my beautiful, dead dolls. Living things—anything with blood running through it—living things can't be trusted, they will always fail you. And they are so noisy, always selfish and demanding. Police, rich people, criminals, convicts; all these people live in uncertainty. I need them for my work and I must endure their constant demands and that awful air of uncertainty that they drag with them. But jewels are different. I can trust jewels. Even though you, The Star of Egypt, are now in my possession, even though you are here resting quietly on my chest, you never are coy, you are never demanding. You must have been the same even resting on the breast of a queen. A jewel is a transparent universe, perfectly satisfied with its own brilliance. No one can enter that universe. . . . I am your owner and master, but even I cannot enter that universe. . . . The same is true for human beings. I detest people I can enter easily. Could any human being resist my entrance as absolutely as a diamond? If there were such a person, I would fall in love with him and try to enter him. The only way to stop me would be to kill him first. . . . But what would happen if he tried to get inside me first? Oh, but that's impossible. My heart is as hard and impregnable as a diamond. . . . But even so, what would happen if he tried to enter in, knowing what I am like? Then to enter me, he would have to kill me first. Otherwise, my body would remain like a diamond, a little world of coldness that never lets anyone else inside.

There is a knock at the door.

AMAMIYA'S VOICE: It's me, Amamiya.

BLACK LIZARD *puts the diamond back in its box, puts the box in a drawer and locks the drawer.*

BLACK LIZARD: Come in!
AMAMIYA: *(He is disguised with a false beard and wears a purser's uniform.)* Excuse me.
BLACK LIZARD: When will we arrive?
AMAMIYA: The sea is very quiet. Right now, we are going around the Izu Peninsula at fifteen knots. We should be able to get to S-port by four in the morning. Fortunately, we haven't been noticed by the coast guard or by any other ships.
BLACK LIZARD: It's spring, so four in the morning should be just about one hour before sunrise. Be sure to get us there before it gets light.
AMAMIYA: Yes, ma'am. *(Opens the door, but hesitates and turns back,)* There is a problem . . .
BLACK LIZARD: What is it?
AMAMIYA: I didn't want to say anything, but ever since we left Tokyo, there have been rumors among the sailors.
BLACK LIZARD: What kind of rumors?
AMAMIYA: They say that there is a ghost on the ship.
BLACK LIZARD: Ridiculous! Has any one seen it?
AMAMIYA: No, no one has seen it. But the men say they've heard a strange voice in the guest cabin.
BLACK LIZARD: What? The room where Sanae is?

AMAMIYA: Yes, just after the ship left port, Kitamura was passing by Sanae's room when he heard someone talking in a low voice. Sanae was gagged all that time, so it couldn't have been her.

BLACK LIZARD: The gag probably came loose and she was cursing me, or something.

AMAMIYA: That's what I thought, but Kitamura went to get the key and when he came back and opened the room, Sanae was still gagged and her arms were still tied. There was no one else in the room. Kitamura said that when he saw no one else was there, he went all cold as though he had just seen a ghost.

BLACK LIZARD: Did he question Sanae?

AMAMIYA: Of course! He took off her gag and asked her about the voice. But Sanae was startled by the question and said that she didn't know anything about it.

BLACK LIZARD: That's a strange story. I wonder if it's true.

She thinks for a while. There is only the sound of the waves. The door to the cabin is open and outside, BLUE TORTOISE *(the new name for* HINA*) comes and stands at attention.*

BLACK LIZARD: *(Sharply)* Who is it? Oh, it's you Blue Tortoise. What's the matter?

BLUE TORTOISE: Something strange has happened. It looks like this ghost has come into the kitchen too. A whole chicken has disappeared.

BLACK LIZARD: A chicken?

BLUE TORTOISE: Now I'll have you know that I believe in running a tight kitchen, especially since you have entrusted me with this great responsibility. I make sure that we always have just the right amount of food. We have never been short even one portion, have we?

BLACK LIZARD: Certainly not.

BLUE TORTOISE: A plucked and boiled chicken is missing. At dinnertime, there were seven chickens in the kitchen, but now there are only six. We are short one chicken!

BLACK LIZARD: There is something funny going on. Amamiya, have the crew spread out and search the ship thoroughly.

AMAMIYA: That's a good idea. I'll have them do it right away.

BLACK LIZARD: Do it immediately!

AMAMIYA *bows obediently and leaves.*

BLUE TORTOISE: There is also a message from Sanae.

BLACK LIZARD: What?

BLUE TORTOISE: I just took dinner to her. When I untied her and took off her gag, I don't know what happened, but for the first time, she ate everything. Then she said that she promised not to scream or yell anymore and asked not to be tied up.

BLACK LIZARD: She promised to be quiet and behave?

BLUE TORTOISE: Yes that's what she said. She said that she has decided not to resist any longer. It was totally different from yesterday.

BLACK LIZARD: That's strange. Well, anyway, tell Kitamura to bring her here, will you?

BLUE TORTOISE: Yes, ma'am.

BLUE TORTOISE *bows and leaves.* BLACK LIZARD *stands and paces anxiously. Finally she sits on the sofa. Just at that point,* KITAMURA *appears with* SANAE, *who looks like she has suffered while she has been a prisoner.*

BLACK LIZARD: *(To* KITAMURA.) You wait outside the door and keep watch. (KITAMURA *nods and leaves the room, closing the door behind him.)* Sanae, my dear. How are you feeling? Please don't just stand there, come and sit here by me.

SANAE: All right. *(Takes a few steps, but then sees the sofa and retreats in terror.)*

BLACK LIZARD: Oh this? You're frightened of this sofa? Well, I guess that's not surprising. There now, why don't you sit in that armchair, instead.

SANAE: I'm sorry that I screamed and yelled and made such a commotion. But I promise to be quiet now. I will do whatever you say.

BLACK LIZARD: So you've finally learned your lesson. Fine. If you are obedient, it will be for your own good . . . But until yesterday you resisted so strongly. You don't even seem like the same Sanae. Why did you change your mind? Did something happen?

SANAE: Nothing has happened, not really . . .

BLACK LIZARD: I heard from Kitamura that there was a voice coming from your room. Was someone in your room? You'll tell the truth if you know what is good for you.

SANAE: No, I didn't see anyone in my room! I didn't hear anything. Honest!

BLACK LIZARD: *(Sharply)* Sanae, you're lying!

SANAE: No, no I'm not!

For a while, the two are silent and there is only the sound of the waves.

SANAE: Where . . . where is this boat going?

BLACK LIZARD: This boat? Shall I tell you where this boat is going? In three or four hours, this boat will arrive at S-port. That is where my private museum is. *(Smiles)* I want to show you my museum as soon as I can. You cannot possibly imagine what a wonderful place it is. As soon as we get there, you and the Star of Egypt will take your places alongside the other treasures there. That is why we are in such a hurry.

SANAE: . . .

BLACK LIZARD: Of course, sending my treasures by train would be much faster. But living things like you are too delicate to be transported over land. Even if it takes longer, going by boat is much safer. Sanae, my dear, this is my own personal boat. You must be surprised, but even a poor little woman like me can own a little boat like this.

SANAE: *(With determination.)* But I . . . I . . .

BLACK LIZARD: "But" . . . ?

SANAE: I'm not going to your museum!

BLACK LIZARD: Perhaps you don't want to, but I will take you there, whether you like it or not.

SANAE: No, I refuse to go to such a place.

BLACK LIZARD: My, what confidence you have. Do you think you can possibly escape from this ship?

SANAE: I'm sure of it. I have faith.

BLACK LIZARD: Faith? Faith in what?

SANAE: Don't you know?

Silence.

BLACK LIZARD: Ah!! Kitamura! Kitamura!

KITAMURA: *(Comes running.)* Yes?

BLACK LIZARD: Take this girl back to her room and tie and gag her as before. You are to keep guard on her inside the room and lock the door from the inside. You are not to move until I say so. Take a pistol with you, just in case. Whatever happens, you are not to let her escape.

KITAMURA: I understand. *(He grabs* SANAE *and is about to pull her out of the room.)*

BLACK LIZARD: Wait a minute! While you are at it, tell everyone that they are to search the ship from top to bottom. I know the true identity of that "ghost." It's none other than Kogorō Akechi.

KITAMURA: What?

BLACK LIZARD: Never mind, just hurry!

KITAMURA *leaves with* SANAE. BLACK LIZARD *is deep in thought, a severe expression on her face. There is the sound of the ship's engines and the sound of the waves. Suddenly* BLACK LIZARD *stands and very carefully examines the sofa that she has been sitting on. She sits again. The sofa starts to seem almost to have a life of its own with a pulse and heartbeat. She stands again and then sits, somewhat uneasily. But she can't stay sitting any longer and stands once more. She gently taps the cushions of the sofa.*

BLACK LIZARD: Akechi! Oh Kogorō Akechi.

She calls several times, but there is no answer.

BLACK LIZARD: Akechi!

AKECHI'S VOICE: *(From inside the sofa.)* I am like your shadow. I will never leave your side. Your trick sofa was very convenient.

BLACK LIZARD: *(Despite herself, her voice shakes.)* Akechi, aren't you afraid? You are surrounded by my people. We are in the middle of the ocean, far away from the police. Doesn't this frighten you?

AKECHI'S VOICE: *(With an unsettling laugh.)* I'm not frightened, I think you're the one that's afraid.

BLACK LIZARD: I'm not frightened; I'm just impressed with you, that's all. How did you know that this was my ship?

AKECHI'S VOICE: I didn't. But I was with you the whole time. It is only natural that I ended up here.

BLACK LIZARD: You were with me?

AKECHI'S VOICE: There's only one man who could possibly have followed you from Tokyo Tower.

BLACK LIZARD: You! You were the souvenir stand man! *(Bites her lips in chagrin.)*

AKECHI'S VOICE: Yes, sorry about that. But it was quite a charming sight to see you trying to deceive me, unaware that you were being deceived yourself.

Quietly BLACK LIZARD *goes to the wall and pushes the signal bell.*

BLACK LIZARD: There was yelling by the bridge and a splash. That was all you?

AKECHI'S VOICE: Just as you guessed. *(During this,* BLACK LIZARD *takes a pencil and writes something on a piece of paper on a nearby table.)* If you hadn't opened the paper screens and looked out, we wouldn't be together here like this now.

BLACK LIZARD: So that was you, wasn't it? How did you follow me from there?

AKECHI'S VOICE: I borrowed a bicycle and rode along the coast. I kept the ship in sight the entire time. *(The* TWO DWARVES *appear.* BLACK LIZARD *holds her finger to her lips to indicate silence and passes the paper with her instructions to them. The* TWO DWARVES *leave quietly.)* Then I got a little boat to bring me to the ship and, in the middle of the night, went through some clumsy acrobatics to get me onto the ship.

BLACK LIZARD: *(Continually glancing anxiously at the door, she sits nervously on the sofa.)* But the top deck was guarded constantly.

AKECHI'S VOICE: Yes it was. That's why it took me so long to get down into the cabins. Then it took a long time to find the cabin where Sanae was being held prisoner. Just when I finally found her—I guess the joke's on me—the boat set sail again.

BLACK LIZARD: Why didn't you try to escape? You knew if you stayed here, you would be found, sooner or later.

AKECHI'S VOICE: The seawater is too cold. And I'm not a very good swimmer.

Instead of drowning in an icy sea, it's a lot more pleasant to burrow down into the warm cushions of this sofa.

BLACK LIZARD: . . .

AKECHI'S VOICE: Look, I've been hiding here since dinner, and I'm tired of it. Don't you think you could let me out and let me look at your pretty face?

BLACK LIZARD: *(Momentarily struck by this entreaty.)* Shh! You mustn't! You mustn't come out. If my men see you, they'll kill you. Be patient a bit longer and stay right where you are.

AKECHI'S VOICE: You're actually trying to protect me?

BLACK LIZARD: Of course. I don't want to lose a good opponent.

At this point, FIVE MEN *with* AMAMIYA *in the lead come into the room carrying a rope, being careful not to make any sound.* BLACK LIZARD *signals with her eyes. The men start from one end of the sofa and wrap it with the rope.* BLACK LIZARD *stands with a nasty smile on her face.*

AKECHI'S VOICE: What's happening? Is there someone in the room?

BLACK LIZARD: Yes. We've just tied up the sofa with rope.

They tie the rope tightly.

AKECHI'S VOICE: Rope?

BLACK LIZARD: Yes. Kogorō Akechi, Japan's greatest detective, has just been wrapped up like a sushi roll.

She laughs and signals for her men to leave. She closes the door herself and comes back by the sofa. She listens closely by the sofa, but all she can hear is a faint moan. She can hear no voice. BLACK LIZARD *has trouble staying still and stands again. She goes to her mirror table and gazes at her reflection, then she sighs. After a while, she faces the sofa again.*

BLACK LIZARD: Akechi, this is farewell. Soon, at the bottom of the cold spring sea, your grave will appear in the form of this sofa. *(No answer.)* Why don't you say anything? These are our last moments together. *(She watches the sofa carefully. Then, unable to hold back any longer, she rushes to the sofa and kneels on the floor beside it. She reaches out as though embracing it.)* Oh how sad! You poor thing! You are so frightened that you cannot speak any more. Listen to that furious heartbeat. Look at the way that twisted body struggles and gropes desperately searching for escape. Oh, how sad! I feel as though you are writhing inside of my own body. Your hands and feet stretch out wildly, but it's no use. The only thing that awaits you now is death. That's all. How you struggle, even though you know there's no hope. You must be covered in sweat. Soon, even that hot sweat will grow cold in the tides of the spring sea. Akechi, now I can say anything I want to you. Now I can tell you all my secret thoughts, because soon the icy seawater will wash my words from your ears. *(She kisses the sofa.)* Did you feel that? The sincere passion in my heart must surely have made my kisses felt, even through the thick Nishijin brocade that covers this sofa. *(She kisses the sofa here and there.)* I want to cover this sofa with my kisses. Did you feel that? Did you feel that? Even though only cold words come from my lips, now you must know the fiery passion that is there. Even though your body will sink to the bottom of the icy sea, my kisses will cover every inch of your body like long strands of red seaweed. Now I can speak honestly to you. Akechi, please do not say anything. Keep silent until the moment you sink into the sea. Akechi, in all my life, I never met anyone like you. I fell in love for the first time; I Black Lizard! I can't forgive you, so I must kill you. I am not killing you because of the trivial complications of a kidnapping case. Do you understand? If I let you live any longer, I will no longer be able to live as Black Lizard. I will never be myself again. That terrifies me. That is why I must kill you. I must kill you because I love you.

She burrows her face in the cushions of the sofa and is silent for a long while. Finally, she stands decisively. She opens the door and calls stage right.

BLACK LIZARD: Take this sofa to the sea for a watery funeral.

AMAMIYA *and the others come.*

AMAMIYA: *(Overjoyed)* Ha, ha! Now even the great detective Kogorō Akechi is just a slab of dead meat.

Wordlessly BLACK LIZARD *slaps him.*

AMAMIYA: *(Rubbing his cheek)* What's wrong?

BLACK LIZARD: You don't even have the courage to betray me, do you? All you can do is enjoy what I have done and laugh. Kogorō Akechi will die now, but that's no thanks to you. And it most certainly is not for your sake. So stop being so full of yourself and get a move on.

She speaks severely. AMAMIYA *and the others carry out the sofa as though it were a casket and exit stage right. Listlessly,* BLACK LIZARD *follows after them.*

After a while, the door of the wardrobe opens behind the place where the sofa was. MATSUKICHI, *one of the stokers of the ship's engines emerges stealthily, his face covered with a filthy beard. He looks at his reflection in the mirror and adjusts the false beard. It is* AKECHI KOGORŌ. *He looks around carefully and finally exits stage right.*

(B) On deck

The stage revolves toward stage left. When it has revolved halfway, the entire stage represents the upper deck of the ship. All of BLACK LIZARD'S FOLLOWERS *stand solemnly in a line.* MATSUKICHI *quietly slips away from the group and exits stage left. Two more stout ropes have been tied around the sofa and they are used to slowly lower the sofa into the sea on the far side of the railing. When the sofa has disappeared from sight, there is a loud splash and the ropes go falling freely into the sea. For a few moments, all are silent.*

BLACK LIZARD: *(Angrily)* Go away, all of you! This is no time to stand around gaping. Go to your posts immediately and stay there!

All are surprised, but quickly scatter and exit. Alone, BLACK LIZARD *leans on the railing and is lost in thought. The stoker* MATSUKICHI *(actually* AKECHI KOGORŌ *in disguise) comes from stage left and approaches fearfully.*

BLACK LIZARD: *(Examining the approaching person carefully)* Matsukichi, is that you?

MATSUKICHI: Please forgive me.

BLACK LIZARD: For what?

MATSUKICHI: I fell asleep down below and didn't hear the bell signaling everyone to assemble.

BLACK LIZARD: *(Her voice suddenly very gentle.)* That's right, you weren't here during the funeral, were you?

MATSUKICHI: I'm terribly sorry. Is there anything I can do to make up for it?

BLACK LIZARD: It's quite all right. Among all the men on this ship, you are the only one who is truly on my side.

MATSUKICHI: *(Surprised)* Huh?

BLACK LIZARD: The men who dumped the sofa off the ship on my orders may be unswervingly obedient. But from that moment, for all eternity, they actually became the mortal enemies of my innermost heart. Now there is only you. Your foolishness, your lateness, this is what has saved you from corruption and yes, it has given me just a little bit of comfort. From now on, I will keep my eye on you. Serve me well.

MATSUKICHI: *(Confused)* Thanks, I guess.

BLACK LIZARD: Your ugly face, your filthy appearance, your stupidity,

Figure 26. *The Black Lizard*, in 1984, with Bandō Tamasaburō as the Black Lizard and Kitaōji Kinya as Akechi in disguise as the old sailor, Matsukichi, on the Black Lizard's yacht. Shimbashi Enbujō. Photograph courtesy of the Waseda University Tsubouchi Hakase Memorial Theatre Museum.

now all that makes me very happy. Come closer.
MATSUKICHI: Okay.
BLACK LIZARD: Can you see my tears?
MATSUKICHI: *(Looks closely at her face.)* Yeah.
BLACK LIZARD: Do you know who these tears are for?

MATSUKICHI *shakes his head.*

BLACK LIZARD: They are for the one man I love more than anyone else. A man who is no longer in this world. Do you know whom I mean?

MATSUKICHI *shakes his head.*

BLACK LIZARD: Of course, you wouldn't know. That makes you all the more precious to me. You can't even read that man's name. For me, his name is like the North Star, shining eternally in some corner of the sky. That name will stay in my head from now on, like an indelible bloodstain. You can't read that man's name! But I can read that name. Oh how clearly I can read that name! Precisely because I can read that name and you cannot, I can speak like this to you now.
MATSUKICHI: Oh.
BLACK LIZARD: Look out at the sea. It's dark, isn't it?
MATSUKICHI: *(Looks down at the sea.)* Yeah.
BLACK LIZARD: But see how brightly the phosphorescent sea creatures are glowing.
MATSUKICHI: . . .
BLACK LIZARD: Matsukichi, in this world there will never be any more miracles.

SCENE 2: AN ABANDONED FACTORY IN THE PORT OF "S"

After Scene 1B fades to black, a drop painted with the interior of an abandoned factory is lowered in front of the previous set. In the factory there are glass windows on all the walls extending up to the high ceiling, but all the glass is broken, leaving not even a single pane intact. The spaces around and between the broken machinery, rusty shafts and wheels, and broken belts are covered with cobwebs. Through a high window shines the pale dawn moon.

From stage right, a group appears, all carrying flashlights. In the lead is BLACK LIZARD *in a cape, behind her is* SANAE *tied up, with* AMAMIYA *holding the end of the rope. Behind them are* BLUE TORTOISE, *the stoker* MATSUKICHI, KITAMURA, FIVE SAILORS, *and the* TWO DWARVES. *Behind them are another* FIVE SAILORS *carrying various kinds of baggage. There is the sound of a steam whistle, indicating that this is close to a port.*

BLACK LIZARD: *(Stops center stage.)* Look at how bright the moon still is. How fortunate that we arrived before dawn. The sea and tides are still protecting me.

BLUE TORTOISE: Why do you say "still"? The seas and all of us will guard such a fine master forever.

BLACK LIZARD: Really? I'm not so sure. Just as that moon will finally disappear in the white clouds of daybreak, I have a feeling that I will vanish very soon as well. *(Laughs.)* I must be getting weak to say such things. Maybe I'm just not the same old Black Lizard anymore. (With a change of mood she turns to SANAE.) Sanae, my dear, can you guess where we are?

SANAE *shakes her head.*

BLACK LIZARD: Our ship anchored in an inlet near the port, then we took small boats to reach here. Now you have finally arrived at your new home. This will be your eternal dwelling. Remember in that hotel in Osaka I promised that I would show you an entirely new world? Here we are. Take a good look. Look up at the iron bars of the skylight up there. The moon shines through the broken panes of glass. There, where the light of the moon falls so faintly, bats have made their nests. They spread their big black wings and fly all around. Aren't they beautiful? When this factory was still in use, many is the time that a worker would get his finger caught in a lathe and lose one of his precious fingers. If you collected one hundred of those fingers, they could be made into display stands for one hundred jeweled rings. Display stands for rings studded with diamonds, rubies, and sapphires. In life, these fingers belonged to rough young men without the slightest connection to beautiful jewels and rings. But in death, these fingers become the most elegant ring stands that you could find anywhere in the world. These fingers that only knew *pachinko* machines, wooden tickets to the public bath, pawn tickets; these fingers that once clutched at the fingers of disreputable women—they become high-class, leisurely, ever so slightly blue fingers. With jeweled rings, these fingers are gorgeous, bending ever so slightly, as though they were overcome with languid boredom . . .

SANAE: Stop it! Stop it!

Screaming, she tries to flee, but AMAMIYA *holds the rope firmly and doesn't let her escape. By chance, their faces touch and, instinctively,* AMAMIYA *kisses her.*

BLACK LIZARD: *(Coldly.)* What do you think you are doing? Let's go. Remember Sanae, my dear, I promised you that I would show you my very special museum.

Figure 27. *The Black Lizard*, in 1968, with Miwa Akihiro as the Black Lizard and Hirose Misa as Sanae. Toyoko Gekijō. Photograph courtesy of the Waseda University Tsubouchi Hakase Memorial Theatre Museum.

With BLACK LIZARD *in the lead, the group exits stage left.*

SCENE 3: THE ART MUSEUM OF TERROR

The scene drop lifts. The stage is pitch dark. There is an enormous trap door high up stage left. This is gradually lifted open and the light of flashlights can be seen from the other side as it opens.

BLACK LIZARD'S VOICE: Turn on the lights on the stairs.
AMAMIYA'S VOICE: Right.

The lights go on brightly on a large round landing a few steps down from the trap door and a set of stairs winding down from the landing to the floor. The rest of the stage is still dark. The group slowly goes down the stairs. Below, there is a second landing with a kind of observation deck protruding toward stage right. BLACK LIZARD *turns a switch and the lights go on brightly on this landing as well. This landing is the place where the jewels are displayed and is like a kind of roof over a cage that is center stage. The jewelry display looks almost like a giant floral crown on the darkened cage. There are strangely designed velvet flowers with branches stretching out in all directions, the branches covered with jewels,. In the center is the largest and most magnificent flower made of black velvet. This is the only flower that is not displaying any jewelry.*

BLACK LIZARD: Dear Sanae, this present from your father is going to make this gloomy looking black flower blossom for the first time.

She takes out the Star of Egypt and places it in that flower. The Star of Egypt lets out a brilliant light that makes even the hundreds of jewels all around seem to lose their luster. All gasp at the sight.

BLACK LIZARD: Oh, but Sanae, there is so much more to show you. *(To the rest of the group.)* You can go rest in your rooms up above. Kitamura, keep guard outside.

Aside from AMAMIYA *and* SANAE, *all bow, go up the stairs again and exit. The trap door closes.* BLACK LIZARD *turns off the jewelry display light and leads the other two down the stairs. When they reach the bottom of the stairs, the staircase light goes off as well.* BLACK LIZARD *shines the light of her flashlight around the cage in the center of the stage and she continues to move stage right. At stage right, there is an area with a magnificent table and chairs.* BLACK LIZARD *goes there.*

BLACK LIZARD: Now Sanae, take a very good look.

At far stage right she presses a switch. In the back wall stage right, there are four alcoves arranged in two rows, top and bottom. The curtain covering one of the alcoves opens and the interior is illuminated. Inside stands a magnificent black man with bulging muscles, posing handsomely, totally naked, his arms folded. The curtain on the next alcove opens and it is illuminated. Inside is a naked blond girl sitting with her legs pulled up seductively by her side. The curtain opens on the next alcove and it is illuminated to show a naked Japanese youth, throwing a discus vigorously with all his muscles bulging.

BLACK LIZARD: Well, what do you think? These statues are extremely lifelike, don't you think? But maybe a bit too lifelike, perhaps. Go ahead, look from closer up. That's it, much closer. *(She forces* SANAE *to go closer to the figures.)* Look, even the pores of the skin are carefully modeled. There is even fine, downy hair around the pores of the skin. Have you ever seen such perfect detail in a statue before? *(With terror,* SANAE *suddenly realizes what the statues really are and retreats in a panic.)* You understand, don't you? You finally understand. *(She smiles and presses a switch. The curtains close on the three alcoves and the lights go out. Then the curtain on the fourth alcove opens and it is illuminated. There is nothing in this alcove.)* Look! Look there! *(She points at the fourth alcove.)* I wanted to put a beautiful Japanese girl there, with a body perfectly pure. Sanae, will you give me what I want?

In shock, SANAE *stands hesitantly, then when she sees that* AMAMIYA'S *attention is diverted, tries to run away.* AMAMIYA *pursues her.*

BLACK LIZARD: Quickly! Throw her into the cage immediately!

The lights go up in the cage under the giant floral crown of the jewelry display. AMAMIYA *catches* SANAE *and brings her back. He pretends that he is going to put her in the cage, but grabs the padlock from* BLACK LIZARD, *shoves her into the cage instead, puts the padlock on the door and locks it. As he takes* SANAE *by the hand and goes running up the stairs,* BLACK LIZARD *screams inside the cage.*

Just as AMAMIYA *and* SANAE *are about to reach the top landing of the stairs, the trap door opens slightly and the stoker* MATSUKICHI *slips out of it. He stops them and strikes* AMAMIYA, *knocking him out. Then he takes* SANAE *by one hand and drags the unconscious* AMAMIYA *with the other and goes down the stairs. He brings them to the cage.*

BLACK LIZARD: Quickly! Here's the key.

She passes the key to MATSUKICHI *through the bars of the cage and he unlocks the door.* BLACK LIZARD *leaves the cage with unruffled dignity. At her signal,* MATSUKICHI *throws* SANAE *into the cage.*

BLACK LIZARD: Throw him into the cage too. *(She points at the unconscious* AMAMIYA.*)* He betrayed me. But I will reward him by allowing him to become a statue as well. I'll just change the design of the composition a little, and instead of a pure young girl, we will have a couple showing the joy of love. In the morning, I will begin the work.

MATSUKICHI *carries the unconscious* AMAMIYA *into the cage and locks the door.*

BLACK LIZARD: *(Walking to stage right.)* Come over here. You've rescued me once again. I will not forget this.

MATSUKICHI *follows her and as they walk stage right, the lights go up on the table and chairs and the lights go down on the cage.*

BLACK LIZARD: Have a seat.
MATSUKICHI: Uhh, okay.
BLACK LIZARD: Please, go right ahead and sit. If I say sit, do so.
MATSUKICHI: Okay.

He sits nervously. BLACK LIZARD *removes her dressing gown to reveal a magnificent dress underneath. She sits with all the dignity of a queen.*

BLACK LIZARD: Your achievements have been truly outstanding. You may only have been a miserable ship's stoker, but now, I promote you into the exalted Order of Reptiles.
MATSUKICHI: What?
BLACK LIZARD: Don't be surprised. You well deserve it. From now on, your name will be Yellow Crocodile. I will give you a reward as well. *(Takes one of the rings from her finger.)* Here, this diamond ring is for you.
MATSUKICHI: A diamond ring!
BLACK LIZARD: But you are shaking. Do not worry. Today I am feeling generous. Take good care of it; this may become a final memento of me.
MATSUKICHI: Huh?
BLACK LIZARD: Don't worry about it, Yellow Crocodile. *(She brushes her hair with her hand.)* I never have thoughts like this, so unlike the usual Black Lizard, but I can't help but feel this way. These terrible thoughts come again and again, no matter what I do. I must be very tired. I finally have everything I want. Perhaps that made me let my guard down a little bit. Somehow, I have let myself get this tired. Probably I have seen too many wonderful dreams come true. Yes, that must be it.
MATSUKICHI: Yeah, uh . . . well, thanks for everything. *(Stands and is about to go.)*

BLACK LIZARD: Wait. Now you are the only person I can trust. I can't trust any of the others. They are the ones who obediently killed Kogorō Akechi on my orders. I gave the orders, but they are the ones who did the actual deed.

MATSUKICHI: . . .

BLACK LIZARD: Have some sympathy for me, Yellow Crocodile. I am alone in this world. After all that work and all that danger, now I sit surrounded by my treasures, but I am alone. Who can I turn to, who?

MATSUKICHI: *(In a surprisingly firm tone of voice.)* You can count on me.

BLACK LIZARD: *(Bursts out laughing. For a while, she cannot control her laughter.)* Oh, you say such funny things, Yellow Crocodile. That is why I like you. I love the foolish things that you say and your dirty stupid face. *(With affection.)* You make me laugh from the bottom of my heart. . . . Well, I should get some sleep. I didn't get any sleep last night. When it's daylight, wake me up. I want to lay my head on my pillow for just a little while and think of nothing. That will make me feel better. I want to sleep like an innocent child.

She stands and claps her hands sharply. From above the stage, the TWO DWARVES *come swinging down on ropes. They land and bow before* BLACK LIZARD.

BLACK LIZARD: Massage my feet as you always do. If my hair falls loose, blow on it with your sweet breath to give me sweet dreams. If while I sleep I grind my teeth nervously in regret, put your delicately perfumed fingers between my teeth. That will soften the hardness of my regret. Come with me.

BLACK LIZARD *takes the* TWO DWARVES *with her and goes to her bedroom behind the door stage right.* MATSUKICHI *bows very deeply to her as she goes. He starts to walk away stage left, but stops and takes a newspaper out of his pocket. He searches for a good place to put it and finally decides to place it right in front of the door to* BLACK LIZARD'S *bedroom. Then, he goes up the grand staircase and exits.*

As MATSUKICHI *exits, the lights go up on the cage.* SANAE *tries to shake the unconscious* AMAMIYA *awake. His jacket has been taken off and he is in his shirtsleeves.*

SANAE: Amamiya! Amamiya!

She tries to make him more comfortable and finally he opens his eyes.

SANAE: You're awake.

AMAMIYA: Where am I?

SANAE: We're in the cage.
AMAMIYA: The cage?!! *(Looks around him.)*
SANAE: Matsukichi knocked you out and then dragged you in here.
AMAMIYA: *(Still groggy.)* Why are you in here too?
SANAE: We are going to die together.
AMAMIYA: What?
SANAE: That's what Black Lizard said. She's going to make us into statues. We are going to show the ecstasy of a man and woman in love. As soon as it gets light, she's going to get to work.
AMAMIYA: *(Suddenly very happy, he shakes* SANAE.) Really? Did Black Lizard really say that?
SANAE: She did. I'm telling you exactly what she said.
AMAMIYA: (Barely *able to control his joy.*) Really.
SANAE: I know what a bad man you are, but I can't hate you. And it is really all my fault that you're in here. Do you really care for me that much?
AMAMIYA: *(Still in a daze.)* Wow.
SANAE: I said, do you really care for me that much? Do you really love me so much that you are prepared to die?
AMAMIYA: Of course. *(Stands.)* Take a good look at my face. Now you know that I'm capable of saving your life. *(Takes off the false beard.)*
SANAE: Oh my goodness!

She gazes at his face. Silence.

AMAMIYA: I see that you remember my face.
SANAE: What do you mean?
AMAMIYA: I can tell by the way you're looking at me.
SANAE: I never suspected there was such a nice face hidden under that beard. It really is you, isn't it, Amamiya?
AMAMIYA: You forget easily, don't you?
SANAE: But I've never seen you without your beard before.
AMAMIYA: *(Mystified, he is lost in thought. Then, abruptly...)* That's it!
SANAE: What?
AMAMIYA: You're sure that you've never seen me without this beard?
SANAE: Positive.
AMAMIYA: Let's pretend that's true for a moment. A while ago you asked if I loved you enough to die for you, didn't you?
SANAE: Yes, I did. After all, what other reason can there be for you to do what you did?
AMAMIYA: But Sanae, I didn't try to save you because I was in love with you. I can't stand rich daughters of the bourgeoisie like you.
SANAE: Then why did you do it?
AMAMIYA: I'll get to that later. But anyway, I want to make it clear that I'm not in love with you or anything. Let's get that clear. After all, we don't

have very long to live.

SANAE: Why don't you love me? What's wrong with me?

AMAMIYA: You're the spoiled daughter of a rich jeweler. You even think that you are a jewel yourself and look down on everyone around you as if it were the most natural thing in the world. I can't stand that kind of arrogance. I don't like the look in your eyes. I don't like all those fancy manners . . . Basically, people like you make me sick. I know what it's like to be poor. The only reason I'm doing what I'm doing is because I got tired of seeing my youth going to waste, struggling to live in the depths of a big city like Tokyo.

SANAE: *(Her eyes shining with excitement.)* Really? Do you really mean that? You don't like me because I'm a bourgeois girl. You can't stand me because I'm the daughter of Shobei Iwase. That's the only reason you hate me, isn't it?

AMAMIYA: That's right.

SANAE: In that case . . . *(Looks around carefully)* I can tell you everything. I promised not to say anything until the day I died, but I am going to go ahead and talk. Anyway, I promised Akechi that I wouldn't talk and now he's dead. There's no hope that anyone will come and rescue me now.

AMAMIYA: You're right. No one's going to save you now.

SANAE: Amamiya!

AMAMIYA: What?

SANAE: I'm not Sanae.

AMAMIYA: What do you mean?

SANAE: I know this will surprise you, but I'm a decoy. I look so much like Sanae that it's frightening. When I first met Sanae, even I couldn't believe my eyes. My lover abandoned me, I had no money, and I was trying to commit suicide when I was saved by one of Kogorō Akechi's men. He had sent his men all over Tokyo searching for someone who looked exactly like Sanae. I knew it was really dangerous, but the money was really good. Since I was ready to die anyway, I said yes immediately. I practiced acting like Sanae for a week. Then one night, they snuck me into the Iwase mansion and I exchanged places with the real Sanae. Almost immediately after that, I was shut up in that sofa and kidnapped by Black Lizard.

AMAMIYA: So that's what happened.

SANAE: My family is poor too. I was already prepared to die, so the second time around is easy. You must be surprised. Now there is no reason to hate me. After all, I'm not Sanae!

AMAMIYA: *(Coolly)* I already realized that. I knew it the moment I took off this beard and you didn't react. After what I put the real Sanae through, she could never forget my face. I knew you were an imposter, but I wanted to make you say it yourself.

SANAE: Why?

AMAMIYA: Listen to me. Until you die, you're going to have to keep it secret that you are a fake. I need the real Sanae with me and you are going to have to play that part.

SANAE: This is a trap, isn't it? You made me confess because you really do like bourgeois girls.

AMAMIYA: I can't stand bourgeois girls real or fake. It doesn't matter whether you are the real Sanae or not. Either way, I'm not interested.

SANAE: Then why did you try to save my life?

AMAMIYA: I need you, I need you to continue to be Sanae until you die. Think about it. When I tried to save you, why did Black Lizard throw me into the cage with you? Do you know why? It's great! Black Lizard was jealous. The only reason she was jealous was because she thinks that you are the real Sanae. Finally I'm important enough to her to be the object of her jealousy. That is what I wanted more than anything else in the world.

SANAE: So if she learns that I'm not the real Sanae, she won't be jealous of you at all?

AMAMIYA: Not a bit.

SANAE: *(Thinks for a while.)* I understand. But at least, there is a way to save your life. I'm going to shout. I'm going to tell them that I'm a stand-in, that I'm not the real Sanae. Then, at least you can live. That will save your life, won't it? I like you. I don't want to see you die. I'm going to shout. Are you ready?

AMAMIYA *quickly covers her mouth.*

AMAMIYA: Don't do anything stupid. You have to continue to pretend to be Sanae until you die. For my sake.

SANAE: For your sake?

AMAMIYA: That is the only way my love will be fulfilled.

SANAE: Your love?

AMAMIYA: Yes, this was the very first time that Black Lizard was jealous of me.

SANAE: You're in love with Black Lizard?

AMAMIYA: Ever since I met her, I didn't want her to look at anyone else. But she's always so cruel to me. Sometimes I think the only reason she saved my life was so that she could torment me. I am her slave, but there is always a cold wind blowing through my empty heart. I am jealous of each and every thing that that woman loves. Sanae, that's why I'm jealous of you.

SANAE: What?

AMAMIYA: And those statues. I'm even more jealous of all of them. I became jealous of them the moment I saw Black Lizard come and secretly kiss her statues. But the worst was when she fell in love with Akechi. Now he's dead and I killed him. Can you imagine how happy I was when I killed him? But from that moment, Black Lizard has gotten even colder. Now I know what I must do. My only wish is to become one of those statues and hope that once in a while she will come and kiss me. But the only way I could do that was to pretend I was trying to help you escape and so she would think that I had betrayed her. Just once, I wanted her to feel just a little bit jealous of me.

SANAE: *(Her heart cooling.)* So that's what it was. That's why you tried to save my life. Just so you could die the way you wanted. You used me.

AMAMIYA: Finally you've got it.

SANAE: Yes, now I understand all too well.

AMAMIYA: So you see why I need you to keep pretending that you're really Sanae.

SANAE: I see that there's no point in trying to save your life now.

AMAMIYA: All you have to do is to let me die the way I want to.

SANAE: I'll give you the kind of death you want, any way you want it. I don't love you enough anymore to want to betray you. But I still love you a little, enough to want to give you what you want.

AMAMIYA: *(Embracing her.)* Thank you. You're a dear. For the first time, you don't seem so bad. We'll be fake lovers. You're a counterfeit Sanae.

SANAE: You're a fake slave.

AMAMIYA: We will be tied together in an imitation of love. We will die a bogus love suicide. Even though we don't love each other at all, we will die together, the same morning, at the same time.

SANAE: Then we will become mounted trophies.

AMAMIYA: And embrace like lovers for eternity.

SANAE: Our fake love . . .

AMAMIYA: Will become the epitome of the undying love between a man and a woman.

SANAE: We will look like the genuine ecstasy of love.

AMAMIYA: No one looking at us would ever doubt it. We will take the shape of true love.

SANAE: Maybe that means that we actually are in love with each other?

AMAMIYA: It's an illusion. It's just a stupid illusion. After all, as long as we live, we are not in love with each other at all. But after we die . . .

SANAE: You're right! We just have to wait a little longer. Then we will truly be lovers!

The stage right door to the bedroom opens abruptly and the lights on the cage go out immediately.

The TWO DWARVES *come out from the bedroom. They notice the newspaper at their feet and present it to* BLACK LIZARD *who happens to emerge at just that moment.*

BLACK LIZARD: A newspaper on the doorstep! What a strangely domestic touch for this hellish hideout. *(She unfolds the paper and looks at it.)* Wait, this is yesterday's paper. What? "The Great Detective Kogorō Akechi Wins Again! Sanae Iwase Returns Home Safely! The King of Jewels is Doubly Happy! Sanae to Marry the Heir to the Hayakawa Fortune! . . ." There's even a picture! How can a responsible paper print such lies. No . . . no, this can't be a lie. In that case, who is in the cage?

Just as she starts to approach the cage, the trapdoor at the top of the stairs opens. BLUE TORTOISE *and* FIVE SAILORS *appear leading* MATSUKICHI *tied with a rope.*

BLUE TORTOISE: Black Lizard! This Matsukichi is a traitor. Kitamura was supposed to be keeping watch, but when we checked on him, he was knocked out and tied up. When we revived him, he said that Matsukichi did it. That's why we've brought Matsukichi here for you to question.

BLACK LIZARD: Matsukichi! You too!

MATSUKICHI: Ma'am, they're lying. I'm innocent!

BLACK LIZARD: *(In tears.)* How could you betray me too?

MATSUKICHI: I would never betray you. I was just worried about the statues.

BLACK LIZARD: The statues? What about the statues?

BLUE TORTOISE: Don't listen to him! It's a trick!

Holding a pistol BLACK LIZARD *backs up and presses the switch stage right. The lights go up on the four alcoves, but the statues are no longer in them. In each alcove there is a* POLICEMAN *with a gun aimed at* BLACK LIZARD. *All of the members of her gang are astonished.* MATSUKICHI *twists free and comes down the stairs, standing with his back to the policemen.* BLUE TORTOISE *and the* FIVE SAILORS *raise their hands.* BLACK LIZARD *tries to shoot* MATSUKICHI *but the pistol only clicks and doesn't fire.*

BLACK LIZARD: Damn! You took out the bullets!

MATSUKICHI: Give me the key to the cage.

Glaring at him with hatred, BLACK LIZARD *hands the key over. One of the policemen presses a switch and the entire stage lights up. The* POLICEMEN *surround* BLACK LIZARD *and her gang. The* TWO DWARVES *shake with terror.* MATSUKICHI *opens the cage and lets out* AMAMIYA *and* SANAE.

SANAE: I can't believe it!

MATSUKICHI: Are you two all right?

AMAMIYA and SANAE: We're in love!

MATSUKICHI: I thought something like this might happen. You can go ahead and leave. *(To* SANAE) Don't forget to have your lover give his statement to the police.

They run to one of the alcoves stage right. They pose briefly as an embracing couple and then exit through a hole in the wall of the alcove that the police made when they came in.

MATSUKICHI *approaches* BLACK LIZARD *and rips off his beard. He is actually* AKECHI.

BLACK LIZARD: You're alive!

AKECHI: It's too bad for the real Matsukichi, though. He drowned when you dropped him into the sea inside that sofa.

BLACK LIZARD: You're alive!

AKECHI: You're under arrest.

BLACK LIZARD: *(Affectionately.)* You terrible man!

She turns and slips away a few steps, opens a compartment in one of her rings and takes poison. All are shocked. BLUE TORTOISE *screams with grief and tries to revive* BLACK LIZARD.

AKECHI: Black Lizard!

BLACK LIZARD: I'm not dying because I was captured.

AKECHI: I know.

BLACK LIZARD: I'm dying because you know all the deepest secrets of my heart.

AKECHI: Nothing is more difficult than to listen to someone revealing their innermost feelings. I'm not used to it.

BLACK LIZARD: How could you have used such underhanded, cowardly tricks! You couldn't possibly trample on a woman's heart more thoroughly.

AKECHI: I'm sorry. . . . But it couldn't be helped. After all, you are a lady gang boss; I'm a detective.

BLACK LIZARD: But in the world of the heart, you were the thief; I was the detective. You were always a thief. I was the detective and I searched for your heart. I looked and I looked and when I finally found it, it was something like a cold hard stone.

AKECHI: I knew all along that your heart was a genuine jewel. A flawless diamond.

BLACK LIZARD: It was a dirty trick to listen in on my confession. You understand that, don't you? But once my innermost feelings were known, it was the end.

AKECHI: The same is true for me. I . . .

BLACK LIZARD: Hush. Let me die without having to know your real feelings. But I am happy.

AKECHI: About what?
BLACK LIZARD: That you're alive.

BLACK LIZARD *dies.* BLUE TORTOISE *clings to her body and weeps. The policemen lock up the* FIVE SAILORS *and the* TWO DWARVES *in the bedroom.* AKECHI *stands in despair.*

Suddenly, the trapdoor at the top of the stairs opens wide and the morning sun comes pouring in. SHOBEI IWASE, HIS WIFE, SANAE *and* SANAE'S FIANCE *enter and line up on the staircase landing stage left.*

IWASE: Akechi! Good job, yes, a good job, a very good job indeed. Now everything is resolved. I must say that I'm very impressed with your skills. Look here is Sanae perfectly unharmed. And here, let me introduce you to young Hayakawa.

AKECHI: You'll find the "Star of Egypt" among those jeweled flowers.

IWASE: Where? Where? *(Rushes down the stairs and finds his diamond, the Star of Egypt.)* Yes, this is the genuine Star of Egypt all right! *(He returns to his family.)*

AKECHI: Now all of your belongings have returned to you. My job is done.

IWASE: I owe all the happiness and prosperity of my family to you. I will never forget it.

AKECHI: Go ahead and forget it. You and your family will continue to prosper and will buy and sell false gems while celebrating your eternal spring. That's just fine. That was the reason I did this job.

IWASE: What do you mean by false gems?

AKECHI: Yes, false gems. *(Looking down tenderly at* BLACK LIZARD.) The only true gem is now dead.

CURTAIN

Appendix: List of Mishima Plays Available in English Translation

1. "Sotoba Komachi," "The Damask Drum" *("Aya no Tsuzumi")*, "Kantan," "The Lady Aoi" *("Aoi no Ue")*, "Hanjo" (all modern *noh* plays) in:
   Donald Keene tr., *Five Modern Nō Plays of Yukio Mishima* (New York: Vintage Books, 1957).

2. "Dōjōji." (modern *noh* play) in:
   Donald Keene tr., *Death in Midsummer and other Stories* (New York: New Directions, 1966).

3. "Yoroboshi The Blind Young Man" *("Yoroboshi")* (modern *noh* play) in:
   Ted Takaya tr. *Modern Japanese Drama: An Anthology* (New York: Columbia University Press, 1979).

4. "Twilight Sunflower" *("Yoru no Himawari")* in:
   Shinozaki & Warren tr., *Twilight Sunflower* (Tokyo: Hokuseido, 1953) and
   (New York: Knopf, 1968).

5. "Madame de Sade" *("Sado Kōshaku Fujin")* in:
   Donald Keene tr. *Madame de Sade* (New York: Grove Press, 1967).

6. "The Rokumeikan" *("Rokumeikan")*, "The Decline and Fall of the Suzaku" *("Suzaku Ke no Metsubo")*, "My Friend Hitler" *("Waga Tomo no Hittora")*, "The Terrace of the Leper King" *("Raiō no Terasu")*, "A Wonder Tale: The Moonbow" *("Chinzetsu Yumiharizuki")* in:
   Hiroaki Sato tr. *My Friend Hitler and other Plays of Yukio Mishima* (New York, Columbia University Press, 2002).

Glossary of Japanese Terms, Historical Personages, and Geographical Locations

(I was greatly assisted in my explanations of kabuki terminology by James R. Brandon and Samuel L. Leiter, eds., *Kabuki Plays on Stage*, vol. 1: *Brilliance and Bravado, 1697-1766* (Honolulu: University of Hawai'i Press, 2002), pp. 353–70, and Samuel L. Leiter and Jiro Yamamoto, *New Kabuki Encyclopedia: A Revised Adaptation of* Kabuki Jiten (Westport, Conn.: Greenwood Press, 1997.)

agemaku In kabuki, a narrow curtain hung at the entrance to the *hanamichi* that slides on rings. For noh-based kabuki dance dramas on the pine board set *(matsubamemono)*, a curtain hung at stage right and lifted, in the manner of the *agemaku* curtain in noh drama.

ai-kyōgen An interval in the middle of a noh play during which *kyōgen* actors perform, affording the main character *(shite)* time to change costume. Most often a single *kyōgen* actor retells the story of the noh play (the *katari ai*) in simple language, maintaining the dignity of the play as a whole. Occasionally one or more *kyōgen* actors engage in comic interplay (the *ashirai ai*), lightening the mood of the noh play.

angura An abbreviation of *andaa guraundo* ("underground"), referring to "Underground Theatre"—contemporary *avant-garde* or experimental theatre performed in basements and in other small venues.

Aoyama Cemetery Located in Tokyo, southeast of the Meiji Shrine Outer Garden, and established in 1872, this cemetery contains the graves of many of Japan's distinguished leaders, including leaders of the Meiji Restoration.

Asahi Shimbun One of Japan's three major daily newspapers, and the one with the best coverage of theatre and literature.

Bungaku-za "The Literary Company." A *shingeki* company founded in 1937 by Kishida Kunio, Kubota Mantarō, and Iwata Toyoo, it is Japan's oldest currently active *shingeki* company, and arguably the most prestigious. The company is committed to an apolitical artistic agenda and was the only *shingeki* company allowed to operate during the Pacific War era. The seminal figure in the postwar Bungaku-za was actress Sugimura Haruko (1907–97). The company staged plays by Mishima beginning in 1950, and Mishima was a member from 1957 to 1963.

bunraku Popular term for a classical puppet theatre form with roots dating back to approximately 1600 that features puppets manipulated by three puppeteers each, and recitation by a *gidayū* singer or singers who are accompanied by the music of the *shamisen*.

buyō (nihon buyō) "Dance"—referring to the dance of kabuki. *Buyō* pieces are also performed outside of the kabuki by a wide range of amateur and professional performers at various venues. *Buyō* has a very large repertory of classical dances, and new dances are frequently choreographed.

Chikamatsu Monzaemon (1653–1724) The most famous playwright of the Edo period, Chikamatsu wrote for both kabuki and the *bunraku* puppet theatre.

Chitose A city in southern Hokkaido, and location of the airport that serves Sapporo as well as several military facilities.

doro-doro The onomatopoeic word for an intermittent, rolling pattern of the offstage large drum that denotes tension, mystery, or the supernatural in kabuki.

Edo The name for the city of Tokyo prior to 1868, when Emperor Meiji established the city as the nation's capital.

Edo period 1600–1868. The time when the Tokugawa shogunate ruled Japan, with their military government *(bakufu)* headquartered in Edo.

Emma Daiō (the King of Hell) A ferocious deity of Chinese origin who judges the fate of dead souls.

Emperor Kammu (731–806, r. 781–806) A powerful emperor who established Kyoto as the Imperial Capital in 794.

Emperor Nintoku An emperor who reigned in the latter half of the fifth century, he is buried near the site of his Imperial Palace in what now is Osaka City. Emperor Nintoku was renowned for wisdom and benevolence.

eroguro An abbreviation of *erochikku gurotesuku* ("erotic and grotesque"), referring to a literary style of the 1920s. Its leading writer was Edogawa Rampo.

"fish *jōruri*" (see *sakana jōruri*)

Fudō A ferocious avatar of the Sun Buddha, worshipped in tantric sects of Buddhism. Fudō is depicted with a sword in his right hand, a rope in his left hand, and surrounded by flames.

fusuma Opaque paper sliding doors used in interiors of traditional Japanese houses, often with art work painted on them.

Gakushūin (the Peers School) Founded in 1877, Gakushūin was put under the direct jurisdiction of the Imperial Household Agency in 1884. It was a school for children of the imperial family and the nobility until 1947, when it became a private institution open to the public. Before 1947 it included elementary and secondary schools as well as a university.

gandōgaeshi A scene-changing technique in kabuki in which the existing set is flipped over backward ninety degrees, revealing a new set on the bottom of the first. Literally "bandit's change," the stage technique was first used in nineteenth-century plays about bandits.

Genroku period (1688–1704) During this time the newly arisen townsman class enjoyed its first period of major prosperity. All of the arts flourished and many of the Edo Period's finest artists were active.

geza The off-stage musicians' room, concealed by a black grille, located stage-right on every kabuki stage. Instruments played in the *geza* include: *shamisen*, drums, gongs, flutes, and various sound effect instruments (i.e., rain rattles, cricket clickers, plover whistles, etc.). Songs are also sung to the accompaniment of these instruments.

gidayū bushi Music of the *bunraku* puppet theatre, also used in kabuki dramas. It includes lyrics sung by one or more chanter accompanied by one or more musicians playing the largest, lowest-pitched *shamisen* in use in Japan. *Gidayū bushi* is also called *takemoto*. This form of music was originated by the *bunraku* chanter, Takemoto Gidayū.

Gojō Higashinotōin An intersection of two major streets in south-central Kyoto. "Gojō" means "Fifth Avenue."

Haiyū-za A major *shingeki* company, founded in 1944 by Senda Koreya, Aoyama Sugisaku, and others.

hakama Wide, pleated trousers worn over kimono. Most are worn by men, but long, red *hakama* are worn by court ladies. *Nagabakama* ("long *hakama*") are worn by samurai indoors on the most formal occasions, and trail on the floor several feet behind the wearer.

hanamichi In kabuki theatres, an approximately four-foot wide runway running at stage level through the orchestra seating from the rear of the auditorium to the stage. It is usually located about six to twelve seats to the right of the left proscenium, and is used for major entrances and exits.

happi A short coat worn by traditional laborers, firemen, etc., often with an organizational logo of some sort on it. *Happi* constitute a kind of traditional laborers' uniform.

Ishikawa Goemon A famous thief of the sixteenth century. After his capture, Goemon was boiled to death in an iron bathtub, giving this sort of tub its name ever since. A cycle of kabuki plays treats Goemon and his relations with famous figures of the late sixteenth century.

Iwashimizu Shrine A Shinto shrine dedicated to Hachiman, god of war. It was founded in 859 and is located on a large hill between Kyoto and Osaka.

Izumi Shikibu A leading lady poet, active at the turn of the eleventh century. Izumi Shikibu was famous for her love affairs with two imperial princes who died while engaged in illicit relationships with her. She wrote an exquisite poetic diary about her affair with the second prince.

Izumo A city in Tottori Prefecture, the location of Izumo Taisha, one of Japan's two most sacred Shinto shrines.

jiuta Songs accompanied by *shamisen* music that date back to the early Edo period. *Jiuta* is a product of the Kamigata Region (Kyoto/Osaka). *Jiuta* music and the dances accompanying them (*Kamigata mai*) were intended for chamber, not kabuki stage performance, and were popular in the Kamigata pleasure districts.

jōruri A generic term for narrative theatre music of kabuki and *bunraku*, sung and accompanied by the *shamisen*. It can refer to music in the styles of *gidayū (takemoto)* [the only *jōruri* used in *bunraku*], *ōzatsuma*, *tokiwazu*, and *kiyomoto*.

kabuki A form of theatre with dance, music, and acting dating from the early Edo period. Originally kabuki was popular theatre, but today is one of Japan's classical theatres.

Kabuki-za Tokyo's major kabuki theatre, built in 1889, and located in the

Higashi Ginza district. Shochiku Corporation bought it in 1914 and has owned and operated it ever since.

Kamigata The old name for the region of Japan in which Kyoto, Osaka, and Kobe are located. Kamigata was the cultural center of Japan until the mid-1700's, when cultural leadership passed to the Kanto region, centering around Edo (now the city of Tokyo).

Kamo River The river running from north to south in eastern Kyoto.

Kannon The Boddhisattva of mercy, often depicted in statuary as a woman.

kataginu A stiff, vest-like garment with wing-like shoulders sometimes worn with *hakama*. Kabuki musicians wear matching *kataginu* and *hakama*. Women only wear *kataginu* when dressing as men—for example, when women sing *jōruri*.

Kawatake Mokuami (1816–93) The leading playwright of nineteenth-century kabuki, Mokuami was famous in the first half of the century for plays about noble outlaws.

ki (hyōshigi) Wooden clappers struck together by the stage manager to signal the opening or closing of the curtain.

Kiyomizu Temple One of the most famous temples of Kyoto, located in the Eastern Hills overlooking Gojō (Fifth Avenue). Kiyomizu is famous as a cherry-blossom viewing site. Its major deity is the Kannon.

kiyomoto A form of allusive narrative *jōruri* used in kabuki. *Kiyomoto* was founded in 1814 and is famous for its high-pitched singing.

Kōkin Wakashū ("A collection of Japanese poems, past and present") A canonical anthology of poems compiled in 902. It is the first anthology of poems in Japanese compiled under imperial orders.

koto The Japanese "harp," a thirteen-stringed, zither-like instrument with a long, hollow, wooden body. It is played by a seated musician, using both hands, with picks on the fingers. It is a concert instrument, and not standard to any kabuki musical ensemble.

kuge aku An evil minister in kabuki, wearing blue striped make-up.

Kumo (Gekidan Kumo) A *shingeki* company founded by Kishida Kyōko,

Akutagawa Hiroshi and others after they split from the Bungaku-za in 1963.

Kumo no Kai An association of artists from various fields founded by playwright Kishida Kunio in 1950.

kyōgen Short, humorous plays performed between noh plays, from the medieval period to the present. The same term is also sometimes used to refer to kabuki plays or kabuki texts.

Lake Biwa Japan's largest fresh water lake, located about fifteen miles east of Kyoto.

mei serifu Famous monologues and dialogues excerpted from kabuki plays. They were sold in short books or anthologies in the Edo period.

Meiji-za A theatre built in 1885 in the Nihombashi district in Tokyo, first with the name Chitose-za. The name was changed to Meiji-za in 1893, and in 1919 Shochiku purchased the theatre.

miseba ("display scenes") Scenes in kabuki plays designed to afford opportunities for actors to display their histrionic talents.

Mount Kurama A mountain north of the city of Kyoto.

Mount Mihara The volcano at the center of Ōshima Island, south of Tokyo. It has erupted frequently in the postwar era, sometimes forcing evacuation of the island.

***mugen* noh** Noh plays in which the leading character, played by the *shite*, is not a mortal human, but a ghost, god, demon, or other spirit.

nagauta A musical ensemble and style used in kabuki. *Nagauta* ("long song") includes singers, shamisen players, and the flute and three drums of the noh orchestra. Most kabuki dance dramas are accompanied by *nagauta*, and *nagauta* musicians work in the *geza* ensemble.

Nakanoshima An island in the Yodo River in the center of downtown Osaka.

The National Theatre (Kokuritsu Gekijō) Opened in 1966, and located southwest of Tokyo's Imperial Palace, the National Theatre presents traditional Japanese performing arts such as kabuki, *bunraku*, music concerts, storytelling, *buyō* dance recitals, and others (but very rarely noh and *kyōgen*, which have their own National Noh Theatre). The National Theatre contains theatre archives, a museum, and a training school, in addition to three theatres. The National Theatre's agenda and funding for kabuki productions promote the revival and presentation of full-length plays, and the creation of new plays for kabuki.

ninja Professional assassins and spies of the pre-Edo period in Japan.

Nissei Gekijō A theatre completed in 1963 in Tokyo's Yurakuchō district.

NLT (New Literary Theatre) A *shingeki* theatre company founded by Mishima Yukio, Matsuura Takeo, and others in 1964 after they split from the Bungaku-za in 1963.

noh A lyrical, masked drama form dating from the thirteenth century. Noh is characterized by sumptuous costumes, highly refined and restrained movements, and intense chanting accompanied only by a shrill flute and percussion. Mishima's "modern noh plays" (*kindai* noh) were written to be performed as *shingeki* plays, not traditional noh plays.

oiemono Kabuki and *bunraku* plays about succession disputes in feudal clans, usually set in the Edo period and often involving the activities of a profligate heir who squanders the family fortune in the pleasure district.

onnagata Kabuki actors (all are male) who specialize in playing women's roles.

Ōshima Island Located 117 kilometers southwest of Tokyo, Ōshima is the largest of the seven Izu Islands. It is a semitropical resort island.

otogizōshi Folk tales dating from the medieval period.

The Peers School (see **Gakushūin)**

Rokumeikan ("The Pavilion of the Baying Stag") A brick building constructed in 1883 in the Hibiya district of Tokyo, designed by the architect Josiah Condler. It was the site of numerous balls and other social events for Westerners and for Japanese officials and their wives. The Rokumeikan came to symbolize the rapid Westernization of the early Meiji period.

Roman Gekijō "The Romantic Theatre Company," founded by Mishima Yukio and Matsuura Takeo when they split from the NLT in 1968.

sakana jōruri Poetic lyrics composed to be sung by *gidayū* singers in which puns using the names of fish are inserted into a story that originally had nothing whatsoever to do with fish. Chikamatsu Monzaemon was a master writer of *sakana jōruri*.

Santo Kyōden (1761–1816) Japan's leading writer of satiric and humorous illustrated fiction (primarily *sharebon* and *kibyōshi*) in the 1780s and 1790s.

Sarusawa Pond A pond in the city of Nara, about 360 meters in circumference, near the temple of Kōfukuji.

seppuku Ritual disembowelment performed by samurai beginning in the 1100s. *Seppuku* was performed for a variety of reasons, including (1) to atone for defeat in battle and to avoid capture and humiliation by the enemy, (2) to remonstrate with one's lord, (3) to atone for one's own failure or failure by a family member, (4) at the order of a superior in lieu of execution for a crime committed. Mishima Yukio committed *seppuku* on November 25, 1970, at the Tokyo headquarters of Japanese Ground Self-Defense Force (the Japanese army) after forcing a general whom he took hostage to assemble his troops and after Mishima unsuccessfully attempted to persuade the troops to revolt and restore the emperor to his former position of authority and reverence.

seven-three spot (see ***shichi-san***)

shamisen A three-stringed instrument with a hollow, dog or cat-skin covered sounding box that is the melodic instrument shared by all of kabuki's musical ensembles. The strings are strummed with a large bone or ivory plectrum held in the right hand. The size and pitch range of *shamisen* vary according to the ensemble. The *shamisen* was modified from the snakeskin-covered *jamisen* imported from the Ryukyus at the turn of the seventeenth century.

shichi go chō ("seven-five meter") Verse written for kabuki or for the *bunraku* puppet theatre composed of alternating lines of five and seven syllables, the standard Japanese classical poetic meter.

shichi-san A location on the *hanamichi,* three-tenths of the distance from the stage to the auditorium. Actors often pause during entrances and exits to act or speak at this spot. The seven-three spot is moved closer to the stage at the Kabuki-za and some other theatres to enable audiences in balcony seats to view action taking place there.

Shield Society (see Tate no Kai)

Shihei (Fujiwara Shihei) Another pronunciation for Fujiwara Tokihira

(871–909), regent of Japan. Because of his rivalry with the scholar-statesman Sugawara Michizane, Shihei became a great villain in popular literature.

Shimbashi Enbujō A major theatre in the Higashi Ginza district of Tokyo that opened in 1925 and was acquired by Shochiku in 1940. It is used primarily for *shimpa* productions.

shimpa A form of theatre born in the 1890s, combining the histrionics of kabuki with modern thematic material. *Shimpa* was Japan's first theatre form in the Meiji period to use actresses regularly, though it used and continues to use *onnagata* as well.

shin kabuki "New kabuki" plays. First performed in 1904, these plays attempt a more psychological exploration than older plays. *Shin kabuki* plays do not use music or dance unless they are called for within the context of the story of the play, and their texts are written in modern Japanese.

shingeki "New theatre." Inspired by Western "realistic" theatre, Japanese dramatists and playwrights worked during the 1910s and 1920s to establish this sort of theatre in Japan. *Shingeki* almost always uses actresses to play women's roles. *Shingeki* became the dominant form of Japanese theatre in the post World War II era.

shite The leading role in a noh play; or, the actor of the leading role in a noh play.

Shochiku (standard abbreviation for Shōchiku Kabushiki Kaisha [The Shochiku Corporation]) Shochiku is an entertainment corporation founded in 1902 by two brothers from Kyoto. Along with Toho, Shochiku is one of the two wealthiest and most influential entertainment conglomerates in Japan. Shochiku gained control over kabuki productions in the first two decades of the twentieth century by acquiring large theatres in major cities and by signing kabuki actors on yearly contracts to perform in them. Shochiku also produces *shimpa* plays, musical reviews, and other large-scale theatre productions. Shochiku was a major film-making corporation until 2000, and continues to be a major distributor and retail purveyor of film.

Shōtoku Taishi (574–622) An imperial prince and statesman who served as regent to Empress Suiko (r. 593–625). Prince Shōtoku solidified the status of Buddhism in Japan, founding several major temples, and wrote Japan's first constitution.

Suo A province at the extreme western end of the island of Honshu, now part of Yamaguchi Prefecture.

Taira no Munemori (1147–85) A minister of state and third son of the tyrant ruler of Japan, Taira no Kiyomori (1118–81), Munemori succeeded to the leadership of the clan in 1181. Munemori was captured during the Battle of Dan no Ura (1185), the Taira's crushing defeat at the hands of the Minamoto army, and was executed soon thereafter.

takemoto (synonymous with *gidayū bushi;* see *gidayū bushi*)

Tate no Kai (Shield Society) A paramilitary organization of young men dedicated to serving the Japanese emperor, founded by Mishima Yukio in 1968. They trained in martial arts and with the Ground Self Defense Forces. Leaders of the Shield Society accompanied Mishima and one even died with him when Mishima committed suicide (***seppuku***) in 1970.

Tōgeki (Tokyo Gekijō) This theatre was built by Shochiku in the Tsukiji district of Tokyo in 1930, and has been used to present *shingeki, shimpa,* and kabuki plays, as well as films. It was an important venue for kabuki in the early postwar years because it was one of a few large theatres not destroyed by wartime bombing.

tokiwazu A style of kabuki narrative music, incorporating singers and *shamisen* players only, developed in the late eighteenth century and now used to accompany dance plays or dance scenes.

Tōru (Minamoto no Tōru [822–95]) A courtier of high ambition who was thwarted by the rival Fujiwara clan. Popular myth held that his ghost haunted various districts of Kyoto.

Tsubomi-kai A kabuki recital, incorporating original plays and dance dramas, produced by *onnagata* actor Nakamura Utaemon VI in the 1950s on an almost yearly basis. The purpose of the Tsubomi Kai was to give playwrights, choreographers, and musicians the opportunity to create new works for Utaemon. Mishima's *Yuya* (1954) and *Asa no Tsutsuji* (1957), premiered as Tsubomi-kai works.

tsuke Two wood blocks beaten alternatively on a wooden board placed on the floor near the stage left proscenium in kabuki. *Tsuke* beats accompany and emphasize stage action, including running, combat, and climactic poses (*mie*).

Tsukiji Shogekijō A theatre built in the Tsukiji district of Tokyo in 1924 by Osanai Kaoru (1881–1928) and Hijikata Yoshi (1898–1959) for the express purpose of presenting *shingeki* plays. Until 1928 the Tsukiji Shogekijō theatre company headed by the two above men produced only plays by Western playwrights.

Tsuruya Namboku IV (1755–1829) The leading kabuki playwright of the early 1800s, Namboku is famous for plays featuring ghosts and horror, the lives of thieves and outcasts, and corruption in the ruling elite.

uchikake A woman's trailing over-kimono, worn on formal occasions. It is usually padded, heavily embroidered, and left open at the front. Today *uchikake* are most often worn by brides at weddings and by kabuki *onnagata*.

utai The vocal music of the noh drama.

waki The secondary character in a noh play, or, the actor who plays secondary characters in noh plays. *Waki* characters are always mortal men.

waki-tsure A companion to the secondary character in a noh play, or, the actor who plays the companion to the secondary character in a noh play. Like *waki*, *waki-tsure* characters are always mortal men.

wakizashi A samurai's short sword (also called *hitokoshi* or *katana*). The long sword was called *tachi*. Edo period samurai typically carried these two swords.

warizerifu ("divided dialogue") In kabuki, dialogue antiphonally spoken, usually by two characters and usually composed in phrases of seven and five syllables (*shichi go chō*), with the final phrase often spoken in unison.

watarizerifu ("passed-along dialogue") A long speech in kabuki divided among a group of characters who speak in sequence and then join together to deliver the last phrase or line in unison.

Yanagibashi Midorikai In the 1950s to 1960s, a regularly produced *buyō* dance recital performed by Tokyo geisha studying dance in the Fujima School.

yatsushi Deriving from the verb *yatsusu*, "to disguise onesself," the *yatsushi* was a kabuki role type/character type developed in the 1680s who was a wealthy young man, usually the heir to a feudal domain, disowned by his parents for conducting extravagent love affairs in the pleasure district, and who was afterward forced to travel in disguise to meet his beloved courtesan in the pleasure quarter.

Contributors

DONALD KEENE, translator and author of the Foreword, is Professor Emeritus at Columbia University. Donald Keene is the scholar more responsible than any other for knowledge outside of Japan about Japanese literature and culture. He has written over one hundred books, including translations of classical and modern novels, plays, and poetry; a four-volume literary history of Japan; studies of authors, poets, and diarists; and, recently, a biography of the Meiji emperor. Donald Keene trained two generations of scholars who are now teaching all over the world and contributing their own scholarship to the world's understanding of Japanese culture.

LAURENCE KOMINZ, editor, translator, and author of the Introduction, is a student of Donald Keene and a Columbia University Ph.D. in Japanese Literature. He is Professor of Japanese Language and Literature at Portland State University and author of *Avatars of Vengeance, Japanese Drama and the Soga Literary Tradition* (1995) and *The Stars Who Created Kabuki: Their Lives, Loves, and Legacy* (1997), as well as numerous articles about and translations of Japanese drama. He studies *kyōgen* acting and *nihon buyō* dance and directs student productions of *kyōgen* and kabuki.

MARK OSHIMA, translator, is a Ph.D. candidate in Harvard University's Department of East Asian Languages and Civilizations. He is a professional singer of *kiyomoto* (stage name, Kiyomoto Shimatayū) and a student of *nihon buyō* (stage name Fujima Toyoaki). Oshima is also a translator/commentator for English "earphone guides" for kabuki and bunraku and writer of English language programs for the Kabuki-za and the National Theatre. He translated Nakamura Matazō's *Kabuki Backstage, Onstage: An Actor's Life* (1990), and kabuki plays *Yotsuya Ghost Stories* and *A Maiden at Dōjōji* in Karen Brazell's *Traditional Japanese Theatre* (1998).

JONAH SALZ, translator, received his Ph.D. in performance studies from New York University. Salz is a Kyoto-based theatre director and producer, and is Professor of Comparative Literature in Ryukoku University's Faculty of Intercultural Communication. His publications include articles on intercultural theatre, the *entre garde*, Beckett, noh abroad, *kyōgen* actor training, and directing. Salz directs the NOHO Theatre Group and Traditional Theatre Training.